I0633930

The Essential Chaucer Reader

Selected Writings of Geoffrey Chaucer

Edited and Translated
By Gerard P. NeCastro, Ph.D.

The Essential Chaucer Reader:
Selected Writings of Geoffrey Chaucer.

Printed and manufactured in the United States.

Published by The Primavera Press. First paperback edition 2013.

Requests for further permissions or information should be made to theprimaverapress@gmail.com.

Library of Congress Control Number: 2013951113.

Author: Geoffrey Chaucer
Editor: Gerard P. NeCastro
Translator: Gerard P. NeCastro

ISBN-10: 0989426319
ISBN-13: 978-0-9894263-1-2

http://www.primaverapress.com

TO ALL OF MY CHAUCER STUDENTS, PAST, PRESENT, AND FUTURE.

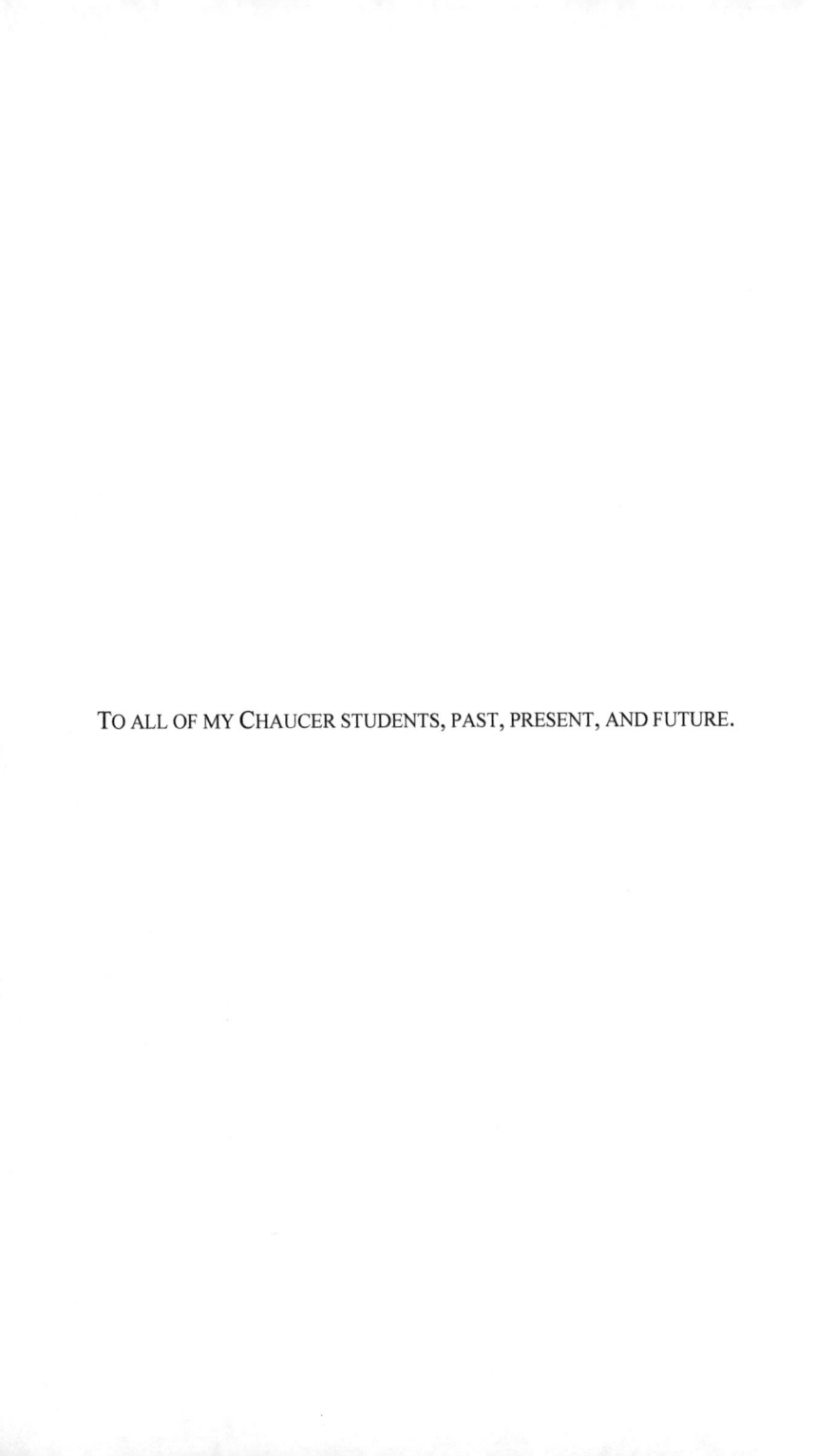

CONTENTS

PREFACE

This volume began with my sister Christina, who was puzzled at my fascination with reading books in ancient languages that most people could not read and would not care to read. For her I set out to translate into modern English the works of Geoffrey Chaucer, which had brought me such joy for many years. There were already available many translations into poetry, old and new, but I knew that many people have difficulty following poetry, and that translators often must compromise on clarity and accuracy in order to make lines fit the rhyme and meter of poetic verse. In order to make Chaucer's work as true to its original meaning and as approachable as possible, I therefore chose to translate his works into prose.

The original project, to set the entire works into a readable translation, took nearly three years, and, after a hiatus of several years, it took another two years to polish the lines. Any success I have had in completing this project is owed to the University of Maine System for its financial support, to countless teachers and scholars for their encouragement along the way, and to my family, especially my wife, for humoring me though thousands of lines of poetry, though they could see that my eyes were "entirely dazed."

It is an honor to have the opportunity to present to you the works of one of the great geniuses our world has known.

ABOUT GEOFFREY CHAUCER

Geoffrey Chaucer was born between 1340 and 1343 to a middle-class merchant family. Though his father and grandfather were wine merchants, his name indicates that earlier generations were probably shoemakers, perhaps of French origin. In his early career, he served at court as a page and then as a soldier. It is well known that he was captured in 1360 at the Siege of Rheims (in the Hundred Years War) and was ransomed by King Edward for £16, but not before he lost his thumb and forefinger, the typical punishment for archers.

In 1366 he was married to Philippa de Roet, a lady-in-waiting to Philippa of Hainault, Queen Consort to Edward III, and together the Chaucers had four children, Thomas, Elizabeth, Agnes, and Lewis (to whom Chaucer's *Treatise on the Astrolabe* is addressed). During the early years of their marriage, Chaucer seems to have studied law at The Inns of Court and traveled on several diplomatic missions, though usually only as a valet. Philippa seems to have died around 1387.

Though he was entrusted with several diplomatic missions to France and Italy, much of his career through the 1380s was as Controller of the Customs House in the London, a position of great responsibility in the bustling port city. He also served as a Commissioner of Peace in Kent and Clerk of the King's Works under King Richard II, and represented Kent in Parliament in 1386. After Richard's deposition and murder in 1399, there are practically no records of Chaucer's life. He died in 1400 and was buried at Westminster Abbey, the first person buried in Poets' Corner.

Chaucer probably started writing poetry at a young age. Many of his shorter poems may have been composed in his early career, and the God of Love in the Prologue to *The Legend of Good Women* says that he wrote a poem about Mary Magdalene long ago. His first major composition was *Book of the Duchess*, a sort of memorial of Blanche, Duchess of Lancaster, for her widower John of Gaunt, the brother of Edward III and uncle of Richard II. It seems that for this poem Chaucer was granted a "tun" of wine (about 250 gallons) each year for the rest of his life. He also translated early in his career Boethius' *Consolation of Philosophy* and Jean de Meun and Guillaume de Lorris' *Romance of the Rose*, both of which were very influential in Chaucer's own poetry.

Before he started work in earnest on *The Canterbury Tales* he attempted several other major compositions: *The Parliament of Fowls*, the first Valentine's Day poem in English in which the birds gather to choose their mates; *The House of Fame*, a literary investigation of fame, rumor, and reputation; *The Legend of Good Women*, a collection of legends, or quasi-saints' lives of women from classical antiquity, retold by the fictional Chaucer as a sort of penance for defaming women in his *Troilus and Criseyde*. By the time he composed his *Troilus and Criseyde*, perhaps the first novel in the English language, Chaucer had reached full maturity as a poet, creating a work that is beautifully crafted, philosophically challenging, and delightfully human. Chaucer's best-known work and the culmination of his career, *The Canterbury Tales*, is a collection of tales told by twenty-five pilgrims on their way from the outskirts of London to Canterbury. Though it, like his *Anelida and Arcite*, *The House of Fame*, and *The Legend of Good Women*, was left incomplete at his death, it has long been considered as one of the very best works of literature throughout the world. Its popularity and its relevance to generation after generation of readers has never decreased.

THE BOOK OF THE DUCHESS

INTRODUCTORY NOTES

Geoffrey Chaucer's *The Book of the Duchess* is the first major poem by the first major author of the English language. Years before he conceived of *The Canterbury Tales*, Chaucer seems to have written a fair number of minor or short poems, and these called his talents to the attention of John of Gaunt, the Duke of Lancaster (1340-1399), who was the son of King Edward III of England, uncle of Richard II, and father of Henry IV. Gaunt was married three times, first and most famously to Blanche in 1359 to Blanche of Lancaster, second to Constance of Castile in 1371, and third to Katherine Swynford in 1396.

Gaunt seems to have maintained a lifelong patronage of Chaucer, who composed *The Book of the Duchess* as a memorial to Gaunt's first wife Blanche (1345-1368), the mother of Henry IV. As noted above, Gaunt was so pleased with the work that he granted Chaucer a yearly "tun" of wine in thanks for his composition of this poem. Eventually, Chaucer and Gaunt were cousins through marriage, as Chaucer's wife Philippa de Roet was the sister of Gaunt's third wife Katherine.

The exact date of the poem as a memorial to Blanche, the Duchess of Lancaster, is a bit tentative. Blanche died on September 12, 1368, and the poem is usually dated somewhere between that date and some point in 1372 when Chaucer was likely at work on *The Parliament of Fowls* and on an ambassadorial mission to Italy. We have three other pieces of information that might set the date at 1374, 1380, or 1376: in 1374 Gaunt commissioned a double tomb and monument for himself and Blanche; in 1380 the work was completed; and the poem itself describes how the dreamer (who arguably is Gaunt himself) has been unable to sleep for eight years. Though most Chaucerian scholars now tend to favor an earlier date of composition, it is hard to resist a scenario for presentation at court of this poem at a memorial service for Blanche.

Whatever the particulars of its composition may be, the poem offers us a memorable glimpse of the sorrowing Gaunt and his attempt to recall Blanche and his courtship with her. We see also how his struggle is underlined as the dreamer (a version of Chaucer, Gaunt himself, or some combination of the two) attempts to understand the grief of the knight, whose name is simply "Black," over the loss of his beloved "White." ("Blanche," of course, is French for white.) *The Book of the Duchess*, though an early work of Chaucer, is no minor accomplishment. The poignancy of the woeful Gaunt is balanced not only by Chaucer's masterful handling of a framing device of a restless narrator who reads the tale of Ceyx and Alcyone, a parallel to that of Gaunt and Blanche, but also by his handling of the relationship between the narrator/dreamer and the woeful knight. Likewise, Chaucer is able to describe Blanche in such a sympathetic but honest fashion that she is brought back into the lives of the members of court who loved her. Though Chaucer may have been as young as twenty-five at the time he wrote *The Book of the Duchess*, he was able to offer us a masterpiece about love and loss that is among the finest works of its kind ever written.

THE BOOK OF THE DUCHESS

I wonder and wonder, by the light of the moon, how I stay alive, for I can hardly sleep at all, day or night. I have so many idle thoughts, all for lack of sleep, that, I swear, I care about nothing at all – whether anything comes or goes. There is nothing dear nor despised for me – it's all alike to me – joy or sorrow, it doesn't matter. For I feel nothing about anything, as if I am some sort of dazed thing, always on the brink of falling over; for sorrowful visions and images are always and everywhere fully in my mind.

And well you should know, it is against nature to live this way, for nature would not allow any earthly creature to endure for such a long time to be without sleep and in sorrow. And as I can not sleep, neither by night nor morning, I am melancholy and afraid that I shall die. Lack of sleep and heaviness[1] have slain my spirit of liveliness, so that I have lost all joy and vigor. My head is so full of fantasies that I don't know what's best to do.

But one might ask me why I can not sleep and what is wrong with me. But nonetheless, whoever asks this truly wastes his question. I, myself, can not tell why. But surely, the truth is that I maintain it is a sickness, I suppose, that I have suffered these eight years; and yet my remedy is never the nearer, for there is but one physician who can heal me – but enough about that. Let's pass over this until later. (What will not come about must be left behind.) It's best to return to our first subject.

So, recently, the other night, when I saw that I could not sleep, I sat up in my bed and bid someone to bring me a book,[2]

[1] Heaviness. Spiritual heaviness (melancholy).

a romance. And he brought it to me to read and drive the night away; for it seemed to me a better activity than playing either at chess or backgammon. And in this book were written fables that clerks and other poets had in old times (when people loved the law of nature) put into rhyme to be read and remembered. This book spoke primarily of queen's lives and king's lives, and many other smaller matters.

Among all this I found a tale that seemed to me an amazing thing. This was the tale. There was a king named Ceyx, and he had a wife, the best who ever lived, and this queen was named Alcyone. So it happened soon thereafter, this king would venture over the sea. To tell it shortly, when he was thus at sea, such a tempest rose up that their mast was broken and it toppled. It cleft their ship in two and drowned them all. They were never found, as the book says, ship nor man nor nothing else. In this way this King Ceyx lost his life.

Now, to speak of Alcyone, his wife: this lady, who was left at home, wondered why the king didn't come home, for it was a long time. Soon her heart began to grieve, as she believed more and more that he did not fare well. She so longed for the king that it is a pitiful thing to tell the exceedingly sorrowful life that she, this noble wife, had, for, alas, she loved him best of all.

Soon she sent messengers to seek him both east and west, but they found nothing. "Alas!" she said, "that I was created! If only I could know whether or not my lord, my love, is dead. Surely, I will never eat one crumb of bread, I make a vow to my god here, unless I might hear of my lord!" Such sorrow this lady took to herself that, truly, I, the person who wrote this book, had such pity and such sorrow to read of her sorrow that, I swear, I fared all the worse the entire morning afterwards to think about her sorrow.

So when this lady received no word and as no man had found her lord, very often she swooned and cried "Alas!" When she was nearly out of her mind for sorrow, she could

---

[2] Book. Probably Ovid's *Metamorphoses*.

think of only one plan of action; she set down on her knees and wept so tenderly that it was a pity to hear. "O, mercy, sweet lady dear!" she said to Juno,[3] her goddess, "Help me out of this distress, and give me grace to see my lord soon, or to know where he may be, or how he fares, or in what manner, and I shall make you a sacrifice and become wholly yours, with good will, body, heart, and all. And, if you would, lady sweet, please send me grace to sleep, and dream in my sleep a clear vision whereby I may know for certain whether my lord is alive or dead."

With that word she hung down her head and fell a-swoon, as cold as stone. Her women caught her up quickly, undressed her, and brought her to bed, and she, exhausted from weeping and lack of sleep, was so weary that a dead sleep fell on her before she noticed, thanks to Juno, who had heard her prayer and made her fall straight asleep. For as Alcyone prayed, just so was the deed done; for Juno immediately called her messenger[4] to do her errand, and he came without hesitation.

When he had come, she instructed him thus: "Go quickly," said Juno, "to Morpheus – you know him well, the god of sleep. Now listen carefully and remember well! Say this on my behalf: that he must go fast into the Great Sea,[5] and bid him that, above all, he take up Ceyx, the king's, body, which lies so pale and lacking all color. Bid him creep into that body and make it go to Alcyone the queen, where she lies alone, and show it to her briefly, so that there is no denying how he was drowned days ago. And make the body speak just as it used to do when it was alive. Go now quickly, and hurry!"

This messenger took leave, went upon his way, and never stopped until he came to the dark valley that stood between two rocks where there never grew wheat nor grass nor trees nor nothing that was anything. There was no beast, man, or

---

[3] Juno. The goddess of women and the wife of Jupiter. Also known as Hera.
[4] Messenger. Probably Iris, as mentioned in Chaucer's sources.
[5] Great Sea. The Mediterranean.

anything else,, but there were, running down from the cliffs, a few springs which made a lifeless, sleeping sound. And the waters ran down next to a cave that was carved under a rock amidst the deep valley. There these gods, Morpheus and Eclympasteyr (the god of sleep's son), who sleep and do no other work, lie and sleep. This cave was also as dark as the pit of hell all around. They had the fine leisure to snore away, as if to contend over who could sleep best. Some hung their chin upon their breast and slept upright, their head hidden, and some lay undressed in their bed and slept all day long.

This messenger came flying fast and cried, "Awake! Awake now!" It was for nought: none heard him there. "Awake!" he said, "who is lying there?" And he blew his horn right in their ears, and cried "Awake!" extremely loud. This god of sleep looked up with his one eye and asked, "Who calls there?"

"It is I," said this messenger. "Juno instructed that you should go." And he told him what he should do (as I have told you before – there is no need to rehearse it again) and went his way when he had said this. Immediately this god of sleep jumped out of his slumber and started to go, and did as he had been bidden to do: he took up the drowned body and bore it forth to Alcyone, his wife the queen, where she lay, exactly three hours before dawn, and stood at the foot of her bed. And he called her by her very name and said, "My sweet wife, Awake! Leave your sorrowful life, for in your sorrow there lies no remedy; for, surely, sweet, I am surely dead. You shall never see me alive. But, good sweet heart, see that you bury my body, for at a certain time you can find it beside the sea. Farewell, sweet, my world's bliss! I pray to God to lessen your sorrow. Our bliss lasts for so short a time!"

With that she cast up her eyes and saw nothing. "Alas!" she said for sorrow, and died within the third morning. But what else she said in that anguish I may not tell you now – it would be too long to dwell on it.

I will return you to my original subject, the reason why I

have told this story of Alcyone and Ceyx the king, for I dare say this much: I would have been entirely buried and dead, because of lack of sleep, if I had not read and heeded this tale. And I will tell you why: for I could not, for comfort or suffering, sleep before I had read this tale of this drowned Ceyx the king and of the gods of sleeping. When I had read this tale well and looked over every bit of, it seemed amazing to me that it would be so, for I had never heard mention before then of any gods that could make people sleep, nor to wake, for I had known only one god.

And in my amusement I said then (and yet I had little desire to play) rather than I should so die through lack of sleep, I would give this Morpheus, or his goddess, Lady Juno, or some other creature, I care not who – "Make me sleep and have some rest, and I will give him, or her, the best gift anyone ever hoped to receive. And into his possession, immediately, if he will make me sleep a little, I will give him a feather-bed of down of pure white doves, arrayed with gold and finely covered in fine black satin from abroad, and many pillows, and every pillowcase of linen from Reynes,[6] to sleep softly – he will not need to toss and turn so often. And I will give him everything that belongs to a bedchamber, and all his rooms I will have painted with pure gold and arrayed with many matching tapestries. All this shall he have (if only I knew where his cave is) if he can make me sleep soon, as he did for the goddess, queen Alcyone. And thus this same god, Morpheus, may gain from me more rewards than he ever won; and to Juno, who is his goddess, I shall so do, I believe, whatever will please her."

I had hardly said that word, exactly as I have told it to you, that suddenly, I know not how, such a desire overtook me to sleep that I fell asleep right on my book, and then I dreamed so inwardly sweet a dream, so wonderful a dream that I believe that no one has ever had the insight to interpret my

[6] Reynes. In France. Famous for its textiles.

dream correctly. No, not Joseph of Egypt,[7] without a doubt, who interpreted the Pharaoh's dream – no more than could the least of us; no, not even Macrobius[8] (who wrote all of the vision that he dreamed, about King Scipio the African, the noble man, of such marvels that happened then), could even interpret my dreams, I believe. Lo, thus it was; this was my dream.

It seemed this way to me: that it was May, and in the dawning of day I lay (I dreamed this) in my bed all undressed and looked about, for I was waked by a great heap of small birds that had startled me out of my sleep through the sound and sweetness of their song. And, as I dreamed, they sat together upon my chamber roof outside, upon the tiles, all over, and sang, each one in its own manner, the most solemn service, in harmony, that ever a person, I believe, has heard, for some of them sang low, some high, and all of one accord. In short, in a word, there was never heard so sweet a voice unless it had been a creation of heaven – so merry a sound, so sweet the tunes, that surely I would not have believed it for all the town of Tunis[9] unless I had heard them sing. For all of my chamber began to ring through the singing of their harmony. There was nowhere to be heard a sound half so sweet in instrument or voice, nor half as agreeable. For none of them pretended to sing, as each of them made great pains to find merry and skillful notes. They spared not their throats.

And the truth be told, my chamber was carefully decorated with pictures, and with glass were all the windows brightly glazed, not a flaw in any of them, so that to behold them it was a great joy. For the entire story of Troy[10] was wrought in

---

[7] Joseph of Egypt. Interpreted the Pharaoh of Egypt's dreams. See Genesis 41.

[8] Macrobius. *The Dream of Scipio*, the African King, was originally written by the Roman Cicero and later expanded via lengthy commentary by Macrobius. In the dream Scipio, visited by the spirit of his grandfather, is shown a vision of the universe. The topic of the work the discordant and limited nature of human existence in a world which is otherwise harmonious.

[9] Tunis. He is punning: Tunis, tunes, towns. Tunis is in northern Africa.

the glasswork thus: of Hector and of King Priam, of Achilles and of King Laomedon, and also of Medea and of Jason, of Paris, Helen, and of Lavinia. And on all the walls were painted with fine colors the entire Romance of the Rose,[11] both text and gloss.[12] My windows were all shut, and through the glass the sun shone upon my bed with bright beams, with many pleasant golden streams. And the sky was so fair, blue and bright, the air was clear and truly temperate, for it was neither too hot nor too cold, and there was not a cloud in the sky.

And as I lay thus, I thought I heard a hunter attempt to blow his horn tremendously loud to tell if the horn were clear or hoarse in its sound. And I heard men, horses, hounds, and other things going up and down, and all the men speaking of hunting – how they would slay the hart with their strength, and how the hart would at length become exhausted from the hunt – I don't remember what else.

As soon as I heard that, how they would go a-hunting, I was rather glad, and right away I took my horse and went forth out of my chamber. I never stopped until I came to the

---

[10] Troy. Of the Trojan War. The ancient war between the Greeks (or Achaeans) and the Trojans, fought over Helen, wife of Menelaus, the King of Sparta, whose wife was seduced and taken by the Trojan Paris back to Troy. The story is best-known from its telling in Homer's *Iliad* and *Odyssey* and Vergil's *Aeneid.* Hector was the military champion of Troy and son to Priam, king of Troy, who was the son of Laomedon. Achilles was the military champion of the Greeks. Aeneas was the Trojan prince, nephew of Priam, who, upon the fall and destruction of Troy, sailed to Italy and founded what eventually became the Roman Empire. There he married Lavinia. Medea, magician and princess of Colchis, who married Jason, leader of the Argonauts who sought and won the Golden Fleece (with Medea's help), but later, after they were married and had two children, he deserted her. Eventually she kills Jason, his lover, and her own two children by Jason.

[11] *Romance of the Rose*. The most famous medieval French poem (which Chaucer translated). In this poem, written by Guillaume de Lorris and Jean de Meun, is encompassed "all the art of love.".

[12] Gloss. A footnote or commentary on the text.

field outside. There I overtook a great company of hunters and foresters, with many chasing hounds and tracking hounds. They rushed to the forest, and I, with them. So finally I asked one of them who led a tracking dog: "Say, fellow, who shall hunt here?" I said, and he answered, "Sir, the Emperor Octavian,"[13] he said, "and he is near here."

"In God's name, in good time!" I said, "Let's go quickly!" and began to ride. When we came to the edge of the forest, every man right away went about doing what hunters are supposed to do. The master-hunter then, without delay, blew three notes with a great horn at the release of his hounds. Within a while the hart is sought, halooed after, and pursued for a great time; and so, at last, this hart deceived them and stole away from all the hounds a secret way. The hounds had overshot him completely and were defeated because of the lack of a scent. And so, at last, the hunter quickly blew his horn.

I walked away from my assigned tree,[14] and as I went, there came near me a whelp, that fawned on me as I stood there. It had followed me and did not know what to do. It came and crept toward me humbly, just as if it had known me. He held down his head and put back his ears and laid his hair down all smooth. I wanted to catch it, but quickly it fled from me and was gone. And I followed him, and it went forth down by a flowery green path, soft under my feet, thick with grass, soft and sweet, with many flowers, and rarely tread upon. So it seemed, for both Flora and Zephirus[15] – the two who make flowers grow, had made their dwelling there, I believe; for it was, to behold it, as though the earth would contend to be more ornate than the heavens, as it had more flowers, seven times as many, as there are stars in the sky. It had forgotten

---

[13] Octavian. Augustus Caesar. Founder of the Roman Empire, which he ruled from 27 BC until his death in 14 AD.

[14] Tree. He was posted, for the purpose of the hunt, at a tree, towards which, supposedly, the hart would be driven.

[15] Flora and Zephirus. Emblems of the beginning of Spring. When Flora is ravished by Zephirus, the West Wind, the flowers return.

the poverty that Winter, through his cold mornings, had made it suffer, and the sorrows he brought; all was forgotten, and that was visible, for all the woods had grown green; the sweetness of the dew had made it grow.

There is no need to ask me if there were many green branches or thickets of trees full of leaves; every tree stood by itself, ten to twelve feet from the next. Such great trees, such immense strength; of forty or fifty fathoms high, neatly maintained, without a stray bough or twig, with crowns equally broad and thick – they were not an inch apart, so that it was entirely shady underneath. And many harts and hinds[16] were both before me and behind. The wood was full of fawns, sorrels, bucks, and does, as were there many roes, and many squirrels that sat high upon the trees and ate, making many feasts in their own fashion. In short, it was so full of beasts that, even if Algus, the noble mathematician,[17] were to sit in his counting house and calculate with his ten numerals – for by those numerals all may learn, if they are sharp enough, to count and calculate – he would still fail to calculate correctly the wonders I dreamed in my dream.

But I roamed very quickly through the wood, until at last I became aware of a man in black, who had turned his back to a huge oak tree and sat. "Lord," thought I, "who may that be? What ails him to sit here so?" Quickly I drew up close to him; then I found him sitting upright, a striking, attractive knight – so was my impression of him – well-proportioned, and moreover rather young, twenty-four years old, with little hair in his beard, and he was clothed all in black.

I stalked directly behind him and I stood there as still as possible, so that, to tell the truth, he didn't see me; so he hung his head down, and with a deadly sorrowful sound he made a complaint[18] of ten or twelve rhymed verses to himself, the

---

[16] Hart and Hind. Male and female deer.

[17] Algus. The inventor of Arabic numerals.

[18] Complaint. A type of poetry which expresses some type of sorrow or hardship.

most pitiful, the most doleful, I ever heard; for, I swear, it is a great wonder that Nature might allow any creature to have such sorrow and not be dead. So piteously pale and lacking any ruddiness, he spoke his lay, a kind of tune, without music, without song; and this was it, for I can repeat it word for word – it began like this:

"I am by sorrow so much undone
That I get joy forever none,
Now that I see my lady bright,
Whom I have loved with all my might,
Is from me dead and is gone.

"Alas, death, what so ails thee,
That thou wouldn't have taken me,
When thou took my lady dear,
That was so fair, so fresh, so free,[19]
So good that all may well see
Of all good folk she had no peer!"

When he had thus made his complaint, his sorrowful heart quickly became faint and his spirits grew dead; his blood had fled, for pure dread, down to his heart, to make him warm – for well it felt the heart had grief – to learn also why it was terrified, by nature, and to make it glad again, for it is the principal organ of the body. And this rush of blood made his entire hue change and grow green and pale, for there was no blood to be seen in any of his limbs.

As soon as I saw this – he fared so poorly, as he sat there – I went and stood right at his feet and greeted him; he spoke nothing, but argued with his own thoughts, and in his mind disputed firmly why and how his life might continue, as his sorrows seemed to him so painful and lay so coldly on his heart. So, his sorrow and gloomy thoughts made him so that

[19] Free. Noble.

he did not hear me – for he had pretty nearly lost his mind; even Pan,[20] whom we call the god of nature, was never so disturbed for his sorrows.

But at last, to tell the absolute truth, he became aware of me, as I stood before him and took off my hood, and had greeted him courteously and humbly, as best I knew how. He said, "I pray you, be not upset. I heard you not, to tell the truth, nor did I see you, sir, truly."

"Ah, good sir, it does not matter," I said, "I am quite sorry if I have at all disturbed you from your thought. Forgive me, if I have made a mistake."

"Yes, but it is easy to make amends," he said, "for no offense has been taken; nothing wrong has been said or done."

Lo, how well this knight spoke, as if it had been another person; he presented himself as neither blunt nor strange. As I noticed this, I began to acquaint myself with him, and he seemed to me, for all his suffering, so agreeable, so very knowledgeable and reasonable. Straightaway I began to search, to look where I might, for a worthy subject for discussion, so that I could get to know him better.

"Sir," I said, "this game is done. I maintain that this hart is gone; these hunters can find him nowhere."

"I do not care about that," he said; "my thoughts are not the least bit on that."

"By our Lord," I said, "I believe you well; that seems plain to me in your face. But, sir, will you listen to one thing? It seems to me I see you in great sorrow; but surely, sir, if you would reveal to me your woe, I would remedy it, if I can or may. You can test it by trying; for, by my word, to make you whole and well, I will give it all of my power. Please tell me of your painful sorrows; by chance it may ease your heart, which seems so sick within."

With that he looked on me askance, as one who says, "No, that will not be."

---

[20] Pan. Lost his beloved Syrinx when she was turned into the reeds. He then created a musical instrument (the pan-flute) by twining together seven reeds.

"Grant mercy, good friend," he said, "I thank you for wishing it so, but it may not be done so soon. No one may lighten my sorrow, which makes my hue to lessen and fade, and which has made me to lose my understanding, so that I am woeful that I was ever born! Nothing can make my sorrows slide away, not all the remedies of Ovid,[21] nor Orpheus,[22] the god of music, nor Daedalus with his ingenious inventions;[23] no physician may heal me, not Hippocrates nor Galen.[24] Woe is me that I should live even another twelve hours! But whoever wishes to try his hand to see if his heart can have pity for my sorrow, let him see me. I am a wretch whom death has stripped naked of all the bliss that ever was made and made lowest of all creatures, so much so that I hate all my days and my nights!

"All my pleasures, indeed, my whole life, are loathsome to me, for myself and my welfare are at odds. Death itself is so surely my foe that if I would say I want to die, he would say no; for when I pursue him, he flees; I wish to have him, but he will not have me. This is my pain without comfort, always dying and not dead, and so much so that not even Sisyphus,[25]

---

[21] Ovid. Author of the *Remedies of Love*, more famous for his *Metamorphoses*.

[22] Orpheus. Well-known for his love of Euridice, who, bitten by a snake, is taken to the underworld, Hades, where she is rescued by Orpheus, whose beautiful lyre music pleases (or puts to sleep) the god of the underworld. As they exit the underworld, Orpheus looks back at his wife, and she must return to Hades, where Orpheus later joins her after his own death. In the medieval version of *Sir Orfeo*, she was snatched by the fairy king, and, after the descent to the underworld, Orfeo and Heurodis live happily ever after.

[23] Daedalus. Mythical inventor (whose name means "cunning inventor"). Invented wings with which his son Icarus could fly. But Icarus flew too close to the sun, the wax on them melted, and he plunged to his death.

[24] Hippocrates, Galen. Famous Greek and Roman physicians. (Thus the Hippocratic Oath.)

[25] Sisyphus. For his misdeeds on earth, he was condemned to eternal punishment in Hades, where he rolled to the top of a hill a large stone, which when it reached the summit rolled down again.

who lies in hell, has no more sorrow to tell. And whosoever might come to know all my sorrow, I swear, unless he should sympathize and take pity on my painful sorrows, that man has a fiendish heart. For whosoever sees me tomorrow may say he has met with Sorrow, for I am Sorrow, and Sorrow is I.

"Alas! And I will tell you why: why my song is turned to lament, my laughter to weeping, my glad thoughts to sad ones; why all my work is also my idleness and my rest; why my wellness is woe, my good is harm; and why my joyful pastimes are turned into wrath, my delight into sorrow. So too my good health is turned into sickness, my security into dread, all my light to dark; my wit is folly, my day is night, my love is hate, my sleep waking, my mirth and meals are fasting; my self-confidence is turned to foolishness and I am entirely disconcerted, wherever I may be; my peace is turned into lawsuits and war.

"Alas, how would I ever fare in war? My boldness is turned to shame, for false Fortune has played a game of chess with me. Alas, the time it happened! The traitoress, false and full of guile, she who promises everything and delivers nothing, who walks upright and still limps, who squints so foully and still looks lovely, the disdainful and gracious one, who scorns so many creatures! She is an idol of false self-portraiture, for she would gladly deceive; she is the monster's head pleasantly disguised, like a dung-heap over-strewn with flowers. Her most innate and representative quality is her lying, for that is her nature; she is false – without sincerity, lawfulness, or moderation, as she is ever laughing with one eye, and weeping with the other. Whatever rises, she knocks down. I liken her to the scorpion, a false, flattering beast, for with his head he makes merry, but as he is flattering you, he will sting and envenom you. Fortune is the hostile charity, who is always false and seems true. So she turns her false wheel around, for it never remains stationary – at one moment you are being served at the table, at another you are a servant standing by the fire. She has blinded many: she is an enchantress, who seems to be one thing and is another.

"The false thief! What has she done? What do you suppose? By our Lord I will tell you: she began to play with me at chess; and with her various little cheating moves, she tricked me and stole away my queen. And when I saw my queen had been taken away, alas, I could not figure out how to continue playing, but said, 'Farewell, sweet, surely, and farewell everything, now and forever!'

"At that moment Fortune said, 'Check her!' And checkmated me, with an errant pawn, in the mid-point of the checker board! Alas, craftier at play was she than Attalus,[26] so was his name, who invented the game of chess. But I wish to God that I could have understood, just once or twice, the chess problems the way that the Greek Pythagoras[27] might have. I should have played better at chess and thereby kept my queen better. But what does it matter? For truly, I say that wish isn't worth a straw! It would have turned out no better for me, for Fortune knows so many tricks that there are few who can beguile her; and she is also the less to blame; myself, I would have done the same, as God is my witness, had I been her; she ought, I suppose, to be more excused than me. For I must say a bit more about this: had I been God and might have done as I wished when she captured my queen, I would have made the same move. For, as surely as God may give me rest, I dare well swear she took the best. But through that move I have lost my bliss; alas, that I was born!

"Forevermore, I truly believe, in spite of all my wishes, my joy is entirely reversed; but yet, what can I do? By our Lord, the only option seems to be to die soon. For I care nothing about anything, but live and die right in this thought; for there is no planet in the firmament, nor in the air nor in the earth or elements, that does not give me a gift of weeping when I am alone. For when I consider everything, how there is

[26] Attalus. Attalus Philometer, king of Cappadocia

[27] Pythagoras. Greek philosopher and ruler who greatly advanced fields of mathematics and geometry.

nothing owing to me in matters of sorrow, and how there exists no merriment that may relieve me of my distress, and how I have lost all my contentment, and how for all that I have no delight, then may I say I have absolutely nothing. And when all this comes into my mind, alas, then I am overcome! For whatever is done can not be changed. I have more sorrow than Tantalus."[28]

And when I heard him tell this tale so pitifully, as I have told you, hardly could I remain there longer, as it gave my heart so much woe. "A, good sir," I said, "do not say so! Have some pity on your Nature that formed you as a creature. Remember Socrates,[29] for he considered anything that Fortune could do to be worth three straws."

"No," he said, "I don't think so."

"Why so, good sir? Yes, by God!" I said; "do not say so, for truly, even if you had lost twelve queens, and you murdered yourself for sorrow, you should be damned in this case, as was Medea, who slew her children on account of Jason;[30] and Phyllis, who was so desperate that she hung herself for Demophoun, for he had broken his appointed day to come to her. Another such rage had Dido, the queen of Carthage, who, because Aeneas was false to her slew herself – for which she was a fool![31] And Echo died because Narcissus would not love her,[32] and likewise have many others done such folly;

---

[28] Tantalus. For stealing the nectar of the gods and for revealing their secrets, he was punished by being placed, hungry and thirsty, in Hades, under fruit trees which moved when he tried to pick them and in a river which receded when he tried to drink it.

[29] Socrates. Greek philosopher who argued that self-control, not Fortune, brought us pleasure.

[30] Medea and Jason. Knowing that her children would be slain by Jason's followers – since she had just slain Jason (unfaithful to her) and his bride – Medea slew her children.

[31] Dido and Aeneas. Their love is the topic of the opening books of Vergil's *Aeneid.* Though he pledged himself to Dido, Aeneas deserted her when he was reminded of his divine mission to found Rome.

[32] Echo and Narcissus. Narcissus, a beautiful youth, would love none but hit own reflection in the water. Echo loved him but died in despair because her

and Samson, who slew himself with a pillar, died for Dalilah.[33] But there is no man alive today who would undergo such woe for a queen!"

"Why so?" he said, "it is not so. You know full little what you mean by your words; I have lost more than you think."

"Lo, tell me how that may be?" I said; "Good sir, tell me entirely, how, why, by what cause, and in what ways you have thus lost your bliss."

"Gladly," he said; "come sit down! I'll tell you upon the condition that you shall wholly, with all your wit, carry out your intention to listen carefully to it."

"Yes, sir."

"Swear your promise to do so."

"Gladly."

"Then you better keep your word!"

"I shall, with great joy, God save me, wholly, with all the wit I have, listen to you as well as I can."

"In God's name!" he said, and began. "Sir," he said, "ever since I first could in my youth by learning or natural understanding in any way comprehend what love was, doubtless, I have ever since been a vassal to and paid tribute to Love, with entirely good intentions, and with great pleasure become his servant, body, heart, and soul, with good will. All this I committed to his service and did homage to him as my lord; and I prayed to him devoutly that he might employ my heart in such a way that it would be a delight to him and an honor to my dear lady.

"And I remained in his service many years before my heart was set anywhere in particular, and I knew not why; I believe it came to me naturally. Perhaps I was most capable in this respect, as is a white wall or slate, for it is ready to accept and receive anything that one will put there, whatever one

---

love was unrequited.

[33] Samson and Dalilah. Biblical story in which the strong man Samson is betrayed by the enemy Dalilah, who seduces him to find out the secret of his strength (his hair).

wishes to paint or portray, no matter how elaborate the works may be.

"And at this time I fared well, so that I was able to have learned all about love, and I learned it as well or better than any other art or science; as love always came first in my mind, I never forgot it. I chose love as my first craft; therefore it has remained with me. Since I took it up at such a young age, my heart had no trouble with it, and time did not erase it, as I had studied too much for that to happen. Up to that time, Youth, my governess, instructed me in idleness; for it was in my early youth, and I knew very little worth knowing then, for all my works were impermanent at that time, and all my thoughts were changeable. Everything that I knew then was equally good; but that is how it was.

"It happened that I came one day into a place where I saw truly the fairest company of ladies assembled in one place that ever a man had seen with eye. Shall I call it chance or grace that brought me there? No, only Fortune, who is so accustomed to lie, the false perverse traitoress! I wish to God I could call her worse, for now she makes me woeful, and I will soon tell you why.

"Among these ladies, to tell the truth, I saw one who was like none of the rest; for I dare swear, without a doubt, that as the summer's bright sun is fairer, clearer, and has more light than any other planet in the heavens, the moon or the seven stars,[34] so had she, for all the world, surmounted them all in beauty, in demeanor, in graciousness, in stature, in cheerfulness – in short, in excellence so well bestowed upon her – what more can I say? By God and his twelve apostles, this was my sweet, her very self. She had such a steadfast countenance, such noble deportment and bearing, and Love, who had listened so carefully to my request, had looked upon me so quickly, that she was, so help me God, so swiftly caught in my mind that I didn't need to ask for advice from anywhere, but

[34] Seven stars. Probably the seven other known heavenly bodies in the Milky Way. Or, perhaps the Pleiades.

only looked to her and to my heart; for when her eyes so gladly beheld my heart, I believe, my own thought then, without a doubt, said it would be better to serve her for nothing than to serve another and be well-rewarded. And it was so, for I will tell you why right now in full detail.

"I saw her dance so becomingly, to sing and join in carols so sweetly, to laugh and play so womanly, to carry herself so graciously, and to speak so friendly and kindly, that surely I believe that never was seen so blissful a treasure as she. For every hair on her head, to tell the truth, was not red or yellow or brown; it seemed most like gold.

"And what eyes my lady had! Stately, kind, glad, sincere, and true, well-proportioned, and not too wide. Thus her eyes looked directly, not aside or askance, but so carefully settled on things that they entirely ennobled everything they beheld. Her eyes seemed to say that she would have mercy[35] on me – fools would think so – but she would never do so hastily. But her look was not counterfeit; it was her own pure way of looking, a way in which the goddess, Lady Nature, had made her eyes open and close moderately; for even if she was delighted, her glances were not spread about foolishly or wildly, even if she was being playful; but, it seemed to me, her eyes said, 'By God, all of my ill-will is gone!'

"In this way she loved to live so fully that dullness was afraid of her. She was not too sober nor too glad; in all things she had more moderation, I believe, than any other creature. She hurt many men with her look, but that sat lightly on her heart, for she knew nothing of their thoughts; but whether she knew it or not, she nonetheless considered it as much as she would a piece of straw! To get her love, no nearer was he who dwelled at home than he who was in India; the first in line was always the last. But she loved good people, above all others, as one may love his brother; and she was very generous in this kind of love, especially in appropriate times and places.

---

[35] Mercy. In the language of courtly love, for a woman to have mercy on a man is to allow him fully into her heart.

"But what a face had she! Alas, my heart is so woeful that I can't describe it! I lack both the English and the wit to unfold it fully; and my spirits are also too dull for me to devise so great a thing. I have no wit that can suffice to comprehend her beauty. But I dare say this much, that she had a fresh, lively complexion, and every day her beauty renewed. And her face was nearly the best of all, for surely Nature had such desire to make that beautiful that truly she was the chief example and pattern of Nature's beauty – and of all her work; for though her image seems so dark and distant, I think I see her always. And, moreover, even if everyone who ever lived were now alive, they would be unable to discover any fault, any wicked sign, in her face, for it was sincere, honest, and kind.

"And such a fine, soft voice had my sweet one, the savior[36] of my life! So friendly, and so well-instructed, so well-grounded in reason, and so agreeable to all good people that, I dare well swear, by the cross, there was never found such eloquent speech, nor so sweet a tongue, nor one that scorned others less, nor could heal them more nor less falseness in her word, that in her simple promise alone was found as true as any bond or oath from any man's hand; nor could she chide anyone, not even one word. (I swear by the holy mass – even if the Pope himself sang it – that there was never any man nor woman harmed by her tongue; and as for her, all harm was hidden from her.) The whole world knows this well.

"But such a lovely neck had that sweet one, every inch perfectly shaped, without a blemish. It was white, smooth, straight, and even, without hollows or collar-bone, as it seems she had none. Her throat, as I remember, seemed a round tower of ivory, full, but not too full.

"And she was called the good faire "White"; truly that was my lady's name. She was both fair and bright; there was nothing inaccurate about her name. She had nice soft shoul-

[36] Savior. Chaucer uses the word "leche," which means Physician or healer.

ders and a long body, and arms as well; every limb was well-rounded and fleshy, but not too much so; nice white hands, and red nails; round breasts; and firm broad hips; and a straight, flat back. I knew of no other fault, as far as I could tell, other than her limbs were not perfectly in proportion.

"She knew how to present herself so well, when she pleased, that I dare say that she was like a bright lamp from which everyone might receive an abundance of light, and never less. In manners and behavior my lady was so excellent that anyone who caught a glimpse of her remembered her fully; for I dare well swear, if she had been one among ten thousand standing in a row at a feast, she would have been, at the least, a chief paragon in the eyes of all; for wherever people gathered together without her, it seemed to me that the company was entirely lacking, like a crown without gemstones. Truly she was to my eye the solitary Phoenix of Arabia,[37] for there is only one of those, and I know of none other like her.

"To speak of goodness, truly she had as much graciousness as ever had Esther[38] in the Bible, and more, if more were possible. And, to tell the truth, she had in this way a wit so congenial, so fully inclined to goodness, that all her thoughts were fixed, by the Cross, without malice and upon gladness; and thus I never saw one less harmful than she. I don't mean that she did not know what harm was, or else she would not have known so well what good was.

"And truly, speaking of truth, if she had not truth, it would have been a pity. She had such a great portion of truth – and I dare well swear it – that Truth himself had chosen her, over one and all, as his principal manor and resting place. And thus she gracefully and calmly persevered, reigning the most moderately I have ever seen, so kind and tolerant was her mind;

---

[37] Phoenix. In legends of the Phoenix, the bird which consumes itself in fire then is reborn of its own ashes, there is much emphasis placed on its solitary nature.

[38] Esther. Biblical model of wifely virtue. See Book of Esther.

and she gladly understood reason; and, of course, she knew goodness well. She used to do good deeds gladly; these were her custom in everything.

"Since she loved justice so well, she would do no wrong to anyone. No creature could do any shame to her, as she loved and honored her own name. She would not encourage anyone with false hopes, nor, be sure of this, would she strive to hold any creature in suspense with half-truths or false-seeming – unless anyone would lie about her. She sent no men to Rumania, Prussia, Mongolia, Alexandria, or Turkey, nor bid him to rush off and go bare-headed into the Gobi Desert and come home the long way, by the Kara-Nor, and say, 'Sir, be sure that you have praiseworthy deeds to report before you return here!' She used no such petty tricks.

"But why do I tell my tale? For this very reason, as I have said: my love was entirely set on her. For surely she was, this sweet wife, my source of contentment, my joy, my life, my good fortune, my health, and all my blessing, the welfare of the world, and my goddess, and I was wholly hers, body and soul."

"By our Lord," I said, "I well believe you! Assuredly, your love was well bestowed; I don't know how you might have done better."

"Better? No creature has ever done half so well," he said.

"I understand it well, sir," I said, "by God!"

"No, *believe* it well!"

"Sir, yes, I do; I believe you well, that truly you thought that she was the best, and the fairest of all to behold, for anyone who looked on her with your eyes."

"With *my eyes*? No, *all* saw her said and swore it was so. And even if they had not, I would still have loved my noble lady best. And even if I had had all the beauty that Alcibiades[39] ever had; all the strength of Hercules; all the worthiness of Alexander;[40] all the riches that ever were in Babylon,

[39] Alcibiades. Athenian politician, remembered mostly for his good looks.

[40] Alexander. Alexander the Great of Macedon, ruler of much of the East-

Carthage, Macedonia, Rome, or Ninevah; all the courage of Hector[41] (whom Achilles slew at Troy, and so too was he slain in a temple, for both he and Antilochus were slain – so says Dares Frygius – for the love of Polixena);[42] or all the wisdom of Minerva, I would forever, without a doubt, have loved her, for I must.

"'*Must?*' No, truly, I speak nonsense now; Not '*must*' – and I will explain why: because my heart *wished* it through good *will*, and because I was obliged to love her as the fairest and the best. She was as good, God rest my soul, as ever was Penelope[43] of Greece, or as the noble wife Lucrece,[44] who was the best (so says the Roman, Titus Livus[45]). She was as good, though nothing like her, except in goodness (though their stories are true); nonetheless she was as faithful as she.

"But why don't I tell you about the first time I saw my lady? I was rather young, to tell the truth, and still in great need of learning; when my heart would yearn to love, it was a great enterprise. As fitting with my young childly mind, I boldly set all my mental energy, as well as my brain could manage, on loving her in the best way I knew how, to honor and serve her in the best way I knew at the time, I swear, without being false or slothful in any way, for I wished to see her more than anything. So greatly did seeing her affect me that when I first saw her in the morning I was cured of all my

---

ern Mediterranean in the Fourth Century B.C.

[41] Hector. Trojan hero. His death at the hands of Achilles is the climax of *The Iliad.*

[42] Antilochus and Achilles. For the killing of Troilus and Hector, they were ambushed at the temple of Apollo where Achilles wished to marry Polixena.

[43] Penelope. Faithful wife of Odysseus, hero of *The Odyssey*. She waited him, though he was gone for over ten years and many men sought her hand.

[44] Lucrece. Faithful wife of Collatinus. Raped by Superbus, who cut out her tongue. She revealed the crime to him in her weaving, then took her life. Superbus' crime was then revenged.

[45] Titus Livius. Livy (59 BC – AD 17), author of *Ab Urbe Condita* (*From the Founding of the City*), which included the story of Lucrece, or Lucretia.

sorrow for the entire day; even into the evening it seemed nothing could grieve me, regardless of how painful my sorrows might be. And yet she sat so in my heart that, I swear, I would not for all the world leave this lady out of my thought; no, truly!"

"Now, I swear, sir," I said, "it seems to me you are in such a position to make your confession without repentance."

"Repentance? No, fy!" he said, "Should I now repent my love? No, surely! I'd be worse off than Achitophel,[46] or Antenor,[47] (the traitor who betrayed Troy), or the false Ganelon,[48] (who secured the treason of Roland and Oliver). No, while I am alive here, I will not forget her – nevermore."

"Now, good sir," I said then, "You have told me well before; there's no need to repeat again how you first saw her, and where. But would you tell me the manner in which you first spoke with her – this I ask you – and how she first came to know your thoughts, whether you loved her or not? And tell me also what you have lost, as I heard you mention earlier."

"Yes!" he said, "you know not what you mean by your words; I have lost more than you think."

"What loss is that?" I said then; "Will she not love you? Is it so? Or have you done something wrong, that she has left you? Is it this? For God's love, tell me everything."

"Before God," he said, "I shall do so. I say, just as I have said, on her was all my love bestowed, and yet she did not know it, not a bit, not for a long time, believe me! For be assured, I wouldn't dare, not for all this world, reveal my thoughts to her, nor would I have upset her, truly. Would you like to know why? She had control over my body: as she held

---

[46] Achitophel. Counseled Absalom to rebel against his father David. The rebellion failed and Absalom was killed in the Battle of Ephraim Wood. See 2 Samuel 17.

[47] Antenor. His treachery caused the downfall of Troy. As a peace offering, he sent the statue of Pallas Athene, the patron of Troy, to Ulysses.

[48] Ganelon. His treachery caused the great French hero Roland to be slain by the Saracens, as told in *The Song of Roland.*

my heart, I could not escape. But to keep myself from idleness, I went about my business in making songs, as best I knew how, and often I sang them aloud; and I made a great number of songs, although I could not make them so well, as I didn't know all the art of it, as did Lamech's son Tubal,[49] who originated the art of song; for as his brother's hammers rang up and down upon the anvil, from this he took the first tune – though Greeks say it was Pythagoras[50] who was the founder of the art (Aurora[51] says so); but what does that matter? Nevertheless, I made songs from my feelings to gladden my heart. And listen, here was the first of all – and perhaps the worst of all:

'Lord, it makes my heart light
When I think on that sweet wight[52]
Who is so lovely to see;
And wish to God it might so be
That she would have me for her knight,
My lady, who is so fair and bright!'

"Now have I told you, to tell the truth, my first song. One day I thought to myself about the woe and sorrow I suffered to that point for her, and yet she knew nothing about it, nor did I yet tell her my thoughts.

"'Alas,' I thought, 'I know no remedy; unless I tell her, I am nothing but dead; and if I tell her, to tell the very truth, I am afraid she will be upset with me. Alas, what shall I do then?'

"I was so woeful in this debate, it seemed my heart would

---

49 Lamech's son Tubal. Actually Jubal: called the "father of all such as handle the harp and organ" (Genesis 4.21).

50 Pythagoras. Greek philosopher and ruler who greatly advanced fields of mathematics and geometry.

51 Aurora. Twelfth-century versified Latin paraphrase and commentary on parts of the Bible by Peter of Riga (1140-1209).

52 Wight. Creature, person.

burst in two! So, at long last, to tell the truth, I determined that Nature never formed in any creature so much beauty, truly, and goodness, without mercy. In hope of that, I made my speech to her, but I told it badly and in a way that I never should have: for necessity, and against my own advising, I had to tell her, or die. I can hardly remember how I began; I can retell it only hazily; and, so help me God, I think it was an unlucky day – there were *ten* wounds of Egypt that day[53] – for I skipped, out of pure fear, over many words in my speech, lest my words would be poorly said. With sorrowful heart and deadly wounds, meekly and quaking for pure fear and shame, and stammering in my speech for fear, and my hue growing entirely pale – I often grew both pale and red – bowing to her, I hung my head; I dared not once look on her, for my wits, manners, and everything were gone. I said 'Mercy!' and no more. It was not amusing; it sat sorely on me.

"So at last, to tell the truth, when my heart returned to me, to summarize, with all my heart I beseeched her to be my sweet lady; and swore, and promised her heartily to be always steadfast and true, and to love her always newly, freshly, and never have any other lady, and to preserve her honor, as best I could. I swore this to her: 'For your honor is all that ever there is for me evermore, my heart sweet! And I'll never be false to you, unless I am dreaming, so help me dear God!'

"And when I had completed my speech, God knows, she valued it not so much as a straw, so it seemed. To be brief, her answer, truly, was this – I can not now counterfeit her words, but this was the main point of her answer: she utterly said 'No.' Alas, the sorrow and the woe I suffered that day, so much so that truly Cassandra,[54] who so bewailed the destruc-

[53] Ten wounds of Egypt. According to a late medieval belief, there were two unlucky days (*di[e]s mal* in French) per month, on which people were afflicted with wounds or plagues (as were the Egyptians in the time of Abraham). Black is having ten of these days at once.

[54] Cassandra. Trojan prophetess, sister of Hector and Troilus. Was given the gift of prophesy by Apollo, who, when she spurned his love, condemned her

tion of Troy and of Ilium, never had such sorrow as I did then. I dared not say another word at that point, for pure fear, but stole away; and thus I lived many a day, so that truly I had no need to go further than the head of my bed to seek sorrow; I found sorrow readily every morning, as my love for her never wavered.

"So it happened, another year passed, and I thought I would try once to let her know and comprehend my woe; and she came to understand well that I intended nothing but good, and honor, and to preserve her name above all things; and that I dreaded her disdain; and was so eager to serve her; and it would be a pity if I should die, since, surely, I intended no harm. So when my lady knew all this, she gave me the noble gift of her mercy entirely, without ever any offense to her honor. Without a doubt, I would have it no other way.

And with that she gave me a ring; I think it was the most memorable thing; of course, there's no need to ask if my heart grew glad! So help me God, I was quickly raised, as if from death to life; of all possible fortunes, I found the best of all, the gladdest, and the most enjoyable. For truly that sweet creature, when I was wrong and she was right, would always forgive me so kindly and graciously. In all my youth, in all events, she took me into her service. And there she was always so true, and our joy was ever renewed; our hearts were so equally paired that never would either of us be contrary to the other for any woe. For truly, both our hearts shared one bliss and one sorrow alike; they were both glad and sad the same; all was one for us, without a doubt. And thus we lived many years so well I can not tell how."

"Sir," I said, "where is she now?"

"Now?" he said, and stopped at once. With that he grew as dead as stone and said, "Alas, that I was born! That was the loss that I told you before that I had lost. Remember how I said earlier, 'You know full little what you mean by your

---

to the fate that no one would believe her predictions. Ilium: the citadel or fortress of Troy.

words; I have lost more than you think.' God knows, alas! She was that very person!"

"Alas, sir, how? How may that be?"

"She is dead!"

"No!"

"Yes, by my word!"

"Is that your loss? By God, that is such a pity!"

And with that word they quickly began to sound the hunting signal to head home; all the hart-hunting was done for that time.

With that I thought that this king began to ride homeward to an adjacent place which was a short way from us – a long castle with white walls, by Saint John, on a rich hill, so I dreamed; but thus it happened. I dreamed just as I tell you: in the castle there was a bell, and as it struck twelve, I awoke and found myself lying in my bed. And the book I had read, of Alcyone and Ceyx the king, and of the gods of sleep, I found wide open in my hand. I thought, "This is so strange a dream that I will, in the course of time, attempt to put this dream into rhyme as best I can, and do so soon."

This was my dream; now it is done.

THE PARLIAMENT OF FOWLS

INTRODUCTORY NOTES

Because Chaucer's *The Parliament of Fowls*, the shortest of his major works, contains the first mention in the English language of Valentine's Day and concerns the mating of birds at the end of winter, it is usually discussed as a celebration of love. If it is a celebration of love, it is not a typical one.

The poem contains many of the trappings of love, including a visit to the garden of love, the gathering of lover birds to select their mates, and the pledges of love by three suitors eagles to one young female eagle. The poem begins, however, with a discussion of the value of old books, a visit from a Roman general, a conversation on the importance of contributing to the general welfare of society (and what happens to those who do not contribute), and the entry gate into a place that might seem to be Hell itself. Likewise, later in the poem the wooing of the young eagle incites a heated discussion that nearly ends in a riot. These factors, along with an ending that one would not anticipate, might make us wonder if this poem is really about the virtue of love.

Despite the convoluted approach to love that Chaucer presents, we can assume without much hesitation that the poem is an allegory for a royal courtship. Most scholars have agreed that it reflects the courtship of Richard II and Anne of Bohemia, which culminated in their marriage in 1382. As the eldest daughter of Charles IV, Holy Roman Emperor, and Elizabeth of Pomerania, the hand of Anne (1366 – 1394) was well-sought by suitors. Though Anne was not received well by the court at first, she grew in the estimation of the court and in the love of Richard.

It is not clear when Chaucer wrote *The Parliament of Fowls*; it was surely written after the courtship began in 1380, but we do not know which stage the courtship was in when he completed the poem. We do know that, in Chaucer's inimitable way, we have a portrait of love that is not ideal, but true to life.

THE PARLIAMENT OF FOWLS

The life so brief, the art so long in the learning, the attempt so hard, the conquest so sharp, the fearful joy that ever slips away so quickly – by all this I mean love, which so sorely astounds my feeling with its wondrous operation, that when I think upon it I scarce know whether I wake or sleep. For albeit I know not Love myself; nor how he pays people their wage, yet I have very often chanced to read in books of his miracles and his cruel anger there, surely, I read he will ever be lord and sovereign, and his strokes will be so heavy that I dare say nothing but, "May God save such a lord!" I can say no more.

Somewhat for pleasure and somewhat for learning I am in the habit of reading books, as I have told you. But why speak I of all this? Not long ago I chanced to look at a book, written in antique letters, and there I read very diligently and eagerly through the long day, to learn about a certain thing. For, as people say, out of old fields comes all this new corn from year to year; and, in good faith, out of old books comes all this new knowledge that people learn. But now to my theme in this matter: it so delighted me to read on, that the whole day seemed to me rather short. This book of which I speak was entitled Tully[1] on the Dream of Scipio. It had seven chapters, on heaven and hell and earth, and the souls that live in those places; about which I will tell you the sub-

[1] Tully. Roman orator, Cicero (Marcus Tullius, 106-43 B.C.), whose *Dream of Scipio*, the conclusion of his *Republic*, was preserved with a long commentary by Macrobius. The narrator is relating the Macrobius version. In the dream the Roman general Scipio the Younger meets his grandfather, Scipio the Elder (Africanus) in a dream in which the younger is shown all the universe.

stance of Tully's wisdom, as briefly as I can.

The book first tells how, when Scipio had come to Africa, he met Masinissa,[2] who clasped him in his arms for joy. Then it tells their conversation and all the joy that was between them until the day began to end; and then how Scipio's beloved ancestor Africanus appeared to him that night in his sleep. Then it tells how Africanus showed him Carthage from a starry place, and disclosed to him all his good fortune to come, and said to him that any man, learned or unlettered, who loves the common profit and is virtuous shall go to a blessed place where there is joy without end. Then Scipio asked whether people that die here on earth have a life and dwelling place elsewhere; and Africanus said, "Yes, without doubt," and added that our space of life in the present world, whatever way we follow, is just a kind of death, and righteous people, after they die, shall go to heaven.

And he showed him the Milky Way, and the earth here, so little in comparison with the hugeness of the heavens; and after that he showed him the nine spheres. And then he heard the melody that proceeds from those nine spheres, which is the fount of music and melody in this world, and the cause of harmony. Then Africanus instructed him not to take delight in this world, since earth is so little and so full of torment and ill favor. Then he told him how in a certain term of years every star should come into its own place, where it first was; and all that has been done by all mankind in this world shall pass out of memory.

Then he asked Africanus to tell him fully the way to come into that heavenly happiness; and he said, "First know yourself to be immortal; and always see that you labor diligently and teach for the common profit, and you shall not fail to come speedily to that dear place that is full of joy and of bright souls. But breakers of the law, in truth, and lecherous people, after they die, shall forever be whirled about the

[2] Masinissa. King of Numidia (Libya).

earth in torment, until many ages be pass; and then, all their wicked deeds forgiven, they shall come to that blessed region, to which may God send you His grace to come."

The day began to end, and dark night, which withdraws beasts from their activity, bereft me of my book for the lack of light; and I set forth to my bed, full of brooding and anxious heaviness. For I both had that which I wished not and what I wished that I had not. But at last, wearied with all the day's labor, my spirit took rest and heavily slept; and as I lay in my sleep, I dreamed how Africanus, in the very same guise in which Scipio saw him that time before, had come and stood at the very side of my bed. When the weary hunter sleeps, quickly his mind returns to the woods; the judge dreams how his cases will fare, and the carter how his carts will go; the rich dream of gold, the knight fights his foes; the sick man dreams he drinks of the wine cask, the lover that he has his lady. I cannot say whether my reading of Africanus was the cause that I dreamed that he stood there; but thus he spoke, "You have done so well to look upon my old tattered book, of which Macrobius thought not a little,[3] that I would requite you somewhat for your labor."

Cytherea,[4] you sweet, blessed lady, who with your firebrand subdues whomsoever you wish, and sends me this dream, be my helper in this, for you are best able! As surely as I saw you in the north-northwest[5] when I began to write my dream, so surely do you give me power to rhyme it and compose it!

This aforesaid Africanus took me from there and brought me out with him to a gate of a park walled with mossy stone;

---

[3] Of which Macrobius thought not a little. Understatement: Macrobius, who preserved the text and wrote a long commentary on it, wrote in the last sentence of the commentary, "there is nothing more perfect than this work" (R).

[4] Cytherea. Venus, the goddess of love.

[5] North-north-west. The reference is unclear, but perhaps means that he seeks inspiration in an unorthodox way. Cf. *Hamlet*: "I am but mad north-northwest. When the wind is southerly, I know a hawk from a handsaw" (II.ii.396-97).

and over the gate on either side, carved in large letters, were verses of very diverse senses, of which I shall tell you the full meaning:

> "Through me people go to that blessed place
> Where hearts find health and deadly wounds find cure,
> Through me men go unto the fount of Grace,
> Where green and lusty May shall ever endure.
> I lead men to blithe peace and joy secure.
> Reader, be glad; throw off your sorrows past.
> Open am I; press in and make haste fast."

On the other side it said:

> "Through me people go where mischance betides,
> Where is the mortal striking of the spear,
> To which Disdain and Coldness are the guides,
> Where trees no fruit or leaf shall ever bear.
> This stream shall lead you to the sorrowful weir
> Where fish in baleful prison lie all dry.
> To shun it is the only remedy."

These inscriptions were written, the one in gold, the other in black, and I beheld them for a long while, for at the one my heart grew hardy, and the other ever increased my fear; the first warmed me, the other chilled me. For fear of error my wit could not make its choice, to enter or to flee, to lose myself or save myself. Just as a piece of iron set between two load-stones of equal force[6] has no power to move one way or the other – for as much as one draws the other hinders.

So it fared with me, who knew not which would be better, to enter or not, until Africanus my guide caught and pushed me in at the wide gates, saying, "Your doubt stands written on your face, though you tell it not to me. But fear

---

[6] Two load-stones. Chaucer names these "adamantes," hard magnetic stones. The narrator is the image of indecision.

not to come in, for this writing is not meant for you or for any, unless he would be Love's servant. For in love, I believe, you have lost your sense of taste, even as a sick man loses his taste of sweet and bitter. Nevertheless, dull though you may be, you can still look upon that which you cannot do; for many a man who cannot complete a bout is nevertheless pleased to be at a wrestling match, and judges whether one or another does better. And if you have skill to set it down, I will show you something to write about."

With that he took my hand in his, from which I took comfort and quickly went in. But Lord, how glad and at ease I was! For everywhere I cast my eyes were trees clad, each according to its kind, with everlasting leaves in fresh color and green as emerald, a joy to behold: the builder oak, and the hardy ash, the elm the pillar and the coffin for corpses, the boxwood for making pipes, the holly for whip-handles, the fir to bear sails, the cypress to mourn death, the yew the bowman, the aspen for smooth shafts, the olive of peace, the drunken vine, the victor palm, and the laurel for divination.

By a river in a green meadow, where there is at all points so much sweetness, I saw a garden full of blossomy boughs with white, blue, yellow and red flowers; and cold fountain-streams, teeming with life, full of small shining fish with red fins and bright silver scales. On every bough I heard the birds sing with the voice of angels in their melody. Some busied themselves to lead forth their young. The little bunnies ran off to play. Further on I noticed all about the timid roe, the buck, harts and hinds and squirrels and small beasts of gentle nature. I heard stringed instruments playing harmonies of such ravishing sweetness that God, Maker and Lord of all, never heard better, I believe. At the same time a wind, scarce could it have been gentler, made in the green leaves a soft noise which accorded with the song of the birds above. The air of that place was so mild that never was there discomfort on account of heat or cold. Every wholesome spice and herb grew there, and no person would age or sicken.

There was a thousand times more joy than one can relate. And it was never night there, but always bright day in everyone's eye.

I saw our lord Cupid forging and filing his arrows under a tree beside a spring, and his bow lay ready at his feet. And meanwhile his daughter, Desire, well tempered the arrowheads in the spring, and by her cunning she piled them after as they should serve, some to slay, some to wound and pierce. Just then I noticed Pleasure and Clothing and Lust and Courtesy and Joy and of Deception who has wit and power to cause a being to do folly – she was disguised, I deny it not. And under an oak, I believe, I saw Delight, standing apart with Gentle Breeding. I saw Beauty without any clothing; and Youth, full of sportiveness and jollity, Foolhardiness, Flattery, Desire, Message-sending and Bribery; and three others – I will not tell their names.

And upon great high pillars of jasper I saw a temple of brass strongly stand. About the temple many women were dancing ceaselessly, of whom some were beautiful themselves and some beautiful in dress; only in their kirtles they went, with hair unbound – that was forever their business, year by year. And on the temple I saw many hundred pairs of doves sitting, white and beautiful. Before the temple-door sat Lady Peace gravely, holding back the curtain, and beside her Lady Patience, with her pale face and wondrous discretion, sitting upon a mound of sand. Next to her were Promise and Cunning and a crowd of their followers within the temple and without.

Inside I heard a gust of sighs blowing about, hot as fire, engendered of longing, which caused every altar to blaze ever anew. And well I saw then that all the cause of sorrows that lovers endure is through the bitter goddess Jealousy. As I walked about within the temple I saw the god Priapus[7]

[7] Priapus. Phrygian god of fertility and gardens, son of Aphrodite by Dionysus or Hermes. He is said to have argued with an ass over the relative size of their genitalia. Naked, they compared themselves, only to find that the ass'

standing in sovereign position, his scepter in hand, and in such attire as when the ass confounded him to confusion with its outcry by night. People were busily setting upon his head garlands full of fresh, new flowers of various colors.

In a private corner I found Venus, who was noble and stately in her bearing, sporting with her porter Riches. The place was dark, but in time I saw a little light – it could scarcely have been less. Venus reposed upon a golden bed until the hot sun should seek the west. Her golden hair was bound with a golden thread, but all untressed as she lay. And one could see her naked from the breast to the head; the remnant, in truth, was well covered to my pleasure with a filmy kerchief of Valence;[8] there was no thicker cloth that could also be transparent. The place gave forth a thousand sweet odors. Bacchus, god of wine, sat beside her, and next was Ceres,[9] who saves all from hunger, and, as I said, the Cyprian woman[10] lay in the midst; on their knees two young people were crying to her to be their helper.

But thus I left her lying, and further in the temple I saw how, in scorn of Diana[11] the chaste, there hung on the wall many broken bows of such maidens as had first wasted their time in her service. And everywhere was painted many stories, of which I shall mention a few, such as Callisto and Atalanta[12] and many maidens whose name I do not know. There was also Semiramis,[13] Candace,[14] Hercules,[15] Biblis,[16]

"sceptre" was larger.

[8] Valence. Valence center of textile trades.

[9] Ceres (Demeter). Goddess of grain, who gives the remedy for hunger.

[10] Cyprian woman. Venus.

[11] Diana. Goddess of the Moon, the hunt, and chastity. He sees many boughs offered to Diana by women in hopes that they might remain virgins. But they have wasted their time in her service.

[12] Calyxte and Athalante. Callisto, favorite hunting companion of Artemis (Diana), duped and ravaged by Zeus, who disguised himself as Artemis, then transformed into a bear by Hera (out of jealousy), or Artemis (for breaking her vow of chastity), or Zeus (to hide her from his wife, Hera). Atalanta, another virgin huntress, whose father, wanting only sons, left her in the forest where she was raised by bears and hunters.

Dido,[17] Thisbe and Pyramus,[18] Tristram and Isolt,[19] Paris,[20] Achilles,[21] Helen,[22] Cleopatra,[23] Troilus,[24] and Scylla,[25] and the mother of Romulus[26] as well – all were portrayed on the other wall, and their love and by what plight they died.

When I had returned to the sweet and green garden that I spoke of, I walked forth to comfort myself. Then I noticed how there sat a queen who was exceeding in fairness over every other creature, as the brilliant summer sun passes the

---

[13] Semiramis. Assyrian queen who built Babylon and conquered Persia and Egypt. Known for beauty, valor, and lust.

[14] Candace. Queen of India who loved Alexander the Great.

[15] Hercules. Great Greek hero, son of Zeus and Alcmene, accidentally killed by his wife Deianeira.

[16] Biblis. Fell in love with her twin brother Caunus, but when she tells him, he departs, horrified. She went mad and searched for him, but is eventually transformed into a spring.

[17] Dido. Queen of Carthage, lover of Aeneas (Trojan hero, later pre-founder of Rome), who killed herself when she saw him depart.

[18] Thisbe, and Piramus. Star-crossed lovers who plan to meet at night at the tomb of King Ninus. Pyramus, discovering her blood-stained cloak in the mouth of a lioness (from whom Thisbe has safely fled) kills himself because he believes that she has been eaten by the lioness; she kills herself for loss of him.

[19] Tristram, Isolt. Famous lovers in the Arthurian tradition. Isolt, though married to King Mark of Cornwall, loves Tristram, who is Mark's most able and dedicated knight.

[20] Paris. Trojan son of Priam; his abduction of Helen from her husband, the Greek King Menelaus, was the immediate cause of the Trojan War.

[21] Achilles. Brooding Greek hero, invulnerable except for his heel (by which his mother held him when she dipped him into the River Styx), who slew the Trojan champion Hector and dragged his body around the city. He died for the love of Polyxena.

[22] Helen. See note on Paris above.

[23] Cleopatra. Famous Egyptian queen, who died for the love of the Roman leader Antony.

[24] Troilus. Trojan son of Priam, brother to Hector and Paris, whose love affair with Criseyde is the topic for Chaucer's *Troilus and Criseyde*.

[25] Scylla. Daughter of Nisus, king of Megara. For love, she helped Minos to defeat her own father, but Minos quickly leaves her.

[26] The mother of Romulus. Rhea Silviaor Ilia, a priestess of Diana who was raped in the forest by Mars. She bore the twins Romulus and Remus, who founded Rome.

stars in brightness. This noble goddess Nature was set upon a flowery hill in a verdant glade. All her halls and bowers were wrought of branches according to the art and measure of Nature.

And there was not any bird that is created through procreation that was not ready in her presence to hear her and receive her judgment. For this was Saint Valentine's day,[27] when every bird of every kind that men can imagine comes to this place to choose his mate. And they made an exceedingly great noise; and earth and sea and the trees and all the lakes were so full that there was scarcely room for me to stand, so full was the entire place. And just as Alan, in *The Complaint of Nature*,[28] describes Nature in her features and attire, so might men find her in reality.

This noble empress, full of grace, bade every bird take his station, as they were accustomed to stand always on Saint Valentine's day from year to year. That is to say, the birds of prey were set highest, and then the little birds who eat, as nature inclines them, worms or other things of which I speak not; but water-fowls sat the lowest in the dale; and birds that live on seed sat upon the grass. There were so many that it was a marvel to see.

There one could find the royal eagle, that pierces the sun with his sharp glance; and other eagles of lower race, of which clerks can tell. There was that tyrant with dun gray feathers, I mean the goshawk, that harasses other birds with his fierce ravening. There was the noble falcon, that with his feet grasps the king's hand; also the bold sparrow-hawk, foe of quails; the merlin, that often greedily pursues the lark. The dove was there, with her meek eyes; the jealous swan,

---

[27] Saint Valentine's day. The first reference of this holiday in the English language.

[28] Alan, in *The Complaint of Nature.* Alain of Lille's work, which is a dramatized remedy for humankind's straying from the laws of Nature, inspires the remainder of this work, especially the following description of the allegorical figure of Nature. In both Chaucer and Alain the birds seem to arise from her gown.

that sings at his death; and the owl also, that forebodes death; the giant crane, with his trumpet voice; thieving chough; the prating magpie; the scornful jay; the heron, foe to eels; the false lapwing, full of trickery; the starling, that can betray secrets; the tame redbreast; the coward kite; the cock, timekeeper of little thorps; the sparrow, son of Venus; the nightingale, which calls forth the fresh new leaves; the swallow, murderer of the little bees which make honey from the fresh-hued flowers; the wedded turtle-dove, with her faithful heart; the peacock, with his shining angel-feathers; the pheasant, that scorns the cock by night; the vigilant goose; the cuckoo, ever unnatural;[29] the popinjay, full of wantonness; the drake, destroyer of his own kind; the stork, that avenges adultery; the greedy, gluttonous cormorant; the wise raven and the crow, with voice of ill-boding; the ancient thrush and the wintry fieldfare thrush.

What more shall I say? One might find assembled in that place before the noble goddess Nature birds of every sort in this world that have feathers and stature. And each by her consent worked diligently to choose or take graciously his lady or his mate.

But to the point: Nature held on her hand a formel[30] eagle, the noblest in shape that she ever found among her works, the gentlest and goodliest; in her every noble trait so had its seat that Nature herself rejoiced to look upon her and to kiss her beak many times. Nature, vicar of the Almighty Lord, who has knit in harmony hot, cold, heavy, light, moist, and dry in exact proportions, began to speak in a gentle voice: "Birds, take heed of what I say; and for your welfare and to further your needs I will hasten as fast as I can speak. You well know how on Saint Valentine's day, by my statute and through my ordinance, you come to choose your mates, as I prick you with sweet pain, and then fly on your way. But

[29] Unnatural. Cuckoos left their eggs in unused nests built by other birds, and were thus considered unnatural.
[30] Formel. Female eagle.

I may not, even if I were to win this entire world, depart from my just order, that he who is most worthy shall begin.

"The tercel[31] eagle, the royal bird above you in degree, as you well know, the wise and worthy one, trusty, true as steel, which you may see I have formed in every part as pleased me best – there is no need to describe his shape to you – he shall choose first and speak as he will. And after him each of you shall choose in order, according to your nature, each as pleases you; and, as your fortune goes, you shall lose or win. But whichever of you love ensnares most, to him may God send her who sighs for him most sorely."

And at this she called the tercel and said, "My son, the choice is fallen to you. Nevertheless under this condition must be the choice of each one here, that his chosen mate will agree to his choice, whomsoever would choose her. From year to year this is always our custom. And whoever at this time can win grace has come here in blissful time!"

The royal tercel, with bowed head and humble appearance, delayed not and spoke: "As my sovereign lady, not as my spouse, I choose – and choose with will and heart and mind – the formel of so noble shape upon your hand. I am hers wholly and will serve her always. Let her do as she wishes, to let me live or die; I beseech her for mercy and grace, as my sovereign lady, or else let me die here presently. For surely I cannot live long in torment, for in my heart every vein is cut. Having regard only to my faithfulness, dear heart, have some pity upon my woe. And if I am found untrue to her, disobedient or willfully negligent, a boaster, or in time love elsewhere, I pray you this will be my doom: that I will be torn to pieces by these birds, upon that day when she should ever know me untrue to her or guilty of faithlessness. And since no other loves her as well as I, though she never promised me love, she ought to be mine by virtue of her mercy; for I can fasten no other bond on her. Never for any woe shall I cease to serve her, however far she

[31] Tercel. A male eagle.

may roam. Say what you will, my words are done."

Just as the fresh red rose newly blown blushes in the summer sun, so grew the color of this woman when she heard all this; she answered no word good or bad, so sorely was she abashed; until Nature said, "Daughter, fear not, I assure you."

Then spoke another tercel of a lower order: "That shall not be. I love her better than you, by Saint John, or at least I love her as well, and have served her longer, according to my station. If she should love for long being to me alone should be the reward; and I also dare to say, if she should find me false, unkind, a gossip, or a rebel in any way, or jealous, let me be hanged by the neck. And unless I bear myself in her service as well as my wit allows me, to protect her honor in every point, let her take my life and all the wealth I have."

Then a third tercel eagle said, "Now, sirs, you see how little time we have here, for every bird clamors to be off with his mate or lady dear, and Nature herself as well, because of the delay, will not hear half of what I would speak. Yet unless I speak I must die of sorrow. I boast not at all of long service; but it is as likely that I shall die of woe today as he who has been languishing these twenty winters. And it may well happen that a man may serve better in half a year, even if it were no longer, than another man who has served many years. I do not say this about myself, for I can do no service to my lady's pleasure; but I dare say that I am her truest man, I believe, and would be most glad to please her. In short, until death may seize me I will be hers, whether I wake or sleep, and true in all that heart can think."

In all my life since the day I was born never have I heard any man so noble make a plea in love or any other thing – even if a man had time and wit to rehearse their expression and their words. And this discourse lasted from the morning until the sun drew downward so rapidly. The clamor released by the birds rung so loud – "Make an end of this and let us go!" – that I well thought the forest would be splintered. They cried, "Make haste! Alas, you will ruin us! When shall your cursed pleading come to an end? How should a judge believe either side for yea or nay, without any proof?"

The goose, cuckoo and duck so loudly cried, "Kek, kek!", "Cuckoo!", "Quack, quack!" that the noise reverberated in my ears. The goose said, "All this is not worth a fly! But from this I can devise a remedy, and I will speak my verdict fair and soon, on behalf of the waterfowl. Let who will smile or frown."

"And I for the worm-eating fowl," said the foolish cuckoo; "of my own authority, for the common welfare, I will take the responsibility now, for it would be great charity to release us."

"By God, you may wait a while yet," said the turtle-dove. "If you the one to choose who shall speak, it would be as well for him to be silent. I am among the birds that eat seed, one of the most unworthy, and of little wit – that I know well. But a creature's tongue would be better quiet than meddling with such doings about which he knows neither rhyme nor reason. And whosoever does so, overburdens himself in foul fashion, for often one not entrusted to a duty commits offence."

Nature, who had always an ear to the murmuring of folly at the back, said with ready tongue, "Hold your peace there! And straightway, I hope, I shall find a counsel to let you go and release you from this noise. My judgment is that you shall choose one from each bird-folk to give the verdict for you all."

The birds all assented to this conclusion. And first the birds of prey by full election chose the tercel-falcon to define all their judgment, and decide as he wished. And they presented him to Nature and she accepted him gladly. The falcon then spoke in this fashion: "It would be hard to determine by reason which best loves this gentle woman; for each has such ready answers that none may be defeated by reasons. I cannot see of what use are arguments; so it seems there must be battle."

"All ready!" then cried these tercel-eagles.

"Nay, sirs," said he, "if I dare say it, you do me wrong: my tale is not done. For, sirs, take it not amiss, I pray, it cannot go thus as you desire. Ours is the voice that has the charge over this, and you must stand by the judges' decision. Peace, therefore! I say that it would seem in my mind that the worthiest in knighthood, who has longest followed it, the highest in degree and of gentlest blood, would be most fitting for her, if she wish it. And of these three she knows which he is, I believe, for that is easily seen."

The waterfowl put their heads together, and after short considering, when each had spoken his large mouthful, they said truly, by one assent, how "the goose, with her gentle eloquence, who so desires to speak for us, shall say our say," and prayed God would help her. Then the goose began to speak for these waterfowl, and said in her cackling, "Peace! Now every man take heed and hearken what argument I shall put forth. My wits are sharp, I love no delay; I counsel him, I say, even if he were my brother, leave him if she will not love him."

"Lo here," said the sparrow-hawk, "a perfect argument for a goose – bad luck to her! Lo, thus it is to have a wagging tongue! Now, fool, it would be better for you to have held your peace than have shown your folly, by God! But to do thus rests not in her wit or will; for it is truly said, 'a fool cannot be silent.'"

Laughter arose from all the birds of noble kind; and straightway the seed-eating fowl chose the faithful turtle-dove, and called her to them, and prayed her to speak the sober truth about this matter, and asked her counsel. And she answered that she would fully show her mind. "Nay, God forbid a lover should change!" said the turtle-dove, and grew all red with shame. "Though his lady may be cold for evermore, let him serve her ever until he die. In truth I praise not the goose's counsel, for even if my lady died I would have no other mate, I would be hers until death take me."

"By my hat, well jested!" said the duck. "That men should love forever, without cause! Who can find reason or wit there? Does one who is mirthless dance merrily? Who should care for him who is carefree? Yea, quack!" said the duck loud and long, "God knows there are more stars than a pair."

"Now fie, churl!" said the noble falcon. "That thought came straight from the dunghill. You can not see when a thing is proper. You do as well with love as owls do with light; the day blinds them, but they see very well in darkness. Your nature is so low and wretched that you can not see or guess what love is."

Then the cuckoo thrust himself forward on behalf of the worm-eating birds, and said quickly, "So that I may have my mate in peace, I care not how long you contend. Let each be single all his life; that is my counsel, since they cannot agree. This is my instruction, and there an end!"

"Yea," said the merlin, "as this glutton has well filled his paunch, this should suffice for us all! You murderer of the hedge-sparrow on the branch, the one who brought you up, you ruthless glutton! May you live unmated, you mangler of worms! It matters nothing to you, though your tribe may perish. Go, be a stupid fool, as long as the world lasts!"

"Peace now, I command here," said Nature, "For I have heard the opinions of all, and yet we are no nearer to our goal. But this is my final decision, that she herself shall have the choice of whom she wishes. Whosoever may be pleased or not, he whom she chooses shall have her immediately. For since it cannot here be debated who loves her best, as the falcon said, then I will grant her this favor, that she shall have him alone on whom her heart is set, and he who has fixed his heart on her shall have her. This judgment I, Nature, make; and I cannot speak falsely, nor look with partial eye on any rank. But if it is reasonable to counsel you in choosing a mate, then surely I would counsel you to take the royal tercel, as the falcon very wisely said; for he is noblest and most worthy whom I created so well for my own pleasure; that ought to suffice you."

The formel answered with timid voice, "Goddess of Nature, my righteous lady, true it is that I am ever under your authority, just as every other creature is, and I must be yours as long as my life may last. Therefore, grant me my first request, and immediately I will speak my mind to you."

"I grant it to you," said Nature; and this female eagle spoke immediately in this way: "Almighty queen, until this year comes to an end I ask for a period of delay, to take counsel with myself; and after that to have my choice free. This is all that I wish to say. I can say no more, even if you were to slay me. In truth, as for now I will in no manner serve Venus or Cupid"

"Now since it can happen no other way," Nature said then, "there is no more to be said here. Then I wish these birds to go their way each with his mate, so that they tarry here no longer." And she spoke to them thus as you shall hear. "To you I speak, you tercels," said Nature. "Be of good heart, and continue in service, all three; a year is not so long to wait. And let each of you strive according to his degree to do well. For, God knows, she is departed from you this year; and whatsoever may happen afterwards, this interval is appointed to you all."

And when this work was all brought to an end, Nature gave every bird his mate by just accord, and they went their way. Ah, Lord! The bliss and joy that they made! For each of them took the other in his wings, and wound their necks about each other, ever thanking the noble goddess of Nature. But first were chosen birds to sing, as was always their custom year by year to sing a roundel[32] at their departure, to honor Nature and give her pleasure. The tune, I believe, was

[32] Roundel. (Or Rondeau.) Poem of ten to thirteen lines; the opening phrase or line is repeated as a refrain in the second and third stanzas.

made in France. The words were such as you may here find in these verses, as I remember them.

Qui bien aime a tard oublie.[33]
"Welcome, summer, with sunshine soft,
The winter's tempest you will break,
And drive away the long nights black!

"Saint Valentine, throned aloft,
Thus little birds sing for your sake:
Welcome, summer, with sunshine soft,
The winter's tempest you will shake!

"Good cause have they to glad them oft,
His own true-love each bird will take;
Blithe may they sing when they awake,
Welcome, summer, with sunshine soft,
The winter's tempest you will break,
And drive away the long nights black!"

And with the shouting that the birds raised, as they flew away when their song was done, I awoke; and I took up other books to read, and still I read always. In truth I hope so to read that some day I shall meet with something of which I shall fare the better. And so I will not cease to read.

Here ends the work of the Parliament of Fowls held on the day of Saint Valentine, according to Geoffrey Chaucer. Thanks be to God.

[33] *Qui bien aime a tard oublie.* Who loves well forgets slowly. This line is included in some of the manuscripts of PF. It seems to be a consolation to the three suitors, and it may also indicate the source of the roundel or tune.

THE LEGEND OF GOOD WOMEN

INTRODUCTORY NOTES

If Chaucer makes anything clear in his early poetry, it was that love did not come easily, and it often did not last long. In his *The Legend of Good Women* he continues to come to terms with love: he explores not only, as we might expect from the title, the lives of women "who were faithful in love," but also, and perhaps more so, the deeds of "false men who betrayed them."

This exploration is mandated in the *Prologue* by Queen Alceste (perhaps a mythological version of Anne of Bohemia, wife of Richard II), who sentences Chaucer to tell stories of good women because the poet has, as Love (Cupid) tells him, written "heresy against [his] religion," especially in his *Troilus and Criseyde*.

As with other works, such as *The House of Fame* and *Anelida and Arcite*, *The Legend of Good Women* was left unfinished. Scholars speculate that Chaucer, both as author and fictional narrator, got tired of the project. Perhaps he set it aside in order to begin *The Canterbury Tales*, which would give him the opportunity to write from varying points of view, not just one.

Though we can not be sure of Chaucer's attitude toward his work, it is clear that he is making a case that these women are martyrs for love. The word "legend" in the title of the work indicates that these women were saints, as a legend or legendary is a collection of saints' lives. As saints' legends were the most popular form of written entertainment in Chaucer's time, his audience would have known to read for the ways in which the women were tortured for love. The difference, of course, seems to be that the women in Chaucer's legends suffer for worldly love (*cupiditas*) while the women in saint's legends suffer for heavenly love (*caritas*). Both types of legends, nonetheless, end unhappily.

On a practical note, the selection presented below includes most of the work, but, for the sake of brevity, is missing these four legends: Hypsipyle and Medea, Philomela, Phyllis, and Hypermnestra.

THE LEGEND OF GOOD WOMEN

THE PROLOGUE

A thousand times I have heard it said that in heaven is joy and in hell pain; and I grant well that it is so. Nevertheless, I know this well, that there is no person dwelling in this land who has been in either hell or heaven, or who can know of them in any other way than as he has heard tell or found it written, for no person can put his knowledge to the test. But God forbid that men should believe far more than they have seen with their eyes! A man shall not deem all things false because he has not beheld them since long ago. God knows, a thing is nonetheless true even if every creature cannot see it. Even Bernard the monk[1] saw not all things, by God!

Then in all reason must we give credence to the books we find, through which ancient things are kept in mind, and to the instruction of these wise ones from ancient times, and believe in these old and true histories of holiness, of kingdoms, of victories, of love, hate, and various other things that I cannot now recount. And if old books were all gone, then the key of remembrance would be lost. Well ought we then to honor and believe old books, where we have no other way to test the truth.

As for me, though I know little, I delight to read in books and revere them in my heart. And to them I give and full credence, and hold them in reverence so heartily faith, that there is scarcely any activity to draw me from my books,

[1] Bernard the monk. Beranard of Clairvaux (1090-1153), Founder of the Cistercian order of monks, a major mystic and scholar in the medieval church

unless it would be some festival, or else, of course, the lovely time of May, when I hear the little birds singing, and when the flowers begin to spring – then farewell to my books and my devotion!

Now I have also this disposition, that of all the flowers in the meadow I most love those white and red flowers, which men in our town call daisies. I have such affection for them, as I have said, that when May has arrived, no day dawns upon me in my bed, but I am up and walking in the meadow to see these flowers opening to the sun when it rises, in the bright morning, and through the long day thus I walk in the green.

That blissful sight softens all my sorrow, so glad I am for it, when I am in the presence of it, to give reverence to her. And I love it, and continually do, and ever shall, until my heart should die. I swear all this; I will not lie about this; no creature ever loved so passionately in his life. All day long I wait for nothing else, and I shall not lie, but to look upon the daisy, that well by reason people may call it the "day's-eye," or else the "eye of day," the empress and flower of all flowers.[2]

And when the sun draws toward the west, then they close and take them to slumber until the morning when the day comes, so sorely they fear the night. This daisy, flower of all flowers, filled with all excellence and honor, always and alike fair and lusty of hue, fresh in winter as well as in summer, gladly would I praise it if I properly could. But I am filled with woe, for it lies not in my power!

For well I know that people have reaped the field of poetry before me and have harvested the corn. I come after, gleaning here and there, and am very glad if perhaps I find

---

[2] F. There are two major versions of the Prologue to the LGW, known as F and G. This translation follows the G version, but adds in italics significant passages from the F version that are not included in G. In order to follow the logic of the narration, some minor rearrangement of material was necessary.

an ear of any goodly words that they have left behind. And if I chance to recount again what they have said in their lusty songs, I hope that they will not be displeased, since all is said in furthering and worship of them who are followers of either the leaf or flower;[3] *but offer help, you who have knowledge and power, you lovers who can write about emotions.*

For trust well, I have not undertaken to sing in honor of the leaf against the flower, or of the flower against the leaf, any more than of the wheat against the chaff.[4] For to me neither is dearer; as yet I am retained by neither. I know not who serves the leaf, who the flower; that is in no way the object of my labor. For this work is all drawn out of another cask, of ancient story, before there was any such strife.

She is the brightness and the true light that in this dark world leads and directs me. The heart within my sorrowful breast fears and loves you so sorely that you are truly the mistress of my mind, and I am nothing. My word, my work is knit so to your service that, just as a harp obeys the hand and makes it sound according to its fingering, so too can you out of my heart bring such voice, just as you wish, to laugh or lament. Be my guide and sovereign lady! As to my earthly god I call to you as well, both in this work and in all my sorrows.

But the reason I spoke of giving credence to old books and revering them is that men should believe authorities in all things where there lies no other means of proof. For my intent is, before I go from you, to make known in English the naked text of many histories or many tales, just as authors

---

[3] Flower and Leaf. The imagery of the flower and the leaf seems to have permeated court life in Chaucer's time, the flower signifying the glamour of the members of the court themselves and the leaf those who worked for or supported them. Cf. the contemporary poem by the name, *The Flower and the Leaf.*

[4] Chaff. Chaucer, following the Church Fathers, distinguishes between the Corn (or wheat) of the story, which is the essential truth, and the Chaff, whish is the story's ornamentation,

tell them. Believe them if you wish.

When the month of May was almost gone, and I had roamed all the summer's day over the green meadow of which I have told you to gaze upon the fresh daisy, and when the sun out of the south drew towards the west, and the flower had closed and gone to sleep, for darkness of the night which she feared, I sped swiftly home to my house; and in a little shady bower that I have, newly embanked with fresh-cut turfs, I asked people to lay my couch, and flowers to be strewn on it, for joy of the new summer. When I had laid me down and closed my eyes, I fell asleep within an hour or two.

Then I dreamed that I was in the meadow, and was roaming about to see that flower, just as you have heard me tell. This meadow was beautiful; it seemed to me to be entirely embroidered with sweet flowers. No herbs or trees or spicy resins could compare with it; for it utterly surpassed all odors and all flowers as well for its rich beauty. The earth had forgotten his poor estate of winter, which had made him naked and dejected and with the sword of cold had struck him so sorely.

Now the mild sun had relieved all that, and clothed him in green all afresh. Rejoicing in the season, the little birds that had escaped the snare and the net mocked the fowler who had frightened them in winter and destroyed their brood, and eased their hearts to sing of him in scorn, and to flout the foul churl who for his greed had betrayed them with his tricks. This was their song, "The fowler we defy, and all his craft!"

On the branches some sang sweet songs of love and spring, in honor and praise of their mates, and for the new, joyous summer; it was a joy to listen. *Upon those branches full of soft blossoms, in their delight they turned themselves often and sang,*

"Blessed be Saint Valentine!

For on his day I chose you to be mine,
My sweetheart, and never have I repented."

And then they joined their beaks, and they paid honor and tenderness to each other, and then did other ceremonies pleasing to love and nature. (I listened carefully to their song, for I dreamed I understood their meaning.)

And those that had been unfaithful – as the tydif bird is, for the sake of novelty – sought mercy for their trespassing, and humbly sang their repentance, and swore on the blossoms to be true, so that their mates would have mercy upon them, and at the last made their accord.

They all found a lord named Danger[5] *for a time, yet Pity, through his strong gentle might, forgave, and allowed Mercy to surpass Justice, through innocence and self-controlled Courtesy. But I do not call innocence folly, nor false pity, for virtue lies in the mean, as Etik*[6] *says. This is the manner to which I am referring.*

And thus these birds, void of all malice, agreed to love, and gave up the vice of hate, and sang all of one accord, "Welcome, summer, our governor and lord!" And Zephyrus and Flora gently gave to the flowers, soft and tenderly, their sweet breath, and made them spread, as god and goddess of the flowery meadow. In this place it seemed to me I might, day by day, dwell always, the jolly month of May, without sleep, without food or drink.

Then at last a lark sang on high. She said, "I see the mighty god of Love! Lo, yonder he comes! I see his wings spread!" Then I looked along the meadow and saw him come, leading by the hand a lady clothed in a royal habit of green. She had a net of gold around her hair, and over that a

---

[5] Danger here refers to the quality in a woman to resist a lover, if only temporarily, for the sake of her honor.

[6] Etik. The reference to the source of this commonplace idea that happiness comes through moderation is not clear. It might be a reference to Horace, but is more likely to the *Ethics* of Aristotle.

white crown with many flowers; for all the world just as the flower of the daisy is crowned with little white leaves, such were the flowers of her white crown, for it was made all of one fine oriental pearl; for this reason the white crown above the green, with the golden ornament in her hair, made her appear like a daisy.

This mighty god of Love was clothed in silk embroidered full of green sprigs; on his head was a garland of rose-leaves, all set with fresh lilies. But the hue of his face I cannot tell, for truly his face shone so bright that the eye was dazzled by the gleam. For several minutes I could not look at him, but at last I saw that he held in his hands two fiery arrows, red as glowing coals. And he spread his wings like an angel. Albeit men say he is blind, but it seemed to me that he could see well enough; for he looked sternly upon me, so that his look even now makes my heart cold.

He held by the hand this noble lady, crowned with white and clothed all in green, who was so womanly, benign and gentle that though men should seek throughout this world they should not find half her beauty in any being formed by nature. Her name was Alceste the gentle. May fair fortune ever come to her, I pray to God! For had it not been for the comfort of her presence, I would have been dead without help, for fear of Love's words and look, as you shall learn hereafter, when the time comes.

On the grass, behind this god of Love, I saw a company of nineteen ladies in royal garb coming at a gentle pace. And after them came such a train of women that I believed that all the possible women who had ever lived in this world since God made Adam from earth composed only one third of them or one fourth. And every one of these women was faithful in love. Now was this a wondrous thing or not? For as soon as they perceived this flower that I call the daisy, they quickly stopped altogether and kneeled down by that very flower and sang with one voice,

"Hail and honor
To faithful womanhood, and this flower
That bears the symbol of our faithfulness!
Her white crown bears for us all the witness."

And after that they went in a circle slowly dancing around it, and sang, as it were in the fashion of a carol, this ballade which I shall tell you.

Ballad

"Hide, Absalom,[7] your bright golden tresses;
And Esther also, lay your meekness down;
And Jonathan, hide your friendly address;
And Penelope and Marcia Catoun,
Make of your wifehood no comparison;
Hide now your beauties, Isolt and Elaine,
Alceste comes, who makes all this pale and vain.

"Thy beautiful body, oh, let it not appear,
Lavinia[8]; and Lucrece too of Rome-town,

[7] Absalom...Alceste. Absalom, Biblical figure known for his beautiful hair, though he died when it was caught in an oak tree; Esther, Biblical wife of Ahasuerus, or Xerxes the Great, who was the model of patience in bringing victory to the Jews; Jonathan, Biblical figure, who, because of his kindness, was favored by King David, who had been Jonathan's rival for the throne of Israel; Penelope and Marcia Cato(un), the long-suffering wives of Odysseus, the Trojan War hero, and Cato the Younger, the Roman statesman; Isolt and Elaine, lovers of Tristram and Lancelot in Arthurian lore, both known for their beauty; Alceste, wife of Admetus, for whom Alceste gave her own life, when Apollo pleaded to the Fates to allow the soon-to-die Admetus to live, and they agreed, on the condition that someone would die in his place.

[8] Lavinia...Thisbe. Lavinia, last wife of Aeneas, founder of Rome; Lucrece, Roman noblewoman best known for taking her life after she was raped by Sextus Tarquinius, an Etruscan prince, rather than living with the shame; Polyxena, Trojan princess, daughter of Priam and Hecuba, who was sacrificed so that the Greeks would have favorable winds for their journey home after the war; Cleopatra, Queen of Egypt, who was first the

And Polyxena, who paid for love so dear,
And Cleopatra, with all your passion,
Hide your truth in loving and your renown,
And Thisbe, who for love had borne such pain;
Alceste comes, who makes all this pale and vain.

"Hero, Dido[9], Laodamia together here,
And Phyllis, hanging for your Demophon,
And Canace, known ever by your heavy cheer,
Hypsipyle, who Jason falsely won,
Make now of your love-pledge no boast or moan,
Hypermnestra, Ariadne, cease complaint;
Alceste comes, who makes all this pale and vain."

This ballad may have been well sung, as I have said earlier, about my noble lady; for certainly al these can not suffice to be equal with my lady in no way. For as the sun will make the fire appear pale, so too my lady, who is so good, so fair, so gracious, surpasses all. I pray to God that goodness may come to her!

When this ballad was all sung, they sat full gently down upon the sweet and soft green grass, in order all in a circle about. First sat the god of Love, and then this lady clad in green with the white crown; and then near them all the rest sat courteously, according to their station. And then, for several minutes, in the entire place not a word was spoken.

Close by, reclining beneath a grassy slope, I waited, still as any stone, to learn what this group intended; until at last

---

lover of Julius Caesar and later of Marcus Antony, and committed suicide when Antony, having been defeated by Octavian, took his life; Thisbe, ill-fated lover who commited suicide when she saw the body of her beloved Pyramus, who took his life when he thought that she had been eaten by a lion.

[9] Dido..Ariadne. All women who had been left behind by their lovers; Dido by Aeneas, Laodamia by Protesilaus; Phyllis by Demophon; Canace by Macareus, Hypsipyle by Jason, Hypermnestra by Lynceus, and Ariadne by Theseus. All of these stories are told in Ovid's Heroides (Heroines).

the god of Love turned his eyes on me and said, "Who is it who rests there?"

And I answered his question and said, "Sir, it is I." And I came nearer, and greeted him.

He said, "What are you doing here in my presence, and so boldly? For truly a worm would be more worthy to come into my sight than you."

"And why, sir," I said, "if it please you?"

"Because," he said, "you are in no way fit. My servants are all wise and honorable; you are my mortal foe, and war against me, and speak evil of my long-time servants. And with your works of translation you plague them and hinder people's devotion in my service, and hold it to be folly to trust in me. You cannot deny it; for in text so plain that it needs no commentary you have translated *The Romance of the Rose*, which is heresy against my religion; and you cause wise folk to withdraw from me, and think in your cool wit that anyone is but a proper fool who loves with passion, too hard and hot. Well I know by this that you begin to drivel, as these old fools when their spirit fails; for then they abuse others, and know not what is amiss with themselves.

"Have you not also made in English the poem which tells how Criseyde forsook Troilus,[10] to show how women have gone astray? But nevertheless answer me this now, why would you not also speak well of women, as you have spoken evilly? Was there no good matter in your memory, and in all your books could you not find some story of good and faithful women?

"Yes, God knows! You have sixty books, old and new, all full of long stories, in which both Romans and Greeks treat of various women, what kind of life they led, and there is always a hundred good to one bad. This God knows, and all scholars as well who use them to seek out such matters. What says Valerius or Livy or Claudian?[11] What says Je-

[10] Troilus. Chaucer's *Troilus and Criseyde.*

[11] Valerius or Livy or Claudian. Valerius. Identity is uncertain, but likely

rome, in his treatise against Jovinian?[12] Jerome tells of pure maidens and faithful wives, of widows steadfast unto death; and he tells not of a few, but I dare say a hundred in succession, until it is piteous and sorrowful to read of the woe they endured for their faithfulness.

"For they were so true to their love that, rather than take a new mate, they chose death in various manners, and died just as the story will relate. Some were burned, some had their throats cut, and some were drowned, because they would not be false. For they all kept their maidenhood, or else widowhood or wedlock. And this was not done for devoutness, but for true virtue and purity, and so that men should put no blame on them. And yet they were heathen, all of them, who so sorely dreaded all disgrace. These women of old so guarded their good name that I believe men shall not find in this world a man who could be so true and kind as was the least woman in those days. Likewise, what do the epistles of Ovid[13] say about true wives and their travail?

"What says Vincent, in his *Historical Mirror?*[14] You may also hear the whole world of authors, Christian and heathen, discuss such matters. There is no need to write all day about them; but again I say, what ails you to write the chaff of stories and overlook the corn?[15] By Saint Venus, by

---

the author of *Epistola Valerii ad Rufinum.* Livy. Titus Livius (59 B.C.-17 A.D.), the Roman historian, author of an extensive *History of Rome.* Claudian. 4th-Century Roman poet, reputed as the last poet of classical Rome, author of *De Raptu Prosperina.* (All three recorded stories of rapes or abuses of women.)

[12] Jovinian. A treatise known as *Jerome against Jovinian*, which is St. Jerome infamous attack on marriage. The work, however, does often praise women in general.

[13] Ovid. Ovid's *Heroides* is a collection of letters written from famous women to the men who have left them.

[14] Vincent of Beauvais' *Speculum Historiale.* Comprehensive history which includes the story of Cleopatra, the first of the nine tales to follow.

[15] Chaff...corn. Chaucer often distinguishes the kernel or fruit of the wheat (or corn), the essential matter, from the chaff, the full description (perhaps non-essential) of the matter.

whom I was born, though you have rejected my faith, as other old fools have done in many days gone by, you shall repent your action in the sight of all men.

Then spoke Alceste, the worthy queen: "God, by your true courtesy, you must listen and see whether he can make any reply to these charges that you have made against him. A god should not thus be moved to anger, but being a deity he should be stable, and righteous and merciful as well. He cannot rightfully vent his ire before he has heard the other party speak. All that is carried to you in complaint is not the gospel truth; the god of Love hears many false tales. For in your court there are many flatterers, and many artful, tattling accusers, who drum many things in your ears out of hatred or jealous imaginings, or to have friendly talk with you. Envy – I pray God may give her bad luck! – forever washes the foul linen in a great court; out of the house of Caesar she departs neither by night nor day (thus says Dante). No matter who departs, never will she be lacking. This man may be accused wrongly, and by rights should be absolved.

"Or else, sir, because this man is unwise, he might translate a thing not out of malice but because he is so used to writing books that he heeds not the substance of them; therefore, he wrote the *Rose*[16] and *Criseyde* entirely innocently and knew not what he was saying. Or else he was told by some person to write those poems, and dared not refuse it, for before this he has written many books. In translating what old scholars have written, he has not sinned so grievously as if he should in malice write scornfully of love from his own point of view.

"A righteous lord should have this in mind, and not be like Lombard tyrants who practice willful tyranny;[17] for a

[16] Rose and Criseyde. Chaucer translated from French The Romance of the Rose, written by Guillaume de Lorris and Jean de Meun, which encompasses "all the art of love." Troilus and Criseyde is Chaucer's lengthy tale (perhaps the first novel in the English language) of doomed love set against the backdrop of the Trojan War.

king or lord by natural right ought not to be tyrannical or cruel like a tax collector, doing all the harm he can. He must bear in mind that they are his subjects, and that his true duty is to show all kindness toward his people, to hear their defenses readily, and their complaints and petitions in due time when they present them. This is the philosopher's[18] saying, that a king shall maintain his subjects through justice; that is his duty, in truth, and to this end a king is sworn deeply and has been for hundreds of years; and he shall maintain his lords in their station, as it is right and reasonable that they be exalted and honored and held most dear, for they are demigods here in this world.

"Thus shall he do to both rich and poor, albeit their conditions may not be alike, and have compassion on the poor. For behold the noble nature of the lion! When a fly annoys or bites him, he gently drives the fly away with his tail; for in his noble nature he does not stoop to avenge himself upon a fly, as a dog and other beasts may do. A noble nature should show restraint and weigh all things by equity, and ever regard his own high station. For, sir, it is no noble act for a lord to condemn a man without speech or answer; in a lord that is a very foul practice. And if it should happen that the man cannot excuse himself, yet with sorrowful heart asks mercy, and humbly in his bare shirt yields himself up wholly to your judgment, then a god with brief consideration ought to weigh his own honor against the other's trespass. For since there is no cause of death here, you ought more readily to be merciful. Lay aside your wrath, and be a little yielding!

"This man has served you with his art and has furthered your religion with his poetry. While he was young he followed you; I do not know if he is now a renegade. But well I know that by what he has been able to write in praise of your name he has caused unlearned people to rejoice in serving

---

[17] Lombard tyrants. A stereotype of the powerful men of 14th-Century Lombardy (Italy), though the stereotype may well be warranted.

[18] The Philosopher. Aristotle.

you. He wrote the book called the *House of Fame*, and the *Death of Blanche the Duchess*[19] as well, and the *Parliament of Birds*, I believe, and all the love of Palamon and Arcite of Thebes,[20] though the tale is little known; and for your holy days many hymns, which are called Ballades, Roundels, and Virelays;[21] and to speak of other laborious works, he has translated Boethius[22] in prose, and *Of the Wretched Engendering of Mankind*,[23] which may be found in Pope Innocent; and he also wrote the life of Saint Cecilia;[24] and also, a long while ago, *Origen upon the Magdalene*.[25] He ought now to have the lesser penalty; he has written many lays and many works.

"Now as you are a god and a king, I, your Alceste, once queen of Thrace,[26] ask you of your mercy never to harm this man so long as he lives. And he shall swear to you, and do so without delay, that he will sin no more thus. But just as you shall direct, so shall he write of women ever faithful in love, maidens or wives, whatsoever you wish. And he shall

---

[19] Death of Blanche the Duchess. Chaucer's *Book of the Duchess.*

[20] Palamon and Arcite of Thebes. Either Chaucer's *Palamon and Arcite* or *The Knight's Tale*..

[21] Hymns, Ballades, Roundels, and Virelays. Four types of formal poetry, the last two borrowed from the French tradition. Few of Chaucer's surviving poems, however, fit these descriptions.

[22] Boethius. Ancius Manlius Severinus (c. 475-525), Roman philosopher, consul and minister to Theodoric, accused of treason. While awaiting execution he wrote *De Consolatione Philosphiae* (*The Consolation of Philosophy*), one of the most important books for the Middle Ages, which Chaucer translated into English (*Boece*).

[23] The Wretched Engendering of Mankind. This work is apparently lost, though it was presumably a translation of Pope Innocent III's *De miseria condicionis humane.*

[24] The life of St. Cecilia. The *Second Nun's Tale* in *The Canterbury Tales.*

[25] Origen upon the Magdalene. Usually regarded as a lost translation of the pseudo-Origen homily *De Maria Magdalena*, though *The Lamentation of Mary Magdalene*, included in the early printed editions of Chaucer, seems to be at least an approximation of this early work.

[26] Thrace. The southeast tip of the Balkan Peninsula, including northeastern Greece, Bulgaria, and Turkey.

further you as much as he spoke amiss in the *Rose* or in *Criseyde*."

Forthwith the god of Love answered her thus: "Madame," he said, "it is long that I have known you to be so charitable and faithful that never, since the world was new, have I found any person who acted better toward me. Therefore, if I wish to safeguard my honor, I neither may nor will refuse your petition. All lies with you; do with him as pleases you, and forgive all, without further delay. For whosoever gives a gift or does a kindness, let him do it in good time, and his thanks will be greater for it. Judge, therefore, what he shall do. Go ahead now, thank my lady here," he said.

I rose, and then got down on my knee and said: "Madame, may God on high reward you because you have made the god of Love forgive his wrath against me; and may He grant me the grace to live so long until I may truly know who you are who have helped me and put me in such a hopeful state. But truly in this matter I thought not to have sinned or to have trespassed against love. For an honest man, in truth, has no part in the deeds of a thief; and a true lover ought not to blame me, though I speak in reproach of a false lover. He ought rather to remain on my side, because I wrote of Criseyde or of the Rose; whatsoever my author meant, it was my intention at least, God knows, to exalt faithfulness in love and to cherish it; and to warn people of falseness and evil by such examples. This was mine intent."

And she answered, "Set aside your arguing, for Love will hear no pleas against himself, just or unjust; learn this from me. You have your pardon; hold yourself to that. Now will I say what penance you shall do for your trespass; understand it now. As long as you live, year by year you shall spend the most part of your life in writing a glorious legend of good women, maidens, and wives, who were ever faithful in love, and you shall tell of the false men who betrayed them, men who all their life do nothing but see how many women they can shame – for in your world that is now seen as a sport. And though you care not to be a lover, speak well of love. This penance I give you. And I will so pray the god of Love that he shall charge his servants in any way to aid you and shall requite your labor. *And when this book has been completed, give it to the queen, on my behalf, at Eltham or at Sheene.* Now go your way; your penance is only a small one."

The god of Love smiled, and then he said, "Do you know whether she is a maiden or wife, a queen or a countess, or of what degree, this woman who has given so little penance to you who have deserved to suffer more sorely? But pity runs soon into a noble heart; that you can see. She manifests what she is."

And I answered, "No, sir, as I hope for happiness, I know no more than that I see well she is kind."

"By my hood," Love said, "that is a true saying; and that you well know, by God, if you well consider. In a book that lies in your chest, do you not have the story of the great goodness of Queen Alceste, who was turned into a daisy? She who chose to die for her husband and to go to hell also instead of him? She whom Hercules rescued, by God, and brought out of hell back to happiness?"

And I replied, "Yes, now I know her! And is this the good Alceste, the daisy, mine own heart's repose?[27] Now I feel well this woman's goodness, that both in her life and after her death her great goodness makes her renown double. Well has she requited me for my affection which I bear toward her flower, the daisy. It is no wonder that Jove should turn her into a star, as Agathon[28] tells, for her goodness. Her white crown bears witness of it; for she had as many excel-

---

[27] Alceste. Chaucer has apparently forgotten that Alceste was introduced eighty lines earlier.

[28] Agathon. This may refer to the Greek dramatist Agatone named in Dante's *Pugatorio* 22.107; it may also refer to Plato's *Symposium*, known as *Agatho's Feast*, which contains the story of Alcestis.

lences as there are small flowers in her crown. In remembrance and honor of her Cybele[29] created the daisy, the flower all crowned with white, as men can see; and Mars gave its redness[30] to her crown, set amidst the white instead of rubies."

At this the queen grew somewhat red from modesty, when she was so praised in her presence. Then said Love, "It was a great negligence to write about the lack of steadfastness of women, since you know their goodness by experience and by old stories as well. Set aside the chaff, and write well of the corn. Why would you not write of Alceste, and leave Criseyde sleeping in peace? For your writing should be of Alceste, since you know that she is a model of goodness; for she taught noble love, and especially how a wife ought to live, and all the bounds that she should keep. Your little wit was sleeping that time. But now I charge you on your life that in your Legend you write of this woman, after you have written of other lesser ones. And now farewell, I charge you no more.

"But before I go, this much I will tell you: no true lover shall go to hell. These other ladies sitting here in a row are in your ballad, if you can recognize them, and in your books you shall find them all. Set them now all in mind in your legend; I mean, of those that are in your knowledge. For sitting here are twenty thousand more than you know, all good women, and true in love for anything that may happen. The sun is drawing west. I must go home to paradise with this entire company. Make the verses of them as you wish, and serve always the fresh daisy.

"I wish you to begin with Cleopatra; and so continue. And so you shall gain my love. *For let us see now what sort*

---

[29] Cybele. In Phrygian relian the Great Mother of the gods, a goddess of fertility.

[30] Redness. Some have suggested that this refers to the red tips of the petals, but it likely refers to the gold in the center. (Red is still often used as the term to refer to gold today.)

of man that lover would be, who would endure so strong a pain for love as she. I know well that you may not set to rhyme all that such lovers did in their time; it would be too long to read and to hear. It will suffice me that you make it in this manner: that you retell the important part of al their lives, following what these ancient authors wish to treat. For whosoever shall tell so many stories, may he tell them shortly, or he shall dwell too long."

And at these words I awoke from my sleep, and I began to write on my Legend even thus.

Here ends the prologue.

THE LEGEND OF CLEOPATRA

Here begins the Legend of Cleopatra, Martyr, Queen of Egypt.

After the death of the king Ptolemy, who had all Egypt under his rule, Cleopatra his queen reigned; until a certain time[1] when a certain situation arose that out of Rome there was sent a senator to win kingdoms and honors for the town of Rome, as was their custom, and to have the world under their obedience; and in truth his name was Antony. As Fortune owed him a disgrace after he had met with prosperity,[2] it so happened that he became a rebel to the town of Rome; and moreover he falsely deserted the sister of Caesar, before she was aware, and at any cost wished to have another wife. For these reasons he fell at odds with Caesar and with Rome.

Nevertheless this same senator was a worthy, noble warrior, in truth, and his death was a great pity. But Love had brought this man into such a madness and so tightly bound him in his snare, all for love of Cleopatra, that he set all the world at no value. Nothing seemed to him so necessary as to love and serve Cleopatra. He cared not to die in arms in defense of her and of her right. And this noble queen in like fashion loved this knight, for his merit and his knighthood; and certainly, unless the books lie, he was in his person, nobility, discretion, and hardiness as worthy as any person alive. And she was as fair as the rose in May. And, as it is best to write briefly, she became his wife and had him as she

[1] A certain time: following the Battle of Philippi (42 B.C.).

[2] Fortune: as the wheel of Fortune continually turns, good and bad fortune always follow one another.

desired.

To describe the wedding and the festival would take too long for me, who have undertaken such an enterprise as to put in verses so many stories, lest I should neglect things of greater weight and importance. For men may overload a ship or a barge. Therefore I will skip lightly to the conclusion, and let the remains slip.

Octavian, maddened by this deed, raised a host of stout Romans, cruel as lions, to lead against Antony for his utter destruction. They went to their ship, and I leave them sailing thus. Antony was wary and would not avoid encountering these Romans if he could; he laid his plans, and on a day both he and his wife and his entire host went forth without delay to their ship; they delayed no longer. Out at sea it happened that the foes met; the trumpet sounds on high, they shout and shoot and with the sun at their back make a fierce onset.

With a grisly sound out flies the huge shot, and furiously they hurtle together, and from the fore-tops down come the great stones. Among the ropes go grappling hooks full of claws. This man and that presses on with poleaxes; one flees behind the mast, and out again, and drives the other over board. One pierces another upon his spear-point; one cuts the sail with hooks like scythes; another brings the wine-cup and bids them be glad; one pours peas upon the hatches to make them slippery; they rush together with pots full of quicklime.

And thus they pass the long day in battle, until at last (as every: thing has an end) Antony is defeated and put to flight, and all his people scatter as best they can.

The queen with all her purple sails fled likewise from the blows that went thick as hail-stones; no wonder she could not endure it. And when Antony saw that chance he said, "Alas the day that I was born! So on this day I have lost all my honor!." And in despair he started out of his wits, and stabbed himself to the heart at once, before he went further from the place.

His wife, who could get no mercy from Caesar, fled to Egypt in dread and anguish. But listen, all you who speak of devotion, you men who falsely swear by many oaths that you will die if your beloved should be so much as angered, behold what womanly faithfulness you may here see.

This woeful Cleopatra made such lament that no tongue can describe it; but in the morning she would delay no longer and commanded her skillful workmen to make a shrine out of all the rubies and fine gems that she could uncover in all Egypt, and she filled the shrine with spices, had the body embalmed, and called for this dead corpse and enclosed it in the shrine. And next to the shrine she had a pit dug, and put in it all the serpents she could find, and thus she spoke: "Now, beloved, whom my sorrowful heart so far obeyed that, from that blissful hour when I swore to be entirely and freely yours – I mean you, Antony, my knight – you were never out of my heart's remembrance as long as I was awake, day or night, in happiness or woe, in the carol or the dance.[3] And then I made this covenant with myself, that, whatever it was you felt, happiness or woe, the same would I feel, life or death, if it lay in my power for the honor of my wifehood. And I will fulfill that covenant while breath remains in me; and men shall see well that never was a queen truer to her love."

And at that word with a resolute heart she leaped naked into the pit among the serpents, and there she chose to be buried. Immediately the serpents began to sting her, and she received her death cheerfully, for the love of Antony who was so dear to her. And this is truth of history; it is no fable.

Now, until I find a man this faithful and steadfast, who will so willingly die for love, I pray to God, may our heads never ache! Amen.

Here ends the Legend of Cleopatra, Martyr.

---

[3] Carol or dance. In the singing or in the dancing part of the festivity.

THE LEGEND OF THISBE OF BABYLON

❦

Here begins the Legend of Thisbe of Babylon, Martyr.

In Babylon, the town around which Queen Semiramis had a ditch and a very high wall built with hard well-baked tiles, this is what happened. In this noble town there dwelt two lords of high reputation; and they dwelt upon a green so close to each other that there was only a stone wall between them, as there often is in great towns. One of these men had a son, one of the most attractive in all that land; and the other had a daughter, the fairest who dwelt then in the eastern world. The name of each was brought to the other by women who were their neighbors. For in that country, even now in truth, maidens are closely and jealously guarded, lest they act foolishly.

This young man was called Pyramus, and the maiden called Thisbe; Ovid says thus. And so their praise was brought to each other by report, so that as they grew in years their love grew. And certainly, as for their age, there might have been marriage between them, except that their fathers would not agree to it. And both alike burned so sorely in love that none of all their friends could hinder them from meeting secretly, sometimes by deceit, and speaking a bit about their longings. Cover the coals and the fire is hotter; forbid love, and it is ten times as raging.

This wall that stood between them was split in two, from the top right down, since long ago when it was built; yet this crack was so narrow and small that it was not visible to the tiniest extent. But what is it love cannot find? You two lovers, to tell the truth, you first found this narrow little crack! And they let their words, with voices as soft as any shrift,[1] pass through the crack, and as they stood there, told all their love-complaints and all their woe every time when they dared. He stood upon the one side of the wall, Thisbe upon the other, to hear the sweet sound of each other's voice; and thus they would deceive their guardians. Every day they would threaten this wall and wish to God it were beaten down. Thus they would say: "Alas, you wicked wall! Through your envy you hinder us entirely. Why will you not split apart, or fall in two? Or at least, if you will not do so, yet would you at least let us meet once, or once permit us to kiss sweetly? Then would we be recovered from our painful cares. But nevertheless we are indebted to you, inasmuch as you allow us to send our words through your mortar and stone. We still ought to be well pleased with you."

When these vain words were uttered, they would kiss the cold stone wall and take their leave and depart. And they were glad to do this in the evening or very early, lest people saw them. And for a long time they did thus, until one day, when Phoebus was clear and Aurora[2] with her hot beams had dried up the dew on the wet herbs, Pyramus came to this crack, as he was accustomed, and then came Thisbe, and by their faith they pledged their honor to steal away that same night, and to beguile all their guardians and flee from the city; and, because the fields were so broad and large, that they might meet at one place at one time, they appointed their meeting to be under a tree where King Ninus was buried. (For old pagans who worshipped idols used then to be buried in fields.) And near this grave was a spring. And, to tell this tale shortly, this covenant was very strongly confirmed. To them it seemed that the sun delayed for a long time before it went down under the sea.

This Thisbe had so great a feeling and desire to see Pyramus that when she saw her time she stole away secretly

---

[1] Soft as any shrift: as soft as any words spoken in the confessional chamber in the sacrament of penance.

[2] Phoebus and Aurora. The sun and the dawn.

at night with her face deceptively wimpled.[3] To keep her pledge she forsook all her friends, Alas! It is pity that a woman should ever be so faithful to trust man, unless she knew him better! She went to the tree at a swift pace, for her love made her so hardy; and down beside the spring she settled herself. Alas! Without more ado a wild lioness, with mouth bloody from strangling some beast, came out of the wood to drink at the spring where Thisbe was sitting. And when Thisbe saw that, she started up, with heart all terrified, and with fearful foot fled into a cave, which she saw well by the moon. And as she ran she let fall her wimple and did not notice it, so sorely was she dismayed, and so glad of her escape as well. And thus she sat in hiding very quietly. When the lioness had drunk her fill, she roamed about the spring, and soon found the wimple, and tore it all to pieces with her bloody mouth. When this was done, she delayed no longer but made her way to the woods.

At last this Pyramus came, but, alas, he had stayed too long at home. The moon shone, and he could see well, and in his way, as he came speedily, he cast his eyes down to the ground, and as he looked down he saw the wide tracks of a lion in the sand, and he suddenly shuddered in his heart and grew pale and his hair stood on end; and he came nearer, and found the torn wimple. "Alas! "he said. "Alas, the day that I was born! This one night will slay both us lovers! How should I ask mercy of Thisbe, when I am he who have slain her, alas! My prayer to you to come has slain you! Alas, to tell a woman to go by night to a place where peril might occur! And I so slow! Alas! If only I had been here in this place a furlong before you! Now may whatever lion there is in this forest tear apart my body; or whatever wild beast there is, now may it gnaw my heart!"

And with these words he sprang to the wimple, and kissed it often, and wept over it sorely and said, "Alas, wimple! There is nothing else, except that you shall feel my

[3] Wimpled. With her face covered by a wimple (a headdress).

blood as well as you have felt the bleeding of Thisbe. And with these words he struck himself to the heart. The blood gushed out of the wound as broad as water when the pipe is broken.

Now Thisbe, who knew nothing of this, thought as she sat in fear, "If it so happens that my Pyramus has come here and cannot find me, he may hold me false and cruel as well." And she came out and searched for him both with her heart and with her eyes, and thought," I will tell him about my dread both for the lioness and for all my behavior."

And at last she came upon her lover, all bloody, beating on the ground with his heels; and at this she started back, and her heart began to toss like the waves, and she grew pale as a boxwood tree. For a short moment she observed him and then well recognized that he was Pyramus, her dear heart.

Who could write what a deadly expression Thisbe had now, and how she tore her hair, and how she tormented herself, and how she lay on the ground and swooned, and how she wept his wound full of tears; how she mingled his blood with her lamentation, and did paint herself with his blood; how she embraced the dead body, alas! How did this woeful Thisbe act then; how she kissed his frosty mouth so cold! "Who has done this! Who has been so ruthless, to slay my beloved! O, speak, my Pyramus! I am your Thisbe who calls you! "And at this she lifted up his head. This woeful man, in whom still remained some life, when he heard the name of Thisbe cried, cast his heavy, death-like eyes upon her and down again, and yielded up his spirit.

Thisbe arose without noise or outcry, and saw her wimple, along with his empty scabbard and his sword, which had put him to death. Then she spoke thus: "My sorrowful hand," she said, "is strong enough for such a task in my behalf, for love shall give me strength and boldness, I believe, to make my wound large enough. Dead I will follow you, and I will be the cause and partner also of your death," she said. "And though nothing except death alone could truly separate you from me, you shall now no more part from me than from death, for I will go with you. And now, you wretched, jealous fathers of ours, we who were once your children, we pray you that without more ill-will we may lie together in one grave, since love has brought us this pitiful end. And may the righteous God grant every lover, that truly loves, more prosperity than ever Pyramus and Thisbe had! And let no woman of gentle blood be so overconfident as to place herself in such hazard. Yet God forbid a woman may be only as true in loving as any man! And for my part I shall without delay make this plain."

And with these words she seized his sword immediately, which was warm and hot with her lover's blood, and struck herself to the heart.

And thus are Pyramus and Thisbe gone. Of faithful men I find in all my books only a few more besides this Pyramus, and therefore I have spoken thus of him. For it is a rare delight to us men to find a man who can be tender and true in love. Here you may see that, whatsoever lover he may be, a woman has mind and daring to do as well as he.

Here ends the legend of Thisbe.

THE LEGEND OF DIDO, QUEEN OF CARTHAGE

Here begins the Legend of Dido, Martyr.

May there be glory and honor, Vergil of Mantua, to your name! I shall follow your lantern as well as I can, while you lead, in telling how Aeneas perjured himself to Dido. I will follow the meaning of your *Aeneid* and of Ovid, and will put the main events into verse.

When Troy was brought to destruction by the wiles of the Greeks, and especially by Sinon, pretending that horse, through which many Trojans were to die, to be an offering to Minerva; and when Hector had appeared after his death, and fire so wild it could not be controlled raged through all the noble tower of Ilium, which was the chief fortification of the city; and when all the land was brought low, and Priam the king slain and brought to nothing; and when Aeneas was charged by Venus to flee, he took Ascanius his son by his right hand and fled. And on his back he bore with him his old father, called Anchises, and on the way he lost his wife Creusa. And he bore much sorrow in heart before he could find his companions. But at last, when he had found them, he prepared himself at a certain place, quickly pushed out to sea, and sailed forth with all his men toward Italy, as destiny directed. But it is not my point to speak of his adventures on the sea here, for it is not related my subject matter; but, as I have said, my tale shall be of him and Dido, until I have finished.

So long he sailed the salty sea, until with difficulty he arrived in Libya with seven ships, and no larger fleet; and he was glad to rush to land, so shaken was he with the tempest. And when he had gained the haven, of all his fellowship he chose a knight called Achates to go with him to survey the land; he took with him no greater company. Forth they went, his comrade and he, without anyone to point the way, and left his ships riding at anchor.

So long he walked in the wilderness until at the last he met a huntress; she had a bow in hand, and arrows; her garments were cut short to the knee; but she was the fairest creature that ever nature had formed. And she greeted Aeneas and Achates, and thus spoke to them, when she met them: "Have you seen," she said, "as you walked wide and far, any of my sisters in this forest with garments tucked up and arrows in their quivers walk near you, with any wild boar or other beast that they have hunted?"

"Nay truly, lady," said this Aeneas; "but it seems to me by your beauty you can not be a woman of this world, I would think, but are the sister of Phoebus.[1] And, if it is so that you are a goddess, have pity on our labor and woe.

"Truly, I am no goddess," she said; "for here in this land maidens walk with arrows and bow in this manner. This is the realm of Libya where you are, of which Dido is lady and queen." And briefly she told him all the reason of Dido's coming to those parts, of which I wish not to write now; there is no need, for it would be a waste of time. For this is the sum and substance: it was Venus, his own mother, who thus spoke with Aeneas; and she told him to turn toward Carthage, and without delay vanished out of his sight. I could follow Vergil word for word, but it would take entirely too long.

This noble queen named Dido, formerly wife to Sychaeus and fairer than the shining sun, had founded this noble town of Carthage, in which she reigned in such great glory that she was believed to be the flower of all queens in

[1] Sister of Phoebus. Diana, or Artemis, goddess of the moon, forest, animals, the hunt, and patron of women in childbirth and of virgins. In the last capacity, she figures into much of Chaucer's work (and Shakespeare's) as the figure of those who choose not to enter into the game of love.

nobility, generosity, and beauty, so much so that anyone would be well who had seen her just once. She was so desired by kings and lords that her beauty had inflamed all the world, so well stood she in grace with every creature.

When Aeneas had come to that place, secretly he made his way to the chief temple of the whole town, where Dido was at her devotions. When he had come into the broad temple, I cannot say if it would be possible, but Venus made him invisible. Thus says the book, I promise you. And when Aeneas and Achates had been over this entire temple, they found painted on a wall how Troy and all the land had been destroyed.

"Alas, that I was born!" said Aeneas, "our shame is known so far over the entire world that now it is depicted everywhere. We who were in prosperity are now defamed, and that so grievously that I care to live no longer." And with these words he burst out weeping so tenderly that it was pitiful to behold.

This lovely lady, queen of the city, stood in the temple in royal state, so splendid and so fair, so young, so joyous, with her glad eyes, that, if the god who made heaven and earth had desired a love, for beauty and goodness and womanhood and seemliness and fidelity, whom should he have loved but this sweet lady? There was no woman half so fitting.

Fortune, who governs the world, speedily brought in so strange a chance that never yet was there so rare a case. For all the company of Aeneas, which he deemed had been lost in the sea, came to shore not far from that city. Therefore some of the greatest of his lords by chance came to the city to that same temple to seek the queen and entreat her for aid, for such renown of her goodness had spread. And when they had related all their distress, and their tempest and their hard case, Aeneas showed himself to the queen and freely told who he was. Who could have been more joyful than his men at this moment, who had found their lord, their ruler?

The queen saw how they did him such honor. She had

often heard of Aeneas before that, and in her heart she had pity and woe that such a noble a man had so lost his heritage. And she could see that he was like a knight, well endowed in person and strength, and likely to be a courteous man; that he was articulate in his speech, had a noble face, and was well formed in brawn and bone. For, taking after Venus, he had such beauty that no man could be half so handsome, I believe. And he well seemed to be a lord. And because he was a stranger she liked him somewhat better; as – God save us – to some people a new thing is often sweet. Before long her heart pitied his woe, and with that pity love also came; and thus out of pity and courtesy he would need to be comforted in his distress.

She said that she was surely sorry that he had had such peril and such mishap. And in her friendly speech she spoke to him thus and said as you may hear: "Are you not the son of Venus and Anchises? In good faith, you shall have all the worship and assistance that I can rightly give you. Your ships and your followers I will protect." She spoke many courteous words and commanded her messengers to go that same day without fail to seek his ships and fill them with provisions; she sent many beasts to the ships, and presented them with wine as well. And she rushed to her royal palace, and she always had Aeneas near her.

What need is there to describe the feast to you? He was never better at ease in his life. The festival was well provided with dainties and with splendor, with instruments of music, song and gladness; and many were the amorous glances and schemes. Aeneas had come into Paradise out of the mouth of hell; and thus in bliss he recalled his state in Troy. After the meal, Aeneas was led to dancing-halls, full of fine hangings and rich couches and ornaments. And when he had sat down with the queen, and spices had been served and wine passed around, he was led before long to his chambers, to take his ease and have his rest, and all his men likewise, to do just as they wished.

There was no well bridled war horse, nor fine jousting steed, nor large easy-to-ride palfrey, nor jewel adorned all over with rich gems, nor fully weighted sacks full of gold, nor any ruby that shone by night, nor noble high-flying falcon for hunting herons, nor hound for hart or wild boar or deer, nor cup of gold, nor florins newly coined, which could be procured in the land of Libya, that Dido did not send to Aeneas. And all that he wished for, she provided for him. Thus could this honorable queen call upon her guests as one who knew how to surpass all in generosity.

Aeneas sent also unto his ship by Achates for his son, and for rich gear, including scepter, clothes, brooches and rings as well, some to wear, and some to present to her who had given him all these noble things. And he told his son to make the presentation and take the gift to the queen. This Achates returned, and Aeneas was eager and glad to see his young son Ascanius. But nevertheless, our author[2] tells us, that Cupid, who is the god of Love, at the prayer of his mother on high had taken on the likeness of the child, to enamor this noble queen of Aeneas. (But as to that text, be it as it may, I pay no attention to it.) But true it is that the queen made such to-do about this child that it is wondrous to hear of; and with good will she thanked him often for the gift that his father sent.

Thus was the queen in delight and joy with all these new, pleasant people of Troy. And she further inquired about the deeds of Aeneas, and learned the entire story of Troy. And the two of them decided to converse and amuse themselves all long day. From this there was bred such a flame that luckless Dido had such a strong desire to become intimate with her new guest Aeneas that she lost her color and her health as well.

Now for the conclusion, the fruit of it all, the reason I have told this story, and shall continue it. Thus I begin; it

[2] Our author. Chaucer typically refers to his source as his author, which in this case is Vergil, author of *The Aeneid.*

happened one night, when the moon had lifted up her beams, that this noble queen went to her rest, sighed sorely, and tormented herself; she waked and tossed, started up many times as lovers usually do, as I have heard. And at last she made her moan to her sister Anna, and spoke thus: "Now, my dear sister, what can it be that makes me so horrified in my dream? This Trojan is so in my thoughts, because it seems to me that he is so well formed and so likely to be a worthy man, and that he know so much goodness as well, that all my love and life lie in his keeping. Have you not heard him tell of his adventures? Now surely, Anna, if you counsel me so, I would gladly be wedded to him. This is all; what more should I say? In him it all lies, to make me live or die."

Her sister Anna, as she saw her advantage, spoke as she thought and somewhat withstood her; but at this point there was so much discourse that it would be too long to retell. To sum it all up, the thing could not be withstood; love will love, it will hold back for no person. The dawn arose out of the sea; this amorous queen charged her attendants to prepare the nets and the spears broad and sharp. She wished to go hunting, this lusty, lovely queen, as this new sweet pain urged her.

On horse went all her lusty company, the hounds were led to the courtyard, and upon chargers swift as thought her young knights hovered all around, and a huge company of her women as well. Upon a stout palfrey white as paper, with a red saddle adorned delightfully, clearly embossed with bars of gold, sat Dido all covered with gold and gems, and she as fair as the bright morning that heals the sick of the night's sorrow. Upon a charger that leapt like flame (though one could turn him with a little bridle-bit) Aeneas sat, like Phoebus in his looks, so splendidly was he arrayed in his fashion; and governed his charger as he would, by the foamy bridle with a golden bit.

And thus I let this noble queen ride forth in her hunting,

with this Trojan by her. The herd of harts was found before long, with “Ho! Faster! Spur on! Loose the dogs! Loose them! Why won’t the lion come, or the bear, so that I might meet him once with this spear?” Thus cried these young people, and on they went killing all these wild harts, and had them as they wished.

Amid all this the heavens began to rumble, the thunder roared with grisly voice; down came the rain thick with hail and sleet and heaven’s fire; so sorely it frightened this noble queen and her attendants as well that each was glad to flee away. And in brief, to save her from the tempest she fled into a little cave, and with her went Aeneas also. I know not if any more went with them; the author makes no mention of that.

And here began the deep devotion between the two of them; this was the first morning of their gladness, and the beginning of their sorrow. For there Aeneas so kneeled, and told her all his heart and his pain, and swore so deeply to be true to her in happiness or in woe, and to exchange her for no other – as a false lover so well knows how to make his complaint – that hapless Dido pitied his woe, and took him for a husband, to be his wife for evermore so long as they should live. And after this, when the tempest ceased, they came out in joy and went home.

Evil Rumor arose, and arose quickly, how Aeneas had gone with the queen into the cave. And people judged as they wished. And when the king named Yrbas knew of it, since he had always loved her and wooed her, to win her as his wife, he made such sorrow and sad expressions that it was pitiful and heart-rending to see. But in love it happens ever so, that one shall laugh at another’s sorrow; now Aeneas laughs, and is in more bliss and wealth than ever he was in Troy.

O unfortunate woman, innocent, full of pity, faith, and tenderness, why did you so trust men? Had you such pity upon their pretended woe, even though you had before you so many old examples? Do you not see how they all perjured themselves? Where do you see one who has not forsaken his beloved or been unkind or done to her some mischief or robbed her or boasted of his acts to her? You can see this as well as you can read it.

Take heed now of this great gentleman, this Trojan, who so well knew how to please her, who pretended to be so true and yielding, so courteous and so discreet in his deeds; who knew so well how to perform all due observances, and attend her pleasure at dances and feasts and when she went to the temple and back again home; and who fasted until he had seen his lady, and wore in his heraldic devices I know not what for her sake; and who would compose songs, and joust and do many deeds at arms, and send her letters, tokens, brooches, rings. Now hear how he shall serve his lady! After he had been in peril of death from hunger and misadventures on the sea, and desolate, fugitive from his country, and all his company scattered by the tempest, she gave her body and her realm as well into his hand, when she might have been a queen of another land besides Carthage and lived in sufficiency of joy. What more would you want?

This Aeneas, who had vowed so deeply, was weary of the business before long, and his hot earnestness had all blown by. Secretly he had his ships prepared and planned to steal away by night. This Dido suspected it and well thought that all was not right; for in the night he lay in his bed and sighed. Without delay she asked him what displeased him: "my dear heart, whom I love best?"

"Surely," he said, "this night my father's spirit has so sorely troubled me in my sleep, and Mercury as well has delivered a message, that it is my destiny to sail soon for I must conquer Italy. For this it seems to me my heart is broken" With this his false tears burst forth, and he took her in his two arms.

"Is that in earnest?" she said. "Will you do so? Have you not sworn to take me as your wife? Alas! What kind of a woman will you make of me! I am a gentlewoman and a queen! You will not thus foully flee from your wife? Alas, that I was born! What shall I do?"

To tell it briefly, this noble Queen Dido sought shrines and made sacrifices; she knelt and cried in such a way that it is pitiful to relate. She implores him and offers to be his slave, his servant of the lowest rank. She fell at his feet and swooned, her shining golden hair disheveled, and cried, "Have mercy! Let me go with you! These lords who are my neighbors will destroy me, only because of you. And, so you will take me now as your wife, as you have sworn, then I will give you leave to slay me with your sword right now this evening, for then I shall die wedded to you. I am with child: grant my child life! Mercy, lord! Have pity in your thought!"

But all this was to no avail for her; for one night he let her lie sleeping and stole away to his followers, and as a traitor he sailed forth toward the great land of Italy. Thus he left Dido in woe and pain; and there he wedded a lady named Lavinia.

When he stole away from Dido in her sleep, he left a garment and his sword also standing right at the head of her bed, as he hastened to reach his ships. When hapless Dido awoke, she kissed this garmentoften for his sake, and said, "O you garment, so sweet while it pleased Jupiter, take my soul now, unbind me from this unrest! I have run through the whole course of fortune." And then she swooned twenty times, without any aid from Aeneas. And when she had made her lament to her sister Anna – of which I cannot write, such pity I have to tell of it – she bade her nurse and her sister to go fetch fire and other things right away, and said she wished to make a sacrifice. And when she saw her time, she leaped on the sacrificial fire, and with his sword she stabbed herself to the heart.

But before she was wounded, before she died, she said this, as my author tells; she wrote a letter without delay, which began in this way: “Just as the white swan,” she said, “begins to sing against the time of his death, so to you I make my lament; not that I hope to get you back, for well I know that is all in vain, because the gods are contrary to me. But since my good name is lost through you, I may well lose a word or a message upon you, albeit I shall be never better for that. For the same wind that blew away your ship has blown away your good faith.” But whosoever wishes to know this entire letter, let him read Ovid; there one shall find it.

Here ends the Legend of Dido,
Martyr, Queen of Carthage.

THE LEGEND OF LUCRECE

❦

Here begins the Legend of Lucretia of Rome, Martyr.

Now I must speak of the exile of kings of Rome by reason of their horrible deeds, and of the last king, Tarquin, as Ovid and Titus Livy[1] relate. But it is not for that reason I tell this tale, but to praise and remember that true wife, the faithful Lucrece, for whose true wifehood and steadfastness not only do these pagans extol her but also he who is called in our legendaries the great Augustine[2] has great pity for this Lucrece, who died in Rome. And of the manner of her death I will treat but briefly, and touch upon only the important matter of this thing.

When Ardea[3] was besieged with Romans who were stern and stout, long lay the siege and accomplished little, so that they remained there half idle, as they judged. And in his sport the young Tarquin began to jest, for he was loose tongued, and said that this was an idle existence, for no man there did more than his wife. He said, "And let us speak of wives; that would be best. Let every man praise his own as it pleases him, and let us ease our hearts with converse."

A knight named Collatine arose and spoke thus: "Nay, there is no need to rely on words, but on deeds. I have a wife," he said, "who is held to be good by all who know her. Let us go to Rome tonight and see."

---

[1] Titus Livy. Titus Livius Patavinus, or Livy (59 BC - 17 AD), author of *Ab urbe condita libri*, commonly known as *The History of Rome*.

[2] Augustine. St. Augustine uses Lucrece in *The City of God* as a defense of the virtue of Christian martyrs who had been raped by Romans but not committed suicide.

[3] Ardea. Capital city of the Rutuli, in Latium about twenty miles south of Rome.

Tarquinius answered, "That is good."

To Rome Tarquin and Collatine came and quickly went to the house of Collatine, and alighted. The husband well knew the whole shape of the house, and secretly they entered in, for there was no porter at the gate, and at the chamber-door they stopped. This noble wife sat beside her bed with hair unbound, for she suspected no harm. And she was working soft wool, our book says, to keep her from sloth and idleness, and she told her servants to perform their duties, and asked them, "What news do you hear? What do people say of the siege and how it shall end? Would to God the walls would fall! My husband has been so long away from this town; for this reason the dread so sorely pains me, it stings to my heart just like a sword, when I think of the siege or of that place. God save my lord, I pray, in His mercy."

And at that she wept tenderly and paid no more attention to her work, but meekly let her eyes fall. And this demeanor well became her. And her tears, full of virtue, embellished her wifely chastity. Her look was worthy of her heart, for they accorded in sign and in truth. And at her words Collatine her husband came bursting in, before she was aware of him, and cried, "Fear not, for I am here!" And immediately she rose up with blissful countenance, and kissed him, as wives used to do.

Tarquin, this proud king's son, considered her beauty and her demeanor, her blonde hair, her form, her manner, her hue, her words of lament, and saw that her beauty was not feigned by any artfulness. And he conceived such desire for this lady that it burned in his heart like a flame, so furiously that his wits were entirely forgotten. For he well imagined that she could never be won; and thus he was continually in greater despair, the more he coveted her and thought of her loveliness. His covetousness turned to blind lust.

In the morning, when birds began to sing, he returned secretly to the camp and walked sadly by himself, ever freshly recalling her image: "Thus lay her hair, and so fresh was her hue. Thus she sat, thus spoke, thus spun. This was her look, this was her beauty and her demeanor." His heart has now received all this thought. And as the sea, all tossed with a tempest, will yet heave for a day or two after the storm has all departed, so too, though her form was absent, the pleasure of it was still present – but not pleasure, but rather evil delight or an unrighteous desire with evil intent. "For in spite of herself she shall be my mistress," he said; "chance always helps the hardy. However it ends, it shall be done."

And he buckled on his sword and departed, and rode forth until he arrived at Rome, and all by himself took his way straight to the house of Collatine. The sun was down, and the day had lost its light. And in he came to a secret corner, and in the night stole out like a thief, when everyone had gone to their rest and none had a thought of such treachery. Whether it was by window or other sly means, he quickly entered in and with sword drawn came speedily where this noble wife Lucrece was lying. And as she awoke she felt her bed pressed down. "What beast is that," she said, "weighs down my bed thus?"

"I am the king's son, Tarquin," he said; "but if you cry out or make a noise, or awake any creature, by that God who formed man alive, I shall thrust this sword through your heart." And at that he leaped at her throat and set the sharp point on her heart.

She spoke no word, she had no strength; what should she say? Her wit had entirely fled. Just as when a wolf finds a solitary lamb, to whom should she lament or make moan? What! Shall she struggle against a hardy knight? Men well know a woman has no strength. What! Shall she cry? How shall she escape the man who has her by the throat, with his sword at her heart? She begged for mercy, and said all she could.

"If you do not yield to me," he said, this cruel man, "may Jupiter save my soul, I will slay your groom in the stable and lay him in your bed, and raise the alarm that I found you in such adultery. And thus you shall die, and also lose your good name, for you have no other choice."

Now at this time these Roman matrons so loved their fair reputation, and so dreaded shame, that, for fear of scandalous talk and fear of dying, she lost her wit and breath at once, and lay in a swoon so deathlike that a man might have smitten her arm or head off; she felt nothing, fair or foul.

Tarquin, heir to a king, who by lineage and justice should bear yourself as a lord and a true knight, why have you done dishonor to chivalry? Why have you basely wronged this lady? Alack! This was a villainous deed of you!

But now to the point: I read in the history that after he departed, the misfortune that occurred was this. The lady sent for all her friends, father, mother, husband together; and with her shining hair all disheveled, in dress such as women then used to wear for the burial of their friends, she sat in the hall with a sorrowful look. Her friends asked what could ail her, and who was dead? And she sat continually weeping; for shame she could not fetch forth a word, nor did she dare to look upon them. But at last she told them of Tarquin, this sorrowful case, all this horrible thing. It would be impossible to tell the lament that she and all her friends made together. Had people's hearts been made of stone, it would have made them pity her, so wifely and so true was her heart. She said that for her guilt or infamy her husband should not have a foul name; that she would not permit in any way. And they all answered, upon their word they forgave her, as was just; it was no fault of hers, it lay not under her control. And they told her many examples.

But it was all for nothing, and thus she directly replied. "Be as it may," she said, "as to forgiving, I will by no means have forgiveness." And secretly she snatched forth a knife, and with it slew herself. And as she fell, she looked and still paid attention to her clothes; for as she fell down she still remained mindful lest her feet or the like would be bare, so well she loved purity and fidelity.

All the town of Rome felt pity for her, and Brutus swore by her chaste blood that for that deed Tarquin should be banished, and all his kinsfolk; and he had the people summoned, and openly told the tale to them all, and openly had her carried on a bier through the entire town, so that men might see and learn the horrible deed of her violation. And never since that day was there a king in Rome; and she was held there to be a saint, and her day was always dearly worshipped in their law.

And thus ended Lucrece the noble wife, as Titus Livy[4] bears witness. I tell the tale because she was so faithful in love, and never by her will changed to any new lover, and for the sake of the constant heart, steadfast and kind, which men may ever feel in these women; where they set their heart, there it remains. For well I know Christ himself tells that in all Israel, broad though the land may be, he found not so great faith as in a woman;[5] and this is no lie. And as for men, look what tyrannical deeds they do every day. Test them who may wish: even the truest of them is too entirely fickle to trust.

Here ends the Legend of Lucretia of Rome, Martyr.

---

[4] Livy. See note near line 287.

[5] Faith as in a woman. Likely refers to Matthew 15.28 in which a woman whose daughter is tormented by a demon persists in asking Christ's aid, to the effect that he heals her.

THE LEGEND OF ARIADNE

Here begins the Legend of Ariadne of Athens.

You Judge in Hell, Minos, lord of Crete, now your turn comes; now you come into the ring! Not for your sake only do I write this history, but to call to mind once more the great untruth in love of you, Theseus, for which the gods of high heaven are angered and have taken vengeance for your guilt; may you grow red with shame! Now I begin your life.

Minos, great king of Crete, who had a hundred great and strong cities, sent his son Androgeus to school at Athens; where it happened that while he was learning philosophy he was slain in that very city, for no reason but envy. The great Minos, of whom I speak, came to avenge his son's death. Long and hotly he laid siege to Alcathoe.[1] Nevertheless, the walls were so strong, and Nisus, king of that city, was so knightly, that he feared little; he took no heed of Minos or his army until one day the chance arose that the daughter of Nisus stood on the wall and saw the entire workings of the siege. It so happened that, watching a skirmish, she set her heart so sorely upon Minos the king for his beauty and his chivalry that she thought she would die. And, to hasten over this long story, she enabled Minos to win that place and to have the city all at his will, to save or destroy whom he wished. But he repaid her wickedly for her kindness, and would have left her drowning in sorrow and woe, had not the gods had pity upon her. But that story would be too long for me now.[2]

---

[1] Alcathoe. The citadel of Megara, near Athens, named after Alcathous, founder of Megara.

This King Minos also won Athens, and Alcathoe and other towns. And this was the outcome: that Minos so harshly pressed the people of Athens that from year to year they had to give him their own beloved children to be slain, as you shall hear. This Minos had a monster, an evil beast, so cruel that, when a man was brought to him, without pause he would devour him; no defense could help. And truly every third year they cast lots, and as the lot fell, on the rich man or the poor, he had to give up his son and present him to Minos to be saved or destroyed, or let his beast devour him at his will. And Minos did this out of hatred; all his pleasure was set to avenge his son and to make the people of Athens his slaves from year to year as long as he should live. And when this town was won he sailed home.

This evil custom continued a long time, until Aegeus, king of Athens, had to send his own son Theseus, since the lot fell upon him, to be devoured, for there was no reprieve. And this woeful young knight was led forth straight to the court of King Minos and was cast fettered into a prison, until the time when he would be devoured.

Well may you weep, woeful Theseus, who is the king's son, thus condemned! It seems to me you were deeply indebted to any who should save you from cold troubles. And now if any woman should help you, well ought you to be her slave and true lover year by year. But now to return to my tale.

The tower where this Theseus was cast, down in the dark bottom, extremely deep, adjoined the wall of an outer chamber belonging to the two daughters of King Minos, who in much mirth and joy and comfort dwelt in their great chambers above, facing the chief street. By chance, I know not

---

[2] Too long for me now. Nisus' daughter Scylla helped Minos by cutting off the purple lock of hair that made her father invincible. After her father was defeated and Minos, disgusted by her treason, set sail, she swam to meet him, but, though she almost caught Minos' ship, she was attacked and drowned by her father who had been transformed into an eagle.

how, it happened that, as Theseus was making his complaint one night, the king's daughter, named Ariadne, and her sister Phaedra as well, heard all his complaint, as they stood upon the wall and looked upon the bright moon; they cared not to go to bed early. And they had compassion for his woe; for a king's son to be in such a prison and be devoured seemed to them a great pity.

Then Ariadne spoke to her noble sister and said, "Phaedra, dear sweet sister, can you not hear how woeful this lord's son is, how piteously he laments his kindred, and the wretched plight he is in, although he is entirely guiltless? Now surely, it is a pity. And if you will assent, by my faith he should be helped, however we can!"

Phaedra answered, "Certainly I am as sorry for him as ever I was for any man; and for his assistance the best counsel I know is that we cause the jailer to come secretly and speak with us directly, and bring this woeful man with him. For if he could overcome this monster, then he would be free; there is no other remedy. Let us test him well to his heart's root, whether, if it may be so that he has a weapon, he might dare to fight this fiend and defend himself, to keep and save his life. For you well know that in the prison where he must descend, the beast is in a place that is not dark, and he has room to wield an axe or a sword or staff or knife; so it seems to me he ought to save himself. If he is a man he will do so. And we shall also make him balls of wax and flax, that when the beast fiercely opens his mouth, he shall cast them into his throat, to encumber his teeth and satisfy his hunger. And as soon as Theseus shall see the beast choke, he shall leap on him to slay him before they would ever meet together. This weapon the jailer shall hide, before that time, secretly within the prison. And because that dwelling-place winds much in and out, and has such intricate paths – for it is shaped like a maze, and for this I have in mind a remedy – that by means of a ball of twine he may directly return the way he went, following the thread continually. And when he has overcome the beast, then he may flee away from this horror and can take the jailer with him, and advance him at home in his country, since he is the son of so great a lord. This is my advice, if he should dare to take it."

Why should I make a longer story? The jailer came, and Theseus with him; and when all was thus agreed, down fell Theseus upon his knee before Ariadne: "True lady of my life," he said, "I, a sorrowful man, condemned to die, will not part from you, after this stroke of fortune, so long as I have life or breath, but I will thus remain in your service, so that as an unknown outcast I will serve you forevermore, until my heart shall die. I will forsake my own heritage, and, as I said, be a page of your court, if you stoop to grant me so great a grace to have my meat and drink here; and for my sustenance I will still labor just as you will have it, so that not Minos, who never saw me with the sight of his eyes, nor any other man, shall be able to recognize me, so cunningly and well shall I bear myself and so skillfully and wretchedly disguise myself, so that I shall be detected by no man in this world.

"This I will do to preserve my life and to remain in the presence of you, who do me this excellent kindness. And I will send this worthy man here, now the jailer, to my father, and for reward he shall be one of the greatest men of my country. And if I yet dare say it, my fair lady, I am a king's son, and a knight. Would to God, if it could be, that you were in my land, all three of you, and I with you to bear you company, then you would see if I lie about this. And if I offer you humbly to be your page and serve you here, if I should not serve you as humbly there I pray to Mars to grant me such favor that a shameful death may there fall upon me, and death and poverty upon all my friends; and that after my death my spirit may roam by night and walk to and fro; and that I may have the shameful name of traitor, by reason of which may my spirit walk! And if I ever claim higher station, unless you stoop to give it to me, may I die a shameful death, as I have said! Have mercy, lady! I can say nothing else!"

Theseus was a handsome knight to behold, and young, only twenty-three years old. Whosoever had seen his countenance would have wept for pity of his woe. Therefore this Ariadne in this way answered to his offer and his appealing look: "For a king's son," she said, "and a knight as well to serve me in such a low degree, may God forbid it, for the shame of all women; and may God grant me that such a thing may never happen, but send you grace and cunning of heart to defend yourself and slay your foe in knightly fashion; and may God grant hereafter that I may find you so kind to me and to my sister here that I regret not to have saved you from death! Yet it would be better if I were your wife, since you are as gently born as I and have a kingdom not far from here, than that I should allow you to die guiltless or let you serve as a page. It is not a reasonable offer for one of your kindred, but what is it that a man will not do for fear? As for my sister, since it is so that she must go with me if I depart, or else suffer death, and I too, arrange for her to be faithfully wedded to your son[3] at your home-coming. This is the final end of this thing. Swear to it here, by all that may be sworn on.

"Yes, my lady," he said, "or else may I be entirely torn to pieces by the Minotaur tomorrow! And here take my heart's blood in pledge, if you will; if I had a knife or spear, I would bear it and vow upon it, for I know only then you will believe me. By Mars, who is chief in my creed, if I should live and not fail tomorrow to win my battle, I would never flee from this place until you should see the very proof of my words. For now if I am to tell the truth to you, in my own country I have loved you for many days, though you knew it

---

[3] Your son. In one version of his story, Theseus and the Amazonian woman Antiope had a son Hyppolotus. Recall that Theseus was not one of the youths sent to be devoured by the Minotaur, but, though older than the rest, volunteered to take the place of one of them.

not, and most desired to see you of any earthly creature living. By my faith I swear and assure you that for these seven years I have been your servant. Now I have you, and you also have me, my dear heart, Duchess of Athens!"

This lady smiled at his steadfastness, and at his earnest words and his look, and spoke all softly to her sister in this way. "Now my sister," she said, "now we are duchesses, both you and I, and assured of royal rank in Athens, and both likely to be queens afterwards; and we have saved from his death a king's son, as it is ever the custom of well-born women to save a man of gentle blood if they can, in an honest cause, and most of all if he is in the right. It seems to me that no person ought to blame us for this, nor give us an evil name."

And to explain this matter briefly, Theseus took leave of her, and every point in this covenant was carried out as you have heard me relate. His weapon, his ball of flax, all the things that I have named, were laid by the jailer right in the house where this Minotaur had his dwelling, near the door where Theseus should enter. And Theseus was led to his death, and he came forth to this Minotaur, and following the instruction of Ariadne he overcame the beast and slew him; and by the ball of flax he came out again secretly when he had slain the beast.

Through the jailer he got a barge and loaded it with his wife's treasure, and he took his wife and her fair sister, and the jailer as well, and with all three of them stole away from the land by night, and turned toward the land of *Oenopia*,[4] where he had a familiar friend. There they feasted and danced and sang. And he had in his arms this Ariadne who had preserved him from the beast. Soon he got himself another ship there, and a great number of his countrymen as well, took his leave, and sailed homeward.

And on an island amid the wild sea, where there dwelt no

---

[4] Oenopia. The modern island of Aegina, about fifteen miles southwest of Athens.

creature except wild beasts, and many of them, he brought his ship ashore. And he remained on that island half a day and said he must rest himself on land, and his mariners did as they desired. And, to tell the matter briefly, while Ariadne his wife lay sleeping, because her sister was fairer than she, Theseus took Phaedra by the hand and went forth to the ship, and like a traitor stole off, while this Ariadne still slept. And toward his country he swiftly sailed – may the wind drive him to twenty devils! – and found his father drowned in the sea.

I wish to speak no more of him, in faith. These false lovers, may poison be their destruction! But I will return to Ariadne, who for weariness was overtaken with sleep. So sorrowfully her heart may awaken! Alas! Now my heart has pity for you! Right at dawn she awakes and gropes in the bed and found nothing. "Alas!" she said, "that ever I was created! I am betrayed!" And she rent her hair, and hastened barefoot to the shore, and cried, "Theseus! My sweet heart! Where are you – that I cannot find you and may be slain thus by beasts?"

The hollow rocks answered her; she saw no man. And the moon still shone, and high upon a rock she climbed speedily, and saw his barge sailing in the sea. Her heart grew cold and she said, "Milder than you I find the wild beasts!" Had he who thus betrayed her not sinned? "O, return," she cried, "for the pity and sin of it! Your ship does not have all its crew!" She stuck her kerchief up on a pole, in case he should indeed see it and remember that she was left and return and find her on the shore. But she did this all for nothing; he had gone his way. And down she fell swooning on a stone; and she arose, and in all her sorrow she kissed the prints of his feet where he had passed.

And then she spoke in this way to her bed: "You bed," she said, "which has received two, you shall answer for two, and not for one only! Where has your greater part gone? Alas, what will become of me, wretched creature! Even if a ship or a boat should come here, I dare not for fear go home to my country. I cannot counsel myself in this situation!"

Why should I tell more of her lament? It was so long, it would be a heavy thing to tell; Ovid records everything in Ariadne's epistle. But I shall tell it quickly to the end. The gods helped her, out of pity; and in the sign of Taurus men may see the gems of her crown shining brightly.[5] I will speak no more of this tale; but this is how this false lover could beguile his true love. May the devil repay him for his trouble!

Here ends the Legend of Ariadne of Athens.

[5] Taurus. Chaucer tampers with this part of the tale. In sympathy Bacchus places the crown of Ariadne on in the heavens as the Corona Borealis (Northern Crown) constellation. As it is opposite Taurus, it shows brightly when the sun is in Taurus.

THE HOUSE OF FAME

INTRODUCTORY NOTES

Chaucer's *The House of Fame* is a sort of puzzle. Though it is similar to his other early works in its form as a dream vision, and its presentation of a narrator who is somewhat incompetent at understanding the world around him, *House of Fame* presents some new twists. Like his other works *The Canterbury Tales*, *Anelida and Arcite*, and *Legend of Good Women*, it is incomplete.

The plot and style of the work is rambling. It begins as a meditation on the logic and value of dreams (discussed more extensively than elsewhere in his works) and moves to the narrator's dream of a temple of glass, the most memorable part of which is a tablet of brass containing the story of Aeneas and Dido. After the retelling of this tale from *The Aeneid* the narrator is seized by an eagle, which takes him, after a lengthy discussion about fame and the inadequacies of the narrator (presumably Chaucer himself), to the House of Fame, where he sees, among other things, one group of plaintiffs after another pleading for Fame herself to bestow the best of fame on them. (Fame is not only the modern concept of fame, but reputation as well.) As we might expect, he is entirely inconsistent in her awarding of that fame. The many vignettes of groups of people being judged in an unearthly setting is often seen as Chaucer's version of Dante's *Inferno*; in fact John Lydgate, a contemporary of Chaucer, called this work "Dante in Englyssh."

After pages of shifting action, the poem ends suddenly with the introduction of "a man of great authority" in the last line of the poem. This has led many scholars to believe that this is an attempt by Chaucer to begin the telling of a number of tales, just as he does in *Legend of Good Women* and *The Canterbury Tales*. One might anticipate that a man such as this might speak at length, tell a story, and, as in Chaucer's other collections of stories, bid others to tell stories.

Regardless of the peculiarities of the poem, Chaucer's *House of Fame* remains a dazzling work of fiction and a compelling discussion of the nature of fame.

HOUSE OF FAME

❦

SELECTIONS

May God turn every dream to good for us! For to my mind it is a wonder, by the Cross, what causes dreams by night or by morning; and why some are fulfilled and some not; why this one is a vision, and this a revelation; why this is one kind of dream, and that one is another, and not the same to everyone; why this one is an illusion and that one is an oracle.

I know not, but whosoever knows the causes of these miracles better than I, let him explain them; for I certainly know nothing about that, and never think to work my wit too busily to understand the kinds of their significance, or the length of time to their fulfillment, or why this is cause of dreams rather than that: whether peoples' temperaments make them dream of what they have been thinking about; or whether, as others say, over-enfeeblement of brain, from sickness or abstinence, imprisonment, or great distress, or of disorder of the natural routine, as when a person is too zealous in study, or melancholy, or so full of inward fear that nobody may offer him relief; or whether the devoutness and meditation of some people often causes such dreams; or whether it may be that the cruel, hard life that these lovers lead, who hope or fear too much, so that their mere fancies cause visions; or whether spirits have the power to make people dream at night; or whether the soul from its proper nature be so perfect, as men judge, that it foreknows what is to be, and warns one and all of each of their risks to come, by means of visions or prefigurings, but our flesh cannot understand these correctly, because the warnings are too dark – I know not what the cause is.

Good luck in this to great scholars, who comment on this matter and others! For I will now make note of no opinion, but only pray that the holy cross will turn every dream to good for us. For never have I since I was born, nor anyone else before me, I firmly believe, dreamed so wonderful a dream as I did the tenth day of December;[1] which, as I can now recall it, I will tell you in full.

After a short invocation, the poem resumes.

The tenth day of December, when it was night, I lay down to sleep just where I was accustomed, and fell asleep very soon, like one who was weary from walking a pilgrimage of two miles to the shrine of Saint Leonard,[2] to make soft what had been hard.

But as I slept I dreamed I was within a temple of glass, in which were more golden images standing on various stands, and more rich decorative niches, and more pinnacles of gemmed work, and more skilful portraits and curious types of figures in old work than ever I had seen. For truly I did not know where I was, but well I knew, truly, that this temple was of Venus;[3] for immediately I saw her figure pictured, floating naked in a sea; and her white and red rose-garland, by God, about her brows; and her comb to comb her hair; her doves, and Sir Cupid, her blind son, and Vulcan,

---

[1] Tenth day of December. Early readings of the poem tried to link this date with some important historical event such as a royal marriage, but none have been convincing. The most valid approaches have noted the fact that December 10 is one of the shortest days of the year and the least suggestive of spring and love. In a sense, the opening of the poem is the opposite of the opening of the *General Prologue* to *The Canterbury Tales.*

[2] St. Leonard. Sixth-Century French saint, patron both against robbers and for prisoners. *The Golden Legend* notes that his name is a combination of "leos" (people) and "nardus" (sweet-smelling herb), "for by the odour of good fame he drew the people to him."

[3] Venus, Cupid, and Vulcan. Venus is the goddess of love, born of the foam of the sea; Cupid, the god of love, her son; Vulcan, the smith of the gods, her husband.

with his brown face.

But as I roamed about, I found a tablet of brass on a wall, where was written: "I will now sing, if I am able, of the arms and the man also, who, fugitive from Troy, first came by his fate into Italy to the Lavinian shore with great suffering."[4] And then after this the story began, as I shall tell you all.

The narration continues of an account of the fall of Troy and the adventures of Aeneas, drawn largely from Vergil's Aeneid with special attention given to the Roman founder's relationship to Dido, the tragic queen of Carthage.

When I had seen all these sights thus in this noble temple, I thought, "Ah, Lord who made us! Never have I seen such magnificence of figures and such wealth as I have seen depicted in this church. But I know not who had them created, nor where I am, nor in what land. But now I will go out just to the gate, and see if I can detect anyone stirring anywhere who can tell me where I am."

When I came out at the doors I gazed around me carefully. Then I saw only a large field as far as I could see, without town or house or tree or bush or grass or plowed ground; for all the field was sand, as fine as men may see yet lying in the desert of Libya. Nor did I see any type of being that is formed by Nature, to instruct or direct me. "O Christ, Who reigns in blessedness," I thought, "save me from hallucination and illusion!"

And devoutly I cast my eyes to the heaven. There at last I noticed then how near the sun, as far up as I could discern with my eye, it seemed to me I beheld an eagle soaring, only it seemed much greater than any eagle that I had ever seen.[5]

---

[4] I will now sing...suffering. These are the first lines of Vergil's *Aeneid.* What follows is a summary of the entire Roman epic poem.

[5] Eagle. Dante in *Purgatorio* 9.19-20 dreams that he is taken up by an eagle.

But for certain, this is as true as death, it was golden, and shone so brilliantly that never had anyone seen such a sight, unless the heaven had gained another sun all new and of gold; so brightly shone the eagle's feathers. And then it began to descend.

After a short "proem" the narrator resumes his dream.

This eagle that I have spoken of, that soared so far on high and shone as with feathers of gold, I began to behold more and more, and to see its beauty and the marvel of it all. But never was a lightning stroke, or that thing that is called the thunderbolt (which sometimes has smitten a tower to powder and burned it by its swift onslaught) so swift in its descent as this bird, when it beheld me in the open in the field. And with his grim and mighty feet, within his long sharp claws, he caught me at a swoop as I fled, and soared up again, carrying me in his strong claws as easily as if I were a lark – how high I cannot tell you, for I did not know not how I came up. For every faculty in my head was so stunned and dazed, for with his swift ascent and my own dread, all my sense of feeling died away, so great was my fear.

Thus I lay long in his claws, until at last he spoke to me in human voice and said, "Awake, and don't be so afraid. Fie upon you!" And then he called me by name, and, to arouse me better, so I dreamed, he said "Awake!" to me, just in the same voice and tone that one whom I could mention uses. And at that voice, to tell the truth, my mind returned to me, for it was spoken to me kindly, as it never was.

And at this I began to stir, and he bore me further in his talons until he felt my heart beating and that I grew warm as well.

Then he began to be mirthful with me and to comfort me with words, and said twice, "By blessed Mary, you are troublesome to carry, and more than you need be, by God! For, so God help me, you shall have no harm from this.

"This thing that has happened to you is for your instruction and your profit. Let's see! Do you dare to look yet? Be fully assured, I tell you plainly, I am your friend." And with that I began to marvel within my mind.

"O God Who made nature," I thought, "am I to die in no other way? Will Jove transform me into a star? Or what may this thing all mean? I am neither Enoch[6] nor Elijah[7] nor Romulus[8] – and not Ganymede,[9] who, as books tell, was borne up to heaven by Lord Jupiter and made the gods' butler."[10]

Indeed, this was my delusion then! But he who carried me noticed that I thought thus, and said, "You think incorrectly in your own mind; for Jove is not intending – I dare well put you fully out of doubt – to make a star of you as yet. But before I bear you much farther I will tell you what I am, and where you shall go, and why I came to do this, so that you will take good heart and tremble not for fear."

"Gladly," I said.

"Now that is well," he said. "First, I who have you in my feet, and whom you fear and marvel, dwell with the god of thunder whom men call Jupiter, who sends me often flying far to do all his commands.[11] And for this cause he has sent me to you. Now listen, by your word! He has pity for you,

---

[6] Enoch. Old Testament Patriarch who was believed to have ascended directly to heaven. See Genesis 5:24.

[7] Elijah. Like Enoch, Elijah was also believed to have ascended directly to heaven.

[8] Romulus. The founder of Rome who was carried to heaven by Mars, the god of war. See Ovid's *Metamorphoses* 14. 816-28.

[9] Ganymede. The servant or butler to Jupiter who was abducted by the god's eagle. Many have noted that Chaucer's father was butler to the king. See Vergil's *Aeneid* V.252-57 and Ovid's *Metamorphoses* 10:155-61.

[10] I am neither Enoch...butler. Dante, when he is taken up by the eagle, remarks the same thing in *Inferno 2.32*: "I am not Aeneas, neither am I Paul; neither I nor others think that I deserve it."

[11] Jupiter...commands. Here the eagle is implicitly compared to Mercury, the messenger god.

truly, because you have served his blind grand son Cupid, and the fair Venus as well, so long and attentively, always without reward. And nevertheless you have set your mind – as small as it may be to making books, songs, and ditties, in rhyme or in cadence, as you best know how, in worship of Love, and of his servants also, that seek and have sought his service; and strive to praise his art, although you had never a portion of it.

"For these reasons, so God bless me, Jove deems it great humility and great virtue, that often you will set your head to aching by night, so diligently composing, and always about Love, in honor and praise of him and to the benefit of his followers; and you have set forth all of their concerns, and despise neither him nor his followers, though you must go into the dance with those he cares little to promote.

"For these reasons, as I said, in truth, Jupiter considers this and other things also, fair sir; that is, that you gain no tidings of Love's followers, whether or not they are glad tidings, nor of anything else that God made. It is not only so that no tidings come to you from far lands, but you hear neither this nor that from your very neighbors who dwell almost at your door. For when your labor is ended and you have made all your calculations, instead of rest and recreation you go home without delay to your house, and as dumb as any stone you sit at another book until your eyes are entirely dazed. Thus, though your abstinence is rather little, you live like a hermit![12]

After further discussion, the Eagle delivers the dreamer to the House of Fame, where the sees hoards of people pleading with the great lady Fame. They bring forth their requests as if they are at court; she judges each of them separately, but there is no consistency to her judgments. The

---

[12] Hermit, abstinence. A hermit would be expected to abstain from all worldly pleasures, but presumably the narrator, though he lives in solitude, does not abstain from such pleasures.

poem ends suddenly, unfinished, with the introduction of "a man of great authority."

THE CANTERBURY TALES

INTRODUCTORY NOTES

Among the greatest books of the world is Chaucer's *Canterbury Tales*, a collection of twenty-four tales told by pilgrims on their pilgrimage to Canterbury from London that has captured the imagination of readers for over 600 years. Though the work was planned as 100 tales, twenty-five pilgrims telling four tales each (two on the way to Canterbury and two on the way home), this incomplete work contains an array of tales and relationships that rivals the intricacy of any work before it or since.

Though it is difficult to judge, because of the incomplete state of the work (and only half of the tales are presented here), what Chaucer's ultimate purpose was, we can say with some certainty that he is attempting to see the complex and sometimes contradictory design under the surface of things. Under his critical though smiling eyes we can see the frail though exuberant humanity of all people, religious and secular, young and old, rich and poor. We see the motivations of lovers and those who are jilted in love, the elegance of epic poetry and the bawdy humor of straightforward fabliaux, the sincerity of the sincere religious and the deception of the abusive churchmen, the genuine hopes for spiritual reform and the rivalry between pilgrims, the joy of life and the sorrow of death. The variety of his work led the great Augustan poet John Dryden, who felt "distracted" by so much choice, to characterize Chaucer's work as containing "God's plenty."

As it is impossible to convey anything more than a few generalizations in an introduction this brief, it is perhaps best simply to wish the reader a joyous literary pilgrimage.

THE CANTERBURY TALES
THE GENERAL PROLOGUE

Here begins the Book of the Tales of Canterbury.

When the sweet showers of April have pierced to the root the dryness of March and bathed every vein in moisture by which strength the flowers are brought forth; when Zephyr also with his sweet breath has given spirit to the tender new shoots in the grove and field, and the young sun has run half his course through Aries the Ram, and little birds make melody (as nature pricks them in their hearts) and sleep all night with an open eye; then people long to go on pilgrimages to renowned shrines in various distant lands, and palmers[1] to seek foreign shores. And especially from every shire's end in England they make their way to Canterbury, to seek the holy blessed martyr[2] who helped them when they were sick.

One day in that season, as I was waiting at the Tabard Inn at Southwark, about to make my pilgrimage with devout heart to Canterbury, it happened that there came at night to that inn a company of twenty-nine various people, who by chance had joined together in fellowship. All were pilgrims, riding to Canterbury. The chambers and the stables were spacious, and we were lodged well. But in brief, when the sun had gone to rest, I had spoken with every one of them

---

[1] Palmers. Pilgrims, who showed that they were pilgrims by carrying palm branches.

[2] The holy blessed martyr. St. Thomas à Becket, Archbishop of Canterbury under Henry II, with whom he had great conflicts; he was martyred at Canterbury Cathedral in 1170 by four of Henry'sfollowers who had perhaps over-interpreted the kings question, "Will no one rid me of this turbulent priest?"

and was soon a part of their company, and agreed to rise early to take our way to where I have told you.

Nevertheless, while I have time and space, before this tale goes further, I think it is reasonable to tell you all the qualities of each of them, as they appeared to me, what sort of people they were, of what social standing, and how they were fashioned. I will begin with a knight.

There was a Knight and a worthy man, who, from the time when he first rode abroad, loved chivalry, faithfulness and honor, liberality and courtesy. He was valiant in his lord's war and had campaigned, no man farther, in both Christian and heathen lands, and ever was honored for his worth. He was at Alexandria[3] when it was won; many times in Prussia he sat in the place of honor above knights from all nations; he had fought in Lithuania and in Russia, and no Christian man of his rank did so more often; he had been in Granada at the siege of Algeciras and in Belmaria; he was at Lyeys and in Attalia when they were conquered, and had landed with many noble armies in the Levant. He had been in fifteen mortal battles, and had thrice fought for our faith in the lists at Tremessen and always slain his foe; he had been also, long before, with the lord of Palathia against another heathen host in Turkey; and he always had great renown. And though he was valorous, he was prudent, and he was as meek as a maiden in his bearing. In all his life he never yet spoke any discourtesy to any living creature, but was truly a perfect gentle knight. To tell you of his equipment, his horses were good but he was not gaily clad. He wore a jerkin[4] of coarse cloth all stained with rust by his coat of mail, for he had just returned from his travels and departed to make

---

[3] Though the knight's battles were all actual battles, he seems to have had no particular allegiance to one nation or creed, as there is no common thread that runs through all of them and no indication of the side(s) on which he fought.

[4] Jerkin. A close-fitting, sleeveless, collarless, hip-length, collarless jacket; worn over a doublet by men.

his pilgrimage.

His son was with him, a young Squire, a lover and a lusty young soldier. His locks were curled as if laid in a press. He was twenty years of age, I suppose, of average height, amazingly nimble and great of strength. He had been, at one time, in a campaign in Flanders, Artois, and Picardy, and had borne himself well, in so little time, in hope to stand in his lady's grace. His clothes were embroidered, red and white, like a meadow full of fresh flowers. All the day long he was singing or playing upon the flute; he was as fresh as the month of May. His coat was short, with long, wide sleeves. Well could he sit on a horse and ride, make songs, joust, dance, draw, and write. He loved so ardently that at night-time he slept no more than a nightingale. He was courteous, modest, and helpful, and carved the meal for his father at table.

He had a Yeoman with him on that journey and no other servants, for that is how he wished to ride. He was clad in a coat and hood of green. Under his belt he bore a sheaf of peacock arrows, bright and sharp, with peacock feathers, and in his hand he bore a mighty bow. He knew how to handle his gear like a good yeoman; his arrows did not fall short on account of any poorly adjusted feathers. His head was cropped and his face brown. He understood well all the practice of woodcraft. He wore a gay arm-guard of leather; on one side he wore a sword and buckler, and on the other a fine dagger, well fashioned and as sharp as the point of a spear; on his breast an image of St. Christopher in bright silver, and over his shoulder a horn on a green baldric.[5] He was a forester indeed, I believe.

There was also a nun, a Prioress,[6] quiet and simple in her smiling; her greatest oath was "by Saint Loy."[7] She was

---

[5] Baldric. A belt, usually of ornamented leather, worn across the chest to support a sword or bugle.

[6] Prioress. Head of a religious house; "first nun" of a convent or abbey.

[7] Saint Loy. St. Eligius, a seventh-century miracle worker with the gift of

named Madame Eglantine. Well she sang the divine service, intoned in a seemly manner in her nose, and spoke French elegantly, after the manner of Stratford-atte-Bow,[8] for she knew nothing of Parisian French. She had been well taught the art of eating, and let no morsel fall from her lips, and wet only her finger-tips in the sauce. She knew how to lift and how to hold a morsel of food so that not a drop fell upon her breast. Her pleasure was all in courtesy. She wiped her upper lip so well that no spot of grease was to be seen in her cup after she had drunk; and very dainty she was in reaching for her food. And surely she was of fine behavior, pleasant and amiable of bearing. She took pains to imitate court manners, to be stately in her demeanor and to be held worthy of reverence. But to tell you of her character, she was so charitable and so tender-hearted she would weep if she saw a mouse caught in a trap if it were dead or bleeding. She had certain small dogs, which she fed upon roasted meat or milk and finest wheaten bread. She would weep sorely if one of them died or was struck sharply with a stick. She was all warm feeling and tender heart. Her wimple was pleated neatly. Her nose was slender, her eyes gray as glass, her mouth small and soft and red. Certainly she had a fine forehead, almost a span[9] high; truly she was not undersized. Her cloak was smartly made, I could tell. About her arm was a coral rosary, the larger beads of green, upon which hung a brooch of shining gold; on it was engraved first an A with a crown, and after that *Amor vincit omnia.*[10]

Another Nun, her chaplain, was with her, and three Priests.

---

prophecy, who foresaw his own death. Note that such oaths were considered sinful by many in Chaucer's day.

[8] Stratford-atte-Bow. A district of eastern London.

[9] Span. The distance from the tip of the thumb to the tip of the little finger when the hand is fully extended, formerly used as a unit of measure equal to about nine inches. A large forehead was a sign of beauty: women in fact often plucked their hairline to achieve one.

[10] Amor vincit omnia. Love conquers all.

There was a Monk, a very fine and handsome one, a great rider about the country-side and a lover of hunting, a manly man in all things, fit to be an abbot. He had many fine horses in his stable, and when he rode, men could hear his bridle jingling in a whistling wind as clear and loud as the chapel-bell where this lord was prior. Because the rule of St. Maurus or of St. Benedict [11]was old and something austere, this same monk let such old things pass and followed the ways of the new world. He gave not a plucked hen for the text that hunters are not holy, or that a careless monk (that is to say, one out of his cloister) is like a fish out of water; for that text he believed was not worth an oyster. And I said his opinion was right; why should he study and lose his wits ever poring over a book in the cloister, or toil with his hands and labor as St. Augustine bids? Of what service would this be to the world? Let St. Augustine keep his work to himself. Therefore he rode hard, followed greyhounds as swift as birds on the wing. All his pleasure was in riding and hunting the hare, and he spared no cost on those. I saw his sleeves edged at the wrist with fine dark fur, the finest in the country, and to fasten his hood under his chin he had a finely-wrought brooch of gold; in the larger end was a love-knot. His bald head shone like glass; so did his face, as if it had been anointed. He was a sleek, fat lord. His bright eyes rolled in his head, glowing like the fire under a cauldron. His boots were of rich soft leather, his horse in excellent condition. Now certainly he was a fine prelate. He was not pale, like a wasted spirit. Best of any roast he loved a fat swan. His palfrey was as brown as a berry.

There was a begging Friar,[12] lively and jolly, a very dignified fellow. In all the four orders there is not one so skilled in gay and flattering talk. He had, at his own expense, married off many young women; he was a noble pillar of his

[11] The rule of St. Maurus or of St. Benedict.

[12] Friar. Friars were like monks, except that, following the example of St. Francis, they had no set home and begged for their entire sustenance.

order! He was well beloved and familiar among franklins[13] everywhere in his countryside, and also with worthy town women, for he had, as he said himself, more virtue as confessor than a parson, for he held a papal license.[14] Very sweetly he heard confession, and his absolution was pleasant; he was an easy man to give penance, when he looked to have a good dinner. For to give to a poor order is a sign that a man has been well confessed; for, he dared to boast, if a man gave, he knew he was repentant. For many people are so stern of heart that they cannot weep, though they suffer sorely. Therefore, instead of weeping and praying, people may give silver to the poor friars. The tip of his hood was stuffed full of knives and pins as presents to fine women. And certainly he had a pleasant voice in singing, and well could play the fiddle; in singing ballads he bore off the prize. His neck was as white as the fleur-de-lis, and he was as strong as a champion. He knew well the taverns in every town, and every inn-keeper and bar-maid, better than the lepers and beggar-women. For it accorded not with a man of his importance to have acquaintance with sick lepers. It was not seemly; there was no profit in dealing with any such poor trash, but only with rich folk and sellers of victuals. And wherever profit might arise he was courteous and humble in his service. Nowhere was any so capable. He was the best beggar in his house, and gave a certain yearly payment so that none of his brethren might trespass on his routes. Though a widow might not have an old shoe to give, so pleasant was his "*In principio*,"[15] he would have his farthing before he went. He gained more from his begging than he ever needed, I believe! He would romp about like a puppy-dog. On days of reconciliation, or love-days, he was very helpful, for he was not like a cloister-monk or a poor scholar

[13] Franklins. Landowners who were not of noble birth,

[14] Papal license. Special permission of the Pope.

[15] *In principio*. In the beginning. (The first words of Genesis and the Gospel of John.)

with a threadbare cope, but like a Master of Arts or a Pope. His half-cope was of double worsted and came from the clothes-press rounding out like a bell. He pleased his whim by lisping a little, to make his English sound sweet upon his tongue, and in his harping and singing his eyes twinkled in his head like the stars on a frosty night. This worthy friar was named Hubert.

There was a Merchant with a forked beard, in parti-colored garb. High he sat upon his horse, a Flanders beaver-hat on his head, and boots fastened neatly with rich clasps. He uttered his opinions very solemnly, ever tending to the increase of his own profit; at any cost he wished the sea were safeguarded between Middleburg and Orwell.[16] In selling crown-pieces he knew how to profit by the exchange. This worthy man employed his wit cunningly; no creature knew that he was in debt, so stately he was of demeanor in bargaining and borrowing. He was a worthy man indeed, but, to tell the truth, I do not know his name.

There was also a Clerk[17] from Oxford who had long gone to lectures on logic. His horse was as lean as a rake, and he was not at all fat, I think, but looked hollow-cheeked, and grave likewise. His little outer cloak was threadbare, for he had no worldly skill to beg for his needs, and as yet had gained himself no benefice. He would rather have had at his bed's head twenty volumes of Aristotle and his philosophy, bound in red or black, than rich robes or a fiddle or joyful psaltery. Even though he was a philosopher, he had little gold in his money-box! But all that he could get from his friends he spent on books and learning, and would pray diligently for the souls of who gave it to him to stay at the schools. Of study he took most heed and care. Not a word did he speak more than was needed, and the little he spoke

[16] Between Middleburg and Orwell. Middleburgh is in the "island" of Walcheren in the Netherlands, nearly opposite the mouth of the River Orwell in Suffolk County, England.

[17] Clerk. Scholar. The term *scholar* is used in most cases in this edition.

was formal and modest, short and quick, and full of high matter; all that he said tended toward moral virtue. Gladly would he learn and gladly teach.

There was also a Sergeant of the Law, an excellent man, wary and wise, a frequenter of the porch of Paul's Church. He was discreet and of great distinction; or seemed so, his words were so wise. He had been a judge at court, by patent and full commission. With his learning and great reputation he had earned many fees and robes. Such a man as he for acquiring goods there never was; anything that he desired could be shown to be held in unrestricted possession, and none could find a flaw in his deeds. Nowhere was there so busy a man, and yet he seemed busier than he was. He knew in precise terms every case and judgment since King William the Conqueror, and every statute fully, word for word, and none could criticize him for his writing. He rode in simple style in a parti-colored coat and a belt of silk with small cross-bars. Of his appearance I will not make a longer story.

Traveling with him was a Franklin. His beard was white as a daisy, and he was sanguine[18] in his complexion. Well he loved a sop of wine of a morning. He was accustomed to live in pleasure, for he was a true son of Epicurus, who held the opinion that perfect happiness was in pleasure itself. He always kept an open house, like a true St. Julian[19] in his own country-side. His bread and his wine both were always of the best; never were a man's wine-vaults better stored. His house was never without a huge supply of fish or meat; in his house it snowed meat and drink, and every fine pleasure that a person could think of. According to the season of the year he varied his meats and his suppers. Many fat partridges were in his cage and many bream and pike in his fishpond. Woe to his cook unless his sauces were pungent and sharp, and his wares ready for service. All day long a great table stood in his hall fully prepared. When the justices met at ses-

[18] Sanguine. Ruddy, reddish. One of the four humors.

[19] St. Julian. Julian the Hospitaller, the Patron Saint of travelers.

sions of court, there he lorded it full grandly, and many times he sat as knight of the shire in parliament. A dagger hung at his girdle, and a pouch of taffeta, white as morning's milk. He had been sheriff and auditor; nowhere was so worthy a vassal.

A Haberdasher, a Carpenter, a Weaver, a Dyer, and an Upholsterer were with us also, all in the same dress of a great and splendid guild. All fresh and new was their gear. Their knives were not tipped with brass but all with fine-wrought silver, like their waistbands and their pouches. Each of them seemed a fair burgess to sit in a guildhall on a dais. Each for his discretion was fit to be alderman of his guild, and had goods and income sufficient for that. Their wives would have consented, I should think; otherwise, they would be at fault. It is a fair thing to be called "madame," and to walk ahead of other folks to vigils, and to have a mantle carried royally before them.

They had a Cook with them for that journey, to boil chickens with the marrow-bones and tart powder-merchant and cyprus-root. Well he knew a draught of London ale! He could roast and fry and broil and stew, make dainty pottage and bake pies well. It was a great pity, it seemed to me, that he had a great ulcer on his shin, for he made capon-in-cream sauce with the best of them.

There was a Shipman, from far in the West; for anything I know, he was from Dartmouth. He rode a nag, as well as he knew how, in a gown of coarse wool to the knee. He had a dagger hanging on a lace around his neck and under his arm. The hot summer had made his hue all brown. In truth he was a good fellow: many draughts of wine had he drawn at Bordeaux while the merchant slept. He paid no heed to silly conscience; on the high seas, if he fought and had the upper hand, he sent them home via water to many lands.[20] But in skill to calculate his tides, his currents and the dangers at hand, as well as his harbors, his moon, and his navigation,

[20] He sent them home…lands. He made his victims walk the plank.

there was none like him from Hull to Carthage.[21] In his undertakings he was bold and shrewd. His beard had been shaken by many tempests. He knew the harbors well from Gothland to Cape Finisterre,[22] and every creek in Brittany[23] and in Spain. His ship was called the Maudelayne.[24]

With us was a Doctor, a Physician; for skill in medicine and in surgery there was no peer in this entire world, for he was well grounded in astrology. He watched sharply for favorable hours and an auspicious ascendant[25] for his patients' treatment. He knew the cause of each malady, if it was hot, cold, dry or moist, from where it had sprung and of what humor. He was a thorough and a perfect practitioner. Having found the cause and source of his trouble, quickly he gave the sick man his cure. He had his apothecaries all prepared to send him drugs and electuaries,[26] for each helped the other's gain: their friendship had not begun recently. He knew well the ancient Aesculapius, Dioscorides, and Rufus as well, the ancient Hippocrates, Haly, and Galen, Serapion, Rhasis, and Avicenna, Averroes, Damascene, and Constantine, Bernard, and Gatisden, and Gilbertine.[27] His own diet was moderate, with no excess, but very nourishing and simple to digest. His study was only a little on the Bible. He was clad in red and blue-gray cloth, lined with taffeta and silk. Yet he was quite moderate in spending, and kept what he gained during the pestilence. Gold is a medicine from the heart in physicians' terms; doubtless that was why he loved gold above all else.

---

[21] Hull. In Yorkshire, on the northern shore of the Humber. Carthage. In modern day Tunisia.

[22] Gothland. Southern Sweden. Cape Finisterre. Peninsula on the west coast of Galicia (Spain).

[23] Brittany. Northwestern province of France.

[24] Maudelayne. Magdalene, as in Mary Magadalene.

[25] Ascendant. Astrological term, meaning the point of the ecliptic, or the sign of the zodiac, that rises in the east at the time of a person's birth or other event.

[26] Electuary. A drug mixed with sugar and water or honey into a pasty mass suitable for oral administration.

[27] Ancient Medical Authorities as well as more contemporary ones.

There was a Good Wife from near Bath, but she was somewhat deaf, and that was pity. She was so skilled in making cloth that she surpassed those of Ypres and Ghent.[28] In all the parish there was no wife who would march up to make an offering before her, and if any did, so angered she was that truly she was out of all charity. Her kerchiefs were very fine in texture; and I dare swear those that were on her head for Sunday weighed ten pounds. Her hose were of a fine scarlet and tightly fastened, and her shoes were soft and new. Her face was bold and fair and red. All her life she was a worthy woman; she had had five husbands at the church-door, besides other company in her youth – but of that there is no need to speak of that now. She had thrice been at Jerusalem; many distant streams had she crossed; she had been on pilgrimages to Rome, to Boulogne,[29] to Santiago in Galicia,[30] and to Cologne.[31] This wandering by the way had taught her many things. To tell the truth, she was gap-toothed; she sat easily on an ambling horse, wearing a fair wimple and on her head a hat as broad as a buckler or target. About her broad hips was a short riding skirt and on her feet a pair of sharp spurs. Well could she laugh and prattle in company. Love and its remedies she knew all about, I dare give my word, for she knew well the art of the old dance.

There was a good man of religion, a poor Parson, but rich in holy thought and deed. He was also a learned man, a clerk, and would faithfully preach Christ's gospel and devoutly instruct his parishioners. He was benign, wonderfully diligent, and patient in adversity, as he was often tested. He was loath to excommunicate for unpaid tithes, but rather would give to his poor parishioners out of the church alms

---

[28] Ypres and Ghent. Two of the major European cloth-making centers of Europe. Both in Flanders.

[29] Boulogne. Important pilgrimage site in Northern coastal France.

[30] Santiago in Galicia. Saint James (Santiago) of Compostela, another important pilgrimage site in Galicia (northwestern Spain).

[31] Cologne. City in western Germany, on the Rhine; another important pilgrimage site.

and also of his own substance; he found sufficiency in little. His parish was wide and the houses far apart, but not even for thunder or rain did he neglect to visit the farthest, great or small, in sickness or misfortune, going on foot, a staff in his hand. To his sheep did he give this noble example, which he first set into action and afterward taught; these words he took out of the gospel, and this similitude he added also, that if gold will rust, what shall iron do? For if a priest upon whom we trust were to be foul, it is no wonder that an ignorant layman would be corrupt; and it is a shame (if a priest will but pay attention to it) that a shepherd should be defiled and the sheep clean. A priest should give good example by his cleanness how his sheep should live. He would not farm out his benefice, nor leave his sheep stuck fast in the mire, while he ran to London to St. Paul's, to get an easy appointment as a chantry-priest, or to be retained by some guild, but dwelled at home and guarded his fold well, so that the wolf would not make it miscarry. He was a shepherd and not a hireling. And though he was holy and virtuous, he was not pitiless to sinful men, nor cold or haughty of speech, but both discreet and benign in his teaching; to draw folk up to heaven by his fair life and good example, this was his care. But when a man was stubborn, whether of high or low estate, he would scold him sharply for it. There was nowhere a better priest than he. He looked for no pomp and reverence, nor yet was his conscience too particular; but the teaching of Christ and his apostles he taught, and first he followed it himself.

With him was his brother, a Ploughman, who had drawn many cartloads of dung. He was a faithful and good toiler, living in peace and perfect charity. He loved God best at all times with all his whole heart, in good and ill fortune, and then his neighbor even as himself. He would thresh and ditch and delve for every poor person without pay, but for Christ's sake, if he were able. He paid his tithes fairly and well on both his produce and his goods. He wore a ploughman's frock and rode upon a mare.

There was a Reeve also and a Miller, a Summoner and a Pardoner, a Manciple and myself. There were no more.

The Miller was a stout fellow, big of bones and brawn; and well he showed them, for everywhere he went to a wrestling match he would always carry off the prize ram. He was short-shouldered and broad, a thick, knotty fellow. There was no door that he could not heave off its hinges, or break with his head at a running. His beard was as red as any sow or fox, and broad like a spade as well. Upon the very tip of his nose he had a wart, and on it stood a tuft of red hair like the bristles on a sow's ears, and his nostrils were black and wide. At his thigh hung a sword and buckler. His mouth was as great as a great furnace. He was a teller of dirty stories and a buffoon, and it was mostly of sin and obscenity. He knew well how to steal corn and take his toll of meal three times over; and yet he had a golden thumb, by God! He wore a white coat and a blue hood. He could blow and play the bagpipe well, and with its sounds he led us out of town.

There was a gentle Manciple[32] of an Inn of Court,[33] of whom other stewards might take example for craftiness in buying victuals. Whether he paid in cash or took on credit, he was so watchful in his buying that he was always ahead and in good standing. Now is it not a full fair gift of God that the wit of such an unlettered man shall surpass the wisdom of a great body of learned men? He had more than a score of masters, expert and diligent in law, of whom in that house there were a dozen worthy to be stewards of lands and revenues of any lord in England, to let him live upon his income, honorably, free from debt, unless he were mad, or live as plainly as he would; and able to help a whole shire in any case that might occur. And yet this Manciple hoodwinked all

[32] Manciple. A purchaser of provisions, usually for a college, abbey, or monastery.

[33] Inn of Court. The inns of court were the places at which those wishing to train for the Bar (legal profession) must reside and to which they must belong.

of them.

The Reeve[34] was a slender, choleric[35] man. His beard was shaven as close as could be, and his hair was cut short around his ears and docked in front like a priest's. His legs were full and lean like a stick; I could see no calf. He could well keep a bin and a garner, and no inspector could get the best of him. In the drought or in the wet he could foretell the yield of his grain and seed. His lord's sheep, poultry and cattle, his dairy and swine and horses and all his stock, this Reeve had wholly under his governance, and submitted his accounts thereon ever since his lord was twenty years of age; and none could ever find him out in arrears. There was no bailiff nor herdsman nor other churl whose tricks and craftiness he didn't know. They were as afraid of him as of the plague. His dwelling-place was a pleasant one on a heath, all shaded with green trees. Better than his lord he knew how to gain wealth, and had a rich private hoard; he knew how to please his master cunningly by giving and lending him from his master's own goods, and to win thanks for that, and a coat and hood as a reward too. In his youth he had learned a good trade and was a fine carpenter and workman. This Reeve sat upon a fine dapple gray cob named Scot. He wore a long surcoat[36] of blue and at his side a rusty blade. He was from Norfolk, near a town they call Baldeswell. His coat was tucked up around him like a friar's, and he always rode last of us all.

A Summoner[37] was with us there, a fire-red cherubim-faced fellow, salt-phlegmed and pimply, with slits for eyes, scabby black eyebrows and thin ragged beard, and as hot and lecherous as a sparrow. Children were terrified at his visage. No quicksilver, white-lead, brimstone, borax nor ceruse,[38] no

---

[34] Reeve. A handyman and a supervisor of laborers for a landowner.

[35] Choleric. Short-tempered or irritable. One of the four humors.

[36] Surcoat. An overcoat or loose-fitting robe.

[37] Summoner. One who summoned people to ecclesiastical court.

[38] Ceruse. White lead pigment.

cream of tartar nor any ointment that would clean and burn, could help his white blotches or the knobs on his cheeks. He loved garlic, onions, and leeks too well, and to drink strong wine as red as blood, and then he would talk and cry out as if he were mad. And after drinking plenty of wine he would speak no word but Latin, in which he had a few terms, two or three, learned out of some decree. That was no wonder, for he heard it all day long, and you know well how a jay can call "Walter" after hearing it a long time, as well as the pope could. But if he were tested in any other point, his learning was found to be all spent. *Questio quid juris,*[39] he was always crying. He was a kind and gentle rogue; a better fellow I never knew; for a quart of wine he would allow a good fellow to have his concubine for a year and completely excuse him. Secretly he knew how to swindle anyone. And if anywhere he found a good fellow, he would teach him in such case to have no fear of the archdeacon's excommunication, unless a man's soul were in his purse; for it was in his purse he should be punished. "The Archdeacon's hell is your purse," he said. (But well I know he lied indeed; every guilty man should fear hiss curse, for it will slay, just as absolution saves, and also let him beware of a *significavit.*)[40] Within his jurisdiction on his own terms he held all the young people of the diocese, knew their guilty secrets, and was their chief adviser. He had a garland on his head large enough for an ale-house sign, and carried a round loaf of bread as big as a buckler.

With him rode a gentle Pardoner,[41] of Roncesvalles,[42] his friend and companion, who had come straight from the court of Rome. He sang loudly, "Come here, love, to me," while

---

[39] *Questio quid juris*. The questions is, which law (pertains to this case)?
[40] *Significavit*. An order for imprisonment.
[41] Pardoner. One who sold indulgences (pardons), which would allow those in sin to redeem themselves in their quest for spiritual salvation.
[42] Roncesvalles. Village in the Pyranees, in the Basque region near the French border; famous as the location of the defeat of the Charlemagne and the death of his great military leader Roland.

the Summoner joined him with a stiff bass; never was there a trumpet of half such a sound. This Pardoner had waxy-yellow hair, hanging smooth, like a coil of flax, spread over his shoulders in thin strands. For sport he wore no hood, which was trussed up in his wallet; riding with his hair disheveled, bareheaded except for his cap, he thought he was all in the latest fashion. His eyes were glaring like a hare's. He had a veronica[43] sewed on his cap, and his wallet, brimful of pardons hot from Rome, lay before him on his lap. His voice was as small as a goat's. He had no beard, nor ever would have; his face was as smooth as if lately shaven; I believe he was a mare or a gelding. But as for his trade, from Berwick to Dover[44] there was not such another pardoner. In his bag he had a pillow-case which he said was our Lady's kerchief, and a small piece of the sail which he said St. Peter had when he walked upon the sea and Jesus Christ caught him. He had a cross of latoun,[45] set full of false gems, and pigs' bones in a glass. But with these relics, when he found a poor parson dwelling in the country, in one day he gained himself more money than the parson gained in two months. And thus, with flattering deceit and tricks, he made the parson and the people his dupes. But to give him his due, after all he was a noble ecclesiastic in church; he could read well a lesson or legend and best of all sing an offertory.[46] For he knew well that when that was done he must preach and file his tongue smooth, to win silver as he well knew how. Therefore he sang merrily and loud.

Now I have told you in few words the social standing, the array, the number of this company at this noble inn

---

[43] Veronica. After St. Veronica who, having wiped the face of the suffering Jesus, received his image on her cloth, a Veronica held the same image, a sign that one had been on a pilgrimage to Rome

[44] From Berwick to Ware. From the northernmost point of England to the southeasternmost point.

[45] Latoun. An alloy similar to brass.

[46] Offertory. Part of the mass in which the gifts of bread and wine are offered for the Eucharist, and typically other gifts, such as cash, are offered.

named the Tabard, close to the Bell tavern, and why they were assembled in Southwark as well,. But now it is time to say how we behaved that same evening, when we had arrived at that inn; and afterward I will tell you of our journey and the rest of our pilgrimage.

But first I pray that by your courtesy you ascribe it not to my ill manners if I speak plainly in this matter, telling you their words and cheer, and if I speak their very words as they were. For this you know as well as I, that whoever tells a tale that another has told, he must repeat every word, as nearly as he can, although he may speak ever so rudely and freely. Otherwise, he must tell his tale falsely, or pretend, or find new words. He may not spare any, even if it were his own brother; he is bound to say one word as well as the next. Christ himself spoke plainly in Holy Scriptures and you know well there is no baseness in that. And Plato, whoever can read him, says that the word must be cousin to the deed.

I also pray you to forgive me though I have not set folk here in this tale according to their social standing, as they should be. My wit is short, you can well understand.

Our host put us all in good spirits, and soon brought us to supper and served us with the best of provisions. The wine was strong and very glad we were to drink. Our Host was a seemly man, fit to be marshal in a banquet-hall, a large man with bright eyes, bold in speech, wise and discreet, lacking nothing of manhood: there is not a fairer burgess in Cheapside.[47] He was in all things a very merry fellow, and after supper, when we had paid our bills, he began to jest and speak of mirth among other things.

"Now gentle people," he said, "truly you are heartily welcome to me, for, by my word, if I shall tell the truth, I have not seen this year so merry a company at this inn at once. I would gladly make mirth if I only knew how. And I have just now thought of a mirthful thing to give you pleasure, which shall cost nothing. You are going to Canterbury:

---

[47] Cheapside. Famous market street in London.

may God help you, and may the blessed martyr St. Thomas duly reward you! I know full well, along the way you mean to tell tales and amuse yourselves, for in truth it is no comfort or mirth to ride along dumb as a stone

"And therefore, as I said, I will make you a game. If it please you all by common consent to stand by my words and to do as I shall tell you, now, by my father's soul (and he is in heaven), tomorrow as you ride along, if you are not merry, I will give you my head. Hold up your hands, without more words!"

Our mind was not long to decide. We thought it not worth debating, and agreed with him without more thought, and told him to say his verdict as he wished.

"Gentle people," said he, "please listen now, but take it not, I pray you, disdainfully. To speak briefly and plainly, this is the point, that each of you for pastime shall tell two tales in this journey to Canterbury, and two others on the way home, of things that have happened in the past. And whichever of you bears himself best, that is to say, that tells now tales most instructive and delighting,[48] shall have a supper at the expense of us all, sitting here in this place, beside this post, when we come back from Canterbury. And to add to your sport I will gladly go with you at my own cost, and be your guide. And whoever opposes my judgment shall pay all that we spend on the way. If you agree that this will be so, tell me now, without more words, and without delay I will plan for that."

We agreed to this thing and pledged our word with glad hearts, and prayed him to do so, and to be our ruler and to remember and judge our tales, and to arrange for our meals at a specific price. We would be ruled at his will in part and whole, and thus with one voice we agreed to his judgment. At this the wine was fetched, and we drank and then each went to rest without a longer stay.

---

[48] Instructing and delighting. The Roman poet Horace said that poetry should aim to both instruct and delight.

In the morning, when the day began to spring, our host arose and played rooster[49] to us all, and gathered us in a flock. Forth we rode, a little faster than a walk, to St. Thomas-a-Watering.[50] There our Host drew up his horse and said, "Listen, gentle people, if you will. You know your agreement; I remind you of it. If what you said at the hour of evensong last night is still what you agree to this morning at the time of matins,[51] let us see who shall tell the first tale. So may I ever drink beer or wine, whoever rebels against my judgment shall pay all that is spent on the journey. Now let us draw straws before we depart further; he who has the shortest shall begin the tales. Sir Knight, my master and my lord," said he, "now draw your lot, for this is my will, Come nearer, my lady Prioress, and you, sir Clerk, be not shy, study not; set your hands to them, every one of you."

Without delay every one began to draw, and in short, whether it were by chance or not, the truth is, the lot fell to the Knight, at which everyone was merry and glad. He was to tell his tale, as was reasonable, according to the agreement that you have heard. What need is there for more words?

When this good man saw it was so, as one discreet and obedient to his free promise he said, "Since I begin the game, in God's name, welcome be the cut! Now let us ride on, and listen to what I say." And at that word we rode forth on our journey. And he soon began his tale with a cheerful spirit, and spoke in this way.

Here ends the Prologue of this book.

---

[49] Rooster. The rooster who crows at dawn and wakes the travelers.
[50] St. Thomas-a-Watering. A stream about two miles outside London.
[51] Evensong and matins. Generally speaking, evensong was the last prayer service of the day and Matins was the first in the morning.

THE KNIGHT'S TALE

Here begins the Knight's Tale.

> *"And now Theseus, drawing close to his native land in a laurelled chariot after fierce battle with the people, is heralded by glad applause and the shouts of the people flung to the heavens and the merry trump of warfare that has reached its end."*[1]

Long ago, as old histories tell us, there was a duke called Theseus; he was lord and ruler of Athens, and in his time such a conqueror that there was none greater under the sun. He had subdued many rich countries, and with his wisdom and his knighthood had conquered all the realm of the Amazons, the land of women, which formerly was called Scythia. He wedded the Queen Hippolyta and brought her home with him to his country in great glory and pomp, along with her young sister Emily. And thus with victory and melody I leave this noble duke riding on to Athens, with his entire host in arms with him.

And if it were not too long to hear, surely I would have told you fully how the realm of the Amazons was won by Theseus and his knightly valor; and, while I was about it, of the great battle between the Athenians and the Amazons; how Hippolyta was besieged, the fair, hardy queen of the Scythians; of her wedding-feast, and of the tempest at her homecoming. But all that I must withhold now; God knows, I have a large field to plough, and my oxen are weak. The

---

[1] The opening quote is from Statius' *Thebiad*, one of Chaucer's sources of the *Knight's Tale*. Trump of war may refer both to the use of trumpet signals in battle and the celebration of victory.

remainder of my tale is long enough, and I would also not hinder any of this company; let every comrade in turn tell his tale, and let us see who shall win the supper. And where I left off I will begin again.

When this duke, who I just mentioned, had drawn close to the town in all his triumph and highest pomp, he cast his eye at one side and noticed a company of ladies, clad in black, kneeling in the highway, two by two. But they made such a cry and such a woe that no living creature in this world ever heard another such lamenting; nor would they stop this crying until they had seized the reins of his bridle.

"What people are you who disturb the festival of my homecoming thus with lamentations?" said Theseus. "Have you so great ill-will toward my honors that you so complain and cry? Or who has done you ill? Tell me if it may be amended. And why you are thus clothed in black?

The eldest lady of them all spoke (after she had swooned with such a deathly look that it was pitiful to see and hear): "Lord, to whom Fortune has granted victory and to live as a conqueror, your glory and honor grieves us not. We beg for aid and for mercy upon our woe and distress. From your nobility let some drop of pity fall upon us wretched women; for surely, there is none of us, lord, who has not been a queen or a duchess. Now are we poor wretches, as you may see, thanks to Fortune and her false wheel that does not ensure prosperity to any estate. And surely, lord, here in the temple of the goddess Clemency we have been this entire fortnight awaiting your coming.

"Now help us, lord, since it is within your power! I, wretch that I am, thus weeping and wailing, was once wife to King Capaneus, who perished at Thebes – cursed be the day! And we who are in this plight and make this lament all lost our husbands while the siege lay about that town. And now, alack, old Creon who is now lord of Thebes, full of anger and iniquity, by his tyrannical malice has drawn the dead bodies of our slain lords upon a heap, to do them indignity, and will allow them by no means to be either buried or burned, but in scorn gives them to hounds to eat."

And with that word, without more ado, they all fell on their faces and cried piteously, "Have some mercy upon us wretched women, and let our woe sink into your heart!"

The noble duke sprang from his charger with a pitying heart, when he heard them speak. His heart nearly broke when he saw them who had once been of high degree so piteous and cast down. And he raised them all up in his arms and comforted them kindly, and swore an oath that, as he was a true knight, he would strive to take such vengeance upon the tyrant Creon that all the people of Greece should tell how Creon was handled by Theseus, as a man that had well merited his death. And very swiftly, without more delay, he unfurled his banner and rode forth to Thebes with his entire host. No nearer to Athens would he travel, nor take his ease half a day, but spent that night along the route to Thebes, and sent Hippolyta the queen and Emily her fair young sister to wait in the town of Athens; and then onward he rode. There is no more to be told.

The red image of Mars[2] with spear and shield so shone upon his broad white banner that all the fields glittered all over. And by his banner was borne his pennant of rich gold, on which was hammered out the Minotaur, which he had slain in Crete. Thus rode this duke, this conqueror, and in his host all the flower of chivalry, until he came to Thebes and dismounted in a beautiful open field where he thought to fight. To tell shortly of this matter, he fought with Creon, King of Thebes, like a worthy knight, and slew him in manly fashion in open battle, and put his people to flight. And then by assault he won the city and tore down wall and beam and rafter. He restored to the ladies the bones of their husbands, to perform their rituals which were then the custom. But it would be entirely too long to tell the clamor and lament of the ladies at the burning of the bodies, and the great honor

[2] Mars. The god of war.

done them by the noble conqueror Theseus, when they departed from him. To be brief is my intent.

When this worthy duke had slain Creon and thus won Thebes, he took his rest in the field all that night and then dealt with all that country as he wished.

After the battle and defeat, the pillagers were busy to search through the heaps of dead, to strip them of harness and garments; and so it happened that in the heap they came upon two young knights, lying near each other, pierced through and through by many grievous, bloody wounds, both bearing arms of one style, richly fashioned; of these two, the one was called Arcite and the other knight Palamon. They were not fully alive nor fully dead, but by their escutcheons and their accoutrements the heralds knew them among the rest to be of the royal blood of Thebes and born of two sisters. Out of the heap the pillagers dragged them, and bore them softly to Theseus' tent. And he sent them immediately to Athens to dwell in prison perpetually; he would take no ransom. And when this worthy duke had done this, swiftly he rode homeward with his entire host, crowned with laurel like a conqueror, and there in joy and honor he lived to the end of his life; what need of more words? And Palamon and Arcite dwelt in a tower in anguish and woe forevermore; no gold could free them.

This passed on by day and by year until it happened, once upon a May morning before daybreak, that Emily, who was fairer to see than the lily upon its green stalk, and fresher than May with its new flowers. Her cheeks competed with the rose – I know not which was the fairer. Emily, I say, as was her custom, had arisen and was already dressed, for May will have no sluggishness at night's end. The season pricks every gentle heart and arouses it out of sleep and says, "Arise, and make your observance." Thus Emily remembered to rise and do honor to May. She was freshly clothed and her yellow hair was braided in a tress behind her back, a yard long, I believe; and in the garden at sunrise she walked up and down gathering the red and white flowers at will, to make a delicate garland for her head; and she sang heavenly, like an angel.

This great tower so thick and strong, where the knights were imprisoned, was the chief dungeon of the castle and joined with the wall of the garden where Emily was amusing herself. Clear was the morning and bright was the sun, and Palamon, the woeful prisoner, had risen and by his jailer's permission, as was his habit, was pacing in a chamber on high, from which he saw all the noble city, and the garden as well, full of its green branches, where this fresh Emily was walking and rambling up and down. Palamon, the sorrowful prisoner, went about pacing to and fro in the chamber, complaining to himself of his misery. Often he cried, "Alas!" And so it happened, by chance or luck, that through a window set thick with many iron bars, great and square as any beam, he cast his eye upon Emily, and therewith he started and cried "Ah!," as though he were stricken through the heart.

And at that cry Arcite quickly started up and said, "Dear cousin, what ails you that you are so pale and deathlike to look upon? Why did you cry out? Who has done you harm? For the love of God, take our prison all in patience, for it may not be otherwise. This adversity was given to us by Fortune. Some evil aspect or disposition of Saturn by some constellation has given us this, though we had vowed it should not be. So stood the heavens when we were born, and we must endure it; this is all."

This Palamon answered then, "Cousin, in truth this thought of yours is vainly imagined. This prison caused not my groan. I have received just now a wound through my eye into my heart, one that will be my death. The beauty of that lady, whom I see yonder in the garden roaming back and forth, is the cause of all my crying and pains. I know not whether she is a woman or a goddess; but in truth I believe it is Venus.[3] With that he fell upon his knees and said, "Venus, if it is your will to transfigure yourself here in this garden thus before me, a sorrowful wretched creature, help us to escape out of this prison. But if my destiny is decreed by eternal word that I shall die in prison, have some compassion upon our lineage that is brought so low by tyranny."

And upon that, Arcite observed where this lady roamed here and there, and the sight of her beauty so hurt him that, if Palamon was sorely wounded, Arcite was hurt as much or worse; and he said piteously with a sigh, "The fair beauty of her who roams in yonder spot here and now slays me, and if I will not have her pity and her grace, at least to see her, I am dead; there is no more to say."

When Palamon heard these words, he looked at him furiously and answered, "Do you say this in earnest or sport?"

"No, in earnest, by my faith," said Arcite. "So God help me, I have very little stomach for sport!"

This Palamon began to knit his brows. "It would be no great honor to you," he said, "to be false or a traitor to me your cousin and one who is sworn deeply to be your brother; as each of us is pledged that never, until death may part us two, even if we die by torture, shall either of us hinder the other in love or in any case, dear brother; rather you shall faithfully advance me in every case, as I shall advance you. This was your oath, and, surely, mine also; I know very well, you dare not deny it. Thus you are pledged to be my trusty friend, and now you would falsely be about loving my lady, whom I love and serve and ever shall until my heart may die. Now surely, false Arcite, you shall not do so. I loved her first and told you my pain, as if to my trusty friend and my brother who has pledged to help me, as I said. Therefore you are bound as a knight to help me if you can, or you are false, I dare say."

Arcite spoke again proudly: "You will be seen to be false before I am; and you are false, I tell you flatly. For with earthly love I loved her before you did. What will you say?

---

[3] Venus. The goddess of love.

You did not know even now whether she were a goddess or a woman. Yours is affection for holiness, and mine is love for a living creature; for this I told you my case, as if to my cousin and sworn brother. You make the case that you loved her first. Do you not know well the old clerk's saying, "Who sets a law on a lover?" By my skull, love is a greater law than can be given to any man on the earth. And therefore all human law and decrees and similar things are broken every day for love by people in every station of life. A man must love in spite of all he could do! He cannot flee it, even if he should die, whether she is a maiden, married, or widow. And you are not likely as well to stand in her grace all your life, and no more shall I; for you know full well that you and I are doomed to prison perpetually, and no ransom shall help us. We strive like the hounds that fought all day for the bone and won nothing; amid all their rage a kite came and bore away the bone from between them. Therefore at the king's court each man for himself is the only rule, my brother. Love if you will, for I love and ever shall, dear brother, and truly this is all. We must remain here in this prison and each of us must take his chance!"

Great and long was the strife between them, if I had the leisure to tell it; but to the point. It happened one day, to tell it to you as briefly as I can, that a worthy duke named Perotheus, a friend to duke Theseus since they were little children, had come to Athens to visit his friend, as he was accustomed, and to amuse himself. For he so loved no other man in this world, and Theseus loved him as tenderly. So well they loved that when the one was dead, in very truth his friend went and sought him down in hell, as the old books say.[4] But I do not wish to write that story. Duke Perotheus loved Arcite well, and had known him at Thebes many years. Finally, at the prayer of Perotheus, Duke Theseus released him from prison without ransom, to go freely where he wished on such terms as I shall tell you. This in short was

[4] Down in hell. It is Theseus who sought out Perotheus in Hades.

the agreement of Arcite, that if ever in his life he were found by day or night in any realm of Theseus and were caught, he should lose his head by the sword. There would be no better remedy or course of action; but he took his leave and hurried homeward. Let him beware, his neck lies as a pledge!

How great is Arcite's sorrow now! He feels death stab him through his heart. He weeps, wails, piteously cries, and watches for a time to slay himself in private. He said, "Alas, the day that I was born! Now is my prison worse than ever; now I am doomed forever not to purgatory but to hell. Alas, that ever I knew Perotheus; if not, I would have dwelt with Theseus evermore fettered in his prison. Then I would have been in bliss, not woe. Though I would never win the grace of her whom I serve, only the sight of her would have sufficed me well enough. O dear cousin Palamon, yours is the victory in this thing. Blissfully may you dwell in prison. In prison? No, in paradise, surely. Well has Fortune cast the die for you, who have the sight of her, as I only have the absence! For it is possible, since you are near her and are a knight, a worthy and an able one, by some chance of changeful Fortune you may at some point attain your desire. But I, who am exiled and so barren of all grace and hope that neither earth, water, fire, nor air, nor any creature made of them, can help or give me comfort – well may I die in despair and distress! Farewell, my life, my joy, and gladness!

"Alas, why do people complain so generally of God's providence or of Fortune, who so often gives them in many ways better luck than they could choose for themselves? One man desires riches, which become the cause of his murder or great sickness. Another would gladly be out of prison; and at home he is slain by his household. In this is infinite peril; we do not know here what thing we pray for. We manage like a man drunk as a mouse; a drunken man knows well that he has a house, but not the right way to that place, and for him the path to it is slippery.

"Surely, so we get along in this world. We seek diligently after felicity, but in truth often go wrong. Thus may we all say, and especially I, that if I, in my imagination and arrogant belief, could escape from prison I would in well-being and perfect joy, where now I am exiled from my happiness. Since I cannot see you, Emily, I am but dead; nothing can cure me."

On the other hand, Palamon, when he knew Arcite was gone, made such sorrow that the great tower resounded with his clamor and lament, and even the fetters about his great shins were wet with his bitter, salt tears. "Alas!" he said, "my cousin Arcite, the profit of all our strife is yours, God knows. You walk now at large in Thebes, and give little thought to my woe. With your wisdom and manhood you may assemble all the people of our kindred and make such sharp war upon this city that by some chance or treaty you may have her as wife and lady for whom I must die. For, to assess our chances, since you are at large, free from prison, and a lord, you have a greater advantage than me, who is dying here in a cage. While I live I must weep and wail with all the woe of a prisoner, and with the pain that love gives me as well, which doubles all my torment." With that the fire of jealousy blazed up within his breast and seized him so madly by the heart that he was livid as a box-tree to look upon, or as the dead and cold ashes.

Then he said, "O cruel gods, that govern this world with the bond of your eternal word, and write your laws and eternal decrees upon tables of adamant, how is mankind more bound unto you than the sheep that cowers in the fold? Man is slain like any beast, and dwells in prison and constraint, and is sick and in adversity, and often guiltless, in faith. What just governance is in this Providence that so torments the innocent? And yet this increases all my pain, that man is bound to his duty, for God's sake to refrain from his desires, where a beast may fulfill all its pleasure. And when a beast is dead, its trouble is past, but after death a man must weep and lament though he has had worry and woe in this world.

Without doubt it may be thus; the answer to all this I leave to theologians, but well I know that on this earth there is great sorrow! Alas! I see a serpent or a thief, one that has done mischief to many faithful men, go at large and where he wishes. But I must be in prison on account of Saturn[5] and the jealous rage of Juno,[6] who has destroyed nearly all the blood of Thebes and laid waste its wide walls. And on the other side, Venus slays me for jealousy and fear of Arcite."

Now for a time will I leave Palamon ever lying in prison, and will tell you now of Arcite.

The summer passed, and the long nights doubled both the bitter pain of the lover and of the prisoner. I know not which has the more woeful plight! For, to tell shortly, Palamon is perpetually doomed to prison, to die in chains and fetters; and Arcite is exiled on pain of death from that country for evermore, and nevermore shall he see his lady. You lovers, I ask now the question, which is in the worse situation, Palamon or Arcite? The one may see his lady daily, but must dwell ever in prison. The other may ride or walk where he wishes, but shall never see his lady more. Now you that know how, judge as you wish, for I will tell now as I began.

Here ends the first part.

Here begins the second part.

When Arcite had made his way to Thebes, he languished many days and said "Alas!" for never again should he see his lady. And shortly to conclude about his woe, no creature that is or shall be while the world shall last ever had so much sorrow. He was bereft of sleep, food, and drink, and grew lean and dry as a stick; his eyes hollow, grisly to see, and his hue sallow, pale as cold ashes; and he was always solitary, wail-

---

[5] Saturn. God of the harvest, also known as Cronos; father of Jupiter (Zeus), Juno (Hera), Ceres (Demeter), Pluto (Hades), and Neptune (Triton).

[6] Juno. Wife of Zeus and patron of married women. Her jealousy, in one sense, is a function of Zeus' profligacy.

ing all night and making his complaint.

If he heard songs or instruments of music, then would he weep and could not be consoled. So feeble and low and changed were his spirits, that nobody could recognize his speech or his voice even if they heard them. And in his behavior he acted not only as if he had the lover's sickness of Eros,[7] but rather like madness sprung from melancholy in the cell of imagination in his brain. In short, both the disposition and habits of this woeful lover, lord Arcite, were turned entirely upside-down.

Why should I describe all day his woe? When he had endured a year or two of this cruel torment in his country Thebes, one night as he lay in his sleep the winged god Mercury seemed to stand before him, and told him to be cheerful. In his hand he bore upright his wand of sleep, and upon his bright hair he wore a hat; in such fashion he came, Arcite took note, as when Mercury put Argus to sleep. And thus he spoke to him: "You shall go to Athens; there an end of your woe is prepared."

And with that word Arcite started up. "Now truly," he said, "howsoever I pay for it, I will go straightway to Athens. Not for the fear of death will I fail to see my lady whom I love and serve. If I behold her once, I do not care if I should die!"

And with that word he picked up a great mirror and saw that his entire hue was changed, and his face was entirely of another fashion; and it ran into his mind then that since his face was so disfigured with his malady, he might well, if he bore himself humbly, live in Athens unknown evermore and see his lady almost daily. And quickly he changed his clothing to that of a poor laborer, and all alone except for a squire, who was disguised in poor fashion as Arcite was and knew Arcite's secret, he took the shortest way to Athens.

And soon he went to the court, and at the gate offered his service to drudge and draw whatever anyone should tell him.

---

[7] Eros. The god of love; Cupid.

And shortly to end this matter, he fell into service with Emily's chamberlain, who was wise and could well detect a good servant. Well could Arcite hew wood and carry water, for he was young and mighty in that, and strong and big of bones to do whatever he was bid. A year or two he was in this service as page of the chamber to Emily the bright, and he called himself Philostrate. But there was never in the court a man of his station who was half so well beloved as him; for he seemed so noble a person that his renown spread throughout the court.

They said that it would be a charity for Theseus to raise this servant's station, and put him in worthy service, where he might employ all of his powers. Thus within a short while the report of his deeds and fair tongue was so spread about that Theseus took him as squire of his chamber, with gold enough to maintain his station. And from year to year men brought him secretly his revenue from his own country as well; but this he spent in such fitting and cunning fashion that no man wondered from where it had come. And in this fashion he led his life for three years, and bore himself so in war and in peace that Theseus held no man dearer. And in this bliss I now leave Arcite, and will speak a little of Palamon.

Seven years in darkness in this horrible fortified prison has Palamon sat, worn away with woe and hardship. Who feels now a double wound and heaviness but Palamon, whom love so torments that he goes out of his wit for woe! And he is a prisoner, not just for a year, but perpetually. Who could properly in English set to rhyme his martyrdom? Not I, in truth. Therefore I pass it over as lightly as I can.

Now in the seventh year, on the third night of May, as the old books tell which relate this history more fully, whether it was by chance or by destiny (as thus, that when a thing is decreed, it shall be), it happened that Palamon, soon after midnight, by the help of a friend broke from his prison and fled the city as fast as he could go. For he had given his jailer a drink of a cordial, made of a certain wine with narcotics and fine opium of Thebes, so that all that night, even if someone should strike him, he could not awake, but remained asleep. And thus Palamon fled away as fast as he ever could. The night was short and dawn was at hand; he had to hide, and to a nearby grove he crept with fearful foot. For in short this was his intent: to hide himself in that grove all day and to take the road toward Thebes at night, and pray his friends to help him make war upon Theseus; and in brief, either he should lose his life or win Emily in marriage. This is the sum of it, and his full intent.

Now will I return again to Arcite, who little knows how near his trouble was until Fortune had brought him into the snare. The busy lark, messenger of day, saluted with her song the gray morning; and Phoebus rose up so fiery that all the orient laughed because of the light; and with his beams he dried in the thickets the silver drops hanging on the leaves. And Arcite, dwelling in the royal court with Theseus, as chief squire, had risen and looked out upon the merry morning. To do observance to May, and keeping in mind the point of his desire, he rode out of the court upon a charger, leaping about like the fire, into the fields a mile or more to occupy himself. And into the grove that I mentioned to you he began by chance to take his way, to make him a garland of sprigs, either of woodbine or hawthorn leaves. And loud he sang in the bright

"May, with your flowers and your green,
So welcome are you, fair fresh May,
I hope to get some green this day."

With lusty heart he sprang from his charger into the grove, and wandered up and down along a path, where by chance Palamon was behind a bush, so that nobody might see him, for he was sorely afraid of his death. He knew not at all that it was Arcite – God knows he would have hardly believed it. But the truth was said many years ago, "The field has eyes, the wood has ears,"[8] A man does well to bear a steady spirit, for people always meet at unexpected times. Little does Arcite know of his old comrade, who was so near that he could hear all that Aricte said, for Palamon sat silently in the bush.

When Arcite had roamed his fill, and sung his roundel[9] lustily, he fell then into a study, as these lovers do in their odd, changeful way, sometimes in the tree-tops, sometimes down among briers, sometimes up, sometimes down, like a bucket in a well. Just as on the Friday sometimes it shines and sometimes it rains hard, so too can fickle Venus overcast the hearts of her followers; just as her day is changeful, so too she changes her aspect; seldom is the Friday like all the rest of the week.

When Arcite had sung he began to sigh, and without more ado sat himself down. "Alas," he said, "alas the day that I was born! How long through your cruelty will you war upon Thebes, O Juno? Alas! all the royal blood of Cadmus and Amphion is brought to confusion. I am of the lineage of Cadmus, the first man that built Thebes and founded the city, and was crowned first king of it; I am offspring of his true line, and of the royal stock. And now I am such a wretch and slave that I serve my mortal enemy as his poor squire. And yet Juno does me this indignity as well, so that I dare not acknowledge my own name. Where I used to be called Arcite, now am I Philostrate, not worth a farthing!

"Alas, cruel Mars! Alas, Juno! Thus has your anger undone all our kindred, except me only, and wretched Palamon whom Theseus martyrs in his dungeon. And over all this, Love has shot his fiery arrow through my true, anxious breast so full of fire, to make a final end of me, so that my

[8] The field…ears. An ancient Latin proverb; no direct source has been identified.

[9] Roundel. (Or Rondeau.) Form of short poetry in which the opening phrase or line is repeated as a refrain in the second and third stanzas.

death was shaped for me before my first shirt was sewn! You slay me with your eyes, Emily; you are the cause of my dying. I set not the value of a peascod upon all the remnant of my care, if only I could do anything to your pleasure!" And with that word he fell down in a trance for a long time.

Palamon, who thought he felt a cold sword glide suddenly through his heart, quaked for anger and could hesitate no longer; but when he heard Arcite's words, started up as if he were a madman up out of the thick bushes with a pale, deathlike face, and "Arcite," he said, "false wicked traitor, now are you caught, who love my lady for whom I have all this pain and woe! You are my own blood and sworn to my confidence, as I have told you often before. And you have deceived Duke Theseus and falsely changed your name. Either you or I shall die. You shall not love my lady; I alone will love her and none other. For I am your mortal enemy Palamon, and though I have no weapon here, but have escaped by grace of Fortune from prison, I doubt not that either I shall slay you or you shall not love Emily. Choose whichever you will, for you shall not escape me."

When Arcite knew him and had heard his tale, with full savage heart he pulled out a sword and as fierce as a lion he spoke: "By the God Who sits in heaven, were it not that you are sick and mad for love and have no weapon here, you should never pass out of this grove unless you were to die by my hand. For I defy the pledge and bond that you say I have made to you. What, you fool – you know that love is free, and that I will love her in spite of all your power. But have here my word, for as much as you are a worthy knight and would gladly contend for her by battle, I will not fail, but without the knowledge of any I will be here tomorrow, by my knightly honor, and bring armor sufficient for you, and you shall choose the best of it and leave the worst for me. And this night I will bring you meat and drink enough, and clothes for your bedding. And if it so happens that you win my lady and slay me in this wood, you may well have your lady, for all that I am concerned.

Palamon answered, "I agree." And thus each of them pledged his faith and parted from the other until the morning. Ah, Cupid,[10] who has no charity! Ah, kingdom that will have no fellow! Truly is it said that neither love nor lordship will have a partner; and indeed Arcite and Palamon found that to be true.

Arcite rode quickly to the town, and in the morning before daylight he secretly prepared two suits of armor, each sufficient and worthy for the battle in the field between them. And as he was alone, he carried this armor before him on his horse, and in the grove, at the appointed time and place, this Arcite and Palamon met. Then the color in their visages began to change. Just as the hunter in the realm of Thrace[11] stands at a gap in the forest with a spear, when hunting bear or lion, and hears him come rushing through the branches, breaking boughs and leaves, and thinks, "Here comes my mortal foe; without fail, either he or I must die, for I must slay him at this moment, or he me, if ill comes to me;" so were they, and so their hue altered, as far off as each could know the other.

There was no "Good-day," no salutation, but straightway, without word or rehearsing, each helped the other to arm, as courteously as if he were his dear friend; and after that they thrust at each other for an amazingly long time with spears sharp and stout. You might judge that Palamon in his fighting were a mad lion and Arcite a cruel tiger. They struck against each other like wild boars that froth white as foam in mad anger; up to the ankles they fought in blood. And in this way I leave them fighting, and will tell you forth of Theseus.

Destiny, God's general vicar, who executes over all the world the providence which He has foreordained, so strong it

---

[10] Cupid. The god of love.

[11] Thrace. The southeast tip of the Balkan Peninsula, including northeastern Greece, Bulgaria, and Turkey.

is that even if the world swore the contrary of a thing, yes or no, yet it shall happen on that day which will not happen again in a thousand years. For certainly our wills here, whether they are on war, or peace, of love or hate, are all ruled by the eye above us. I am put now in mind of this by the mighty Theseus, who is so zealous on the hunt, and chiefly in May for the great hart, that no day dawns upon him in bed, that he is not clad and ready to ride with huntsman, horn, and hounds before him. For in hunting he has such delight that all of his joy and passion is to be himself the great harts' destroyer, for after Mars now he serves Diana.[12]

Clear was the day, as I have told, and Theseus in all joy and mirth rode a-hunting royally, with his fair Hippolyta and Emily clothed all in green; and to the grove, not far away, in which men told him was a hart, he held the straight course, and over a brook and so forth on his way toward the glade where the hart was accustomed to have his flight. The duke would have a run or two at him with hounds such as he might wish to order.

When he had come to the opening he shaded his eyes from the sun and looked about, and immediately noticed Palamon and Arcite who fought furiously, as if they were two boars. The bright swords went back and forth so hideously that with the least blow it seemed they would fell an oak; but who they were he knew not at all. The duke smote his charger with his spurs and at a bound was between the two, and pulled out a sword and cried, "Hoo! No more, upon pain of losing your heads! By mighty Mars, he whom I see strike another stroke shall die immediately! But tell me what sort of men are you who are so bold as to fight here without a judge or other officer, as if you were in a legal duel?"

Palamon answered hastily, "Sire, what need is there of more words? Both of us have deserved the death. We are two woeful wretches, weary of our own lives, and as you are

[12] Diana. Goddess of the moon; a huntress; the patron of virgin women.

a just lord and judge, grant us no mercy nor escape, but slay me first, for the love of holy charity; but slay my fellow as well. Or slay him first, for though you little know it, this is your mortal foe; this is Arcite, who is banished from your land on pain of death, for which he deserves to die; this is he who came to your doors and called himself Philostrate. Thus he has deceived you many years. And you have made him your chief squire, and this is he who loves Emily.

"And since the day of my death is come, I fully confess that I am that woeful Palamon who wickedly broke from your prison. I am your mortal foe, and it is I who bear so hot a love to Emily the bright that I wish to die now before her eyes. Therefore I ask my death and my judgment. But slay my companion in the same way, for we both have deserved to die."

The worthy duke answered then, "This is a speedy judgment. Your own mouth by your confession has condemned you, and I bear witness to it. There is no need to torture you on the rack. You shall die, by mighty Mars the red!"

The queen on account of her true womanliness began to weep, and so did Emily and all the ladies in the troop. It was a great pity, as they all deemed, that such a mischance should ever occur, for they were gentle youths, of great station, and only for love was this combat. They beheld their bloody wounds wide and sore, and one and all they cried, "Have mercy upon us women, lord!" and upon their bare knees down they fell, and would have kissed his feet where he was, until at the last his mood was softened, for pity runs soon into a noble heart.

And though at first he quaked for anger, yet he considered in brief the trespass of them both and the cause of it; and although his anger arraigned them of guilt, yet his reason held them excused. Thus he considered that every man will help himself in love, if he is able, and deliver himself from prison as well. And his heart had pity upon the women as well, who continued weeping, and at that moment he thought in his noble heart, and said softly to himself, "Fie upon a lord who will have no mercy, but be a lion in word and deed to those who repent and tremble, as well as to a proud, scornful man who ever upholds what he has done. That lord has little of discernment who knows no difference in such a case, but measures pride and humility alike."

And, in brief, when his anger was thus departed, he began to look up with shining eyes and spoke these words aloud: "Ah, the God of Love! God bless! How mighty and great a lord he is! Against his might no obstacles can help; well may he be called a god by reason of his miracles, for of every heart he can make what he will. Lo, here are this Palamon and this Arcite, who have freely left my prison, and might have lived royally in Thebes, and know that I am their mortal foe and that their death lies in my power; yet love, in spite of their two eyes,[13] has brought them here both to die! Look now, is not that a high folly? Who can be a fool unless he is in love? Behold how they bleed, for God's sake in heaven! Are they not well arrayed? Thus has their lord, the god of love, paid their wages and their reward for serving him! And yet they who serve love deem themselves wise, for anything that may happen!

"But this is the best sport of all, that she for whom they have this mirth thanks them therefore no more than me; for she knows no more of this heated display than a cuckoo or a hare! But all things must be attempted, both good and bad; young or old, a man must sometimes be a fool. I know it by myself, for in my time, years ago, I was a servant of love. And therefore, since I know of love's pain, as one often caught in his snare, and how sorely it can clutch a man, I forgive you this trespass entirely, at the request of the queen kneeling here and of Emily as well, my sweet sister; and you shall both now swear to me never again to hurt my country nor war upon me by day or night, but be my friends in all that you can. I forgive you this trespass, every bit!"

[13] In spite of their two eyes. I.e., in spite of themselves.

Fairly and well they swore to him as he asked, and prayed him for mercy and to be their good lord; and he granted them his grace and said thus: "To speak of royal lineage and riches, each of you is worthy, doubtless, to wed in due season, either a queen or a princess; but nevertheless, to speak of my sister for whom you have all this strife and jealousy, you know yourselves she may not wed two at once, though you fight forevermore. One of you, willy-nilly, must go whistle in an ivy-leaf; this is to say, she may not have both of you, no matter how jealous you may be. And therefore I give you these terms, that each of you shall have his destiny as it is ordained for him, and hear now in what manner.

"Lo, here I set your terms! My will is this, for flat conclusion, not to be replied to, and take it for the best, if you like it; that each of you go where he would like, freely, without ransom or control, and this day fifty weeks, neither more nor less, each of you shall bring a hundred knights, armed in all perfection for the lists, ready to contend for her in battle. And this I promise you, without fail and upon my word as a knight, that whichever of you both that has the strength, that is to say, whether he or you with your hundred that I spoke of can slay your adversary or drive them out of the lists,[14] to him shall I give Emily, to that one whom Fortune grants so fair a grace. The lists I shall make here, and God so surely have mercy upon my soul as I shall be a fair and faithful judge! No other terms shall you make with me, but that one of you shall be either dead or prisoner. And if this seems to you well said, speak your mind, and be content. This end and conclusion I set you!"

Whose look is light now but Arcite's? Who springs up for joy but Palamon? Who could tell or write of the joy there when Theseus granted so fair a grace? But down on their

[14] Lists. Area at a tournament where the participants lined up for jousting; the long runway with a barrier between the two horses and riders. The term is also used to mean jousting matches or tournaments in general.

knees went every creature and thanked him with heart and soul, and most chiefly the Thebans many times over. And thus with good hope and joyful hearts they took their leave, and rode homeward to Thebes, with its broad old walls.

Here ends the second part.

Here follows the third part.

I believe I would be judged negligent if I forget to tell of Theseus' outlay, who went busily to work to build up royal lists; such a noble theatre I dare to say was nowhere in this world. The circuit was a mile around, with a wall of stone and a ditch outside of it. Round was the shape, in a circle, full of steps to the height of sixty paces, so that when a man was set on one step he hindered not his neighbor behind from seeing. Eastward stood a gate of white marble, and even such another such one opposite westward; and, to conclude briefly, within a similar space was no such fabric on the earth. For there was no crafty man in the land that knew geometry or arithmetic, nor any expert portrayer nor carver of images, that Theseus gave him not meat and hire to plan and build the theatre. And to do his rites and sacrifice, he built an oratory and an altar eastward above the gate, in honor of Venus, goddess of love; and westward, in commemoration of Mars, he built another such one, that cost a huge load of gold. And northward, in a turret on the wall, Theseus ordered to be made in noble fashion an oratory rich to behold, of white alabaster and coral red, in honor of Diana the chaste.

And I have yet forgotten to describe the noble carving, the portrayals, the devices, the emblazonings and the figures in these three oratories. First, in the temple of Venus you might have seen created upon the wall, in imagery piteous to behold, the broken sleeps and cold sighs, the sacred tears and lamentations, the fiery pangs of desire that love's servants endure in this life; the oaths which secure their covenants; Pleasure and Hope, Desire and Foolhardiness, Beauty and

Youth, Mirth, Riches, Love-charms and Violence, Deceits, Flattery, Extravagance, Anxiety and Jealousy (who wore a garland of yellow marigolds, with a cuckoo sitting on her hand); feasts, instruments or music, singing with dancing, pleasures and gay garments, with all the circumstance of love which I have described and shall describe, were painted by order upon the wall, and more than I can make mention of.

In truth all the mount of Citheron, where Venus has her principal dwelling, was drawn upon the wall, with all the garden and the lustiness of it. Idleness, the porter, was not forgotten, nor the lovely Narcissus of long ago, the folly of King Solomon, the great strength of Hercules; the enchantments of Medea and Circe, the hardy fierce heart of Turnus, nor the rich Croesus, captive and in servitude. Thus may you see that neither wisdom nor riches, beauty nor cunning, strength nor hardihood can hold rivalry with Venus, for she can guide the entire world as she wishes. Lo, all these folk were so caught in her snare until for woe they cried often "Alas!" One or two examples shall suffice here, though I could explain a thousand more. The naked statue of Venus, glorious to look upon, was floating in a great sea, and from the navel down all was covered with green waves, bright as any glass. She had a lyre in her right and, and on her head a rose-garland, fresh and fragrant, and seemly to see. Above her head fluttered her doves, and before her stood her son Cupid, blindfolded, as he is often shown, with two wings upon his shoulders. He carried a bow and bright, keen arrows.

Why should I not tell you as well the portrayals on the wall in the temple of mighty Mars the red? The walls were painted, in length and breadth, just as the inner parts of the grisly, great temple of Mars in Thrace, in that cold, frosty region where Mars has his supreme habitation. On the wall was painted first a forest, in which dwelt neither beast nor man, with barren old trees, knotty and gnarled, with sharp and hideous stumps.

Through the forest ran a rumbling and a rushing noise, as though every bough should break in the tempest. Beneath a hill, under the slope, stood the temple of Mars mighty in arms, forged all of burnished steel, the portal deep and narrow, ghastly to see; and out from it came such a raging blast as made all the gates to shake.

The light from the north shone in at the door, for there was no window in the wall through which one could discern any light. The doors were all of everlasting adamant, bound across and length-wise with tough iron, and every pillar that strongly held the temple aloft was the size of a tun and of bright and shining iron.

There I saw first the dark contriving of Felony and all the scheming; cruel Anger, red as a coal; the pick-purse, and pale Dread as well; the smiler with a knife under the cloak; the stable burning in its black smoke; the treacherous murder in the bed; the open war with wounds all bleeding; and Strife with bloody knife and sharp menace. That sorry spot was entirely full of shrieks.

Further on I saw there the slayer of himself with his hair bathed in his heart's blood; the nail driven in the temples by night; cold death upon his back, with mouth gaping. In the midst of the temple sat Misfortune, with dejection and sorrowful face. Farther yet I saw Madness laughing in his frenzy, armed Complaint, Outcry and fierce Fury; the corpse in the bushes with throat cut; a thousand slain, but not by pestilence; the tyrant with his prey taken by force, and the town utterly left in ruins. Yet again I saw the dancing ships burned, the hunter strangled by the wild bears, the sow devouring the child in the very cradle, the cook scalded, despite his long spoon. Nothing was forgotten that comes by the evil aspects of Mars. The carter run over by his cart lay low under the wheel. There were also, of Mars' clan, the barber, the butcher, and the smith forging sharp swords upon his anvil. And above, in a tower, was depicted conquest sitting in great state, with the sharp sword hanging above him by a subtle thread of twine. The slaughter of Julius Caesar was painted there, and of great Nero and Antony.[15] Albeit they were unborn at that time, yet their deaths, through the menacing of Mars, were depicted in clear heraldry, though it was long before their time. So was it shown in those portrayals just as it is drawn large in the stars of heaven, who shall be slain and who die for love. One or two examples from old histories shall suffice; I cannot describe them all even though I would.

The statue of Mars stood armed upon a chariot, grim as a madman, and over his head shone two figures of stars called in scholars' writings Puella and Rubeus;[16] in this guise was the god of arms shown. A wolf stood before him at his feet, red-eyed and devouring a man. With subtle pencil were these figures depicted, to the glory of redoubtable Mars.

Now to the temple of Diana the chaste I will get me as fast as I can, to give you the full description if it. The walls up and down were painted with examples of hunting and of modest chastity.

There I saw how woeful Callisto, when Diana was angered with her, was turned from a woman to a bear (and she was made the lode-star afterwards). Thus was it painted, I can tell you no more; her son is a star also, as one may behold. There I saw Daphne, turned into a tree; I mean not the goddess Diana, but the daughter of Peneus, that was named Daphne. There I saw Actaeon transformed into a hart, for vengeance because he saw Diana naked; I saw also how his hounds caught and devoured him because they knew him not. There was painted also how Atalanta hunted the wild boar, with Meleager and many others, for which Diana wrought woe for him. There I saw many other wondrous sto-

[15] Julius Caesar…Nero and Antony. Three Roman emperors.
[16] Puella and Rubeus. Figures used in the practice of geomancy, the practice of divination through the interpretation of lines, shapes, or textures on the ground.

ries, which I wish not call to mind.

This goddess sat high on a hart, with small hounds about her feet, and underneath her feet she had a waxing moon that would soon wane. Her statue was clothed in green, bow in hand and arrows in a quiver. Her eyes she cast down low, where Pluto[17] controls his dark realm. Before her was a woman in labor, and because her child was so long unborn she called piteously upon Lucina,[18] "Help, for you can aid me better than any other." He who depicted her could make his likenesses beautiful and lifelike, and he paid many florins for his colors.

Now were these lists all made, and Theseus, who at his own great cost had thus every bit appointed the temples and the theatre, was very well pleased. But I will pass on a little from Theseus, and speak of Arcite and Palamon.

The day of their returning approached, when each should bring a hundred knights, as I have told you, to contest in battle; and to Athens each of them came to keep his covenant, with a hundred knights all well and duly armed for the combat. And truly many people said that never since the world began, as far as God has made sea or land, was so noble a fellowship, of a few men, in the knightly exploits of their hands. For every creature that loved chivalry and would gladly have an exalted name had prayed to be in those jousts. Joyful was he who was chosen. For you know well that, if such a case presented itself tomorrow, every lusty knight that had his strength and was acquainted with love would be eager to be there. To fight for a lady, God bless, it would be an enjoyable sight to see!

And so it was with many knights that came with Palamon. One would be armed in a coat of mail, a breastplate and a light tunic; some would wear a pair of broad plates on front and back; some would have a Prussian shield or target; some would be armed well on their legs, and have an ax or a

[17] Pluto. God of the underworld.

[18] Lucina. Goddess of childbirth; a form or manifestation of Diana.

steel mace. There is no new guise that is not old. Armed they were, even as I have said, each one in his own fashion.

There you might have seen, coming with Palamon, the great king of Thrace, Lycurgus himself. Black was his beard and manly his face. His eyes glowed of a hue between yellow and red, and like a griffin he looked about, with shaggy hairs in his dogged brows, his limbs great, his brawn hard, his shoulders broad, his arms round and long. And as the manner was in his country, high he stood upon a chariot of gold, with four white bulls in the harness. Instead of an armorial tunic over his harness, he had an ancient bearskin, coal-black, with yellow nails bright as any gold. His long hair was combed down behind, and shone black as any raven's feather; on his head was a diadem of gold as great as an arm, of huge weight, set full of bright stones, of fine rubies and diamonds. About his chariot marched white mastiffs, twenty and more, as great as any steer, to hunt the lion or hart, and they followed him with collars of gold and ringed leashes filed smoothly, and muzzles fast bound. He had a hundred well-armed lords in his troop, with stern and stout hearts.

With Arcite, as one may read in the histories, came riding, like Mars, the god of arms, the great Emetreus, king of India, upon a bay steed trapped in steel and covered with a diapered[19] cloth of gold. His tunic, blazoned with his arms, was of cloth of Tartary,[20] laid with pearls, white, round, and great. His saddle was of burnished gold, freshly forged. A short mantle hung upon his shoulders, stiff with red rubies sparkling as fire. His crisp hair ran in rings, yellow, glittering as the sun. His nose was high, his lips full, his eyes bright citron, and his color sanguine, with a few freckles between yellow and black sprinkled in his face; and as a lion he cast his looking about. His age I estimate at five-and-twenty; his

---

[19] Diapered. Ornamented with a geometric or floral pattern.

[20] Tartary. Russia or Siberia. Most editors suggest that the cloth was likely from imported from China via Tartary.

beard was well begun to spring, and his voice as a thunderous trumpet. Upon his head he wore a garland of green laurel, fresh and lively to see; and upon his hand he bore for his pleasure a tame eagle, white as any lily. He had with him a hundred lords, all armed richly in all their gear, except for their heads. Dukes and earls and kings were gathered in this noble company, trust me well, for the advancement of knighthood and for love's sake. On every side about this king ran many tame lions and leopards.

And in this way on that Sunday about prime[21] these lords one and all arrived in the city and alighted. This worthy Duke Theseus, when he had brought them into his city and lodged them, each according to his rank, took such pains to feast and entertain them and do them all the honor that even now men deem that no man's wit could improve upon it. The service at the banquet, the minstrelsy, the great gifts to high and low, the rich array of Theseus' palace, what ladies were fairest and best on the dance, or which could best dance and sing, or who spoke of love most tenderly, who sat first or last on the dais, what hawks were perched above, what hounds lay on the floor – of all this I make no mention now, but only the pith of it, that it seems to me is best to tell. Now comes the point; listen if you will.

Sunday night, before daybreak, when Palamon heard the lark sing (though it would not be day for two hours, yet the lark sang, and Palamon as well), he arose with holy heart and high spirit to go on his pilgrimage to the blessed and gracious Cytherea, I mean Venus, worthy of all reverence; and in her hour he walked forth on foot to the tournament grounds, and into her temple. And down he kneeled, and with humble bearing and aching heart he spoke as I shall tell you.

"Fairest of fair, daughter to Jove and spouse to Vulcan,[22] O Venus my lady, you who gladdens the mount of Citheron,

---

[21] Prime. 9 A.M.

[22] Vulcan. Smith to the gods; also a god himself.

have pity on my bitter burning tears and receive my humble prayer at your heart, by that love you bore to Adonis. Alas, I have no language to express the torments of this hell! My heart cannot reveal my woes, I am so bewildered that I can say nothing. But mercy, lady bright, who well knows my thought and sees my pain; consider all this and have pity, and so surely shall I evermore be your true servant with all my might, and hold warfare ever with chastity. That vow I make, so you will help me.

"I care not to boast of arms, nor ask tomorrow to have victory, nor renown in this combat nor vain praise for my exploits trumpeted up and down. But I fully wish to have possession of Emily and die in your service. Choose yourself the manner how; I know not whether it would be better to have victory of them, or they of me, so long as I have my lady in my arms. For though Mars may be the god of battle, your virtue is so great in heaven that, if you wish, I shall have my love. Your temple evermore will I honor, wherever I go, and on your altar I will maintain a fire and do sacrifice. And if you deny me, my sweet lady, then I pray that tomorrow with a spear Arcite may pierce me through the heart. Then, when I am dead, I will care not if Arcite should win her as his wife. This is the sum and end of my prayer: grant me my love, blessed lady."

When his prayer was done, Palamon immediately made his sacrifice very devoutly, with all ceremony, though I will not describe his rites now. But at last the statue of Venus shook, and made a sign by which he understood that his prayer that day was accepted. For though the sign showed delay, yet he knew well that his request was granted and went home with a glad heart.

About the third hour after Palamon set forth for Venus' temple, up rose the sun, and up rose Emily, and hastened forth to the temple of Diana. Her maidens she had with her prepared the fire, the incense, the vestments, horns full of mead, as was the custom, and all the rest that appertained to the sacrifice; nothing was lacking. While the temple, full of beautiful hangings, smoked with sweet odors, this Emily with mild heart washed her body with water from a spring. But how she performed her rite, unless it were something in general, I dare not tell. (Yet it would be a pleasure to hear more. For a man of blameless mind there would be no harm; it is good that a man be unrestricted in his speech.) Her bright hair was combed and loose, and on her head was set a crown of green oak, fair and pleasing.

She kindled two fires on the altar, and completed her rites as one may read in Theban Statius[23] and other old books. When the fire was kindled she spoke thus to Diana with pious expression.

"Chaste goddess of the green woods, to whom heaven and earth and sea are visible, queen of the deep, dark realm of Pluto; goddess of maidens, who many years has known my heart and what I desire, keep me now from your wrath and vengeance, which Actaeon cruelly bore. Chaste goddess, you well know that I desire to be a maiden until I die, never do I wish to be a lover or wife. I am a maiden, you know, yet of your band, and love hunting and the chase and to walk in the savage woods, and not to be a wife or to be with child. I wish to know nothing of the company of men. Now lady, I ask you by your own three forms:[24] help me, since you can, and grant me this one grace; send love and peace between Arcite and Palamon, that love me so sorely; and so turn away their hearts from me that all their hot desire and love and busy torment and flames be quenched or turned elsewhere.

"And if you will not favor me, or my destiny be ordered that I must have one of the two, send me the one who desires

---

[23] Theban Statius. Roman poet and author of the *Thebiad*, indirectly one of Chaucer's primary sources for *Troilus and Criseyde*.

[24] Three forms. As named above, goddess of the hunt, of the underworld, and of virgins. Some editors include also the attribute, or form, of the moon.

me most. Goddess of pure chastity, behold the bitter tears that drop from my cheeks. Since you, a maiden yourself, are protector of us all, keep and defend my maidenhead, and as long as I live I will serve you as a maiden."

The fires burned steadily upon the altar while Emily was thus praying, but suddenly she saw a marvelous sight. For just then one of the fires was quenched and restarted again, and soon after that the other fire was quenched and quite extinct. And as it was extinguished it made a whistling as do these wet brands when they burn, and at the end of the brand out ran, as it were, many bloody drops. At this Emily was so sorely aghast that she began to cry aloud and was nearly mad; for she knew not what it signified, but only called out for fear and so wept that it was pitiful to listen.

And at this moment Diana appeared in the guise of a huntress with bow in hand and said, "Daughter, cease your heaviness. It is decreed among the high gods and written and confirmed in eternal words, that you shall be wedded to one of those who has had so much care and woe for you; but to which one I may not tell. Farewell, I may remain no longer. The fires burning on my altar, before you leave here, shall declare to you your lot in this love matter."

And with that word the arrows in the goddess' quiver clattered and rung aloud, and she forth went and vanished. At this Emily was astonished, and said, "Alas! What does this signify? I put myself in your protection, Diana, and in your control." And she went straight home. This is the sum of it; there is no more to say.

In the next hour of Mars after this Arcite went forth on foot to the temple of fierce Mars, to do his sacrifice with all the rites of his pagan faith. With devout heart and high reverence he said his prayer to Mars thus.

"O strong god, who in the cold realms of Thrace are honored and held as lord, and in every country and every realm has the entire bridle of war in your hand, and disposes fortune in war as you wish, accept from me my devout sacrifice. If my youth may have such merit, and my might be worthy to serve your godhead, and I may be one of yours, then pity my pains, I pray. For that pain and those hot flames in which you once burned for desire, when you had at will all the beauty of fair, young, fresh Venus (although one time it went amiss with you, when Vulcan caught you in his cords, alas!), for that sorrow that was in your heart then, pity my bitter pains as well.

"You know I am young and unlearned, and hurt more with love, I believe, than ever was any living creature. For she who gives me all this woe cares never if I sink or float. And well I know I must win her with force of arms upon the field, before she will promise me mercy; and well I know without help or grace from you my strength cannot avail. Then help me tomorrow in my fight, and recall for yourself that fire that once burned you, lord, as this fire now burns me; and grant that tomorrow I may conquer.

"May mine be the travail, yours be the glory! Your supreme temple will I most revere of any place, and ever most toil in your strong calling and to do your pleasure; and in your temple I will hang up my banner and all the arms of my fellows, and evermore until the day I die I will maintain an eternal fire before you. And I will bind me to this vow also; my beard and my hair I will give you, that now hang down long and never yet felt offence of razor or shears, and I will be your true servant while I live. Now, lord, have pity on my bitter sorrows, and give me victory; I ask of you no more."

The prayer of Arcite the strong being done, the temple-doors and also the rings that hung on them clattered loudly, at which Arcite was somewhat aghast. The fires burned brightly upon the altar and illumined all the temple, and then the ground gave out a sweet smell. And Arcite lifted his hand and cast more incense into the fire, and did other rites. And at last the statue of Mars began to ring his hauberk. And with that sound Arcite heard a low and dim murmur which said "Victory!", for which he gave laud and honor to Mars.

Thus with joy and high hope of faring well, Arcite went immediately to his lodging, as glad as a bird is for the bright sun.

Immediately such strife for that grant began in heaven between Venus, goddess of love, and Mars, the stern god mighty in arms, that Jupiter was hard at work to calm it, until the pale and cold and hostile Saturn, who knew so many earlier dealings, soon found in his vast experience a plan to content both sides. Truth to tell, age has great advantage; in age is both wisdom and experience. One can outrun the old, but not outwit them. Now, to appease strife and dread, albeit that is against his nature, Saturn began to find a remedy.

"My dear daughter Venus," he said, "my course which circles so widely has more power than any mortal comprehends. Mine is the drowning in the pale sea, mine the imprisoning in the dark cell, mine the strangling and the hanging by the throat; the murmurs, the groaning, the churls' rebellion, the secret poisoning. I make vengeance and full chastisement when I dwell in the sign of the Lion.[25] Mine is the ruin of high mansions, the falling of towers and walls on the miner and the carpenter. When Samson[26] shook the pillar, it was I who slew him. And mine are the cold maladies, the dark treasons and ancient plots; my aspect begets the plague.

"Weep no more now. I will do my duty that your own knight Palamon shall have his lady as you have promised him. Though Mars may help his knight, nevertheless at last there must be peace between you; albeit you are not of one nature, which always causes such division. Weep you no more; I am your grandfather, ready at your command, and I

[25] Lion. Zodiacal sign of Leo.

[26] Samson. Old Testament Israelite strongman whose strength was in his hair (or his promise to God that he would not cut his hair). When his hair had grown again, after Delilah betrayed him and cut it off, he knocked down the temple pillars, killing his enemies (the Philistines) and himself. The story of his troubles with Delilah is told in Judges 16. 15 and retold in the Monk's Tale 2015-94.

will fulfill your pleasure."

Now will I leave the gods of heaven, Venus, goddess of love, and Mars; and tell you as plainly as may be the main substance, for which I began.

Here ends the third part.

Here follows the fourth part.

Great was the festival in Athens, and for that lusty season of May every creature was in such mirth that they jousted and danced all that Monday, and spent it in Venus' high service. But because all should be up early to see the great tourney, they went to rest early that night.

When day began to spring in the morning, there was clattering and noise of horses and armor in the lodgings everywhere, and to the palace rode many troops of lords upon steeds and palfreys. There you could have seen armor devised rare and richly, and wrought well in gold-work, embroidery, and steel; bright shields, horses' trappings, steel caps, gold-beaten helmets, hauberks, armorial tunics; lords on their chargers in splendid vesture above their armor; knights-retainers, and squires nailing on spearheads, buckling helms, strapping shields and lacing with thongs.

Where there was need, none were idle. Foamy steeds were gnawing on golden bridles, armorers were spurring to and fro in haste with file and hammer; there were yeomen on foot, and many burgesses, with short staves in hand, as thick as they could walk in a crowd; pipes, trumpets, drums, clarions, that sound bloody blasts in battle; the palace up and down full of people holding talk, here three, there ten, surmising about these two Theban knights.

Some said it shall be so, some said thus, some sided with him of the black beard, some with the thick-haired, some with the bald; some said that one looked grim and would fight indeed, and that one had a battle-ax that weighed twenty pound. Thus the hall was full of conjecture from the time the sun began to spring.

The great Theseus, awakened from his sleep with the minstrelsy and noise, held yet his chamber in his rich palace until the Theban knights with equal honor were fetched there. Duke Theseus was seated at a window, arrayed as if he were a god on his throne. The people pressed in that direction to see him and pay him high reverence, and to hear his pronouncement and behest. A herald on a scaffold proclaimed silence until all the people's noise was hushed, and then he declared the mighty duke's will.

"The lord duke, of his high prudence, has considered that it would be mere destruction to noble blood, if men should now in this event fight in the fashion of mortal battle. Therefore, to ordain that they shall not perish, he will modify his first purpose. On pain of death, therefore, no man shall send or bring into the lists any manner of missile, or pole-ax, or short knife; no man shall draw or bear by his side any short sword with sharp point for stabbing; no man shall ride against his adversary with a sharply ground spear more than one run, but on foot he may thrust, if he will, to defend himself. He who is bettered shall be captured, not slain, but brought to the stake that shall be ordained on either side; to that place he must go by the rules and remain there. And if should happen that the chieftain on either side be taken, or else be slain, the tournament shall last no longer. God speed you! Go forth, lay on hard! With maces and long swords fight your fill. This is the lord duke's decree, and now go your ways."

The voice of the people reached the sky, so loud they cried with joyful voice: "God save so good a lord, who will have no bloody destruction!" Up go trump and melody, and the bands of knights ride to the tournament grounds in order through the broad city, which was entirely hung not with serge[27] but with cloth of gold. Like a lord indeed rode this noble duke, the two Thebans on either side; next rode Emily and the queen, and then another company ordered according

[27] Serge. Worsted wool.

to their station.

Thus they passed through the city and came early to the tournament grounds. It was not yet full prime[28] of day when Theseus was set down in high state, and Hippolyta the queen, and Emily, and the other ladies in rows of seats. All the crowd pressed to their seats. And then through the western gates, under the shrine of Mars, Arcite and his hundred entered now with a red banner; and at the same moment Palamon and his men entered from the east under the shrine of Venus, with a white banner and hardy bearing and face. In the entire world, if one should seek up and down, there would be no two such companies, so even, without inequality. None, however, was so discerning as to be able to say that either had advantage over the other in valor, rank or age. And they arranged themselves in two fair formations.

When all their names had been read, so that there might be no deception as to their number, then were the gates shut and a herald cried on high, "Do now your duty, proud young knights!"

The heralds stopped their spurring about, trumpets and clarions rang aloud; there is no more to say but that in either line the spears were put firmly in their resting place, in went sharp spurs into flanks, and everyone saw who could ride and who could joust. Shafts were shivering upon thick shields, one man felt the stab through the breast-bone, up sprung spears twenty foot on high, out came swords bright as silver, and hewed and split helms, out burst the blood with stern red streams, with mighty maces they crushed bones. One thrust through the thickest of the throng, there stumbled mighty steeds and down went knight and all, one on foot thrust with his spear-stump. One was hurtled down with his horse, and rolled like a ball under foot. One was hurt through the body, and then seized and, against his will, brought to the stake, and there he must remain by agreement; and there one was brought from the other party.

---

[28] Prime. 9 A.M.

At times Theseus made them rest and refresh themselves, and drink if they wished. Often in that day those two Thebans met together and each created woe for his adversary; each unhorsed the other twice. There is no tiger in the vale of Gargaphia,[29] when her little cub is stolen, so cruel on the hunt as Arcite's jealous heart was against Palamon. Nor is a lion in Belmary so vicious after the blood of his prey, when he is hunted or mad with hunger, as Palamon to slay Arcite his foe. The jealous strokes bit on their helmets, and out ran the red blood on both their flanks.

Eventually there must be an end of every deed. For before the sun went to rest, the strong king Emetreus took the opportunity to seize upon Palamon as he fought, and made his sword to bite deeply into his flesh; and by the arms of twenty he was drawn, ever resisting, unto the stake. Striving to rescue him, the strong king Lycurgus was borne down, and for all of his valor king Emetreus was knocked a sword's length out of his saddle, so Palamon hit him before he was overpowered. But it was all for nothing, as Palamon was dragged to the stake. His hardy heart could not help him; when he was caught he had to obey, by force and by agreement as well. Who but woeful Palamon sorrows now, who may now no more go to the fight?

And when Theseus had seen it, he cried to the people who continued to fight, "Ho! No more, it is done! I shall be a faithful judge and not a partial one. Arcite of Thebes shall have Emily, whose good fortune has granted him to win her nobly." And straightway for joy of this began such an uproar among the people, so loud and high, it seemed the tournament grounds would fall.

What now can fair Venus in heaven do? What can she say? What can this queen of love do? She wept so, for lack of her desire, that her tears fell into the ground. "I am ever disgraced, without doubt," she said.

"Hold your peace, daughter," Saturn replied. "Mars has

[29] Gargaphia. Likely a valley in Boetoia in central Greece.

his will, and his knight all that he prayed for, and you shall be eased before long, by my head!"

The trumpets, the heralds that called and cried on high, and all the loud minstrelsy, made high festival for joy of Lord Arcite. But hold your peace a little now, and hearken what miracle occurred just then.

This fierce Arcite had doffed his helmet to show his face, and on a charger spurred down the long field, looking upward at Emily. And she cast a friendly eye on him in return, for women, to speak generally, follow ever the favor of fortune. And in his heart she made all his joy.

Out of the ground burst an infernal Fury, sent from Pluto at the request of Saturn, for fear of which Arcite's horse suddenly turned and leapt aside and, as he leapt, foundered and, before Arcite could notice, pitched him on the crown of his head. He lay on the ground as if lifeless, his breast all crushed by his saddle-bows; as black was his face as any raven or coal, just as the blood that run in it. Quickly he was carried away with mourning to Theseus' castle. Then was he cut out of his harness, and brought fairly and soon into a bed, for he was yet alive and conscious, crying always for Emily.

Duke Theseus with his entire retinue and guests had come home to his city of Athens with all pomp and great festivity. Although this misadventure had occurred, he would not dishearten them all. People said also that Arcite should not die; he should be healed of his hurt. And they were as glad of another thing, that of them all none was killed, though they were sorely wounded, and especially one whose breast-bone was pierced by a spear. For other wounds and for broken bones some had charms and some had salves; they drank sage and remedies of herbs to preserve their limbs.

For all this, the noble duke cheered and honored every man, as he well could; and made revelry all night long, as was due, for the foreign lords. Nor was there held to have been any defeat, but only as in a joust or a tourney; there was no defeat, in truth, for it is but a misadventure to fall, or to be held by twenty knights and carried unyielding and by force unto the stake, one man alone without a defender, dragged forth by arm, foot and toe, and his steed also driven forth with staves by yeomen and pages on foot. It could not mark him with disgrace; none could call it cowardice.

Therefore, to stop all rancor and malice, Duke Theseus then bade it to be proclaimed that the victory belonged to both sides equally, and either side as alike as the other's brother, and gave gifts to all according to their station, and held a high festival for three days. And he honorably escorted the kings out of his town a full day's journey. And every man went home directly; there was no more than, "Farewell, have a good day!" Of this battle I will speak no more, but tell of Arcite and of Palamon.

The breast of Arcite swelled, and the malady around his heart increased more and more. The clotted blood corrupted, in spite of any doctor's aid, and remained so in his trunk that neither blood-letting nor cupping[30] nor drink of herbs could help him.

The animal or expulsive virtue, which derives from that force called natural, availed not to expel or drive out the venom. The pipes of his lungs began to swell, and every muscle in his breast and below was sorely harmed with venom and corruption. Neither vomit upward nor other medicine would help to save his life. Crushed was that entire region; Nature no longer had dominion.

And certainly wherever Nature will not act, farewell medicine! Go bear the man to church! This is the sum of it: Arcite must die; therefore he sent after Palamon, his dear cousin, and after Emily, and then said as you shall hear.

"The woeful spirit in my heart cannot declare one point of all my bitter sorrows to you my lady, that I love most; but since my life can last no longer, to you above every creature I bequeath to you the devotion of my soul. Alas, for the woe!

---

[30] Cupping. Taking blood from the patient by using a cupping glass.

Alas, for the strong pains that I have suffered for you, and for such a long time! Alas, the death! Alas, my Emily! Alas for our parting! Alas my heart's queen! Alas my bride, my heart's lady, ender of my life! What is this world? What does one ask for? At once with his love, at once in his cold grave alone, without any company! Farewell, my Emily, my sweet foe, and for the love of God take me softly in your two arms and listen to my words.

"Many days I have had strife and rancor here with my cousin Palamon, for the love of you and for jealousy. And may Jupiter, so wise, guide my soul, to speak kindly of a lover and faithfully on all points, that is to say, of fidelity, honor and knighthood, prudence, humility, station and noble lineage, nobility and all such virtues – so may Jupiter have concern for my heart, as I know of none now in this world so worthy of love as Palamon, who serves you and will his entire life. And if you shall ever wed, forget not the noble Palamon."

With that word his speech began to fail, for from his feet up to his breast had crept the cold of death that had vanquished him; and in his arms likewise the vital strength was lost and entirely gone. The intellect that dwelt in his sick and sore heart began to wane just as the heart felt death. Dusk grew before his two eyes, and breathing failed, but yet he cast his eye on his lady. His last word was "Mercy, Emily!" His spirit changed house and went to a place where I have never been – I cannot tell where.

Therefore I leave off; I am no diviner; I find nothing about souls in this volume that I follow. Nor do I care to repeat the opinions of those who write where spirits dwell. Arcite is cold. May Mars guide his soul. Now I will tell more about Emily.

Emily shrieked and Palamon roared, and Theseus took his swooning sister and bore her away from the corpse. What good is it to take all day to tell how she wept both morning and night? At such times, when their husbands have departed from them, that mostly they grieve, or fall into such sickness, to such a degree that at last they certainly die. Infinite were the sorrow and tears of people both old and of tender age throughout the town for the death of this knight; children and adults wept for him. There was not such great weeping, surely, when Hector was brought, freshly slain, to Troy. Alas for the piteous sight – scratching of cheeks, rending of hair! "Why did you have to die," these women cried, "if you had plenty of gold, and Emily?"

No man could cheer Theseus except Aegeus, his old father, who knew this world's transmutation as he had seen it change back and forth, joy after woe, woe after gladness; and he showed them examples and similar instances. "Just as a man never died that had not lived on earth in some fashion, so too a man never lived in this world," he said, "that had not died at some time. This world is only a thoroughfare full of misery, and we are pilgrims that pass back and forth; death is an end to every pain and grief in this world." Above this he said much more to the same effect, wisely exhorting the people to be consoled.

Duke Theseus deliberated with all anxious care where the sepulchre of good Arcite might best be made and most honorably to his rank. And at last his conclusion was that where first Palamon and Arcite had the battle between them for love, in that same sweet and green grove where Arcite made his complaint and bore his amorous desires and the hot flames of love, Theseus should make a fire in which the funeral rite should be performed. Then he gave orders to hew and hack the aged oaks, and lay them on rows in pieces well disposed for burning. With swift feet his officers ran and rode quickly at his command.

And then Theseus sent after a bier and overspread it all with cloth of gold, the richest that he had, and in the same he clad Arcite, with white gloves on his hands, a crown of green laurel on his head, and in his hand a bright sharp sword. He laid him on the bier with uncovered face, weeping all the while, as it was a pity to behold. And so that all the people might see the corpse, when it was day it was brought into the hall, which resounded with the sound of lament.

Then came this woeful Theban Palamon, with torn beard and rough hair all sprinkled with ash, and then Emily, surpassing others in weeping, the most pitiful in all the procession. So that the service might be the richer and more noble, Duke Theseus ordered that three steeds be led forth, with trappings of steel all glittering and bearing the armor of Lord Arcite. Upon these large white steeds sat people, of whom one bore his shield, another held his spear upright in his hands, and the third bore his Turkish bow, with quiver and trappings of burnished gold; and all rode forth slowly with sorrowful manner toward the grove.

The noblest of the Greeks there present carried the bier upon their shoulders, with slow pace and eyes wet and red, through all the city via the chief street, which was spread all with black, and hung very high with the same black. On the right hand went Aegeus the old, and on the left Duke Theseus, with vessels of pure gold in their hands full of honey, milk, wine and blood. Then came Palamon, with a great troop, and then woeful Emily, with fire in her hand, to do her duty at the funeral, as was then the custom.

Much labor and great preparation was there for the service and the making of the pyre, which reached heaven with its green top and stretched its arms twenty fathoms in breadth; that is to say, the boughs reached that far. First there were laid many loads of straw. But how the pyre was built up on high, the kinds of the trees as well (such as oak, fir, birch, aspen, alder, holm, poplar, willow, elm, plane, ash, box, chestnut, linden, laurel, maple, thorn, beech, hazel, yew, and dogwood), and how they were felled I shall not tell!

And how the gods ran up and down, disinherited of their habitation, in which they had long time dwelt in peace and rest, nymphs, fauns, and hamadryads of the woods; and how all the beasts and birds fled for fear when the wood was felled; and how the ground was aghast of the light that was not accustomed to see the bright sun; and how the fire was laid first with a bed of straw, and then with dry sticks cloven in three, and green wood, and then with spicery and cloth of gold and gems, and garlands hanging with many flowers, and myrrh and incense and sweet odors; and how Arcite lay among all this and amid what treasures; and how Emily, as was the custom, applied the funeral torch, how she swooned when the fire was made and what she spoke and what she thought; what jewels were cast into the fire when it was burning high; how some cast shields and some spears and certain of their vestments, and cups full of wine, milk and blood into the furious fire; and how the Greeks in a huge company rode three times around the fire toward the left with loud shouts, clattering their spears three times; how the ladies cried aloud three times, and Emily was led homeward; how Arcite was burned to cold ashes; and how the wake was held all that night, and how the Greeks played in the funeral games – all this I care not to tell, nor who wrestled best, naked and anointed with oil, nor who bore him best in a hard clinch; nor will I tell how they went home to Athens when the games were done.

But I will go shortly to the point and make an end of my long tale. In the process of certain years all the lament and mourning of the Greeks was ended by one general accord.

Then, as I find, a parliament was held in Athens upon certain matters and cases, among which points there was consultation concerning an alliance with certain countries, and how to have full submission of the Thebans. Thereupon this noble Theseus sent after gentle Palamon, who little knew what was the cause; but in his black clothes and with his sorrow he came hastening at the command.

Then Theseus sent for Emily. When they were seated and all the place hushed, and Theseus had delayed a moment, before a word came from his wise bosom, he fixed his eyes where he wished, and sighed softly with a grave face, and then spoke his will thus.

"When the great First Cause and Mover created the fair chain of love, great was the deed and high His intent; well He knew why, and what He designed in that. For with that fair chain of love He bound, to certain limits that they could not flee, the water and the earth, the fire and the air. That same Prince and Mover" he said, "has established in this wretched world below for all who are engendered here a certain duration of days, beyond which they may not pass, albeit indeed they may shorten those days. There is no need to cite authority here, for it is proven by experience; I wish to declare only that which is in my mind. Then may men well perceive by this order of things that this same Mover is stable and eternal.

"Well may a man know, unless he is a fool, that every part derives from its whole. Therefore Nature took not her origin from any fragment or part of a thing, but from a being stable and perfect, descending from there so far until she would become corruptible. Therefore by His wise providence He has so well ordered His works that things processes of all kinds shall endure only by renewal and not eternally. This is surely true. You may well understand and plainly see.

"Lo, the oak, which has such a long span of youth after it first begins to spring, and, as we may see, has so long a life, yet at last it wastes away. Consider also how the hard stone under our feet, on which we tread and pass, still wears down as it lies along the way. The broad river at last grows dry. The great towns we see diminish and pass. Then you may see that all these earthly things come to an end. Of man and woman we see well also that at one time or another, in youth or age, they must die, king and serving-boy alike; one in the deep sea, another on the broad plain, another in his bed. Nothing helps; all go that same way. I may well say then that all things must die.

"Who has ordained things in this way but Jupiter the

king, prince and cause of all creatures, converting all things again to their proper source from which they were derived? And to strive against this helps no creature on earth of any degree.

"Then it seems wise to me to make a virtue of necessity, and to accept well what we cannot avoid, and most chiefly that which is decreed for us all. And whoever complains commits folly and is a rebel against the governor of all things.

"And certainly it is the greatest honor to a man to die in the flower of his excellence, when he is secure of his fair reputation and has brought no shame to himself or his friend. And when he has breathed his last in honor, his friend ought to be gladder about his death than if his name had grown pale with age and his valor all forgotten. For a man's glory, then, is it best to die when he is highest in fame.

"To think the contrary of all this is stubbornness. Why would we complain? Why are we filled with sadness because good Arcite, the flower of chivalry, has departed in the course of duty and in honor from this life, this foul prison? Why do his bride and cousin complain here about the welfare of one who loved them so well? Will he thank them for it? No, God knows, not a bit! They hurt both his soul and themselves as well, and profit themselves not at all.

"How shall I conclude after this long discourse, except to say that that after woe I counsel that we should be merry and thank Jupiter for his grace! And, before we depart from here, I counsel that of two sorrows we make one perfect joy that shall last evermore; and look now to where there is the most sorrow, for there will we first begin and make amends.

"Sister," he said, "with the full agreement of my parliament, this is my decree: that by your grace you shall have pity on noble Palamon, your own knight, who serves you with will, heart, and strength, and always has since first you knew him, and that you shall take him for your lord and husband. Extend to me your hand, for this is our mandate. Show now your womanly pity. In faith, he is a king's brother's son; and though he has been a poor squire, he has served you so many years in such great adversity, believe me this ought to be considered. For gentle mercy ought to go beyond mere justice."

Then he said directly to Palamon, "I believe there is need of little preaching to make you agree to this. Draw near, take your lady's hand!"

Quickly there was made between them the bond called marriage or matrimony by all the council and all the baronage. And thus with all bliss and melody has Palamon wedded Emily, and may God that created all this wide world send all the joy and love to him who has paid for it so dearly.

Now Palamon is living in complete happiness, in bliss, in wealth, and in health. And Emily loves him so tenderly, and he serves her so gently, that never was there a word between them of jealousy or any other displeasure. Thus ends Emily and Palamon.

And may God save all this lovely company! Amen.

Here is ended the Knight's Tale.

THE MILLER'S TALE

Here follow the words between the Host and the Miller.

When the Knight had ended his tale, in the entire crowd there was nobody, young or old, who did not say it was a noble history and worthy to be called to mind; and especially each of the gentle people. Our Host laughed and swore, "So may I thrive, this goes well! The bag is unbuckled, let see now who shall tell another tale, for truly the sport has begun well. Now you, Sir Monk, if you can, tell something to repay the Knight's story with."

The Miller, who had drunk himself so completely pale that he could scarcely sit on his horse, would not take off his hood or hat, or wait and mind his manners for no one, but began to cry aloud in Pilate's voice,[1] and swore by arms and blood and head, "I know a noble tale for the occasion, to repay the Knight's story with."

Our Host saw that he was all drunk with ale and said, "Wait, Robin, dear brother, some better man shall speak first; wait, and let us work thriftily."

"By God's soul!" he said, "I will not do that! I will speak, or else go my way!"

"Tell on, in the Devil's name!" answered our Host. "You are a fool; your wits have been overcome."

"Now listen, one and all! But first," said the Miller, "I make a protestation that I am drunk; I know it by my voice. And therefore if I speak as I should not, blame it on the ale of Southwark,[2] I pray you; for I will tell a legend and a life

[1] Pilate's voice. Pilate in the mystery or Corpus Christi plays of the Middle Ages apparently spoke in an exaggerated fashion.
[2] Southwark. Borough of London.

of a carpenter and his wife, and how a scholar made a fool of the carpenter."

"Shut your trap!" the Reeve answered and said, "Set aside your rude drunken ribaldry. It is a great folly and sin to injure or defame any man, and to bring woman into such bad reputation. You can say plenty about other matters."

This drunken Miller answered back immediately and said, "Oswald, dear brother, he is no cuckold who has no wife. But I do not say, therefore, that you are one. There are many good wives, and always a thousand good to one bad. You know well that yourself, if you have not gone mad. Why are you angry now with my tale? I have a wife as well as you, by God, yet for all the oxen in my plough I would not presume to be able to judge if I may be a cuckold; I would like to believe well that I am not one. A husband should not be too inquisitive about God's private matters, nor of his wife's. He can find God's plenty there; he need not inquire about the remainder."

What more can I say, but this Miller would withhold his word for nobody, and told his churl's tale in his own fashion. I am sorry that I must repeat it here. And therefore I beg every gentle creature, for the love of God, not to judge that I tell it thus out of evil intent, but only because I must truly repeat all their tales, whether they are better or worse, or else tell some of my matter falsely. And therefore whoever wishes not to hear it, let them turn the leaf over and choose another tale; for they shall find plenty of historical matters, great and small, concerning noble deeds, and morality and holiness as well. Do not blame me if you choose incorrectly. The Miller is a churl, you know well, and so was the Reeve (and many others), and the two of them spoke of ribaldry. Think well, and do not blame me, and people should not take a game seriously as well.

Here ends the Prologue.

Here begins the Miller's Tale.

A while ago there dwelt at Oxford a rich churl fellow, who took guests as boarders. He was a carpenter by trade. With him dwelt a poor scholar who had studied the liberal arts, but all his delight was turned to learning astrology. He knew how to work out certain problems, to determine by scientific operations; if, given certain times, there should be drought or showers, or what should happen in any matter; I cannot recall them all.[3]

This scholar was named gentle Nicholas. He was well skilled in secret love and consolation; and he was also sly and secretive about it; and as meek as a maiden to look upon. He had a chamber to himself, without any company, in this lodging-house and handsomely decked with sweet herbs; and he himself was as sweet as the root of licorice or any setwall.[4] His *Almagest*,[5] and other books great and small, his astrolabe,[6] which he used in his art, and his counting-stones for calculating, all lay neatly by themselves on shelves at the head of his bed.

His clothes-press was covered with a red woolen cloth, and above it was set a pleasant psaltery,[7] on which he made melody at night so sweetly that the entire chamber was full of it. He would sing the hymn *Angelus ad Virginem*,[8] and after that the King's Note.[9] Often was his merry throat blessed. And so this sweet scholar passed his time by help of what income he had and his friends provided.

This carpenter had newly wedded a wife, eighteen years

---

[3] Them all. I.e., all of the things the scholar could calculate.

[4] Setwall. A spice similar to ginger.

[5] Almagest. Ptolemy's astrological treatise (second century, Alexandria).

[6] Astrolabe. Instrument, used especially at sea, for measuring the position of celestial bodies. It has been replaced by the sextant. Chaucer also wrote a *Treatise on the Astrolabe* explaining the use of the instrument.

[7] Psaltery. A stringed instrument, usually set on the musician's lap.

[8] *Angelus ad Virginem*. A hymn to Blessed Mother, Mary, on the event of the Annunciation.

[9] King's Note. Perhaps the medieval song "King William's Note."

of age, whom he loved more than his own soul. He was jealous, and held her closely caged, for she was young, and he was much older and judged himself likely to be made a cuckold.

His wit was rude, and he didn't know Cato's teaching that instructed that men should wed their equal. Men should wed according to their own station in life, for youth and age are often at odds. But since he had fallen into the snare, he must endure his pain, like other people.

This young wife was fair, and her body moreover was as graceful and slim as any weasel. She wore a striped silken belt, and over her loins an apron white as morning's milk, all flounced out. Her smock was white and embroidered on the collar, inside and outside, in front and in back, with coal-black silk; and of the same black silk were the strings of her white hood, and she wore a broad band of silk, wrapped high about her hair.

And surely she had a lecherous eye; her eyebrows were arched and black as a sloe berry, and partly plucked out to make them narrow. She was more delicious to look on than the young pear-tree in bloom, and softer than a lamb's wool. From her belt hung a leather purse, tasseled with silk and with beads of brass.

In all this world there is no man so wise who could imagine such a wench,[10] or so lively a little doll. Her hue shone more brightly than the noble[11] newly forged in the Tower.[12] And as for her singing, it was as loud and lively as a swallow's sitting on a barn. In addition, she could skip and make merry as any kid or calf following its mother. Her mouth was sweet as honeyed ale or mead, or a hoard of apples laid in the hay or heather. She was skittish as a jolly colt, tall as a mast, and upright as a bolt. She wore a brooch on her low collar as broad as the embossed center of a shield,

---

[10] Wench. Woman of a lower class.
[11] Noble. A coin worth six shillings, eight pence.
[12] Tower. The Tower of London, which housed the mint.

and her shoes were laced high on her legs. She was a primrose, a pig's-eye,[13] for a lord to lie in his bed or even a yeoman to wed.

Now sir, and again sir, it so chanced that this gentle Nicholas fell to play and romp with this young wife, as scholars are very artful and sly, on a day when her husband was at Osney.[14] And secretly he caught hold of her genitalia and said: "Surely, unless you will love me, sweetheart, I shall die for my secret love of you. And he held her hard by the thighs and said, "Sweetheart, love me now, or I will die, may God save me!"

She sprang back like a colt in the halter, and wriggled away with her head. "I will not kiss you, in faith," she said. Why, let me be, let me be, Nicholas, or I will cry out, 'Alas! Help!' Please mind your manners and take your hands away!"

But this Nicholas began to beg for her grace, and spoke so fairly and made such offers that at last she granted him her love and swore by Saint Thomas of Kent[15] that she would do his will when she could see her chance.

"My husband is so jealous that unless you are secretive and watch your time, I know very well I am no better than dead. You must be very sly in this thing."

"No, have no fear about that," said Nicholas. "A scholar has spent his time poorly if he can not beguile a carpenter!"

And thus they were agreed and pledged to watch for a time, as I have told. When Nicholas had done so, petted her well on her limbs, and kissed her sweetly, he took his psaltery and made melody and played fervently.

Then it happened on a holy day that this wife went to the parish church to work Christ's own works. Her forehead shone as bright as day, since she had scrubbed it when she had finished her tasks.

---

[13] Primrose, a pig's-eye. Two small flowers.

[14] Osney. Town near Oxford.

[15] Saint Thomas of Kent. Thomas à Becket.

Now at that church there was a parish clerk named Absolon. His hair was curly and shone like gold, and spread out like a large broad fan; its neat part ran straight and even. His complexion was rosy, and his eyes as gray as goose-quills. His leather shoes were carved in such a way that they resembled a window in Paul's Church. He went clad precisely and neatly all in red hose and a kirtle of light watchet[16] blue; the laces were set in it fair and thick, and over it he had a lively surplice, as white as a blossom on a twig. God bless me, but he was a sweet lad!

He knew well how to clip and shave and let blood, and make a charter for land or a deed of release. He could trip and dance in twenty ways in the manner of Oxford in that day, and cast with his legs back and forth, and play songs on a small fiddle. He could play on his cittern[17] as well, and sometimes sang in a loud treble. In the whole town there was no brew-house or tavern where any tapster might be that he did not visit in his merrymaking. But to tell the truth he was some-what squeamish about farting and rough speech.

This Absalom, so pretty and fine, went on this holy day with a censer, diligently incensing the wives of the parish, and he cast many longing looks on them, and especially on this carpenter's wife. To look at her seemed to him a joyful employment, as she was so sweet and proper and lusty; I dare say, if she had been a mouse and he a cat, he would have pounced on her immediately. And this jolly parish-clerk had such a love-longing in his heart that at the offertory he would take nothing from any wife; for courtesy, he said, he would take none.

When at night the moon shone very beautifully and Absalom planned to remain awake all night for love's sake, he took his cittern and went forth, amorous and jolly, until he came to the carpenter's house a little after the cocks had crowed, and pulled himself up by a casement-window.

---

[16] Watchet. Bilberry or blueberry.

[17] Cittern. Stringed instrument; predecessor to the guitar.

Dear lady, if your will so be,
I pray you that you pity me,

he sang in his sweet small voice, in nice harmony with his cittern.

This carpenter woke, heard his song and said without hesitation to his wife, "What, Alison! Don't you hear Absalom chanting this way under our own bedroom-wall?"

"Yes, God knows, John," she answered him, "I hear every bit of it."

Thus it went on; what more do you want to know? From day to day this jolly Absalom wooed her until he was all woe-begone. He remained awake all night and all day, he combed his spreading locks and preened himself, he wooed her by go-betweens and agents, and swore he would be her own page; he sang quavering like a nightingale; he sent her mead, and wines sweetened and spiced, and wafers piping hot from the coals, and because she was from the town he offered her money.[18] For some people will be won by rich gifts and some by blows and some by courtesy. Sometimes, to show his cheerfulness and skill, he would play Herod on a high scaffold.[19]

But in such a case what could help him? She so loved gentle Nicholas that Absalom may as well go blow the buck's-horn. For all his labor he had nothing but scorn, and thus she made Absalom her ape and turned all his earnest to a joke. This proverb is true – It is no lie. People say it is just so: "The sly nearby one makes the far dear one loathed." For though Absalom may go mad for it, because he was far from her eye, this nearby Nicholas stood in his light. Now bear yourself well, gentle Nicholas, for Absalom may wail and

---

[18] Offered her money. Perhaps in order that she might buy things with it.

[19] Play Herod on a high scaffold. Playing Herod in the Corpus Christi plays was an honor, well-known because Herod was a boisterous madman to whom the audiences responded with delight.

sing "Alack!"

And so it happened one Saturday that the carpenter had gone to Oseney, and gentle Nicholas and Alison had agreed upon this, that Nicholas would create a ruse to beguile this poor jealous husband; and if the game went as planned, she should be his, for this was his desire and hers also. And immediately, without more words, Nicholas would delay no longer, but had food and drink for a day or two carried softly into his chamber, and instructed her say to her husband, if he asked about him, that she did not know where he was; that she had not set eyes upon him all that day and she believed he was in some malady, for not even by crying out could her maid rouse him; he would not answer at all, not for anything.

Thus passed forth all that Saturday; Nicholas lay still in his chamber, and ate and slept or did what he wished, until Sunday toward sundown. This simple carpenter had great wonder about Nicholas, what could ail him. "By Saint Thomas," he said, "I am afraid all is not well with Nicholas. God forbid that he has died suddenly! This world nowadays is so ticklish, surely; to-day I saw carried to church a corpse that I saw at work last Monday. Go up, call at his door," he said to his boy, "or knock with a stone; see how it is, and tell me straight."

This boy went up sturdily, stood at the chamber-door, and cried and knocked like mad: "What! How! What are you doing, master Nicholas? How can you sleep all day long?"

But all was for nothing; he heard not a word. Then he found a hole, low down in the wall, where the cat would usually creep in; and through that he looked far into it and at last caught sight of him. Nicholas sat ever gaping upward as if he were peering at the new moon. Down went the boy, and told his master in what plight he saw this man.

The carpenter began to cross himself and said, "Help us, Saint Frideswide![20] People know little what shall happen to

[20] Saint Frideswide. Abbess, protector, and patron of Oxford, whose relics were the cause of many miracles.

them. This man with his astronomy is fallen into some madness or some fit; I always thought how it would end this way. People were not intended to know God's secrets. Yes, happy are the unlearned ones who never had schooling and knew nothing but their beliefs!

"So fared another scholar with his astronomy; he walked in the fields to look upon the stars, to see what was to happen, until he fell into a clay-pit that he did not see! But yet, by Saint Thomas,[21] I am very sorry about gentle Nicholas. By Jesus, King of Heaven, he shall be scolded for his studying if I may. Get me a staff, Robin, so that I can pry under the door while you heave it up. I believe we shall rouse him from his studying!"

And so he went to the chamber door. His boy was a strong lad, and quickly heaved the door up by the hinges, and it immediately fell flat upon the floor. Nicholas sat ever as still as a stone, ever gaping into the air. This carpenter believed he had fallen into despair, and seized him mightily by the shoulders and shook him hard and cried wildly, "What, Nicholas! What, ho! What, look down! Awake, think on Christ's passion; I cross thee[22] from elves and unearthly creatures!" And at that point he said the night-spell, toward the four corners of the house and on the outside of the threshold of the door: -

"Jesus Christ and sweet Saint Benedict
Bless this house from every wicked sprit.
For the night-hag, the white *pater noster*;[23]
Where did you go, Saint Peter's sister?"[24]

---

[21] Saint Thomas. Probably the apostle, who would not believe that Jesus had been resurrected until he saw him.

[22] I cross thee. I give you the sign of the cross. The Christian tradition is to draw with one's hand in the air or over a person or object the shape of a cross, saying "in the name of the Father, the Son, and the Holy Spirit.

[23] The white pater-noster. Variation on the Our Father prayer.

[24] Saint Peter's sister. Not clearly identified.

At last this gentle Nicholas began to sigh sorely and said, "Alack! Shall the entire world be destroyed again now?"

"What are you saying?" said the carpenter. "What now! Think on God, as we do, we men that work."

"Fetch me a drink," said Nicholas, "and after I will speak privately of a certain thing that concerns you and me both. I will tell it to no other man, you can be sure."

The carpenter went down and came again bringing a large quart of mighty ale; and when each of them had drunk his share, Nicholas shut his door fast and set the carpenter down beside him.

"John, my dear host," he said, "you shall swear to me here on your honor that you will reveal this secret to no creature; for it is Christ's own secret that I show you, and if you tell it to any you are a lost man. For this vengeance you will receive, therefore: if you betray me, you shall run mad!"

"No, may Christ and His holy blood forbid!" said this simple man. "I am no blabber, and though I say it myself, I am not wont to prate. Say what you will, I shall never utter it to any man, woman or child, by Him That harrowed hell!"[25]

"Now, John, I will not deceive you," said Nicholas; "I have found by my astrology, as I have been looking at the shining moon, that now on next Monday, about a quarter through the night, there shall fall a rain so wild and mad that never was Noah's flood half so great. This world shall all be drowned in less than an hour, so hideous shall be the downpour. Thus shall all mankind perish in the flood."

"Alas, my wife! And shall she drown?" this carpenter answered, and nearly fell over for sorrow. "Alas, my Alison! Is there no remedy?"

"Why yes, before God, if you will work according to wise advising," said gentle Nicholas; "but you may not work out of your own head. For thus says Solomon, and he was

---

[25] Harrowed hell. When Christ died on Good Friday, he went to hell to retrieve the souls of all the good people who had died before him, thus harrowing (raiding or pillaging) the souls from hell.

right trustworthy, 'Work all by counsel, and you shall never repent.' And if you will work after good advice, I undertake without mast or sail to save both her and you and me. Have you not heard how Noah was saved, when our Lord had warned him that the entire world should be destroyed with water?"

"Yes," said the carpenter, "I heard it long, long ago."

"Have you not heard also," said Nicholas, "the woe that Noah and his sons had before he could get his wife aboard? He had rather than all his black rams then, I dare be bound, that she had had a ship all to herself! Do you know then what is best to do? This thing calls for haste, and on an urgent matter one may not preach or delay. Go immediately and get us directly into this house a kneading-trough or else a brewing-tub for each of us (but make sure that they are large), in which we may swim as if in a barge and have in enough provisions for a day – we will need no more. The water shall slacken and run off about nine o'clock on the next day. But Robin your boy must not know of this, and I cannot save your maid Jill either. Do not ask why, for even if you ask me I will not tell God's secret. It ought to suffice you, if your wits are not turning, to have as great a grace as Noah had. I shall save your wife, I promise you. Go your way now, and make haste.

"But when you have obtained these three kneading-tubs for us three, then you shall hang them from the rafters high in the roof, so that nobody will notice our device. And when you have done this, and laid our provisions in them nicely, and an axe as well to strike the cord in two when the water comes, and when you have broken a hole on high in the gable toward the garden over the barn, so that we may freely go on our way when the great shower is past - then you will float as merrily, I will be bound, as the white duck after her drake. Then will I call out, 'How, Alison! How, John! Be merry; the flood will soon pass.' And you will answer, 'Hail, Master Nicholas! Good morning, I see you well, it is daylight now!' And then we shall be lords over the entire world until we die, just as Noah and his wife!

"But one thing I warn you of strictly. Be well advised on that night when we have entered aboard ship that none of us speaks a word, neither calls nor cries, but we must be in our prayers. For that is God's own precious command. And your wife and you must hang far apart, so that there will be no folly between you, no more in looking than in action. Now that all this plan is explained to you; go, and may God help you! Tomorrow at night, when people are all in bed, we will creep into our kneading-tubs and sit there, awaiting God's grace. Go your way now; I have no time to make a longer sermon of this. Men say thus: "Send the wise and say nothing." You are so wise that there is no need to teach you. Go, save our lives, I entreat you."

This simple carpenter went his way often crying "alack!" and "alas!", and told the secret to his wife. And she was wary, and knew better than he what this quaint plan was about. But nevertheless she acted as if she would die, and said, "Alas! Go your way at once and help us to escape, or else we are all lost; I am your true, faithful wedded wife. Go, dear spouse, and help to save us!

Lo, how great a thing is feeling! Men may die of imagination, so deep may the impression be. This simple fellow began to quake; he thought he could truly hear Noah's flood come wallowing like the sea to drown his honey sweet Alison; he wept, wailed and made sorrowful expression, and he sighed with many a sorry gust. He went and got himself a kneading-trough, and after that a tub and a cask, sent them secretly to his house and hung them in the roof. With his own hand he made three ladders, to climb by the rungs and uprights into the tubs hanging among the beams; and supplied tub and trough and cask with bread and cheese as well as good ale in a large jug, sufficient for a day. But before he had made all this gear, he sent his serving boy and girl to London about his business. And as it drew toward night on the Monday, he lit no candle, but shut the door and ordered all things as they should be; and, in brief, up they all three climbed, and sat still for the space of time that it would take to walk a furlong.[26]

"Now mum, and say a *pater noster*!" said Nicholas; and "Mum!" said John, and "Mum!" Alison. This carpenter sat still and said his prayers, ever listening for the rain, if he could hear it.

The dead sleep, for very weariness and apprehension, fell on this carpenter right about curfew-time or a little later, as I suppose; he groaned sorely in the travail of his spirit, and eke snored, for his head lay uneasily. Down the ladder stalked Nicholas, and Alison sped down very softly; and they were in mirth and glee, until the bells began to sound for lauds, and friars in the chancel began to sing.

This parish-clerk, amorous Absalom, always so woe-begone for love, was at Oseney on that Monday to amuse himself and make merry, with a party; and by chance he secretly asked a cloister-monk after John the carpenter. The monk drew him aside out of the church. "I know not," he said; "I have not seen him work here since Saturday. I believe he has gone where our abbot has sent him for timber, for he is accustomed to go for timber and remain at the grange a day or two. Or else he is at home, certainly. In truth I cannot say where he is."

This Absalom grew very merry of heart, and thought, "Now is the time to wake all night, for certainly since daybreak I have not seen him stirring about his door. On my soul, at cockcrow I shall knock secretly at his window which stands low upon his chamber-wall. To Alison now will I tell the whole of my love-longing, and now I shall not fail at the least to have a kiss from her. I shall have some sort of comfort, in faith. My mouth has itched all day long; that is a sign of kissing at least. All night also I dreamed I was at a festival. Therefore I will go sleep an hour or two, and then I will

[26] Furlong. One-eighth of a mile, or 220 yards.

wake all night in mirth."

When the first cock had crowed, up rose this frisky lover, and arrayed him handsomely in the finest detail. But first he chewed cardamom and licorice to smell sweetly, before he had combed his hair, and put a true-love charm under his tongue, for by this he hoped to find favor. He rambled to the carpenter's house and stood still under the casement, which was so low it reached to his breast. He softly coughed with a gentle sound: "Where are you, sweet Alison, honeycomb?[27] My fair bird, my darling! Awake, sweet cinnamon, and speak to me. You think very little upon my sorrow, and how I sweat for your love wherever I go! No wonder though I languish and sweat! I mourn like a lamb after the dug. In faith, darling, I have such love-longing that I mourn like the true turtle-dove. I cannot eat, no more than a maiden."

"Go from the window, Jack-fool," she said. "On my soul, there will be no singing "Come kiss me now." I love another better than you, by Jesus, Absalom; otherwise, I would be at fault. Go on your way, or I will cast a stone at you, and let me sleep, in the name of twenty devils!"

"Alas!" he said. "and welaway! Oh, that true love was ever so badly abused! Then kiss me, since it may be no better, for Jesus' love, and for the love of me."

"Will you then go your way with that?" she said.

"Yes, surely, sweetheart," said this Absolon.

"Then make yourself ready," she said, "I am coming now."

And to Nicholas she said silently, "Now hush, and you shall laugh your fill."

This Absolon set himself down on his knees and said, "I am a lord of the highest degree; for after this I hope there will come more. Sweetheart, your grace, and sweet bird, your favor!"

She unlatches the window, and does so in haste. "Take

[27] Honeycomb. Some of the language in this speech is borrowed from the Biblical Song of Songs.

this," she said, "come now, and move quickly, lest our neighbors see you."

This Absolon wiped his mouth dry. Dark as pitch, or as coal, was the night, and at the window she put out her hole, and Absolon, who knew no better or worse but with his mouth he kissed her naked ass so sweetly, before he was aware of this.

He started aback, and thought something was amiss, for well he knew a woman has no beard. He felt something all rough and long-haired, and said, "Fy! alas! What have I done?"

"Tee hee!" she said, and shut the window, and Absolon went forth with troubled steps.

"A beard! A beard!" said handy Nicholas, "By God's body, this goes fair and well."[28]

This foolish Absolon heard every bit, and on his lips he began to bite angrily, and said to himself, "I shall pay you back."

Who rubs now, and who chafes now, his lips with dust, with sand, with straw, with cloth, with chips, but Absolon, who says over and over, "Alas! I commend my soul unto Satan"? But I would rather be revenged for this insult" he said, "than own this entire town. Alas," he said, "alas, that I did not turn aside!"

His hot love was now cold and entirely quenched; for from that moment that he had kissed her ass, he cared not a straw for things of love, for he was healed of his sickness.[29] Often the things of love he defied, and wept as does a child that is beaten.

This Absalom walked slowly across the street to a smith called Master Gervase, who forged plough-instruments at his forge. He was busily sharpening coulter and share[30] when

---

[28] Fair and well. Absolon's tone is sarcastic at this point.

[29] Sickness. I.e., his love-sickness.

[30] Coulter and share. The share, or ploughshare, is the main cutting blade on a plough; it is set behind the coulter set at the front of the plough.

Absalom knocked very gently and said, "Unlock the door, Gervase, and do it quickly."

"What! Who are you?"

"It is me, Absalom."

"What, Absalom! By the cross, why are you up so early? Eh, God bless! What ails you? Some pretty girl, God knows, has brought you to stir so early. By Saint Neot,[31] you know well what I mean!"

This Absalom cared not a peascod for all his mocking, and returned not a word in kind. He had more wool on his distaff[32] than Gervase knew, and said, "Dear friend, that hot coulter in the chimney – lend it to me. I have something to do with it; and I will bring it you again right away.

"Surely," answered Gervase, "even if it were gold or nobles in a bag all uncounted, you should have it, as I am a faithful smith! Eh, the Devil, what do you want to do with it?"

"That is as it may be," said Absalom. I shall tell you tomorrow;" and he took up the coulter by the cool handle. Softly he went out the door and went to the wall of the carpenter's house. He coughed first, and knocked upon the window as well, as he did before.

"Who is there that knocks so?" Alison answered. "I warrant it a thief!"

"Why nay," he said, "God knows, my sweet, I am your Absalom, my sweetheart. I have brought you a ring of gold; my mother gave it me, on my life! It is very fine and nicely engraved. I will give you this, if you kiss me!"

This Nicholas thought he would amend all the sport; he should kiss him before he escaped! Back he put the window in haste, and out he put himself. Thereupon spoke this clerk Absalom, "Speak, sweet bird, I know not where thou art;" and then he was ready with his hot iron and smote Nicholas therewith.

---

[31] St Neot. A saint of Glastonbury.

[32] More wool on his distaff. I.e., more troubles on his mind.

Off went the skin, about a hands-breadth around, the hot coulter burned his rump so, and for the pain he thought he would die. "Help! Water, water! Help, help, for God's sake!" he cried like a madman.

The carpenter started out of his slumber; he heard one cry wildly "Water!", and thought, "Alas! Noah's flood is coming now!" He sat up without a word, and with his axe struck the cord in two, and down went tub and all; they stopped for nothing until they came to the floor, and there he lay in a swoon.

Up started Alison and Nicholas, and cried "Help!" and "Alack!" in the street.

The neighbors young and old ran to stare upon John as he lay yet in a swoon, for with the fall he had broken his arm. But he had to deal with his own trouble, for when he spoke he was talked down by gentle Nicholas and Alison. They told everyone that he was mad, that he was so terrified of "Noah's flood" in his fantasy that through his folly he had bought himself three kneading-tubs and had hung them in the roof above; and had prayed them for God's sake to sit with him in the roof, to keep him company.

People laughed at his odd quirk; into the roof they peered and gawked, and turned all his trouble into mirth. For whatever the carpenter answered, it was all for nought; nobody listened to his words. He was so sworn down by the great oaths of the others that in the entire city he was considered mad. Every scholar then agreed with every other scholar: "the man is mad, my dear brother!" And every creature laughed over this commotion.

Thus the carpenter wife was fornicated with, despite all his watching and jealousy; and Absolon kissed her nether eye; and Nicholas was scalded in the rump.

This tale is done, and may God save this entire company.

Here ends the Miller's Tale.

THE REEVE'S TALE

The Prologue of the Reeve's Tale

When people had laughed at this plight of Absalom and of gentle Nicholas, various people said various things, but for the most part they laughed and made merry over the tale, and I did not see anyone take it badly except Oswald the Reeve. Because he was a carpenter by trade, a little anger was still lingering in his heart, and he began to grumble and to condemn it a little.

"By my soul, I could pay you back well," he said, "with a tale about the hoodwinking of a bold miller, if I wished to speak of ribaldry. But I am old and do not wish to make sport; my grass-time is over, all my fodder now is hay; this white pate writes me as an old man, and my heart is as dried up as my hair. If not, I am like a medlar[1] that grows softer and worse until it lies rotten among muck or straw. We old men, I fear, we move along in such a way that we cannot be ripe until we are rotten.

"We dance as long as the world will pipe to us, for we are always pricked by our desire to have a hoary head and a tail as green as a leek. Though our strength may be gone, our will always desires for folly, for when we cannot do it we will still talk about it. Still there is fire, if you rake over our old ashes. We have four burning coals – boasting, lying, anger and greed. These four sparks belong to old age. In truth, our old limbs may be feeble, but our desire does not fail us.

"As many a year as has passed since my tap of life began to run, I have always kept my colt's tooth. Truly, when I was born, Death drew out the tap of life and let it run, and ever

[1] Medlar. Small fruit resembling a crab apple.

since it has so run until now the cask is nearly empty. The stream of life now trickles in upon the rim. The poor old tongue may well ring and chime of wretchedness long past; with old folk nothing is left except senility."

When our Host had heard this homily, he began to speak as lordly as a king. "What does all this wisdom amount to?" he said. "Are we to talk all day of Holy Scripture? The Devil made a shipman or a doctor out of a cobbler, and the Devil made a reeve into a preacher! Do not dally with the time. Tell us your tale. Lo, Deptford,[2] and it is half-way to prime;[3] lo, Greenwich,[4] where there are many rascals! It is surely time to begin your tale."

"Now, sirs, I pray you all not to take it badly," said this Oswald the Reeve, "though I may answer this Miller and make a fool of him. For it is lawful for a man to shove away force with force. This drunken Miller has told us here how a carpenter was beguiled, perhaps in mockery, because I am one. And by your leave I shall requite him directly, even in his own churlish language. I pray to God, may his neck break! He can well see a sliver in my eye, but cannot see a beam of wood in his own.

Here begins the Reeve's Tale.

At Trumpington, not far from Cambridge, there runs a brook over which stand a bridge and a mill. And this is the very truth that I tell you. For a long time there was a miller dwelling there, as proud and gay as any peacock. He could play the bagpipes, fish, mend nets, turn cups,[5] wrestle well, and shoot. He wore by his belt a very sharp-bladed sword, and a long cutlass, and in his pouch he carried a jolly dagger.

---

[2] Deptford. About five miles from London.

[3] Half-way to Prime. This might mean half-way between the prayer service of Lauds, at dawn, and Prime, an hour or so later, around 6:00, but most scholars agree that it means around 7:30.

[4] Greenwich. About one-half mile beyond Deptford.

[5] Turn cups. This may mean that he can make wooden cups on a lathe or that he can drink (turn over his cup) well.

There was no man who dared to touch him for fear of peril! And in his hose he carried a Sheffield knife as well. His skull was as bald as an ape's, his face was round, and his nose a pug. He was a notable swaggerer at markets. No creature dared to lay a hand on him, for he swore he should pay dearly for it. He was a thief of grain and ground meal, and a sly and tiresome one at that, in truth. He was called Simkin the Bully.

He had a wife, of noble blood; the parson of the town was her father, who gave as her dowry many pieces of brass kitchen ware, so that Simkin might marry into his kin. She had been brought up in a nunnery; Simkin would have no wife, he affirmed, unless she were well nurtured and a virgin, for the sake of his social rank as a yeoman. And she was proud and pert as a magpie. The two together were a fair sight on holy days; he would walk before her with the tail of his hood wound about his head, and she came after him in a red petticoat, and Simkin wore hose of the same color.

No creature dared call her anything but "madam." There was no man so bold that he would walk near her or dared once to flirt or dally with her, unless he wished to be slain by Simkin with a cutlass or knife or dagger. For jealous people are always perilous – at least they would have their wives believe so. And because she was somewhat smirched in her name,[6] she was as repellent as water in a ditch, and full of disdain and of insolence. She thought ladies should treat her with respect, on account of her lineage and of the nurturing she had gained in the nunnery.

They had between them a twenty-year-old daughter and no other children, except one of six months; it lay in a cradle, and was a proper lad. This young lady was sturdy and well grown, with broad hips and round high breasts, and a pug-nose and eyes gray as glass. Her hair was rather pretty, I will not deny it.

---

[6] Smirched in her name. She is the illegitimate daughter of a priest or parson.

Because she was attractive, the parson of the town intended to make her his heir of both his movable property and his house. And he made plenty of fuss about her marriage; his purpose was to present her well into some family of exalted lineage and blood. For Holy Church's goods must be spent on the blood that is descended from Holy Church; therefore, he meant to dignify his holy blood, even if he had to devour the Holy Church.[7]

This miller surely collected a great toll on the wheat and malt from all the surrounding lands. And most notably there was a great college that is called King's Hall at Cambridge, all the wheat and malt for which were ground by him. It happened one day that the manciple[8] of the college fell ill of some sickness; they deemed that surely he could never recover. Therefore this miller stole a hundred times more of the meal and corn than any other time. Before this he stole only courteously, but now he was a thief outrageously. The warden reproached him for this and made much ado about it, but the miller did not care one straw about it, and blustered fiercely and said it was not so.

Now there dwelt in this Hall that I tell of two young poor scholars. They were bold and headstrong and lusty in sport, and they eagerly begged of the warden, only for the fun and joy of it, to grant them a leave for only a little while to go to the mill and see their corn ground. And truly they would wager their own heads that the miller would steal half a peck of corn from them by cunning or plunder it from them by force. And at last the warden gave them leave. One of them was named John, and the other, Alan. They were born in the same town; it was called Strother, far in the north. I cannot

[7] Devour the Holy Church. This odd sentence is meant to be humorous. The Miller is playing on the idea that the Church must take care of its people: in this case the profligate father of his wife, i.e., the parson, must pay for his indiscretion.

[8] Manciple. A purchaser of provisions, usually for a college, abbey, or monastery.

tell exactly where.

This Alan, the scholar, prepared everything that he needed to take, cast the sack of corn over a horse, and went forth with John. And they wore good swords and bucklers by their thighs. John knew the way; so they needed no guide. And he laid down the sack at the mill door.

Alan spoke first: "All hail, Simon, in faith! How is your wife, and your fair daughter?"

"Alan, welcome, by my head!" Simkin said. "And John too! How are you, and what are you doing here?"

"Simon," replied John, "by God, need has na peer.[9] It behooves him to serve himself that has na equal, as scholars say, or else he is a fool. I believe our manciple will die soon, so the jaws waggle in his head. And therefore I have come with Alan to grind our corn and carry it home. I pray you help us along from here as fast as you can."

"In faith it shall be done," Simkin said. "What will you do while it is being milled?"

"By God, I will be here right by the hopper," John said, "and see how the corn gaes in. By my father's soul, I never yet saw how the hopper wags to and fra."

"And do you wish to do swa?" answered Alan. "Then, by my pate, I will be beneath, and see how the meal falls down into the trough; that sail be my amusement. In faith, John, I must be of your class, I am as poor a miller as you."

This miller smiled at their simplicity. "All this is only done as a stratagem," he thought; "they deem no man can beguile them. But I vow by my trade, for all the craftiness in their philosophy, I shall still blear their eyes. The more cunning trick they try, the more I will take when I steal. I shall give them bran yet in the place of flour. "The greatest schol-

[9] Na peer. As noted a bit earlier in the story, John and Alan are from northern England, which Chaucer shows in their dialect. In this translation, many of Chaucer's touches have been maintained, such as na (no), swa (so), fra (fro), sall (shall), gane (gone), alsa (also), bath (both), ga or gae (go), ane (one), twa (two), sang (song), and sawl (soul).

ars are not the wisest men," as the mare once said to the wolf.[10] I would not give a weed for their art.

Out the door he secretly went when he saw his time. He looked up and down until he found the scholars' horse where it stood tied under an arbor behind the mill; and went softly to the horse and swiftly stripped off the bridle. And when the horse was loose, he started forth with a "Wehee!" through thick and thin toward the fen, where wild mares ran.

This miller went back. He did not say a word, but did his business and chatted with the scholars until their corn was ground nicely and well. And when the meal was sacked and fastened, John went out and found his horse gone, and began to cry, "Help! Alack! Our horse is lost! Alan, for God's sake, man, step on your feet, come out at once! Alas, our warden has lost his palfrey!"

Alan forgot everything, including the meal and wheat. His careful management of the situation entirely escaped his mind. "What!" he began to cry. "Which way is he gane?"

The wife came leaping in with a run. "Alas!" she said, "your horse is going to the fen with wild mares, as fast as he can gallop. Curses on the hand that bound him so poorly, he should have tied the rein better."

"Alas!" said John. "By the Cross, Alan, lay down your sword, and I will mine alsa. I am nimble, God knows, as a deer. By God, he shall not escape us bath! Why had you not pit the nag in the barn? A curse on you, Alan. You are a fool."

These poor scholars ran hard toward the marsh, both Alan and John. And when the miller saw they were off, he took half a bushel of their flour, and told his wife to go and knead it in a loaf.

"I believe the scholars were afraid of what I might do. A miller can still," he said, "trim a scholar's beard for all his

---

[10] Mare to the wolf. The mare told the wolf, who wanted to buy her foal, that the price was written on her hind foot. When he tried to read it, she kicked him. (Benson)

art; now let them go where they will. Lo, there they go! By my pate, it's not so easy for them to get that horse. Yes, let the children play!"

These poor scholars ran up and down, with "Whoa, whoa! Gee! Stop, stop! Ha! Look out behind! Gae whistle you while I head him off here!" But, in brief, they could not with all their power catch their nag, he always ran so fast, until at length they caught him in a ditch when it was dark night.

Wet and weary, like a beast in the rain, poor John came, and Alan with him. "Alack the day I was born!" said John. "Now we are brought to mockery and ridicule; our corn is stolen. People will call us fools, bath the warden and all our friends, and especially the miller. Alack the day!"

Thus John lamented as he walked along the road toward the mill, leading Bayard the horse by the bridle. He found the miller sitting by the fire, for it was night. They could go no further then, but begged him for the love of God to give them lodging and food, for their payment.

"If there be any," the miller replied, "such as it is, you shall have your part in it. My house is small; but you have studied book learning, so you know how to make twenty feet of space a mile wide through argumentation. Let see now if this house may suffice, or make it bigger by your talking, as you scholars usually do."

"Now, Simon," said John, "you are always merry, by Saint Cuthbert, and that was fairly answered. I have heard it said that a man shall choose ane of twa things: either just as he finds or just as he brings. But especially I pray you, dear host, get us some food and drink and be friendly, and we will pay faithfully and completely. One can lure no hawks with an empty hand; lo, here is our silver, all ready to spend!"

This miller dispatched his daughter into town for ale and bread, and roasted a goose for them, and secured their horse so that it would not go astray any more. He made them a bed in his own chamber, nicely decked with sheets and blankets, only eight or ten feet from his own bed. His daughter had a bed to herself right in the same chamber very close at hand. It could be no other way, and the reason is that there was no larger room in the place.

They supped and talked and amused themselves, and drank ever deeper of the strong ale, and about midnight went to rest.

Well had this miller varnished his head with the beer, for he had drunk himself all pale and lost all the red in his flesh. He belches and speaks through his nose as if he had a frog in his throat or a cold. His wife went to bed also, as light and frisky as any jay, so well had she wet her jolly whistle. The cradle was put at the foot of her bed, so that she might rock it and nurse the child.

And when all that was in the crock had been drunk, the daughter went to bed. And Alan and John went to bed as well. None of them took anything else; they needed no sleeping potion! Truly, the miller had so gulped his ale that he snorted in his sleep like a horse. His wife bore him a full strong bass; one could have heard their snoring two furlongs away. The daughter snored also, to keep them company.

Alan the scholar, hearing all this tunefulness, poked John and said, "Are you sleeping? Have you ever heard such a sang before this? Lo, what a compline[11] they are singing among them. May Saint Antony's fire[12] fall on their bodies! Wha ever heard such an amazing thing? Yea, may they come to the best of bad ends! This lang night I shall get na sleep; but yet na matter, all shall be for the best. For, John, if I could sleep with that young lady over there, the law would allow us some compensation. For, John, there is a law that says that if a man be harmed in one point, he shall be re-

---

[11] Compline. The last prayer office of the day, after darkness falls.

[12] St. Anthony's Fire. Ergotism, a disease that comes from eating grain infected by the ergot fungus and affects the sufferer with inflamed skin. (Chaucer only mentions "wylde fyr," but most have assumed that he means St. Anthon's Fire.

lieved in another. Our corn is stolen, without a doubt, and all day we have had an bad time; and since all that cannot be remedied, I shall have some easement to counter my loss. By my sawl, it shall nat be otherwise.

"Be careful, Alan," John answered. "The miller is a dangerous man, and if he would start out of his sleep he might do us bath an injury.

"I do not count him as much as a fly," Alan replied, and up he rose. He crept up to the young woman (she lay upright[13] and fast asleep) until he was so close to her that, if she were to see him, it would be too late for her to cry out. And, to make a long story short, they were soon one. Go ahead and play, Alan, for I will now speak of John.

John lay still for about a furlong's length[14] or two, and pities himself, and feels woeful. "Alan" he said, "this is a wicked trick. I would say now that I am just a fool. Yet my friend has gained something for his trouble; he has the Miller's daughter in his arms. He took a risk and has accomplished his purpose, and I lie here like a sack of chaff[15] in my bed; and when this prank is retold another day, I shall be thought a fool, a weakling. I will rise and risk it, by my faith! 'One who is not bold is not lucky!' as they say." And up he rose, and softly he went to the cradle, took it up with his hand, and bore it to the foot of his own bed.

Soon after this the wife stopped snoring, awoke, went out to pee, returned again, could not find her cradle, and groped here and there but did not find it. "Alas," she said, "I almost went to the wrong place; I almost went to the scholar's bed. Ah, God bless! Then I would have made a bad mistake. And she went forth and found the cradle. She groped along with

---

[13] Upright. Some editors take upright to mean on her back, but many people did sleep upright, believing that sleeping flat on the bed was bed for their health.

[14] Furlong's length. The length of time it would take to walk a furlong (an eighth of a mile, 220 yards); a few minutes.

[15] Chaff. The discarded part of a grain, used to feed livestock.

her hand, found the bed, and thought all was well since the cradle stood next to it. And she did not know where she was since it was dark.

And softly and carefully she crept into bed with the scholar, and lay perfectly still, and would have fallen asleep. In a while John the scholar leapt up and with all his energy laid on this wife. She had not had such a good time for a long time. He pierced hard and deep, as if he were a madman.

These two scholars led this jolly life until the cock crowed the third time.[16] Alan grew weary in the time before dawn, for he had labored all night long, and said Farewell Malyne, sweet one! The day has come; I can stay no longer. But forever, wherever I may ride or go, I am your own scholar, I swear!"

"Dear sweetheart," she said, "now go, and farewell! But before you go, I will tell you one thing. When you pass the mill going homeward, right at the entrance behind the door you will find a loaf that was made of a half a bushel of your own meal, which I helped my father to take. And now, good friend, may God save and keep you." And with that word she began to weep.

Alan rose up and thought, "Before it is day I will go creep in next to my fellow;" and then his hand touched the cradle. "By God," he thought, "I have gone all wrang; my head is all giddy tonight, and therefore I am not walking straight. I know well by the cradle, here lie the miller and his wife, and I have gone the wrong way."

And with the Devil's own luck, he went forth to the bed where the miller lay. He thought to have crept in next to his fellow John, but he crept in by the miller and caught him by the neck and said softly, "John, you swine's head, awake, for Christ's soul, and listen to this noble game! For, by the lord who is called Saint James, in this short night I have coupled three times with the miller's daughter lying flat on her back,

[16] Cock crowed. This usually occurs about an hour before dawn.

while you have, you coward, been afraid."

"You – false knave!" said the miller. "Ah, false traitor, false scholar! You shall die, by God's dignity!" And he caught Alan by the throat. Alan caught him in turn furiously, and struck him on the nose with his fist. Down ran the bloody stream onto the miller's breast, and on the floor they wallowed like two pigs in a poke, with nose and mouth crushed and bleeding.

Up they got, and down again, until the miller stumbled against a stone and fell down backward upon his wife, who knew nothing of this ridiculous fight. With a shock she started up, and cried, "Help, Holy Cross of Bromholm![17] Lord, I call to you! *In manus tuas*![18] Awake, Simon, the fiend has dropped on us. My heart is crushed! Help, I have been killed! Some one lies on my head and body; help, Simon! The false scholars are fighting!"

John started up as fast as ever he could, and groped to and fro by the wall to find a staff. She started up also, and knew the room better than John did, and directly found a staff by the wall. She saw a little shimmer of light where the moon shone in through a hole, and by it she saw the two of them, but in truth knew not which was which, except that she saw something white in her eye.

When she caught a glimpse of a white thing, she thought one of the scholars had worn a night-cap, and drew nearer with the staff and thought to strike this Alan a shrewd rap, but struck the miller on the bald pate. Down he went, crying, "Help, I am dying!" These scholars beat him well, and let him lie. They dressed and quickly took their horse and their meal and went their way. And at the mill they took their loaf also, baked with half a bushel of flour

Thus was the proud miller well beaten, and has lost his toll for grinding their wheat, and paid every penny for the

---

[17] Holy Cross of Bromholm. A famous shrine in Norfolk.

[18] *In manus tuas.* Luke 23:46: *Into your hands* I commend my spirit. The phrase was uttered by Christ on the cross just before his death.

supper of Alan and John who beat him well. Lo, such a thing it is for a miller to be false! And therefore this proverb is entirely true: "An evil-doer should not hope for good deeds." And may God Who sits on high in glory save all this company, high and low. Thus have I requited the Miller in my tale.

Here is ended the Reeve's Tale.

THE WIFE OF BATH'S TALE

The Prologue of the Wife of Bath's Tale

Experience, though it may be of no authority[1] in this world, would be quite sufficient for me, in speaking of the woe that is in marriage; for, gentle people, since I was twelve years old – thank God, Who lives forever – I have had five husbands at the church-door (for I have been wedded so often); and all were worthy men in their ranks. But in truth I was told not long ago that since Christ went only once to a wedding, in Cana of Galilee,[2] by that same example he taught me that I should be wedded only once. Lo! Hear what a sharp word Jesus, man and God, spoke on a certain occasion beside a well, in reproof of the Samaritan woman.[3] He said, 'You have had five husbands; and that man who has you now is not your husband.' Thus he said, certainly. What he meant by it I cannot say; but I ask, why the fifth man was no husband to the Samaritan woman.

"How many could she have in marriage? At this point I have never in my life heard a designation of the number. Men may divine and interpret up and down, but well I know, surely, God expressly instructed us to increase and multiply. I can well understand that noble text. Likewise, I know well he said also that my husband should leave father and mother

---

[1] Experience…authority. The Wife is trying to make the case that she can make her case based on her life experience, as opposed to the authority of learnèd men.

[2] Wedding at Cana. John 2:1-12. Jesus performed his first miracle at the wedding in Cana, at which he turned water into wine.

[3] Samaritan woman. John 4:1-42. The Wife of Bath is largely accurate in her retelling of the story, though her reaction is suspect.

and take me. But he did not mention any number, not bigamy or octogamy. Why should men speak villainously of them?

"Lo, Sir Solomon[4] the wise king! I believe he had more than one wife, and I wish to God it were lawful for me to be refreshed half so often! What a gift of God he had in all his wives! No man who lives in this world now has so many. God knows this noble king, to my thinking, had a merry life with each of them, so joyous was his lot! Blessed be God that I wedded five! And they were the best that I could pick out, both in their bodies and of their coffers. Study in a variety of schools makes perfect scholars, and much practice in a variety of employments truly makes the perfect workman. I have the schooling of five husbands: I would welcome the sixth, whenever he shall come! In truth, I will not keep myself wholly chaste; when my husband has departed from the world, then some other Christian man shall wed me. For then, the apostle[5] says, I am free, in God's name, to wed where I wish.

"He says that it is no sin to be wedded; it is better to be wedded than to burn. What do I care if people speak badly of cursed Lamech[6] and his bigamy? Well I know Abraham[7] was a holy man, and Jacob[8] as well, as far as I know, and each of them had more than two wives. And many other holy men did as well.

"When have you seen that in any time great God forbade marriage explicitly? Tell me, I pray you. Or where did he command virginity? You know as well as I, without a doubt,

---

[4] Solomon. OT King, second son of David, who ruled Israel about 970-933 in great prosperity; known for his great wisdom.

[5] Apostle. Paul.

[6] Lamech. Genesis 4:23ff. A descendant of Cain and the first bigamist, he was married to Adah and Zillah.

[7] Abraham. Genesis. Biblical patriarch of the Hebrew nation who had two wives, Sarah and Hagar, and one concubine, Keturah.

[8] Jacob. Genesis. Abraham's grandson, who also had two wives, Leah and Rachel.

that the apostle, when he speaks of maidenhood, says that he had no instructions on it. Men may counsel a woman to be single, but counseling is not commanding; he left it to our own judgment. For if God had commanded maidenhood, then with that same word had he condemned marrying. And certainly, if no seed were sown, from where then should virgins spring? Paul dared not command a thing for which his master gave no order. The prize is set for virginity – win it who can. Let us see who runs best.[9]

"But this command is not to be taken by every creature, but only where Almighty God wishes to give it through his might. The apostle was a virgin, I know well, but nevertheless, though he wrote that he wished every creature to be like him, all that is only advice to be a virgin; and he gave me leave and indulgence to be a wife. So likewise, if my spouse should die, there is no shame or charge of bigamy to marry me. It would be good, he said, to touch no woman, for it is a peril to bring together fire and hay. You know what this example may mean.

"This is the sum of it all: the apostle held virginity to be more perfect than marriage because of weakness. I call them weak unless man and wife would lead all their life in chastity. I grant it well, I have no malice even if maidenhood were set above remarriage. It pleases them to be clean, body and soul; of my own estate I will make no boast. For you well know that not every vessel in a lord's house is made of gold; some are of wood, and do their lord service. God calls people to him in various manners, and each one has his own gift from – one this, one that, as it pleases God to provide. Virginity is a great perfection, and devoted chastity as well.

"But Christ, the fountain of perfection, did not instruct every person to go sell all that he had and give to the poor, and in such a fashion follow him and his footsteps. "He spoke this to those people who wished to be perfect; and by

[9] Who runs the best. Virginity is seen here as the prize awarded to the winner of a race.

your leave, gentle people, I am not one of those. I will use the flower[10] of my life in the acts and fruits of marriage.

"Tell me also, for what purpose were members of procreation made, and made in such a perfect manner? Trust well, they were not made for nothing. Whosoever wishes to interpret may do so, and interpret things up and down that and say that they were made for purging urine and that both our small things were also to know a female from a male and for no other cause – did someone say no? Those with experience know well it is not so. So that scholars will not be angry with me, I say this: that they are made for both; that is to say, for duty and for ease of procreation, providing we do not displease God. Why should men otherwise set down in their books that man shall yield to his wife her debt? Now with what should he make his payment, if he did not use his blessed instrument? They were made then upon a creature to purge urine, and for procreation as well.

"But I do not say that every person who has such equipment is bound to go and use it for procreation. For that reason people should men take no heed of chastity. Christ was a virgin and created as a man, as were many saints since the beginning of the world; yet they always lived in perfect chastity. I will not envy virginity at all. Let virgins be called bread of purified wheat-seed, and let us wives be called barley-bread; and yet, as Mark can tell, our Lord Jesus refreshed many people with barley-bread.[11] I will persevere in such a state as God has called us to; I am not particular. In wifehood I will use my instrument as freely as my Maker has sent it. If I am unaccommodating to my husband, may God give me sorrow. My husband shall have it both evening and morning, whenever it pleases him to come forth and pay his

---

[10] Flower. Best years.

[11] Barley bread. Mark. Perhaps John 6:9 (the story of the loaves and fish): "One of his disciples, Andrew, the brother of Simon Peter, said to him, 'There is a boy here who has five barley loaves and two fish; but what good are these for so many?'"

debt. I will not stop. I will have a husband who will be both my debtor and servant, and have his tribulation upon his flesh, while I am his wife.[12] As long as I live, I, and not he, have the power over his body. The apostle told it to me in this very way, and instructed our husbands to love us well.[13] This entire subject pleases me well, every bit."

Up started the Pardoner, and without delay. "Now lady," he said, "by God and St. John, you are a noble preacher in this matter! I was about to wed a wife; alas! Why should I pay for it so dearly upon my flesh? I would rather not wed any wife this year."

"Wait! My tale is not yet begun," she said. "No, before I go you shall drink out of another barrel that will taste worse than ale. And when I have told my story to you about the tribulation in marriage, in which I have been expert all my life (that is to say, I myself have been the whip), then you may choose whether you will sip of that same barrel that I shall broach. Be mindful, before you come too close; for I shall tell you half a score of examples. 'Whosoever will not be warned by other men, by him shall other men be corrected': these same words writes Ptolemy; read his *Almagest*."[14]

"Lady," said this Pardoner, "I would pray you, if it were your pleasure, to tell your tale as you began, hold back for no man, and teach us young men from your experience."

"Gladly," she said, "if it may please you. But I beg all of

---

[12] Tribulation…wife. 1 Corinthians 7:28: If you marry, however, you do not sin, nor does an unmarried woman sin if she marries; but such people will experience affliction in their earthly life, and I would like to spare you that.

[13] Apostle…well. Paul, 1 Corinthians 7:3-5: "A wife does not have authority over her own body, but rather her husband, and similarly a husband does not have authority over his own body, but rather his wife. Do not deprive each other, except perhaps by mutual consent for a time, to be free for prayer, but then return to one another, so that Satan may not tempt you through your lack of self-control."

[14] *Almagest*. An Astrological treatise by the second-century author, Ptolemy of Alexandria.

you in this company, if I speak according to my fancy, do not take it amiss. For my intent is but to make sport. Now, sirs, I will continue.

"May I never see another drop of ale or wine, if I did not tell the truth about my husbands, as three of them were good, and two of them were bad. The three men were good, rich, and old, and they hardly could keep their obligation to me, by which they were bound to me. By God, you know well what I mean by this. May God help me, I laugh when I think how pitifully I made them work at night! And, by my faith, I found it useless. I did not need to make an effort or pay them any respect to win their love. They loved me so well, by God above, that I set no value on their love. A wise woman will always attempt to win love where she has none; but since I had them wholly in my hand and had all their land, why should I bother to please them, unless it were for my profit and pleasure? I ruled them so, by my faith, that many nights they sang 'alas!'

"Not for them, I believe, was fetched the bacon that some men win at Dunmow in Essex.[15] I governed them so well by my rules that each of them was blissful and glad to bring me beautiful things from the fair. They were glad when I spoke friendly to them, for God knows, I chided them without mercy. Now listen, you wise wives who can understand, hear how craftily I behaved myself.

"Thus shall you speak, and thus you shall put them in the wrong, for there is no man who can swear and lie half so boldly as a woman. I say this for the benefit of wise wives when they have made a little misstep. A wise wife, if she knows what is good for her, shall make a man believe that the jackdaw is mad,[16] and shall use her own maid as a wit-

---

[15] Bacon. "A side of bacon was awarded to spouses who lived a year and a day without quarreling" (Benson).

[16] Jackdaw is mad. An allusion to the tale in which a husband uses a bird, a chough or jackdaw, to report his wife's actions (not unlike *The Manciple's Tale*).

ness to confirm it.

"But now hear how I spoke: 'Old sir fogey, is this how you would have things? Why is my neighbor's wife so fine? She is honored everywhere she goes, while I have no decent clothes and must sit at home. Are you in love? What are you doing at my neighbor's house? Is she so lovely? What do you whisper with our maid? God bless! Leave behind your tricks, old sir lecher! And if I have a friend or a gossip, completely innocent, and I walk to his house or amuse myself there, you chide me like a fiend. You come home as drunk as a mouse and sit on your bench preaching, with no good reason. You say to me, it is a great evil to wed a poor woman, for the cost; and if she were rich, of noble birth, then you say that it is a torment to suffer her pride and her melancholy. And if she were pretty, you say that every lecher will have her, you arrant knave! She who is assailed on every side cannot remain in chastity for long.

"'You say that some folk desire us for our wealth, some for our figure, some for our beauty, some because she can sing or dance, some for our manners and mirth, and some for their hands and slim arms. Thus all goes to the Devil, by your account.

"'You say that a castle wall can not be defended when it is assailed so long from every side. And if a woman be foul, then you say that she covets every man she sees, and will leap on him like a spaniel, until she find some man to do business with her. There is no goose in the lake, as you say, that is too grey to look for a mate. And you say that it is a hard matter to control a thing that no man would be willing to keep.

"'Thus you say, old fool, when you are going to bed; that no wise man need marry, nor any man who hopes for heaven. With a wild thunder-clap and fiery lightning-bolt may your withered neck be snapped in two! You say that leaky houses, smoke, and chiding wives, make men flee from their own homes. Ah, God bless! What ails such an old man to scold like this?

"'You say that we wives will cover our vices until we are safely married, and then we show them. That is a villain's proverb! You say that oxen, asses, horses, and hounds are tested for some time before men buy them, and so are basins, wash-bowl, spoons, stools, pots, clothes, attire, and all such household stuff; but people make no test of wives until they are wedded. And, you old rascally dotard, you say, we will then show our vices.

"'You say also it displeases me unless you praise my beauty and gaze ever upon my face and call me "fair lady" everywhere; and unless you make a feast on my birthday, and dress me gay and freshly; and unless you do honor to my nurse, and to my maid in my bower, and to my father's family – all this you say, you old barrel-full of lies.

"'And yet you have gathered a false suspicion of our apprentice Jankin, for his crisp hair shining like fine gold, and because he escorts me back and forth. I would not have him, even if you should die tomorrow! But tell me this – and bad luck to you! – why do you hide the keys of your chest from me? By God, they are my goods as well as yours! Why do you intend to make a fool of the mistress of your house? Now by the lord who is called St. James,[17] however you may rage, you shall not be master both of my body and of my goods; you must give up one of them, in spite of your eyes.

"'What good does it do if you inquire after me or spy upon me? You want to lock me in your chest, I believe! You should say, "Wife, go where you wish, take your pleasure, I will believe no tales; I know you for a true wife, Lady Alice." We love no man who takes note or care where we go; we wish to have our freedom. May he be blessed of all men, that wise astrologer, Sir Ptolemy, who says this proverb in his book *Almagest*: "Of all men, he who never cares who has the world in hand has the greatest wisdom." You are to un-

[17] St. James. Probably St. James of Compostella. His shrine, like that of St. Thomas à Becket in Canterbury, was a popular destination for pilgrims.

derstand by this proverb that you have enough: why do you need to care how well-off other people are? For in truth, old fogey, you shall have plenty pleasing thingss in the evening. He who will forbid a man to light a candle at his lantern is too great a miser; by God, he should have light, nevertheless. So you have enough; you need not complain.

"'You say also that if we make ourselves amorous with clothing and with costly dress, it would be a peril to our chastity; and yet – may the plague take you! – you must confirm it with these words of the apostle: "Ye women shall apparel yourselves in garments made with chastity and shame," he said, "and not with tressed hair and splendid gems and pearls, nor with gold, nor rich clothes."[18] I would not give a fly for your text or your rubric.[19]

"'You said also I was like a cat; for a cat, if someone were to singe the cat's skin, will always dwell at home; but if she were sleek and elegant in her fur, she will not remain in the house an hour, but before any day would dawn, will go forth to show her skin and go a-caterwauling. This is to say, sir rogue, if I am finely dressed, I will run out to show my clothes.

"'Sir old fool, what ails you to spy after me? Even if you were to ask Argus[20] to be my sentry with his hundred eyes as best he can, in faith, he shall not keep watch over me unless it suits me. Still I could deceive him, as I hope to prosper!

"'You say also that there are three things that trouble this entire world, and that no creature can endure the fourth. Oh, dear sir rascal, may Jesus shorten your life! Still you preach and say a hateful woman is considered one of these adversities.

---

[18] 1 Timothy 2.9-10. Similarly, (too,) women should adorn themselves with proper conduct, with modesty and self-control, not with braided hairstyles and gold ornaments, or pearls, or expensive clothes, but rather, as befits women who profess reverence for God, with good deeds.

[19] Rubric. Usually a heading in a book written in red.

[20] Argus. Guardian with 100 eyes who watched over Io, one of Zeus' loves, at the command of Hera, Zeus' wife. Ovid's *Metamorphosis*. 1.165.

"'Are there no other things you can use for comparison without an innocent wife being one of them? You compare woman's love to hell, or to barren land where no water can lie. You compare it also to wildfire; the more it burns, the more it desires to consume everything that can be burned. You say that just as worms destroy a tree, so too a wife destroys her husband; those who are tied to women know this.

"Gentle people, in this very way, as you can see, I would firmly swear to my old husbands, that they said this in their drunkenness; and all was false, except I got Jankin and my niece to be my witnesses. O Lord! The pain and woe I did them, though they were innocent, by God's sweet suffering! For I could bite and whinny like a horse. I knew how to complain, even if I was guilty; or else I would have often been undone. He who first comes to the mill, grinds first; I complained first, and thus our war was ended. They were very glad to excuse themselves hurriedly of things that they never had done in all their lives. I would accuse my old husband of visiting prostitutes, even when they were so sick that they could scarcely stand.

"Yet I tickled his heart because he thought that I had such great fondness for him. I swore that all my walking about at night was to spot wenches whom he slept with. Under that pretext I had many fun times; for all such wit is given to us when we are born. God has given deceit, weeping, and spinning to women by nature, so long as they live.

"And thus I boast of one thing for myself: in the end I had the better in every way, by cunning, or by force, or by some type of device, such as continual murmuring or grumbling. And most chiefly at night they had ill fortune; then I would scold and grant him no pleasure. I would not stay in bed any longer if I felt his arm over my side, until he had paid his ransom to me. And therefore I tell this to every man: let he who can, prosper, for everything has its price. Men may lure no hawks with an empty hand. For the sake of gain I would give them their way, and pretend to have an appetite; and yet I never had pleasure in bacon, from Dunmow or elsewhere. And so I would be chiding them all the time; even if the pope had sat beside them, by my word, I would not spare them at their own table. I repaid them word for word; so may the Almighty Lord help me, if I were to make my testament right now, I would not owe them a word that has not been repaid. By my wits I made it so that they were glad to surrender, as their best option, or we would have never been at peace. For even if my husband looked like a mad lion, he was nonetheless bound to fail in his purpose.

"Then would I say, 'Good dear, take note how meekly Wilkin our sheep looks; come near, my spouse, let me kiss your cheek. You should be all patient and mild, and have a sweet tender conscience, since you thus preach of the patience of Job.[21] Always endure, since you can preach so well; and unless you do, we must teach you for sure that it is pleasant to have a wife in peace. Truly, one of us two must bend to the other and since a man is more reasonable than a woman, you must be patient. What ails you to grumble and groan in this way? Is it because you want to have my body all to yourself? Why, take it all! Have every bit! By Peter, I curse you, but you love it well! If I would sell my *bel chose*,[22] I could walk as fresh as a rose, but I will keep it for your own taste. You are to blame, by God! I tell you the truth. We had this sort of words between us; but now I will speak about my fourth husband.

"My fourth husband was a reveller, that is to say, he had a paramour – and I was young and full of frolic, stubborn and strong, and jolly as a magpie. I could dance well to a little harp, and sing like any nightingale, when I had taken a draught of sweet wine. Metellius,[23] the filthy churl, the

---

[21] Job. Biblical figure who had all the worldly gifts one could ever want and head them all stripped away from him as a test of his virtue. He is known for his patience; thus the phrase, "the patience of Job."

[22] Bel chose. Literally, beautiful thing.

[23] Metellius. The story is told in Valerius Maximus's *Factorum dictorum-*

swine, who with a staff bereft his spouse of her life, because she drank wine, would not have frightened me from drink, if I had been his wife! And when I think of wine I must think of Venus;[24] for just as surely as cold engenders hail, a lecherous mouth leads to a lecherous body. There is no defense in a woman who is full of wine, as lechers know by experience.

"Lord Christ! But when I think about my youth and mirth, it tickles me at the root of my heart! To this very day it does my heart good that I have had my fling in my time. But alas! Age, which envenoms all things, has bereft me of my beauty and energy. Let them go. Farewell! May the Devil go with them! The flour is gone, and there is no more to say; now I sell the bran[25] as best as I can. But even now I will strive to be very merry.

"Now I will tell of my fourth husband. I say I had great resentment in my heart that he had pleasure in any other. But by the Lord and Saint Joce,[26] he was paid back! I made a cross from the same wood for his back; not with my body, in any foul manner, but truly I offered people such generous hospitality that for anger and absolute jealousy I made him fry in his own grease. By God, I was his purgatory on earth, for which I hope that his soul is in glory now.[27]

"For God knows, he sat often and sang, when his shoe pinched him bitterly: No creature knew, except God and he, how sorely I twisted him in so many ways. He died when I returned home from Jerusalem, and lies buried under the cross-beam,[28] albeit his tomb is not quite as elaborately

---

que memorabilium liber (Book of memorabilia of words and deeds).

[24] Venus. In a general sense, she is referring to activity Venus associated with Venus, i.e., sex.

[25] Flour…bran. She is distinguishing from the essential or best part of the wheat (the flour) from the less essential part (the bran).

[26] Saint Joce. St. Judocus. There is no clear reason for calling on him here. He is a patron saint of sailors.

[27] In glory now. The fact that she, by making him jealous, sent him through Purgatory means that his sins were purged and thus prepared for Heaven.

crafted as the sepulcher of Darius that Apelles[29] so skilfully made. It would have been a waste to bury him at such an expense! Farewell to him; he is now in his grave and in his coffin – God rest his soul!

"Now will I speak of my fifth husband – may God never allow his soul to enter hell! And yet he was the most villainous to me, as I can still feel on my ribs all in a row, and ever shall to my ending day. But he was so fresh and merry, and could sweet-talk so well that, even if he had beaten me on every bone, he could soon win my *bel chose* again. I believe I loved him best, because he was sparing in his love.

"We women have, to tell the truth, an odd fantasy on this matter; whatever thing we can not easily win we will cry after continually and crave. Forbid us something, and we desire that thing. Press on us hard, and then we will flee. With much reserve we offer our merchandise; a large crowd at the market makes our wares expensive; wares offered at too low a price will be thought to have little value. Every wise woman knows this.

"My fifth husband – may God bless his soul – which I took for love and not for riches, was sometime an Oxford scholar; and he had left school, and went to board with my good friend, who dwelt in our town. May God keep her soul! Her name was Alisoun. She knew my heart and my private thoughts better than our parish priest, by my soul! To her I revealed all my secrets.

"For had my husband peed on a wall, or done something that would have cost him his life, I would have told every bit of his secret to her, and to another worthy wife, and to my niece, whom I loved well. And I did so often, God knows, which often made his face red and hot for true shame, and he would blame himself for telling me so great a secret.

---

[28] Cross-beam. The "rood-beam" supported the cross in a church between the chancel and nave.

[29] Darius...Apelles. Probably Darius I Sixth-century Iranian ruler known for his elaborate sepulcher; apparently crafted by Apelles.

"And so it happened that once, in Lent, (as I so often did, I visited my friend, for I still always loved to be merry, and to walk from house to house in March, April, and May, to hear various tales) that Jankin the clerk, my friend dame Alice, and I walked into the fields. All that spring my husband was in London; I had a better opportunity to play, and to see and to be seen by lusty folk. What did I know about how my fortune was to be shaped or in what place? Therefore, I made my visits to holy day vigils, to processions, to sermons, to these pilgrimages, to miracle-plays,[30] and to weddings, and wore my gay scarlet gowns. These worms and moths and mites never ate a bit of them, upon my peril! And do you know why? Because they were well used.[31]

"Now I will tell what happed to me. I say that we walked in the fields, until in truth we had such flirtation together, this clerk and I, that in my foresight I spoke to him, and told him how he should wed me, if I were widowed. I am not speaking in boast, for I was certainly never without provision for marriage – nor for other things as well. I think that a mouse's heart is not worth a leek if the mouse has but one hole to run to; and if that one fails, then all is over.

"I persuaded him to think that he had enchanted me; my mother taught me that trick. And I said also I dreamed of him all night; he would have slain me as I lay on my back, and my whole bed was full of real blood; but yet I hoped that he should bring good fortune to me, for blood signifies gold, as I was taught. And all of it was false; I dreamed not a bit of it, but I followed my mother's teaching all along, as well as in other things besides.

"But now, sir, let me see; what shall I say now? Aha! By God, I have it again. When my fourth husband lay on his bier, I wept ever and made a sorrowful expression, as wives

---

[30] Miracle plays. Popular festival dramas on various biblical topics, often played in a sequence or cycle of plays.

[31] Well used. Her clothes never sat in storage, so the insects never had time to get at them.

must, for it is the custom; and I covered my face with my kerchief. But since I had been provided with a new mate, I wept rather little, I vow.

"In the morning my husband was borne to church by the neighbors, who mourned for him, and our scholar Jankin was one of them. So may God help me, when I saw him go after the bier, I thought he had so clean and fair a pair of legs and feet that I gave him all my heart to keep. He was twenty winters old, I believe, and if I am to tell the truth, I was forty. But I always had a colt's tooth. I was gap-toothed;[32] I bore the print of Saint Venus' birthmark,[33] and that became me well. I was a lusty one, and fair, and rich, and youthful, and merry of heart, may God help me.

"For certainly, I am dominated by the planet Venus in my senses, and my heart is dominated by the planet Mars. Venus gave me my love for pleasure and my wantonness, and Mars my sturdy hardihood. My ascendant was Mars in Taurus. Alas, alas! That ever love was thought a sin! I followed ever my inclination by virtue of my constellation. That made it that I could not withhold my chamber from any good fellow. Yet I have the mark of Mars upon my face and in another private place as well. May God be my salvation indeed, I never loved discreetly, but always followed my appetite, whether he was short or tall, black or white, it did not matter to me, as long as he pleased me, how poor he was, nor of what station.

"What should I say but at the end of a month this jolly clerk Jankin, who was so debonair, wedded me with great splendor? And I gave him all the land and wealth that I had ever been given; but afterwards I repented myself sorely, for

[32] Gap-toothed. A gap between one's front teeth was thought a sign of amorousness.

[33] Saint Venus' birthmark. Chaucer sometimes refers to mythological figures such as Venus or Cupid as Saint or Sir; by birthmark, the Wife of Bath means that she was made in the image of Venus, as she will then explain in terms of astrology.

he would allow nothing that I desired. By God, he struck me once on the ear! That was because I tore a leaf out of his book and my ear grew entirely deaf because of the blow. I was as stubborn as a lioness, and a very chatterbox with my tongue, and I would walk as I had done before from house to house, though he had sworn I should not. For this reason he would often make homilies and teach me old Roman histories how Symplicius Gallus left his wife and forsook her for all his days, just because he saw her one day looking out of his door with her head uncovered.

"He told me the name of another Roman who forsook his wife also because without his knowledge she went to a summer game. And then he would seek in his Bible that proverb of the Ecclesiast[34] where he commands and firmly forbids that a man should allow his wife to go wander about. Then indeed he would say just this,

'He who builds his house out of sallows,[35]
And spurs his blind horse over fallows,[36]
And allows his wife to seek hallows,[37]
Then should be hanged upon the gallows.'

But all for nothing; I did not care one acorn for his proverbs or his old saying, and I would not be scolded by him. I hate anyone who tells me my faults; and, God knows, so too do more of us than I. This made him insanely furious with me, but I would not tolerate him in any case.

"Now, by Saint Thomas,[38] I will tell you the truth, why I tore a leaf out of his book, for which he struck me so that I became deaf. He had a book which he read night and day for

[34] Ecclesiast. I.e.., the author of Ecclesiasticus, or Sirach. 25. 24-25. Allow water no outlet, and be not indulgent to an erring wife. If she walks not by your side, cut her away from you.
[35] Sallows. Willow twigs
[36] Fallows. Fallow or uncultivated fields
[37] Hallows. Holy places, shrines.
[38] St. Thomas. Probably St. Thomas à Becket of Canterbury.

his amusement. He called it Valerius and Theophrastus;[39] he always laughed uproariously at this book. And there was also once a scholar at Rome, a cardinal, named Saint Jerome, who composed a book against Jovinian; and besides this in my husband's book there were Tertullian, Chrysippus, Trotula, and Heloise, who was an abbess not far from Paris, and also the Proverbs of Solomon, Ovid's *Art of Love* and many other books; and all these were bound in one volume.

"And every night and day, when he had leisure and freedom from other outside occupations, it was his habit to read in this book about wicked women; of them he knew more lives and legends than there are of good women in the Bible. For, trust well, it is an impossibility that any scholar will speak well of women, unless it would be of the lives of holy saints; but never of any other woman. Who painted the Lion,[40] tell me? By God, if women had written histories, as scholars have in their chapels, they would have written about men more evil than all the sons of Adam could redress.

"The children of Mercury and the children of Venus are contrary in their actions; Mercury loves wisdom and knowledge, and Venus revelry and extravagance. And, because of their contrary natures, each of these planets descends in sign of the zodiac in which the other is most powerful; thus Mercury is depressed in Pisces, where Venus is exalted, and Venus is depressed where Mercury is exalted. Therefore no woman is praised by any scholar. When the scholar is old and entirely unable to give Venus service that is even worth his old shoe, then he sits down and in his dotage writes that women cannot keep their marriage vow!

---

[39] Valerius and Theophrastus. These authors as well as Jerome, Tertulian, and Chrisippus all wrote anti-feminist tracks that preached of the wickedness of women and that it was best for men to avoid them entirely. Trotula was a woman physician who wrote of the diseases of women. In her writings Heloise explains why she wishes not to marry.

[40] Who painted the lion. In an Aesop fable, a sculptor depicts a man defeating a lion, upon which a lion muses that the sculpture would look much different if the lion had sculpted it.

"But now to my tale – why I was beaten for a book, by God, as I told you. One night Jankin, our husband, sat by the fire and read in his book, first about Eve, for whose wickedness all mankind was brought to misery, for which Jesus Christ Himself was slain, Who redeemed us with His heart's blood. Lo! Here you may read explicitly about woman, that she was the ruin of all mankind.

"Then he read to me how Samson lost his hair in his sleep; his sweetheart cut it with her shears, through which treason he lost both his eyes.[41] Then I tell you he read me about Hercules and his Dejanira,[42] who caused him to set fire to himself. Nor did he in any way forget the penance and woe which Socrates had with his two wives, how his wife Xantippe cast piss on his head; this blameless man sat still as a stone, wiped his head, and dared say no more than, "before thunder ceases, the rain comes."

"Of his cursedness my husband found a relish in the tale of Pasiphae, queen of Crete.[43] Fie! Speak no more of her horrible lust and desire – it is a grisly thing. He read with good devotion about Clytemnestra,[44] who for her wantonness treacherously caused her husband's death. He told me also for what cause Amphiaraus perished at Thebes; my husband had a legend about his wife Eriphyle, who for a brooch of gold secretly informed the Greeks where her husband had

---

[41] Samson. A Hebrew champion with supernatural strength, when Delilah cut off his hair when he was sleeping, he lost all his strength, after which he is tortured and blinded by the Philistines. When his hair grew back, he got revenge by destroying the Philistine temple with his bare hands, but died in the tumult. The story of his troubles with Delilah is told in Judges 16. 15 and retold in *The Monk's Tale* 2015-94.

[42] Hercules and his Dejanira. Dejenira, the jealous wife of Hercules, hoping to regain his fidelity, smears the poisoned blood of the Centaur Nessus on Hercules's lion-skin shirt, thinking that the blood is really a magic potion that will make him always faithful. It, however, kills him. The story is retold in *The Monk's Tale* 2119-35.

[43] Pasiphae…Crete. Gave birth to the Minotaur, whose father was a bull.

[44] Clytemnestra. Wife of the Greek king Agamemnon, who led the Greeks against the Trojans. Upon his return, she and her lover murdered him.

hidden himself; for this reason he met a sorry fate at Thebes. He told me of Livia and Lucilia, who both caused their husbands to die, the one for hate, the other for love. Livia,[45] late one evening, poisoned her husband, because she had become his foe; the wanton Lucilia[46] so loved her husband that she gave him a love-drink, that she might always be in his mind, but of such power that he was dead before morning.

"And thus in one way or the other husbands came to sorrow. And then he told me how one Latumius lamented to Arrius, his friend, how there grew in his garden such a tree on which, he said, his three wives had hanged themselves with desperate heart. 'Oh dear brother, give me a shoot from this same blessed tree,' said this Arrius, 'and it shall be planted in my garden!'

"He read about wives of later times, some of whom have murdered their husbands in their sleep, and had sex with their lovers while the corpse lay all night flat on the floor. And some have driven nails into their husband's brains while they slept. And some have given them poison in their drink. He spoke more evil than a heart can devise.

"And in all this he knew more proverbs than blades of grass grow in this world. He said, 'It is better to have your dwelling with a lion or a foul dragon, than with a woman accustomed to scorning.' 'It is better,' he said, 'to dwell high on the roof, than down in the house with an angry woman; they are so wicked and contrary that they forever hate what their husbands love.'

"He said, 'A woman casts her shame away when she casts off her undergarments.' And furthermore, 'A beautiful woman, unless she is also chaste, is like a gold ring in a sow's nose.' Who would think or imagine the woe and pain in my heart.

"And when I saw that he would never leave reading all night in this cursed book, all of the sudden I plucked three

---

[45] Livia. Convinced by her lover Sejanus to murder her husband.

[46] Lucillia. Married to the Roman poet Lucretius.

leaves out of his book, even as he was reading, and I also struck him on the cheek with my fist so that he fell down backward into our fire. And he started up like a mad lion, and struck me on the head with his fist so that I lay as if dead on the floor.

"And he was aghast when he saw how still I was, and would have fled on his way, until at last I came out of my swoon. 'Oh, have you slain me, false thief,' I said, 'and have you murdered me thus for my land? Before I die, I will still kiss you.' And he came nearer and kneeled down gently and said, 'Dear sister Alisoun, so God help me, I shall never strike you again! You yourself are to blame for what I have done. Forgive me for it; and I beg you for that.' And yet again I hit him on the cheek, and said, 'Thief, I am revenged this much. Now I will die; I can speak no more.'

"But at last with great pain and grief, we fell into agreement between ourselves. He put the full bridle into my hand, to have the governance of house and estate, and over his tongue and hands as well. And I made him burn his book then and there.

"And when I had taken for myself all the sovereignty, through a master-stroke, and when he said, 'My own faithful wife, do as you will the rest of your days; be the guard of your honor, and of my dignity also,' we never had a dispute after that day. God help me so, I was as loving to him as any wife between Denmark and India, and as true also; and so was he to me. And I pray to God, Who sits in glory, so bless his soul for His sweet compassion! Now I will relate my story, if you will listen."

The Friar, when he had heard all this, laughed and said, "Now, Madame, so may I have joy, this is a long preamble for a tale!"

When the Summoner heard the Friar make an outcry, he said, "Lo! By God's two arms! A friar will evermore be meddling. Lo, good men! A fly and a friar will fall into every dish and every affair. Why do you speak of preambling? What! Amble or trot, or hold your peace, or go sit down! You hinder our sport in this way."

"Yes, is that what you want, sir Summoner? Now by my faith," said the Friar, "I shall tell, before I go, such a tale or two of a summoner that all the people here shall laugh."

"Now, Friar, I curse your face," said this Summoner, "and I curse myself, unless I tell stories, two or three, of friars, before I get to Sittingborne,[47] that shall make your heart grieve, for I know well your patience has already left you."

"Peace, and now!" cried our Host; and said, "Let the woman tell her tale. You act like people who are drunk with ale. Please, Madame, tell your tale; and that is best."

"All ready, sir, just as you wish," she said, "if I have the permission of this worthy Friar."

"Yes, Madame," he said, "tell your tale now, and I will listen."

Here ends the Prologue of the Wife of Bath.

Here begins the Tale of the Wife of Bath.

In the old days of King Arthur, of whom Britons speak great glory, this land was entirely filled with fairy power. The elf-queen danced often with her merry company in many green meadows. This long ago was the belief, as I find in books. I speak of many hundred years ago; but in our times no man can see elves anymore.

For now the great charity and the prayers of begging friars and other holy friars, who, as thick as motes in a sunbeam, reach every land and every stream, blessing halls, chambers, kitchens, bowers, cities, towns, castles, villages, barns, stables, dairies – all this causes there to be no elves. For where a fairy was accustomed to walk, there the begging friar himself walks now, in the mornings or the afternoons, and says his matins[48] and his holy things as he goes along in

---

[47] Sittingbourne. Between Rochester and Canterbury; about forty miles from London.

[48] Matins. Morning prayers.

his begging. Women may go up and down safely; in every bush or under every tree, there is no incubus,[49] except him, and he will do nothing but dishonor them.

And so it happened that this King Arthur had in his court a lusty young knight, who one day came riding from the river; and it happened that he saw walking ahead of him a maiden, whom he ravished, in spite of all her resistance. For this violation there was such clamor and such appeal to King Arthur, that the knight was condemned by course of law to die; and so it was the statute in place then was so severe that he would have lost his head, if the queen and other ladies had not so long begged the king for mercy, until he granted him his life at that point and placed him entirely at the queen's will, to choose whether she would save him or let him die.

The queen thanked the king very heartily; and after this, upon a day when she saw the opportunity, she spoke in this way to the knight: "You stand now," she said, "in such a plight that you have even now no guarantee for your life. I grant you life, if you can tell me what thing it is that women desire most. Beware, and guard your neck-bone from iron! And if you cannot tell it right now, I will still give you leave to go for twelve months and a day, to search out and learn an answer sufficient for this point. And before you depart, I must have security that you will yield up your body in this place."

This knight was woeful, and he sighed sorrowfully. But what! He could not do just as he pleased. And, with such a reply that God would provide for him, at last he chose to depart and come at the very end of the year; and he took his leave and went forth along his way.

He sought every house and place where he hoped to find such luck as to learn what women love most. But he could arrive at no place where he could find two creatures agreeing

---

[49] Incubus. Evil spirit which, according to legend, readily mated with women and usually impregnated them.

together on this matter. Some said that women best love riches; some said honor; some said mirth; some, fancy clothes; some, pleasure in bed, and to be widowed often and re-wed. Some said that our hearts are most eased when we are flattered and gratified.

They came very near the truth; a man shall best win us by flattery, I will not deny it, and we are caught by attentiveness and diligence, both great and small. And some said how we love best to be free and to do just as we wish, and that no man should reprove us for our faults, but say that we are wise and never foolish at all. For in truth there is nobody among us who will not kick if someone would claw us on a sore place, just because he tells us the truth. Try this, and he shall find out that it is true. For though we may be full of vice within, we wish to be considered wise and clean of sin.

And some said that we have great delight to be accounted stable and trustworthy and steadfast in one purpose, and never reveal what men tell us. But that sort of talk is not worth a rake-handle, by God! We women can conceal nothing. Take witness of Midas. Would you like to hear the tale?

Ovid, among other little things, says that Midas had two ass's ears growing upon his head under his long hair, which deformity he hid artfully from every man's sight, as best he could, so that nobody knew of it, except his wife. He loved her most and trusted her; and he asked her to tell of his disfigurement to no creature. She swore to him, "No," not even to gain all the world would she do that villainy and sin, to bring her husband so foul a name; for her own honor she would not do it.

But nevertheless she felt she should die, to hide a secret so long; it swelled so sorely about her heart, it seemed to her, that some word needed to burst from her. And since she dared tell it to no human creature, she ran down to a nearby marsh; her heart was ablaze until she arrived there.

And as a bittern booms[50] in the mire, she laid her mouth

[50] Bittern booms. A bittern is a small tawny brown heron that lives in the

down unto the water: "Betray me not, you water, with your sound,' she said; 'I tell it to you, and to nobody else. My husband has two long ass's ears. Now my heart is whole and well again; now it is out. In very truth I could keep it in no longer.'

By this you may see that though we wait a time, we can conceal no secret forever; it must come out. If you wish to hear the remainder of the tale, read Ovid;[51] you can find it out there.

This knight, about whom my tale chiefly is, when he saw he could not come by it, that is to say, what women love most – the spirit in his breast was so sorrowful. But home he went, as he could not remain. The day had come when he had to turn homeward. And as he went, deep in care, it happened that he rode under the edge of a forest, where he saw twenty-four ladies and more in a dance. Eagerly he drew toward this dance, in hope of learning some piece of wisdom. But in truth, before he arrived there entirely, the dance vanished – he did not know where it went. He saw no living creature there, except a woman sitting on the grass – no one could imagine a fouler creature.

At the approach of the knight this old woman arose and said, "Sir knight, there is no path that lies this way. Tell me, by your faith, what do you seek? Peradventure it may be better for you; these old people know many things."

"My dear mother," said this knight, "in truth I am just a dead man, unless I can say what thing it is that women desire most. If you could instruct me, I would repay you well for your work."

"Pledge me your word here on my hand," she said, "that you will do the first thing that I require of you, if it should lie in your power; and before it is night I will tell it you."

"Take my pledge here," said the knight, "I agree."

"Then," she said, "I dare to boast that your life is safe;

---

marshes or mires and is distinguished by its booming cry.

[51] Ovid. Specifically *Metamorphoses*. Book 11, ll. 100ff.

for upon my soul I will guarantee that the queen will say as I do. Show me the proudest of the whole court, who wears a kerchief or other head-dress and who dares say no to what I shall teach you.[52] Let us go on, without further words." Then she whispered a word in his ear, and told him to be glad and have no fear.

When they had arrived at the court, this knight said he had kept his day, as he had promised, and his answer was ready. At that time many noble wives were assembled to hear his answer, and many maidens, and many widows (because they are wise); and the queen herself sat as judge. And then this knight was summoned.

Silence was commanded to every creature, and the knight was ordered to tell in public what thing mortal women most love. This knight stood not like a dumb beast, but without delay answered the question with manly voice, so that all the court heard it.

"My liege lady, over all this world" he said, "women wish to have sovereignty both over their husband and their love, and to have mastery over him. This is your greatest desire, though you may slay me for this. Do as you wish; I am here at your will."

In all the court there was neither wife nor maiden nor widow to contradict what he replied, but all declared he was worthy to have his freedom. And at that word, the old woman, whom the knight had seen sitting on the grass, started up.

"Mercy, my sovereign lady!" she said. "Do me justice, before your court departs. I taught the knight this answer, for which he pledged me his word that he would do the first thing I should require of him, if it lay in his power. Before the court, then, I pray you, sir knight," she said, "that you take me as your wife; for you well know that I have saved your life. If I speak falsely, say no to me, upon your faith!"

---

[52] Show me…teach you. In other words, she dares him to show her anyone who would disagree with her.

This knight answered, "Alas and alack! I know full well that this was my promise. But for the love of God, please choose another request! Take all my goods, and let my body go."

"No, then,' she answered, "I curse us both. For though I may be ugly, poor, and old, I would like none of all the metal or ore that is buried under the earth or lies upon it, only that I would be your wife, and your love also."

"My love!" he said, "No, my damnation! Alas that any of my kindred should be so foully disgraced by such a match!"

But all this was for nothing. This is the conclusion, that he was constrained, and had to wed her. And he took his old wife and went to bed.

Now perhaps some men would say that through my negligence I take no care to tell you all the joy and all the preparations that there were at the celebration that day. To this point I shall briefly answer, and say there was no joy nor celebration at all; but only heaviness and much sorrow. For he wedded her secretly the next morning. And he was so miserable that he hid himself the rest of the day like an owl, as his wife looked so ugly.

Great was his misery when he was alone with his wife; he tossed about and turned back and forth. His old wife lay always smiling, and said, "Ah, God bless, dear husband! Does every knight act this way with his wife? Is this the way of King Arthur's household? Is every knight of his so hard to please? I am your own love and your wife also, and I have saved your life, and surely, I have never yet done you any wrong. Why do you act this way on this first night? You act like a man who has lost his wit. What is my guilt? Tell me, for the love of God, and if I have the power, it shall be amended."

"Amended!" said this knight. "Alas! No, no! It can not be amended forevermore! You are so loathly and so old, and come of so low a lineage as well, that it is small wonder that I toss and turn. I wish to God my heart would burst!'

'Is this,' she said, 'the cause of your unrest?'

'Yes, certainly, and no wonder,' he said.

"Now, sir," she replied, "I could amend all this before three days had passed, if I wish, so that you might bear yourself toward me well.

"But when you speak of such gentility[53] as is descended from ancient wealth – so that you knights should therefore would be gentlemen of breeding – such arrogance is not worth a hen. Look who is always most virtuous, openly and secretly, and most inclines to do what gentle or noble deeds he can; take him for the gentlest man. Christ wishes that we claim our gentility from Him, not from our ancestors' ancient wealth. For though all their heritage of our ancestors, by reason of which we claim high rank, may descend to us, yet they cannot at all bequeath to any of us their virtuous living, which made them to be called gentle or noble men and to bid us follow to them and do in like manner.

"The wise poet of Florence, who is named Dante, speaks well on this matter. Lo, this is what Dante says in his poetry: "Seldom does a man climb to excellence on his own slim branches, for God, from his goodness, wills that we claim our gentility from Him." For we may claim nothing from our ancestors, except for temporal things that can be injured and impaired.

"Every creature also knows this as well as I, that if gentility were planted by nature in a certain family all down the line, openly and privately, then they would never cease to do the fair duties of gentility; they could never do any base or vicious deed. Take fire and bear it into the darkest house between here and the mount of Caucasus, and let the doors be shut and leave that place. Nevertheless the fire will burn and blaze as fairly as though twenty thousand men witnessed it; on peril of my life, it will keep to its natural duty until it dies.

"Here you may well see how nobility hangs not from an-

---

[53] Gentility. Nobility.

cient possessions, since people do not always perform its works, as does the fire, according to its nature. For, God knows, one may often see a lord's son do vicious and shameful deeds; and he who wishes to be esteemed for his gentility because he was born of a noble house and had virtuous and noble ancestors, and yet himself will not perform the deeds of gentility or nobility nor follow after his noble ancestor who is dead, he is not gentle, even if he is a duke or an earl; for base and sinful deeds make a commoner. For gentility then would be nothing but renown of your ancestors for their high worthiness, which is something that has nothing to do with you. Your gentility comes only from God. Then our true gentility comes from divine grace, and was in no fashion bequeathed to us with our earthly station.

"Think how noble was that Tullius Hostilius,[54] as Valerius[55] tells, who rose out of poverty to high nobility. Read Seneca,[56] and Boethius[57] as well; there you shall see expressly that he who does noble deeds is noble. And therefore, dear husband, I conclude in this way: albeit my ancestors were untutored, yet may the high God – and so I hope – grant me grace to live virtuously. Then I am noble, when I begin to live virtuously and to abandon evil.

"And you reproach me for poverty; but the great God in whom we believe chose freely to live in poverty. And surely every man, maiden, or wife, may well know that Jesus, King of Heaven, would not choose a wicked manner of living. Truly cheerful poverty is an honorable thing, so will Seneca say, and other clerks. Whoever keeps himself content with his poverty, I count as rich, even if he does not have a shirt! He who covets is a poor creature, for he wishes to have that

---

[54] Tullius Hostilius. In legend, he rose to become the third king of Rome.

[55] Valerius. Valerius Maximus, a Roman author of a collection of commonplace anecdotes.

[56] Seneca. Roman author. [Epistle] 44.

[57] Boethius. Late Roman philosopher, author of the influential *Consolation of Philosophy*, which Chaucer translated.

which is not within his power. But he who has nothing, nor covets things, is rich, albeit you count him as only a serving-lad.

"True poverty sings a song of its own. Concerning poverty, Juvenal says merrily:

> 'The poor man, when he goes along the way,
> Before the thieves, he can still sing and play.'

Poverty is a hateful good, I suppose, a great remover from the busyness of the world, and a great teacher of wisdom to one who takes it in patience. All this is poverty, though it may seem wretched; and a possession that no creature will challenge. When a man is humbled, often poverty allows him to know his God and himself as well. It seems to me that poverty is a magnifying glass through which he may see who his true friends are. And therefore, sir, I pray, so that I will not grieve you, scorn me no more for my poverty.

"Now, sir, you reproach me for my old age. And surely, sir, though there may be no authority in any book to tell you so, yet you honorable gentlefolk say that men should do courtesy to an old creature, and for your gentle manners call him Father. And I could find authorities to show this, I believe.

"Now you say I am old and foul: then have no fear that you will be a cuckold. For ugliness and age, upon my life, are great wardens over chastity. But nevertheless, since I know your delight, I shall fulfill your appetite.

"Choose," she said, "one of these two things: to have me foul and old until I die, and to you a true, humble wife, never in all my days displeasing you; or else to have me young and beautiful, and take your chance on how many visits there will be to your house – or perhaps to some other place – which will be for my sake. Now choose yourself which one you will have."

This knight thought hard about it and sighed deeply; but

at last he spoke in this manner: "My lady and love, and my dear wife, I put myself into your wise governance. Please choose which may be the greatest pleasure and greatest honor to you and me also; I care not which of the two, for it is sufficient to me to please you."

"Then I have the mastery over you," she said, "since I may choose and govern as I wish"

"Yes, surely, wife," he said; "I believe that is for the best."

"Kiss me," she said, "we will be angered no longer. For by my faith I will be both unto you – that is to say, both beautiful, yes, and good. I pray to God that I may die mad, but I would be as good and faithful as ever a wife was since the world was new. And if I am not as beautiful to see in the morning as any lady, queen or empress, between the east and the west, do with my life and death as you will. Lift up the curtain, and see how it is."

And when the knight saw truly that she was so fair and so young, he clasped her in his two arms for joy, his heart bathed in a bath of bliss. A thousand times in a row he kissed her. And she obeyed him in all that might cause him delight or pleasure.

And thus they lived in perfect joy to the end of their lives. And may Jesus Christ send us husbands meek, young, and lusty, and the grace to outlive them that we wed.

And I pray Jesus also to shorten the days of those who will not be ruled by their wives. And old, angry misers – may God send them a true pestilence soon!

Here ends the Wife of Bath's Tale.

THE CLERK'S TALE

❦

Here follows the Prologue of the Clerk of Oxford's Tale.

Sir Clerk[1] of Oxford," said our Host, "you ride as quiet and demure as a newly married maiden, sitting at the wedding feast. This day I have not heard one word from your tongue, I believe you are pondering some complex argument; but "everything has its time,"[2] just as Solomon says.

For God's sake, be of merrier countenance; it is not the time to study now. Tell us some merry tale, by your faith. For everyone who has entered into a game must agree to the rules of the game. But preach not like friars in Lent, to make us bewail our old sins, and do not let your tale put us to sleep.

Tell us some merry happening. Put away your learned terms and colors[3] of rhetoric and figures; keep them in reserve until a time when you may be composing in high style, such as when men write to kings. I pray you to speak so plainly now that we may understand what you say.

This worthy scholar answered gently, "Host, I am under your authority. You have now the governance over us, and therefore I bind myself by obedience to you, as far as reason asks. I will tell you a tale that I learned at Padua from a scholar, and a very worthy one, as is shown by his words and deeds. He is now dead and nailed in his coffin. I pray God rest his soul.

---

[1] Sir Clerk. The term "clerk" refers here to a scholar. Herein the term scholar is used instead of clerk.

[2] Everything has its time. "All things have their season, and in their times all things pass under heaven." Ecclesiastes. 3.1.

[3] Colors. Figurative language, such as simile, metaphor, and hyperbole.

Francis Petrarch,[4] the laureate poet, is the name of this scholar, whose sweet rhetoric illumined all Italy with poetry, as John of Lignano[5] did with philosophy and law and other learned arts.

But death, which will not allow us to dwell here but as it were a twinkling of an eye, has slain them both, and will yet slay all of us.

But to continue as I began of this worthy poet who taught me this tale I say that first, before he comes to the body of his tale, he composes a prologue in a high style,[6] in which he describes Piedmont and the country of Saluzzo, and speaks of the Apennines, the high hills that are the bounds of West Lombardy, and especially he speaks of Mount Viso,[7] where the Po out of a small spring takes its first source and rising, and ever grows in its course eastward toward the Emilia,[8] Ferrara, and Venice,[9] which would take a long time to describe. And truly to my judgment it seems an irrelevant thing, except that he wished to convey this information. But this is his tale, which you may hear now.

Here begins the Tale of the Clerk of Oxford

On the western side of Italy, down at the root of the cold Viso, there is a lively plain, abundant in its harvest, where you may behold many towers and towns founded in the time of the old fathers, and many other delightful sights. This noble country is called Saluzzo, where long ago a marquis was

---

[4] Petrarch. Chaucer may have met Petrarch on his first trip to Italy in 1372-73.

[5] Giovanni da Lignano. Professor of canon law at Padua (and Bologna), who once visited England. (D. 1383)

[6] High style. Perhaps in contrast to the low style (in prose and simple language) of Giovanni Boccaccio who told the tale of Griselda (the topic of the tale that the Clerk is about to tell) as the tenth tale of the tenth day of his *Decameron*.

[7] Mount Viso. Also called Monviso, the highest of the Italian Alps.

[8] Emilia. Eastern Italy.

[9] Venice. Where the Po empties into the Adriatic Sea.

lord, as were his worthy ancestors before him, and his lieges great and small were all obedient and ready to serve him. Thus he lived in delights, and had done for a long time, through the favor of Fortune, beloved and feared both by his lords and the common people. And to speak of lineage as well, he was of the gentlest birth of Lombardy, a handsome person and strong and young, and full of honor and courtesy, discreet enough to guide his country, except that he was to be blamed in certain things. And this young lord's name was Walter.

I blame him in this: that he considered not what might happen to him in the time to come, but put all his thought on present delight, such as hawking and hunting all the time. Very nearly all other cares he let slip, and, what was worst of all, he would not wed a wife, for anything that might happen. This point only his people bore so sorely that one day they flocked to him in groups, and one of them, who was the wisest in learning, or else from whom the lord would take it least badly when he told him what his people thought, or else who could best expound such a matter, said this to the marquis:

"O noble marquis, your humanity gives us confidence and fortitude, as is often needed, to tell you our heaviness, so much so that we can now tell you of the heaviness of our hearts. Please accept now, lord, through your nobility, accept the complaint that we lay before you with piteous heart, and do not let your ears disdain my voice. Although I have nothing more to do in this matter than any other person here, yet, my beloved lord, in as much as you have always showed me favor and grace, I dare even more so to ask of you a little time to listen, so that we may show our request, but only to the extent that you, my lord, shall do fully as you wish. For surely, lord, we so delight in you and in all your work, and have always done so, that we could not devise for ourselves how we might live in greater felicity, except for one thing, lord, if it should be your will, that you desire to be a wedded man; then your people would rest in their most excellent hearts. Bow your neck under that blissful yoke of sovereignty, not of servitude, which men call espousal or wedlock.

"And think, lord, among all your prudent thoughts, how our days pass away from us in various ways; for though we sleep or wake, or roam, or ride, time forever flees away; it will tarry for no person. And though your fresh youth may still be in flower, age always creeps in, as still as a stone, and death menaces all ages and strikes each estate, and nobody escapes. And just as certainly as each one of us knows that we shall die, so uncertain are we of that day when death shall fall on us. Accept, then, this loyal intention from us, who never yet refused your command. And, lord, if you will agree, we will in short time choose you a wife born of the noblest and greatest of all this land, at the least, so that it ought to seem for God's honor and yours, as well as we can judge. Deliver us out of this anxious fear, and for the sake of the high God take a wife. For if it should so happen, God forbid, that through your death your line should fail, and that a strange successor should take your heritage, ah, may woe be to us living. For these reasons we beseech you to wed quickly."

Their meek prayer and piteous countenance struck pity into the marquis' heart. He said, "My own dear people, you would constrain me to that which I never once thought of. I have rejoiced in my liberty, which is seldom found in marriage where I was free, I must now be in servitude.

"But I see your loyal meaning, nevertheless, and trust your wisdom, and have always trusted it. For this reason, by my free will I will agree to wed, as soon as I am able. But as to the offer which you have made today to choose me a wife, I release you from that choice, and ask you to offer it no more. For, God knows, children are often unlike their worthy elders before them. Goodness comes all from God, not from the strain of which they were begotten and born. I trust in

God's goodness, and therefore my marriage and well-being and peace I commit to Him; He may do as pleases Him.

"Let me alone to choose my wife: I will bear that responsibility upon my own back. But I pray you and charge you upon your lives that whatever wife I take, you will give me assurance to honor her, as long as she lives, in word and deed here and everywhere, as if she were an emperor's daughter. And furthermore you shall swear this: that you will neither grumble nor strive against my choice. For since I am to forgo my liberty at your request, upon my soul I will take a wife where my heart is set. And unless you will agree to this, speak no more of this matter, I ask you."

With hearty will they swore and agreed to this whole thing, and no creature said no, beseeching him before they went that through his grace he would set for their sake a certain day for his wedding, as soon as he could. For still the people remained somewhat in feared lest this marquis would not after all wed a wife. Such a day as pleased him, on which he would truly be wedded, he granted them, and said that he did all this only at their request.

And with humble and submissive minds and reverently kneeling upon their knees they all thanked him; and thus they had achieved their desire, and all went their way home. And upon this he commanded his officers to purvey the feast; and he gave to his personal knights and squires such orders as he wished; and they obeyed his commandments, and each did his full duty to give honor to the feast.

Here ends the first part.

Here begins the second part.

Not far from that honorable palace where this marquis prepared for his marriage, stood a village in a pleasant site, where poor people of that place had their huts and beasts, and drew their sustenance from their own labor, as the earth yielded them its plenty. Among these poor people dwelt a man thought to be the poorest of the whole village; but God almighty can sometimes send his grace into a little ox's stall.[10] This man was called Janicula by the men of that village.

He had a daughter named Griselda. This young maiden to the eye was plenty beautiful; but to speak of virtuous beauty, she was in this respect one of the most beautiful under the sun. She was bred in poverty, and no lecherous desire ran through her heart; she drank more often from the spring than of the cask, and because she wished to satisfy the demands of virtue, she knew labor well, but no idle ease.

And though she was tender of age, yet in the breast of her virginity was enclosed a mature and steadfast temper, and she cherished her old poor father in great reverence and love. Spinning in the field, she watched a few sheep, and would never be idle until she slept. And when she came home, she would often bring cabbages or other vegetables, which she shredded and boiled for their sustenance, and made her bed, which was hard and not a bit soft. She always sustained her father's life with all the diligence and obedience that a child could show to a father's honor.

Upon Griselda, this poor maiden, the marquis often set his eye, by chance as he rode at his hunting; and when it so happened that he could see her, he cast his look upon her not with wanton glances of folly, but would often consider her countenance in a serious fashion, commending her womanhood in his heart, and her virtue, surpassing any creature of so young age as well in look as in deed. For though the common people have no great insight into virtue, he considered very well her goodness and intended to wed her only, if ever he should wed.

The day of the wedding came, but no creature could tell who the woman was to be; for this marvel many wondered and said when they were in private, "Will our lord still not leave his vanities? Will he not wed? Alas the day! Why will he so deceive us and himself?"

But nevertheless for Griselda's sake this marquis had had

---

[10] Ox's stall. I.e., as was the case in the birth of Christ.

brooches and rings made of gems set in gold and azure; and for her clothing, and for all the other adornments that pertain to such a wedding, he had had the measurement taken of a maiden similar to her in stature. The morning drew toward nine o'clock on the day when this wedding should be, and the palace was put all in order, the hall and chambers, each according to its use. There you could see the store-rooms stuffed with plenty of the choicest food to be found as far as Italy stretches.

This richly arrayed royal marquis, the lords and ladies in his company who had been bidden to the feast, and the young knights of his retinue with the sound of mingled melody proceeded directly to the village of which I have spoken. Griselda, completely unaware, God knows, that all this pageantry was made for her, went to fetch water at a spring, and came home as soon as she could; for indeed she had heard that the marquis was to wed that same day, and if she could she would gladly have seen some of that sight. She thought, "I will stand in our door with other maidens, my friends, and see the marchioness; and therefore I will attempt to do as soon as possible the labor that I must do at home. And then at leisure I may see her, if she should take this way to the castle."

And as she was about to cross over her threshold, the marquis came and began to call her. And without delay she set down her water-vessel in an ox's stall beside the threshold, and fell down upon her knees, and remained kneeling with a serious countenance until she heard the lord's will.

This thoughtful marquis spoke to this maiden in a serious tone and said, "Where is your father, Griselda?"

And she answered with reverence and humble expression, "Lord, he is close at hand." And she went in without staying longer and fetched her father to the marquis.

He then took this old man by the hand, and when he had taken him aside, said this: "Janicula, I can no longer hide the pleasure of my heart. If you promise it, whatever happens, before I depart I will take your daughter as my wife as long as she lives. You love me, and are born my faithful follower, I know well, truly; and I dare well say, all that pleases me pleases you. And especially, therefore, tell me what you think about that point I have spoken of just now; if you will agree to my proposal that you will take me as your son-in-law?"

These sudden words so astonished the old man that he grew red and abashed and stood all quaking. He could scarcely say a word except only this: "Lord," he said, "my will is your will; and I wish nothing against your pleasure. You are my very dear lord. Govern this matter just as you wish."

"Yet I would like," said this marquis softly, "that in your chamber I and you and she might have a conference; and do you know why? Because I wish to ask if it would be her will to be my wife, and to conduct herself according to my wishes. And all this shall be done in your presence; I will not speak outside of your hearing.

And while they were in the room carrying out their treaty, of which you shall hear after this, the people drew near the house and marveled how kindly and attentively she looked after her dear father.

But Griselda herself might well be marveling most of all, for never before had she seen such a sight; it is no wonder if she were astonished to see so great a guest come there, such as she was not accustomed to; she gazed at him with a pale face.

But briefly to hurry this tale forth, these are the words which the marquis spoke to this true gentle faithful maiden: "Griselda," he said, "you shall understand well that it pleases your father and me that I should wed you; and it is also possible, as I suppose, that you will grant it. But these questions I will ask first. Since it is to be done in so hasty a fashion, will you now assent, or consider further? I ask this: are you ready with good heart to do all I wish, that I may freely cause you to laugh or to grieve as seems best to me, and that you never shall complain about it day or night, and that when I say 'yes,' you will never say 'no,' neither by word nor frowning expression? Swear this, and here I swear our alliance."

Wondering at these words and trembling for fear, she said: "Lord, undeserving and unworthy am I of that which honor that you offer me. But as you wish, so too do I wish. And here I swear that willingly I shall never disobey you in deed or thought, even if I were to die for it and yet were loath to die."

"This is enough, my Griselda," he said. And he went forth with a serious countenance through the door, and she came after him. And to the people he said, "This is my wife who stands here. Whoever loves me, honor and love her, I beg. There is no more to say."

And because she should bring into his house nothing of her old clothing, he ordered that women should unclothe her right there. These ladies were not very joyous to handle the clothes in which she was clad; but nevertheless from foot to head they clothed afresh this maiden bright of hue. Then they combed her hair which lay unarranged and uncared for, and with their slender fingers placed a crown on her head, and covered her with gemmed ornaments, great and small. Why should I make a long tale of her array? When she was translated into such richness, the people hardly knew her for her beauty.

This marquis married her with a ring brought for that purpose, and then set her upon a snow-white and gently-pacing horse, and conveyed her to his palace amid joyful people who led her and met her. And thus they spent the day in revelry until the sun went down.

And to move this tale forth quickly, I say that God by His grace sent such favor to this new marchioness that none would have believed she had been rudely born and fostered, as in a hut or ox-stall, but rather in an emperor's palace. In the eyes of every creature she grew so beloved and deserving of honor that people where she was born, who had known her year by year from her birth, scarce believed that she was daughter to Janicula, of whom I have spoken; but dared have sworn she was quite another creature.

For though she had always been full of worth, she increased in excellence of precious virtues rooted deep in goodness of nature. She was so discreet and fair of speech, so benign and so worthy of reverence, and had such power over the people's hearts, that every person who looked upon her face loved her. The nobility of her fame was published not only in the town of Saluzzo, but in many surrounding regions. If one spoke well of her, another said the same. So spread the report of her high goodness that men and women, young and old, went to Saluzzo to look upon her.

Thus Walter, wedded lowly – no, royally actually – with good fortune and honor, lived at home well at ease and in God's peace, and outside the home he had plenty of favor. And because he had seen that under lowly social rank virtue is often hidden, the people believed him to be a prudent man, and that is seldom seen. This Griselda through her natural wit not only knew all the acts of wifely domesticity, but also, when the case required it, she could promote common profit.[11] There was no discord, rancor, or heaviness in all that land which she knew not how to appease, and to bring wisely all those in trouble into rest and satisfaction. Even if her husband were absent, if people of gentle birth or others of her country were angered, she would quickly reconcile them. She had such wise and mature words, and judgments of such equity that people thought she had been sent from heaven to save people and to redress every wrong.

Not long after this Griselda was wedded, she bore a daughter, though she had rather have borne a baby boy. The marquis and the people were glad about this. For if a daughter came first, she might by likelihood succeed in bearing a

---

[11] Common profit. Public or common good.

son, since she was not barren.

Here ends the second part.

Here begins the third part.

It happened, as it sometimes does, that when this child had nursed only a little while, this marquis so longed in his heart to test his wife, and to know her steadfastness, that he could not cast out of his heart this marvelous desire to test his wife.

Needlessly, God knows, he intended to frighten her. He had tested her enough already, and found her good at all times. What need was there to test her more and more? Though some men praise it for a subtle mark of wit, as for me I say that it is not fitting to test a wife when there is no need, and to put her in anguish and fear.

To this end the marquis plotted in this manner. He came alone by night to the place where she lay, and, with stern face and troubled countenance, said this: "Griselda, that day when I took you out of your poor condition and put you in the estate of high nobility: you have not forgotten that, I believe. I say, Griselda, I trust that this present dignity in which I have placed you does not makes you forgetful that I took you in poor, lowly estate, and gave you all the present happiness you now experience. Take heed of every word I say, for there is no creature who can hear it but the two of us.

You know well yourself how you came here into this house; it has not been a long time. And though you are cherished and dear to me, you are in no way so to my gentle people. They say it is a great shame and woe to them to be subjects and to be in servitude to you, who were born in a little village. And, in truth, especially since your daughter was born, they have spoken these words. But I desire to live my life in quiet and peace with them as before. I cannot be careless in this matter. I must act for the best with your daughter; not as I wish, but only as my people desire. And yet I am loath to do this thing, God knows. And without your knowledge I will not act; but I desire that you give me your consent in this thing. Show now in your action the patience you promised me and swore in your village, that day when your marriage was made.

When she had heard all this, she changed neither in word nor face nor bearing; it seemed as if she were not grieved. She said, "Lord, all lies in your pleasure. My child and I with hearty obedience are all yours, and you may save or destroy your own possession; act according to your own will. May God so save my soul, nothing can please you that can displease me; I desire to have nothing, and fear to lose nothing, except only you. This will now is in me, and shall always be. No length of time or death can destroy it, or change my heart to another place."

This marquis was glad about her answer, yet he pretended as if he were not. His expression and his look were dreary when he went from the chamber. Soon after this he secretly told his full purpose unto a trusty man, and sent him to his wife.

This man was a kind of officer, whom he had often found faithful in weighty matters; such people can discreetly execute things, bad as well as good. The lord well knew he loved and feared him. And when this officer knew his lord's will, he entered the chamber.

"Madame," he said, "though I may be doing a thing to which I am constrained, you must forgive me of it. You are so wise that you know well that lords' behests must not be avoided. These commands may well be bewailed or lamented; but one must obey the lord's pleasure, and so I shall. There is nothing more to say. I am commanded to take this child." And he said no more, but caught up the child pitilessly and made motions as though he would have slain it before he departed.

Griselda had to endure all and comply in all things, and sat meek and quiet as a lamb and let him do his will. This man had a bad reputation; his face was suspect, as were his words; suspect also was the time in which he carried this out.

Alas, she thought he would have slain her daughter, whom she loved so, right then. But still she neither wept nor sighed, consenting to what the marquis willed. But at last she began to speak, and meekly prayed the officer that, as he was a worthy man and of gentle stock, she might kiss her child before it died.

And with a calm face she laid this little child in her bosom, and she then blessed it, lulled it, and afterwards kissed it. And then she said in her gentle voice, "Farewell, my child. I shall never see you again. But since I have marked you with the cross of that Father – blessed may He be – Who died for us on a cross of wood. Your soul, little child, I commit to Him, for this night you shall die for my sake."

I believe that to a nurse it would have been hard to see this pitiful act; well might a mother have cried, "Alas!" Yet she was so calm and steadfast that she endured all adversity, and meekly said to the officer, "Take here your little young maiden again. Go now, do my lord's command," she said. "But by your grace I will pray you one thing, that, unless my lord forbade you, at least you bury this little body in some spot where no beasts or birds may tear it to pieces." But to that he would speak no word, and took the child and went his way.

This officer came back to his lord and told him Griselda's words and demeanor, point for point, in short and plain, and presented him with his sweet daughter. This lord felt some pity, after his fashion, but nevertheless, as lords do when they will have their way, held still to his purpose, and told this officer that he should secretly wind and wrap this child softly and tenderly with all his care, and carry it in a crib or cloth; but, upon pain of having his head struck off, he should let no man know his purpose, nor from where he came or where he went. And he should take it to the lord's dear sister at Bologna, who at that time was countess of Panigo, and should explain this matter to her, beseeching her to do her best to foster this child in all matters of gentle breeding. And he bade her to hide whose child it was from every creature, no matter what might happen. And the sergeant went, and carried this thing out.

But now we return to this marquis. For now he went intently examining whether he could see by his wife's bearing, or perceive by her speech, that she was changed. But he never could find her as anything but steadfast and gentle at all times. In every way she was as glad, as humble, and as busy in service and in love to him as she was accustomed to be, and she spoke not a word of her daughter.

No accidental evidence of any affliction she felt was seen in her, nor did she ever mention her daughter's name, in earnest or in game.[12]

Here ends the third part.

Here follows the fourth part.

Four years in this manner passed, before she was with child again; but now, as God willed, she bore by this Walter a baby boy, gracious and fair to see. And when people told it to his father, not only he but all his land was merry for this child, and thanked and praised God. When it was two years old and parted from the breast of its nurse, one day the desire seized the marquis to test his wife yet again, if he could. Ah, needless was the test! But wedded men know no moderation, when they find a patient creature.

"Wife," said this marquis, "before this, you have heard that my people dislike our marriage, and especially is it worse than ever in our lives now since my son is born. The murmuring slays my heart! For the voice comes to my ears so bitterly that it nearly destroys my spirit. They say this now: 'When Walter is gone, then shall the blood of Janicula succeed and be our lord, for we have no other.' Such words my people surely say. Well ought I to take heed of such murmuring, for in truth I fear it, though they speak not

---

[12] In earnest or in game. I.e., on any account.

openly in my presence; I wish to live in peace, if I could. For this reason I am fully resolved to serve him secretly by night as I served his sister. I warn you of this, lest you suddenly act distractedly in your grief; be patient, I pray you."

She said, "I have said, and ever shall, that I wish nothing and refuse nothing, in truth, except as you wish. I grieve not at all though my daughter and son have been slain, as it was at your command. I have had no part in my two children except sickness first, and then woe and pain. You are our lord: do with your own just as you wish. Ask no advice from me, for just as I left at home all of my clothing when I first came to you, so I left my will and all my freedom, and took your clothing. Therefore, I pray you, do your pleasure; I will obey your will.

"And surely, if I had foreknowledge to understand your desire before you told it to me, I would do it without neglect. But now that I know your desire and what you wish, I hold firmly to all your pleasure. For if I knew that my death would do you pleasure, I would die very gladly to please you. Death can hold no comparison to your love."

And when this marquis saw the constancy of his wife, he cast down his two eyes, and marveled that she could suffer all this treatment in patience. And he went forth with dreary countenance, but in his heart was great gladness. This ill-favored officer, just as he had seized her daughter, in the same way or worse (if a man could contrive worse) caught up her son, who was so full of beauty. And likewise she was so patient that she made no heavy expression, but kissed her son and made the sign of the cross over him. The only exception was this: she prayed the man that, if he could, he should bury her little son in the earth, to save his tender limbs from fowls and beasts.

But she could get no answer from him; he went his way as if he did not care. But he brought the child very tenderly to Bologna. This marquis more and more wondered at her patience; and if he had not truly known before this that she loved her children perfectly, he would have thought that she had endured this with such a calm expression out of some deception, and from cruelty or malice. But in truth he knew that next to him she loved her children best of the whole world.

But now I would gladly ask of women if these tests should not have sufficed. What more could a harsh husband contrive to test her wifehood and steadfastness, while he continued at all times in his harshness? But there are people of such disposition that, when they have taken a certain course, they cannot stop, but just as if they were bound to a stake, they will not slacken from that first purpose. Just so, this marquis intended fully to test his wife, as he was first inclined.

He watched to see by word or bearing if she were changed toward him, but never could find variance; she was always the same in heart and expression. And the older she grew, the truer in love she was to him, if that were possible, and the more painstaking. It seemed that in the two of them there was but one will, for as Walter wished, the same was her pleasure as well. And, God be thanked, all happened for the best. She well showed that for no earthly discomfort should a wife wish anything, except as her husband may wish.

The evil reputation of Walter spread often and widely, that by a cruel heart he had wickedly murdered both his children in secret, because he had wedded a poor woman. Such murmur was commonly among them; it is no wonder, for no word came to the people's ears except that they were murdered. Therefore, though his people before had loved him well, the scandal made them hate him. To be a murderer is a hateful report! But nevertheless he would not stop from his cruel purpose in earnest or in game;[13] his mind was fully set upon testing his wife.

When his daughter was twelve years of age, he sent his

[13] In earnest or in game. I.e., on any account.

messenger to the court of Rome, which had been informed of his will already in secret fashion, commanding them to contrive such bulls[14] as should answer his cruel purpose: how the pope, as if for the quiet of his people, ordered him wed another if he wished. I say he commanded that they should counterfeit the papal bulls, making mention that he had leave to abandon his first wife, as if by the pope's dispensation, to stop the rancor and strife between his people and him; thus said the bull, which they made public to all. The common people, and no wonder, knew full well that it would be so. When these tidings came to Griselda, I believe her heart was sad; but she, this humble creature, always just as constant, was entirely ready to endure the adversity of Fortune, awaiting always his desire and pleasure, to whom, heart and all, she was given as to her true earthly sufficiency.

But, to tell this story shortly, the marquis wrote a special letter in which he showed his full intention, and dispatched it secretly to Bologna. He especially prayed the earl of Panigo, who had wedded his sister, to bring his two children home again openly in honorable state. But he asked him one thing above all, that even if people should ask, he should tell no creature whose children they were, but say that the maiden was to be wedded soon to the Marquis of Saluzzo. And this earl did just as he was asked.

For on the day set he went on his way toward Saluzzo, along with many lords in a rich company, to escort this maiden; her young brother riding beside her. This blooming maiden was arrayed in preparation for her marriage with many clear gems; her brother, seven years old, was also arrayed freshly, as befitted him. And thus with great magnificence and joyful mood they rode from day to day on their journey, shaping their course toward Saluzzo.

Here ends the fourth part.

Here follows the fifth part.

---

[14] Bulls. Official communications from the pope.

Meanwhile, and after all his wicked behavior, to test his wife still more, to prove her disposition to the utmost, and to learn fully whether she were as steadfast as formerly, one day in front of others this marquis spoke these words roughly to her: "Surely, Griselda, I have had pleasure enough in having you as a wife, for your goodness, loyalty and obedience, not for any lineage or wealth of yours. But now, when I well reflect, I know in very truth that in greatness of rank there is great servitude in many ways; I have not the freedom of every ploughman. My people cry day after day and force me to take another wife. And the pope also, to allay rancor, consents to this. And in truth I must tell you this: that my new wife is on her way. Be strong of heart, and leave her place. And the dowry that you brought me, take it again; I grant you that grace. Return to your father's house. No person may have prosperity always. I counsel you to endure the stroke of Fortune or of chance with a steady heart."

And she answered again patiently, "My lord, I know, and knew always, that no man may make comparison between your magnificence and my poverty; no man can say no to that. I never held myself worthy in any way to be your wife; no, nor your chamber-maid. And I take almighty God as my witness, and – may He so surely gladden my soul – in this house where you made me a lady I never held myself to be the lady or mistress, but humble servant to your honor, above every earthly creature; and so I shall ever be as long as I shall live.

"Through your kindness you have so long held me in honor and dignity of which I was not worthy; for that I thank God and you, and I pray Him to reward you. There is no more to say. Gladly will I return to my father, and dwell with him to the end of my life. Where I was fostered from childhood, I will lead my life until I die, a widow pure in body, heart and all. For since I gave you my maidenhead and am your undoubted loyal wife, God forbids that such a lord's wife take another man as husband or mate. And with your new wife may God through His grace grant you happiness and prosperity; I will gladly yield her my room where I was accustomed to be happy, for since it pleases you that I shall go, my lord, who were once all my heart's repose, I will go when you desire.

"But as for your offer such dowry as I first brought, it is well in my mind that it was only my wretched unsightly clothing, which now would be hard to recover. O good God! How noble and kind you seemed by your speech and expression that day when our marriage was made! But to tell the truth – at least I find it to be truth, for it is proved in me – love old is not as it was new.

"But certainly, lord, I would die for it, for nothing shall ever make me repent in word or deed giving you my heart with full purpose. My lord, you know that you had me stripped of my poor clothes in my father's home, and by your grace clad me richly. Truly I brought nothing else to you, except faithfulness and nakedness and maidenhead. And here I return my clothing forevermore, and my wedding-ring as well. The remnant of your jewels, I dare assure you, are ready within your chamber.

"Naked I came out of my father's house, and naked must I return.[15] All your pleasure I gladly would follow, yet I hope it would not be your will that I go out of your palace smockless. You could not do so unseemly a thing as permit that body in which your children once lay to be seen entirely bare before the people as I walk. For this reason, I pray you, let me not go like a worm by the road. Recall, my own lord so dear, I was your wife, though unworthy. As reward for my maidenhead, therefore, which I brought and do not bear away again, promise to give me as payment only such a smock as I was accustomed to wear, so that I may cover the body of her who was your wife. And here, lest I offend you, I take my leave of you, my own lord."

---

[15] Naked I . . . return. This line echoes Job 1.21. "Naked I came forth from my mother's womb, and naked shall I go back again."

He replied, "The smock which you have on your back, let it remain there and bear it forth with you." But for the compassion and pity he felt he could scarcely speak these words, and needed to go out. Before the people she strips herself, and goes forth toward her father's house in her smock, with her head and feet entirely bare.

The people follow her, weeping in their way, and as they go they curse Fortune at all points. But she kept her eyes dry of tears, and in this entire time spoke no word. Her father, who soon heard these tidings, cursed the day and hour that nature formed him to be a living being; for in truth this old poor man was always suspicious of her marriage, and ever since the beginning he judged that when this lord had accomplished his desires, he would think it a disgrace to his estate to descend so low, and would discard her as soon as he could.

He went quickly to meet his daughter, for by the noise of the people he knew she was coming, and weeping sorely he covered her with her old coat, as well as he could. But he could not cover her entire body, for the cloth was coarse and much older than it was on the day of her marriage.

Thus for a certain time this flower of wifely patience dwelt with her father, in such a way that neither by her words nor by her expression, before the people or in their absence, did she show that injury had been done her; nor did she seem to have any remembrance of her high estate. And it was no wonder; for in her great estate her spirit had always been in complete humility; hers had been no delicate palate or pleasure-loving heart, no pomp or semblance of royalty, but she was always full of patience and kindness; she was always discreet, humble, and honorable, as well as meek and constant to her husband at all times. People speak of Job,[16]

[16] Job. Biblical figure who had all the worldly gifts one could ever want and head them all stripped away from him as a test of his virtue. Like Griselda, he is known for his patience; thus the phrase, "the patience of Job."

and most of all of his humility, as scholars can well explain when they wish to speak concerning holy men. But in truth, though scholars praise women rather little, no man can behave as humbly as a woman can, nor can be half as loyal as a woman can be, unless it has happened very recently.

Part Six

This earl of Panigo had come from Bologna, from which the report spread among great and small. And it was known in the ears of all the people that he brought with him a new marchioness in such magnificence and splendor that never had the eye of man seen so noble an array in all of West Lombardy. The marquis, who planned and knew all this, before the earl came, sent his messenger to this same simple poor Griselda. And she came at his command with humble heart and glad expression and with no swelling thoughts in her mind, and set down on her knees, and greeted him reverently and discreetly.

"Griselda," he said, "it is fully my intention that this maiden, who shall be wedded to me, be received tomorrow in my house as royally as it is possible; and that every creature according to his degree shall be seated, served, and entertained as best as I can arrange it. In truth I have no women able to put the rooms in order according to my preferences; and therefore I gladly would like it if all the oversight of it were yours. You know also from before all my pleasure. Though your clothes may be poor and wretched-looking, do you your duty, at the least."

She said, "Not only, lord, am I glad to do your pleasure now, but in all things I desire also to serve you and to please you in my degree without fainting, and shall evermore. Never, for joy or woe, shall the spirit in my heart cease to love you best with all my loyal purpose.

And with that word she began to prepare the house and to set tables and make beds, and took pains to do all she could, asking the chambermaids for God's sake to hurry and shake and sweep fast. And she, the hardest-working of all, arranged the hall and every chamber.

About mid-morning this earl alighted, and with him these two noble children, whose array, so richly furnished, the people ran to gaze upon. And then first they said among themselves that Walter was no fool though he desired to change his wife, for it was for the best. For, as they all judged, she was more beautiful than Griselda, and of more tender years; and fairer fruit and more pleasing should spring from them, because of her high lineage. Her brother also was so handsome of face that the people were pleased to see them, commending now the choice of the marquis.

"O stormy people! Changeable as a weather vane, unstable, ever faithless, indiscreet, delighting always in new rumor! Forever you wax and wane like the moon. Ever full of gabbing that is not worth a farthing! Your judgment is false, and your constancy turns out badly; anyone who trusts in you is a great fool." So said the serious people in that city, when the people were gazing this way and that, because they were glad, only for the novelty of it, to have a new lady of their town. I make no more mention of this; but I will address myself again to Griselda, and tell of her constancy and zeal.

Griselda was very busy in all that pertained to the feast. Not at all was she ashamed of her clothing, though it was rude and somewhat torn. But with glad countenance she took herself to the gate with the other people, to greet the marchioness, and after that continued her tasks. And she received the guests with such glad appearance and discernment, each according to his degree, that none perceived any fault; but they always wondered who she might be, who was in such poor attire, and yet so well understood stately ceremony, and they praised the worthiness of her prudence.

Meanwhile she did not cease to commend so well this maiden, and her brother, with all her heart and gracious temper, so that none could have praised them better.

At last, when these lords went to sit down to their meal, the marquis called Griselda while she was busy in his hall.

"Griselda," he said, as if it were in jest, "how do you like my wife, and her beauty?

"Very well, my lord," she answered; "for in good faith I never saw a more beautiful one. I pray God to give her prosperity, and much pleasure to you both until your life's end. One thing I ask you and warn you also: that you do not goad this tender maiden with any tormenting, as you have others. For she has been fostered more tenderly, and, to my thinking, she could not bear adversity as could a creature fostered in poverty."

And when this Walter saw her patience, and glad expression without any malice, though he had so often afflicted her, and how she was ever steady and constant as a wall, continuing at all times her innocence, this stern marquis began to incline his heart to take pity upon her wifely steadfastness.

"This is enough, my Griselda. Be no more aghast," said he, "nor displeased. I have tested your loyalty and your kindness both in a great rank and in poverty, as well as ever woman was tested. Now I know, dear wife, your steadfastness." And he took her in his arms and began to kiss her. And she in her wonder did not understand it; she did not hear what he said to her. She acted as if she had just started out of a sleep, until she came to her senses out of her dazedness.

"Griselda," he said, "by God Who died for us, you are my wife, nor have I another, nor ever had, may God save my soul! This is your daughter whom you supposed to be my wife; the other, in faith, shall be my heir, as I have always intended. You bore him truly in your body. I have kept them secretly at Bologna; but take them back, for now you cannot say that you have lost either of your two children. And people that have said otherwise of me, I warn them well that I have done this deed out of neither malice nor cruelty, but to test your womanhood; not to slay my children – God forbid

– but to keep them secretly until I knew all your mind and will."

When she heard this, she fell down in a swoon for piteous joy, and after her swooning she called both her young children to her; and, piteously weeping, embraced them in her arms and tenderly kissed them, just as a mother, with her salt tears bedewing their hair and their faces. Ah, what a pitiful thing it was to see her swooning and to hear her humble voice!

"Lord have mercy," she said, "I thank you that you have saved me my dear children. Now I do not care even if I should die right here; since I stand in your love and grace, no matter when my spirit departs. O, my tender, dear young children! Your sorrowful mother believed very well that cruel hounds or some foul vermin had eaten you; but God in his mercy, and your benign father, have caused you to be tenderly guarded." And in that same moment suddenly she fell to the ground. And in her swoon she held her two children so firmly in her embrace that only with much skill and difficulty they removed the children from her arms. Ah, many tears trickled down many pitying faces among them that stood nearby; scarcely could they remain about her.

Walter cheered her and soothed her sorrow; she rose up from her trance embarrassed, and every creature expressed joy and congratulations to her, until she regained her senses once more. Walter so earnestly strove to please her that it was a delight to see the gladness between the two, now that they were joined again. These ladies, when they saw their time, took her and went into a chamber and stripped off her poor garments, and in cloth of gold that shone bright, with a crown of many rich stones upon her head, they led her into the hall, where she was honored as was her due. Thus came this piteous day to a joyous end, for every creature strove to spend the day in mirth and revel, until the stars' light shone in the sky. Far more splendid in every man's sight was this feast, and of greater cost, than was the revel at their wedding.

These two lived many years in great prosperity, harmony, and peace. The marquis married his daughter richly to a lord, one of the worthiest of all Italy. And he kept his wife's father in rest and peace at his court, until the soul crept out of his body. Griselda's son, after his father's day, succeeded to his inheritance in quiet and peace, and was fortunate also in marriage, though he did not put his wife to a great test.

The world is not so strong, there is no denying it, as it was in olden times; listen, therefore, to what my author[17] says. This story was not told so that wives will follow Griselda's example in humility, for that would be intolerable even if they wanted to, but so that everyone, according to his station, will be steadfast in adversity as Griselda was. It was with this purpose that Petrarch wrote this story, which is set down in high style.

Since one woman was so patient towards a mortal man, the more we should receive with patience all that God sends us, for it is reasonable that He should test those whom He created. However, He will not tempt anyone whom he had redeemed, as St. James will tell you if you read his epistle.[18] Undoubtedly God tests people every day and permits us often to be beaten in various ways, for our own good, with the sharp lashes of adversity – not so that He may know our qualities, for surely He knew all our weaknesses before we were ever born. His arrangements are all for our profit; let us live then in virtuous patience.

Hear but one more word, ladies and gentlemen, before I stop. Nowadays it would be very hard to find two or three like Griselda in a whole town. For if they were put to such tests, their gold is so badly alloyed with brass[19] that, though

---

[17] My author. The source (or sources) for this tale, i.e., Boccaccio and Petrarch, though the conclusions of the three versions vary greatly.

[18] St. James . . .epistle. See James 1.13.

[19] Gold is so badly alloyed with brass. In other words, they are not pure or

the coin appears to be good, it is more likely to break in two than bend. And so, for the love of the Wife of Bath – may God keep her and all her sex in supremacy: it would be a pity otherwise – with all lusty spirit, fresh and vigorous, I shall sing you a song which I think will please you. So let us stop this serious talk; listen to my song which goes like this:[20]

Chaucer's Envoy[21]

Griselda is dead, and her patience, too, and both are buried together in Italy. Therefore, I openly declare that no married man should be so harsh as to try his wife's patience in hope of finding another Griselda, for he shall certainly fail.

Oh, noble wives, full of high wisdom, let no humility nail down your tongue, and let no scholar have cause or reason to write so marvelous a story about you as the tale of patient Griselda, lest Chichevache,[22] the cow, swallow you into her belly. Follow the example of Echo,[23] who never keeps quiet but always answers back. Don't be tricked in your innocence; take the control into your own hands. Engrave this lesson deeply in your memories, for it will work to the common profit of all.

You wives, strong as big camels, stand up for your own rights; don't allow men to do injustices to you. And weak wives, feeble in battle, be fierce as a tiger yonder in India;

---

made entirely of the best elements.

[20] Like this. The next section, usually titled in modern editions as "Chaucer's Envoy," adopts a completely different tone. One might imagine the Clerk speaking in a woman's voice, in imitation of the Wife of Bath. It should be apparent that the words the Clerk sings here are not his voice, since it refutes what he has just said and tells the audience not to listen to clerks (scholars). The advice offered in these lines also closely aligns with that which the Wife of Bath has offered in her Prologue.

[21] Envoy. Usually a short song of parting in which the poet tells his poem to fly off to his intended audience.

[22] Chichevache the cow. A lean cow fabled to have fed on patient wives, so it consequently (so the story goes) had little to eat.

[23] Echo. Mythological maiden, unrequited lover of Narcissus, whose voice repeated the last syllable of each of her utterances.

always chatter like a windmill, I advise you. Don't fear men or pay them respect, for though your husband may be dressed in armor, the arrows of your crabbed eloquence will pierce his breast and his helmet. I advise you to bind him with jealousy and you will make him cower like a quail. If you are pretty, show your face and your dress where people are present; if you are ugly, be generous in your spending; always work hard to make friends. Be as gay in spirit as a linden leaf, and let him worry and weep, wring his hands and wail!

Behold the Merry Words of the Host.[24]

When the Clerk had finished his story, our host swore and said: "By God's bones, I'd rather my wife at home had heard this story just once than have a barrel of ale! That's a good story for that purpose. You people know what I'd like, but leave behind what can not be."

Here ends the Tale of the Clerk of Oxford.

[24] Merry words of the host. This part does not appear in all manuscripts, but is considered by most editors to be worthy of inclusion.

THE MERCHANT'S TALE

The Prologue of the Merchant's Tale

"About weeping and wailing,[1] care and sorrow, I know plenty," said the Merchant, "both day and night, and so do others who are wedded, I believe. Well I know it is so with me. I have a wife, the worst one possible; for even if the Fiend were coupled to her, I dare well swear she would outmatch him. Why should I rehearse to you all the points of her great malice? She is an evil creature in every way. There is a long and large difference between Griselda's[2] meekness and the surpassing cruelty of my wife.

"If I were unbound, never again would I come into the snare,[3] by my head! We wedded men live in worry and sorrow. Try it, those who wish to, and they shall find, by Saint Thomas of India,[4] that I tell the truth, at least for the greater part – I speak not of all. May God save us, if it should be so!

"Ah, good sir Host! I have been wedded these two months, and not more, by God! And yet I believe that he who has been wifeless all his life could in no way, even if

---

[1] Weeping and wailing. The epilogue of the *Clerk's Tale*, the tale preceding this one, has just ended with a note that women should work to get the upper hand in marriage and let their husbands worry, weep, wring their hands, and wail over the trouble that their wives give them. This last part of the epilogue to the *Clerk's Tale*, however, is spoken in an ironic tone, since the tale itself presents the point of view that women should be subservient to their husbands.

[2] Griselda. In an earlier tale, the Clerk has told of patient Griselda, a woman who endured the many hardships and cruelties set forth for her by her own husband, who was testing her loyalty.

[3] The snare. I.e., of marriage.

[4] St. Thomas of India. St. Thomas the Apostle, who, according to legend, traveled to India to convert thousands to Christianity.

men would tear him to the heart, tell so much sorrow as I now could tell here of my wife's cursedness!"

Our Host said, "Now, Merchant, may God save your soul, since you know so much about that business, I pray you heartily, tell us a part of it."

"Gladly," he replied, "only from my own pain will I, for my sorry heart I can tell no more."

Here begins the Merchant's Tale.

Some time ago there dwelt in Lombardy[5] a worthy knight, born in Pavia, in which town he lived in great prosperity; and for sixty years he was wifeless and always pursued his carnal pleasure on women where his appetite was set, just as these fools do who are laymen.[6] And when he was past sixty years, this knight had such a mind to be a wedded man – whether it was from holiness or dotage, I cannot say – that he did all he could, day and night, to determine how he might become wedded. He prayed to our Lord to grant him once to know that very blissful existence that is between husband and wife, and to live under that holy bond with which God first bound man and woman.

"No other way of life," he said, "is worth a bean. For wedlock is so simple and pure that it is paradise on earth." Thus spoke this old knight, who was so wise.

"And certainly, as true as God is King, it is glorious to take a wife, especially when a man is old and white-haired; then a wife is the fruit of his treasure. Then he ought to take a young and beautiful wife, on whom to beget himself an heir; and lead his life in joy and bliss, while these bachelors sing 'alas,' when they find any adversity in their affairs of love, which are but childish vanity.

---

[5] Lombardy. The central northern region of Italy.

[6] Laymen. Secular, as opposed to clerical or religious professions. As the merchant is a layman, some scholars take this line as evidence that this tale should have been told by a religious person on the pilgrimage such as the monk. Others see it as a touch of self-deprecating irony.

"And in truth it is fitting that bachelors often have pain and woe; they build on brittle ground, and find brittleness when they look for certainty. They live just as a bird or a beast, in freedom, under no restraint, while a wedded man in his degree lives a life blessed and ordered, secured under the yoke of marriage.

"Well may his heart abound in all gladness and bliss. For who can be as obedient as a wife? Who is as faithful as his mate, and as attentive to care for him, sick and well? For well or for woe, she will not forsake him. She is not weary to love and serve him, though he may lie bedridden until he may die. And yet some scholars deny it, of whom Theophrastus[7] is one. But what does it matter if Theophrastus wishes to lie? He says, 'Take no wife, for the sake of your thrift, to spare expense in your household a faithful servant is more diligent than your own wife to keep your goods. For all her days she will claim a half. And if you are sick, as God is my witness, your true friends or a faithful lad will care for you better than she that ever waits, and has waited many days, for your goods.' This man writes this evil saying, and a hundred more – may God curse his bones! But heed no such vain opinions; reject Theophrastus and listen to me.

"Truly, a wife is God's gift. All other forms of gifts, such as lands, rents, pasture, common or personal property, all are gifts of Fortune, I declare boldly, which pass away as a shadow upon the wall. But without doubt, and, to speak plainly, a wife will last and abide in your house (longer than you would wish, perhaps). Marriage is a great sacrament; he who has no wife, I believe him to be a lost man, who lives helpless and desolate – I am speaking of lay people.[8]

---

[7] Theophrastus. Author of the lost book *Liber de Nuptiis* (*The Book of Marriage*), an anti-feminist tract that is mentioned in the Wife of Bath's Prologue (see note on this below) and that is used by St. Jerome in *Jerome adversus Jovinianum* (*Jerome Against Jovinian*), another famous anti-feminist tract.

[8] Lay people. As noted above, this may be an indication that this tale was originally intended for a religious teller.

"And hear why – I don't say this lightly – it is because woman was created to be man's help. When he had made Adam, and saw him all alone, and stark naked, the great God, from his great goodness said, 'Let us now make a helper for this man, like him.' And then he made Eve for him. Here you may see and prove by this that a wife is man's help and comfort, his terrestrial paradise and his amusement. So obedient and excellent she is that they cannot do other than live in unity. They are one flesh; and one flesh, I would say, has but one heart in wellness and woe.

"A wife! Ah, Holy Mary! God bless! How could a man who has a wife feel any adversity? Surely, I cannot say. The bliss that is between the two of them no tongue can tell or heart can think. If he is poor, she helps him labor; she keeps his goods and never wastes a bit. All that her husband desires pleases her well! She never says 'no' when he says 'yes.' He says, 'do this'; she answers, 'all ready, sir.' O, blessed order, precious wedlock, you are so pleasant and virtuous and so highly commended and approved, that every man who maintains himself to be worth a leek ought to thank his God that has sent him a wife, or else pray God to send him a wife to last until he dies. For then is his life set in security.

"He cannot be deceived, I believe, so he works according to his wife's counsel; wives are so faithful and discreet that he may hold his head up boldly. Therefore, if you wish to be like the wise, always do as women counsel you.

"Lo, how Jacob[9] by the good counsel of Rebecca, his mother, as these scholars tell, bound the kid's skin about his neck, and thus won his father's blessing. Lo, Judith,[10] as the

---

[9] Jacob. Old Testament figure whose mother Rebecca advised him to wear a kid's skin in order to deceive his father Isaac into passing the family blessing, i.e., inheritance, to him instead of his twin brother Esau, the older son. Jacob's twelve sons then become the fathers of the twelve tribes of Israel. Jacob's name means "deceiver."

[10] Judith. Old Testament figure who slays the Assyrian general Holofernes before he is able to rape her. Her act of courage leads the Israelites to vic-

history tells; she by wise counsel guarded God's people and slew Holofernes while he slept. Lo, Abigail,[11] how she by good counsel saved her husband, Nabal, when he was to have been slain. And look also how Esther[12] by good counsel delivered the people of God from woe, and made Mordecai to be advanced by Ahasuerus.

"There is nothing superlative in degree, as Seneca[13] says, 'above a humble wife.' 'Endure your wife's tongue,' as Cato[14] bids. 'She shall command, and you shall permit it, and yet of her courtesy sometimes she will obey.' A wife is the keeper of your household. Well may the sick man wail and weep who has no wife to keep his house. I warn you, if you wish to act wisely love your wife well, as Christ loves His church. If you love yourself, you will love your wife. No man hates his own flesh, but he fosters it all the days of his life; and therefore I bid you to cherish your wife, or you shall never prosper. However men may mock and jest, of all mortal people husband and wife hold the safest road. They are so closely knit that no harm can happen – and especially from the wife's side."

Thus in the days of his age, this January, of whom I speak, meditated on the lusty life and the virtuous repose of honey-sweet marriage. And one day he sent for his friends to tell them all his intention.

---

tory. (In some Protestant Bibles the Book of Judith is included in The Apocrypha.)

[11] Abigail. Old Testament woman who persuaded David, who desired her, not to take vengeance on her husband, but married David when Nabal died. See 1 Samuel 25.1-35.

[12] Esther. Beautiful Jewish woman, who is chosen as queen by the Persian King Ahasuerus (Xerxes I or II) after he has rejected his previous wife, Vashti. The duplicitous Haman plotted the massacre of the Jews, but Esther and her cousin Mordecai stopped him. Haman was hanged, and Mordecai became the king's chief minister. See Esther 7.1-10.

[13] Seneca. Actually, the quote is from Fulgentius in the *The Mythographies* 1.22.

[14] Cato. Author of the *Distiches of Cato*, a work of proverbs that was popular in the Middle Ages.

With grave countenance he told his tale, and said, "Friends, I am white-haired and old, and, God knows, almost on the brink of the grave; now must I consider my soul a bit. I have wasted my body on folly, but – blessed be God! – that shall be amended for I will be a wedded man, and that will soon be so, surely, in all possible haste. I pray you, help me to plan for my speedy marriage to some fair maiden of tender years, for I will not delay; and on my side, I will try to seek out to whom I may be quickly wedded. But inasmuch as you are more numerous than I, you rather than I should be able to seek out such a thing, and in such a way that it would be best for me to make an alliance.

"But of one thing, my dear friends, I warn you: in no manner will I have any old wife. In truth, she shall not be over twenty years of age; I gladly would have old fish and young flesh.[15] Better is a pike than a pickerel, and better the tender veal than old beef," he said. "I will have no woman thirty years of age; such creatures are but dried beanstalks and coarse fodder. And these old widows – God knows – they know so much of Wade's boat,[16] create so many small annoyances when they wish, that I should never live in peace with a widow. For studying in diverse schools will make subtle scholars; and woman has studied in many schools. But certainly men can guide a young thing, just as men can mold warm wax with the hands. Therefore I tell you plainly and in short, I will have no old wife, for this very reason.

"For if it turned out so ill that I could have no joy in her, then I would lead a life of adultery and go straight to the Devil when I die. And I would beget no children by her; yet I tell you all, I'd rather hounds would eat me than that my

---

[15] Old fish and young flesh. An old proverb. The complete saying is "old fish and young flesh feed a man best."

[16] Wade's boat. Many editors have tried to explain this phrase by referring to Germanic mythology, but nobody has been able to pinpoint the exact meaning of the clause. The point may be that these women know so much about something that there is nothing to know about.

heritage should fall into strange hands. I dote not, I know the reason why men should wed, and furthermore I know that many men speak of wedlock who knows no more than my page for what reasons man should take a wife. If he cannot live chaste all his days, let him take a wife in piety, for the sake of procreating children, to the honor of God in heaven and not only for love and passion; and because they should shun lechery and yield their debt when it is due; furthermore, each of them should help the other in misfortune, as a brother shall a sister, and live holily in chastity.

"But, sirs, by your leave, I am not such for, God be thanked, I feel my limbs strong and sufficient to play all a man's part. I know best what I can do. Though I may be white on my head, I fare like a tree that blossoms before it yields fruit; a blossoming tree is not dry or dead. I feel myself white only on my hair; my heart and limbs are as green as the laurel is throughout the year. And since you have heard my whole mind, I pray you agree to my will."

Diverse men told him diversely many old examples about marriage. In truth, some blamed it, some praised it; but in the end, to speak briefly, as altercation every day occurs between friends in dispute, there arose strife between his two kinsmen, of whom the first was called Placebo,[17] the second Justinus.

Placebo said, "Brother January, you had very little need, my lord so dear, to ask counsel of anyone present, save that you are so wise that by your great prudence you wish not turn aside from the word of Solomon. This advice he said to us, 'Do all things by counsel and then you shall not repent.' But though Solomon spoke such words, my own dear lord and brother, I hold your own counsel the best, so may God save my soul! For, my brother, take this from me: I have been a courtier all my life now, and God knows, though I am unworthy, I have stood in high position with lords of great estate; yet I never had strife with any of them. Truly, I never

[17] Placebo. In Latin the word means "I will please or accept."

contradicted them.

"I know well my lord knows more than I; what he says I hold to be sound, and say the same, or things similar. Any counselor who serves a lord of high degree is a complete fool, if he dare take upon himself, or even think, that his counsel should surpass his lord's wisdom. No, by my faith, lords are no fools; you yourself have showed here today so well and in such holy fashion your lofty wisdom, so devoutly and well, that I approve and confirm all your words and your opinion every bit. By the Lord, there is no man in this entire town nor in all Italy who could have spoken better; Christ is well pleased with this counsel. And in truth it shows a high spirit in any man who is advanced in age, to take a young wife; by my father's soul, your heart hangs on a jolly nail! Do in this just as you wish, for in conclusion I think it best."

Justinus, who sat quietly throughout and listened, answered Placebo in this fashion. "Now, my brother, be patient, I ask you; since you have spoken, listen to me. Seneca, among his other wise words, says that a man ought very well to consider to whom he gives his land or his goods. And since I ought to consider well to whom I give my goods away, much more ought I to consider to whom I give my body; for well I warn you it is no child's play to take a wife without due thought. A man must inquire, I believe, whether she may be wise, sober, drunken, proud (or otherwise a shrew), a scolder, a waster of your goods, rich, poor, or even man-crazy.[18]

"Albeit no man shall find or imagine any in this world that trots perfectly in all things, neither man nor beast, nevertheless, it should suffice that any wife will have more good traits than ill vices. And all this demands leisure to inquire into. For, God knows, I have wept many private tears since I have had a wife. Let whoever will praise the life of a wedded man, in truth, I find in it only cost and care, and duties bare of all bliss.

---

[18] Man-crazy. Lustful.

"And yet, God knows, my neighbors around me, and especially many troops of women, say I have the most steadfast and meekest wife living. But I know best where my shoe pinches me. But for all of me, you may do just as you will; you are a man of years, consider how you enter upon marriage, and especially with a young and pretty wife.

"By Him that made water, air, earth, and fire, the youngest man in all this company has enough to do to keep his wife to himself, trust me. Not for three years can you wholly content her; a wife demands many duties. But I ask you, do not be ill-pleased with me."

"Well, have you done your speech?" said January. A straw for your Seneca and your proverbs; I care not two blades of grass for your school-terms. Wiser men than you have agreed to my plan, as you have heard just now. Placebo, what do you say?"

"I say," he said, "that it is truly a cursed man who hinders matrimony." And at these words they immediately arose and fully agreed that January should wed when he wished and whomever he desired.

High-flown fancies and anxious thoughts about his marriage began to occupy January's soul from day to day, and night by night many lovely shapes and many pretty faces passed through his heart. Whoever would take a well-polished mirror and set it in the general market-place, would see many forms pass across the mirror; and in the same fashion January began to consider in his thoughts the maidens who dwelt near him.

He knew not where his thoughts should settle. For if one had beauty of countenance, another stood so highly in the people's grace for her steadiness and kindness that she most had the general approval. And some were rich and had a bad reputation.

But nevertheless, between earnest and game, at last he decided on one, and let all the others pass out of his heart, and by his own authority chose her; for love is always blind.

And when he was laid in his bed, in his heart and mind he portrayed her fresh beauty and tender age, her small middle, her long and slender arms, her wise demeanor, her good breeding, her womanly bearing, and her steadiness. And when his choice was fixed upon her, it seemed to him that it could not have been bettered; for when he was resolved, he thought every other man's wit so poor that none could speak against his choice; so he imagined.

He sent to his friends with his urgent request and asked them to do him the pleasure of coming to him speedily. He would relieve them, one and all, of their labor, and there was no more need for him to go on searching; he had made up his mind where he would place his affections.

Placebo came immediately, and all his friends as well. And first of all January begged of them the grace that none of them should offer argument against the purpose which he had taken; which course was pleasing to God, and a sure foundation for his well-being. He said there was in the town a maiden who had a great name for beauty, though she was of low degree; but beauty sufficed him. This maiden, he said, he wished to have, to lead all his life with her in ease and holiness; and he thanked God that he might have her entirely, that no creature should share his bliss, and asked them to do their duty that he failed not of success; if they would do this, his spirit would be at rest.

"Then," he said, "there is nothing to mar my bliss, save that one thing pricks in my conscience, which I will rehearse to you here. Long I have heard it said that no man can have two perfect joys," he said, "that is, on earth and in paradise. For even if he may avoid the seven sins and every branch of that tree, yet there is such perfect felicity and ease and joy in marriage, that now in my old age I am ever aghast that I shall now lead so merry a life, so delicious, without woe and contention, that I shall have my heaven now on earth. For since the true heaven is bought so dearly with tribulation and great penance, how should I, then, who shall live in such happiness as all wedded men have, come to the bliss where Christ lives eternally? This is my fear, and please, my two brethren, resolve this question for me, I pray."

Justinus, who despised January's folly, answered without delay in his mockery; and to abridge his long tale he would cite no authority, but said, "Sir, so that there may be no obstacle other than this, God may in His mercy work such a great miracle for you that, before you receive the last sacrament of the Holy Church, you may have reason to repent the married life, in which you say there is no woe or contention. And may God forbid otherwise, that he would send a wedded man grace to repent more often than a single man! And therefore the best counsel I know is, despair not, sir, but have in your memory that perhaps she may be your purgatory. She may be God's instrument and God's scourge; then shall your soul skip up to heaven swifter than an arrow out of a bow. I hope to God that hereafter you shall learn that there is no such felicity in marriage, and never shall be, that will hinder your salvation, as long as you satisfy your wife's desires in moderation, as is just and reasonable, and please her not too amorously, and keep yourself from other sin as well. My tale is done, for my wit is thin, but be not aghast at this, my brother. But let us wade out of this matter. The Wife of Bath[19] has declared full well in little space, if you have understood, upon marriage, which you have in hand. And now fare you well, and may God have you in His grace!"

And after these words Justinus and Placebo each took leave of him and each other. And when they saw it must be so, by discreet and wise negotiation they planned so that this maiden, who was named May, should be wedded to this January as soon as she could. I believe it would delay you

---

[19] Wife of Bath. Another Canterbury pilgrim; she has told her own life story at length, of her five marriages and the troubles in them, especially how as a young woman she tortured and deceived her three much older husbands; she has also told the tale of a knight who discovers what women want most, which is sovereignty over men.

too long if I told you of every bond and document by which she was put into legal possession of his land, or of all her rich preparation. But finally the day had come when they both made their way to the church to receive the holy sacrament. The priest came forth with stole over his shoulders, and bade her be like Rebecca and Sara[20] in faithfulness to marriage vows and in discretion; and said his prayers as is the custom, and signed them with the cross and prayed to God to bless them, and made all very secure with holy rites.

Thus were they wedded with all ceremony, and at the feast he and she sat upon the dais with other honorable people. All full of joy and happiness was the palace, and full of instruments of music and the most dainty cuisine in all Italy. Before them stood instruments of such sound that neither Orpheus nor Amphion[21] of Thebes had ever made such melody. With every course came such bursts of minstrelsy that Joab[22] never trumpeted half so clear to men's hearing, nor Theodamas at Thebes,[23] when the city was in dread. Bacchus[24] poured out the wine for them on every side, and Venus[25] laughed upon every one of them, for January was now her knight and would make trial of his spirit as well in marriage

---

[20] Rebecca and Sara. Two faithful wives of the Old Testament. Rebecca was the wife of Isaac and mother, in her advanced age, to Jacob and Esau. Sara was the wife of Abraham and the mother, also in her advanced age, to Isaac.

[21] Orpheus nor Amphion. Two mythological musicians. Orpheus was the long-suffering husband of Eurydice and traveled to the underworld to retrieve her, but ultimately in vain. Amphion was the leader of Thebes who was given a lyre by Mercury. With his music he later moved the rock that would become the city walls by the power of his music.

[22] Joab. Son of David's sister Zeruiah and the ruthless commander of David's armies; he gave commands through the use of trumpets. See 2 Samuel 2.28, 18.16, an d 20.22.

[23] Theodamas at Thebes. Augur for the Argive besiegers of Thebes after Amphiaraus's death; his first prayer as augur was followed at once by the trumpets of the attacking Thebans, and more trumpets followed a raid on the Thebans that he later inspired. (RC)

[24] Bacchus. The god of wine.

[25] Venus. Goddes of love, especially physical love.

as in freedom; and with her torch in her hand she danced about before the bride and all the company. I dare well say, in truth, that Hymen, who is the god of marriage, never saw in his life so merry a wedded man. You, Martian,[26] the poet who describes to us that merry wedding of Philology and Mercury, and the songs that the Muses sang, hold your peace; too small are both your pen and your tongue to describe this wedding. When tender youth weds stooping age, there is such mirth that it cannot be written; try it yourselves, and then shall you know whether or not I am lying in this.

May, who sat with so benign a countenance, to look upon her seemed as if she were enchanted; so meek was her look, Queen Esther never looked with such eyes upon Ahasuerus.[27] I cannot describe to you all her beauty, but thus much I may tell, that she was like the bright morn of May filled with all beauty and January was ravished into a trance every time he beheld her face. "Now would to God it would become night," he thought, "and that the night would last forever! Would that all these people were gone!"

And finally he did all he could, saving his honor, to hasten them in crafty fashion from the feast. And the time came when there was reason to rise. And after that, people danced and drank deep, and cast spices all about the house, and every man was full of joy and happiness – all but a squire, called Damian, who many days had carved[28] before the knight. He was so ravished with his lady May that for the very pain he was nearly mad; he almost fainted and swooned where he stood, so sorely had Venus wounded him with her brand as she bore it in her dancing. And quickly he got him-

---

[26] Martian. Martianus Capella, fifth-century poet, author of *The Marriage of Philology and Mercury*, a sort of compendium of the Seven Liberal Arts.

[27] Queen Esther never looked with such eyes upon Ahasuerus. See note on Esther above.

[28] Carved. I.e., carved the meat and served January's household.

self to bed. I speak no more of him as at this time, but there let him weep and lament his fill, until fresh May will have pity on his pain.

O perilous fire, that breeds in the bedstraw! O household foe that proffers his service! O traitor servant, false appearance of domestic faithfulness, like the sly faithless serpent in the bosom, may God shield us all from knowing you! O, January, drunken in joy of marriage, see how your Damian, your own squire and your man born, has in mind to do you dishonor. God grant you to spy out your household foe, for there is no worse pestilence in this world than a household foe ever before you.

The sun had run his diurnal arc; his body could no longer sojourn on the horizon in that latitude; night with his dark rough mantle began to overspread the hemisphere. Wherefore all this lusty throng parted from January, with thanks on every side. Home to their houses they rode full of energy, where they did their things just as it pleased them, and went to rest when they saw their time. Soon after, this impatient January wished to go to bed and tarry no longer. He drank punches, cordials and sweet wine of Italy with stinging spices, and many choice medicinal syrups, such as the cursed monk Constantine, has written of in his book *De Coitu*;[29] he was not a bit backward to partake of all of them. And to his close friends he said, "For God's love, in courteous fashion let the house be emptied as soon as may be." And they did just as he desired. The people drank and soon drew the curtain.

The bride was brought to bed as still as a stone; and when the bed had been blessed by the priest, every person left the chamber, and January held tight in his arms his fresh May, his paradise, his mate. He sings to her, and he kisses her repeatedly. With the thick bristles of his rough beard,

---

[29] Constantine. Constantine the African (1015-1087), Benedictine monk and medical scholar who translated the Arabic text known as *De Coitu* (*On sex*).

like the skin of a dogfish, sharp as briars – for he was freshly shaved in his manner – he rubs her all about her tender face, and said, "Alas, I must trespass on you, my spouse, and greatly offend you before the time comes that I will go to sleep. But nonetheless, consider this," he said, "there is no workman, whoever he may be, that may work both well and hastily; this will be done perfectly at leisure. It doesn't matter how long we play; in true wedlock the two of us are coupled, and blessed be the yoke that we are in, for in our actions we can not sin. A man may commit no sin with his wife, nor hurt himself with his own knife, for we have permission of the law to play."

Thus he labored until the day began to dawn, and then he took a sop of bread in fine cleared wine and sat upright in his bed and sang loud and clear, and kissed his wife and made lecherous sport. He was all coltish, and as full of wantonness and chatter as a flecked magpie. The slack skin about his neck shook while he sang, so he chants and croaks. But God knows what May thought in her heart, when she saw him sitting up in his shirt and nightcap, with his lean neck; she did not think his playing was worth a bean.

Then he said, "I will take my rest; now the day has come, I can keep my eyes open no longer." And down he laid his head and slept until prime.[30] And afterwards in due season up rose January, but fresh May, as the good custom is for wives, remained in her chamber up to the fourth morning. For all must have rest sometime, or else they cannot long endure; no living creature can, be it fish or bird, or man or beast.

Now will I speak of the wretched Damian, who, as you shall hear, is languishing for love. And therefore I speak to him in this manner: I say, "O hapless Damian, alas! Answer my demand now, how shall you tell your woe to your lady, the fresh May? She will say "no," and if you speak, she will reveal your sorrow. May God be your help! I can say no

[30] Prime. 9:00 A.M.

better!

This sick Damian so burned in the flames of Venus that he was dying of desire. He could endure no longer in this state, but put his life in jeopardy, and secretly he borrowed a pen-case, and wrote all his pain in a letter, in the style of a complaint or a lay,[31] to his fair fresh lady. And he put it into a purse of silk which hung over his shirt, and laid it next to his breast.

The moon, which on that noon when January wedded fresh May was in the second degree of Taurus, had now glided into Cancer. May had remained in her chamber this long, as is the custom among these nobles; a bride shall not eat in the hall until four days, or three at the least, have passed; then she was to go to the banquet. The fourth day being completed from noon to noon, when the high mass was ended, this January sat in the hall, with May as fresh as a bright summer's morning. And so it happened, this good man considered his squire and said, "Blessed Mary! How is it that Damian attends not upon me? Is he still sick, or what is the matter?

His squires, who stood beside him, made excuses for him because of his sickness, which hindered him from the performance of his duties; no other cause could keep him away.

"That worries me; he is a gentle squire, by my faith!" said January. "If he were to die, it would be a trouble and a pity; he is as wise, discreet, and secret as any man of his degree that I know, and he is manly and willing to serve, and most deserving to prosper. After this meal, as soon as I can, I myself and May also will visit him, to give him all the comfort I know how.'

And for these words every man blessed him, since through his noble kindness he would thus comfort his squire in sickness; for it was a gentle deed.

"Lady," said this January, "after this meal when you

[31] Complaint. A lament in poetic form. Lay. A song, usually one in which there is a setting for the lover's complaint.

have gone from this hall to your chamber with your women, mind that you all go see this Damian. He is a man of gentle blood. Make him some entertainment and tell him that I will visit him when I have rested a little. And hurry along, for I will wait until you have come to me again." And after these words he called to him a squire, who was the marshal of his hall, and told him certain things that he wished.

This fresh May with all her women held her way straight to Damian. Down by his bed-side she sat, comforting him in as kind a way as she could. This Damian, when he saw his opportunity, put into her hand secretly his purse and his letter in which he had written his desires, without more ado than that he sighed deeply, and softly said to her, "Mercy, and I pray that you will not expose me. I am dead if this thing be known."

This purse she hid in her bosom and went her way; you get no more from me on this meeting. And now she came to January, and sat softly upon his bed-side. He took her and kissed her often, and laid himself down to sleep. She made excuse to leave the room, and when she had read through this love letter, at last she tore it all to bits and cast them away in the privy.

Who ponders carefully now but fair fresh May? She came back to the side of old January, who slept until the cough awakened him. Then he asked her to strip herself naked; he wished of her, he said, to have some pleasure. He said her clothes got in the way. And she obeyed, whether she wanted to or not.

But lest prudish people be upset with me, I dare not let you know whether it seemed to her paradise or hell; and here I leave them until evensong rang and they had to arise.

Whether it was by destiny or chance, by some mystic influence or by nature or through the constellations, that the heavens stood in such a configuration that the time was fortunate (for as these scholars say, everything has its time) to give a letter in the service of Venus to any woman, to get her

Jove – as to all this I cannot say. But great God in heaven, who knows no act is without cause, let Him judge all, for I will hold my peace.

But the truth is that this fresh May received that day such an impression of pity for this sick Damian that she could not drive from her heart the thought of bringing him ease. "In truth," she thought, "I care not whom this thing may annoy, for here I assure him to love him best of any creature, even if he has no more than his shirt."

Lo, pity runs swiftly into a gentle heart! Here you may see how excellent a generosity there is in women, when they take counsel well. There may be some tyrant, indeed there are many, with hearts as hard as stone, who would have let him die in that place rather than have granted him their grace; and would rejoice in their cruel pride, and care not though they committed homicide.

This gentle May, full of pity, made a letter with her own hand, and in it she granted him her full grace; there was nothing lacking except a day and place where she might meet him, for it should be just as he would have it. And one day, when she saw her time, May went to visit this Damian, and craftily thrust this letter down under his pillow; let him read it if he wished. She took him by the hand and squeezed it hard, but so secretly that there was not a creature that knew of it, and bid him to be entirely well soon, and went forth to January, when he sent after her.

Up rose Damian the next morning; all his sickness and sorrow were gone. He combed his hair, he preened and adorned himself, he did all that delights and pleases his lady; and toward January he performed as dutifully as ever did any bow-hunting dog. He was so pleasant to every one (for cunning is all, whoever knows how to use it), that every creature was glad to speak well of him; and fully he stood in his lady's favor. And thus I leave Damian going about his business, and I will proceed with my tale.

Some scholars maintain that felicity consists of pleasure,

and if this be so, in truth, this noble January shaped his course by all his power to live in the highest happiness in honorable fashion as is fitting for a knight. His house and all his manner of life were made as honorable and befitting his degree as a king's. Among others of his noble possessions, he made a garden, walled entirely with stone; so beautiful a garden I know of nowhere.

For, beyond a doubt, I believe truly, he who wrote the *Romance of the Rose*[32] could not well describe the beauty of it; nor would Priapus,[33] though he may be god of gardens, be sufficient to tell the beauty of the garden and of the well-spring under an ever-green laurel. Often Pluto and his spouse Proserpina,[34] and all elfdom, amused themselves and made melody about that spring, and danced, as men have told. This aged knight, noble January, took such pleasure in walking and entertaining himself there that he would allow no person except himself to bear the key; for he always carried a little silver key to the small gate, with which, when he wished, he opened it.

And in the summer season, when he wished to pay his wife her marital debt, he would go there with May his wife and none but the two of them. And in this fashion January and his blooming spouse lived many merry days. But earthly joy does not last forever, for January or any creature.

O sudden chance, O you Fickle Fortune, so deceitful like the scorpion, that with your head flatter when you are about to sting; your tail with its venom is death. O brittle joy! O sweet, strange venom! O monster that can paint your gifts so craftily under the color of steadfastness, so that you deceive

---

[32] Romance of the Rose. Lengthy thirteenth-century French poem by Guillaume de Lorris and Jean de Meun (and translated by Chaucer) encompassing "all the art of love." The poem gives a full description of the Garden of Love, which is an enclosed garden.

[33] Priapus. Over-endowed fertility god, whose identity as a god of gardens is known only through a reference in Boccaccio's *Teseida*, an analogue of Chaucer's *Knight's Tale*.

[34] Pluto and Proserpina. King and queen of the underworld.

both great and small! Why have you thus deceived January, who had taken him as your full friend? And now you have robbed him of both his eyes, for sorrow of which he would gladly die.

Alas! This noble, lordly January, amidst all his prosperity and lustiness, has grown blind, and so suddenly. He wept and wailed sorely, and with this, lest his wife should fall into some folly, the fire of jealousy so burned his heart that he would gladly some man had killed both him and her. For he desired not that either in the days of his life or after his death she should be loved or wedded, but ever live as a widow in black clothes, solitary as the turtle-dove that has lost her mate.

But at the last, to tell the truth, his sorrow began to assuage after a month or two; for when he knew that it could not be otherwise, he took his adversity in patience, except that he could not help but to be more jealous all the time. This jealousy was so inordinate that neither in the hall nor in any other house, nor in any other place, would he allow her to walk or ride, unless he had at all times his hand on her.

Therefore this fresh May wept often, who loved Damian so warmly that either she must soon die or else she must have him. She looked at all times for the day when her heart would break.

On the other side, Damian had become the most sorrowful creature that ever was, for neither by day nor by night could he speak a word to fresh May upon his subject, or upon any such matter, unless January were to hear it, who had his hand upon her at all times. But notwithstanding this, by writing back and forth and by secret signals, he knew her mind; and she knew also the purpose of his intention.

O January, what does it matter even if you could see as far as ships sail? It would be just as well to be deceived when blind as be deceived when a man can see. Lo, Argus[35]

---

[35] Argus. A giant with a hundred eyes (also named Panoptes, all-seeing), whom Hera set to guard Io, the mistress of her husband Zeus' mistress Io.

with a hundred eyes, as much as he could pry or pore, still he was hoodwinked; and, God knows, so are others that believe truly that it is not so. But to pass over all that is a pleasure, and I say no more.

This fresh May, of whom I have been speaking, pressed into warm wax the little key, which January carried, the key to the small gate through which he often went into his garden. And Damian, who knew her plan well, secretly counterfeited the key. There is no more to say, but there shall soon occur some marvel through this key, which you shall hear, if you will wait.

O noble Ovid, God knows you speak truly! What deception is so long and painful that a lover will not find out in some way? People may learn from Pyramus and Thisbe;[36] though they were watched everywhere at all times and strictly, they had an understanding, whispering through a wall, in such a way that none could have detected such a trick.

But now to my tale. Before eight days had passed, before the month of July, it happened that through the urging of his wife January caught so great an appetite to amuse himself in his garden, with none but the two of them, that one morning he said to May, "Rise up, my wife, my noble lady, my sweetheart; the turtle dove's voice is heard, my sweet dove; the winter is gone, with its drenching rains. Come forth, now, with your dove-like[37] eyes!"

"How lovelier are your breasts than wine! The garden is enclosed all around; come forth, my white spouse; surely you have wounded me in my heart, O wife! I have known no blemish in you. Come forth, and let us take our indulgence. I

Zeus sent Hermes to kill the giant, and Argus was transformed into a peacock.

[36] Pyramus and Thisbe. Star-crossed lovers whose attempt to flee their families and be together ends in their deaths. Chaucer tells their tale in *Legend of Good Women*, 706-923.

[37] Dove-like. Borrowing imagery and language from the Song of Songs, Chaucer uses the more familiar Latin term "columbine" in this case.

chose you for my wife and my solace."

Such old words of folly he used. To Damian she made a sign that he should go ahead of them with his key. This Damian then opened the gate and in he darted, and he did so in such a way that none could see or hear him. And soon he was sitting quietly under a bush. This January, as blind as a stone, holding May by his hand and with no other person, went into his fresh garden, and quickly clapped the gate shut.

"Now wife," he said, "here is none but you and I – you, who are the creature I love best. For by that Lord that sits in high heaven, I would rather die on a sword than harm you, dear faithful wife! For God's sake, think how I chose you, not for any greed, in truth, but only for the love I bore you.

"And though I am old and can not see, be true to me, and I shall tell you why. Three things you shall win by this, surely: first, Christ's love; and honor for yourself; and all my heritage, town and tower. I give it to you, make out the charters as you wish; this shall be done tomorrow before the sun goes down, so surely may God bring my soul to heaven. First I ask that you will kiss me as a sign of this covenant, and though I am jealous, do not blame me.

"You are so deeply imprinted in my thought that when I consider your beauty and with it my old unsuitable age, surely, though I die for it, I cannot endure to be out of your company, for the sake of love; and this is the very truth. Now wife, kiss me, and let us roam about the garden."

This fresh May, when she heard these words, answered January mildly; but first of all she began to weep. She said, "I have a soul to guard as well as you, and also my honor, and that tender flower of my wifehood, which I secured to your hand when the priest bound my body to you. Therefore, I will answer thus, by your leave, my dear lord: I pray to God, may the day never dawn when I would not die, as foully as woman can, if I ever do such shame to my family, or so smirch my honor by being false. And if I commit that offence, let me be stripped and put in a sack, and drowned in the nearest river. I am a gentlewoman, and not a wench.[38] Why speak you thus? But men ever are faithless and women are always being blamed by men; you have no other pretext, I believe, than to speak of distrust and reproach to us."

And at that word she saw where Damian sat in the bush, and she began to cough and made signs with her finger that Damian should climb up a tree which was laden with fruit; and up he went. For truly he knew her purpose well and every sign that she could make, far better than January, her own husband. For she had told him in a letter all of this matter and how he was to act. And thus I leave him sitting up in the pear-tree, and January and May roaming pleasantly.

Bright was the day and blue the firmament; Phoebus sent down his beams of gold, to gladden every flower with his warmth. At that time he was in Gemini, I believe, but little removed from his descending in Cancer, which is the exaltation of Jupiter. And so it happened this bright morning-time that in the further side of that garden was Pluto, who is the king of Fairyland, and many ladies with him, following his wife, Queen Proserpina, one after another, straight as a line. You may read the story in Claudian,[39] how he fetched her away in his grisly chariot, while she was gathering flowers in the meadow.

This king of Fairyland then sat himself down upon a bank of green and fresh turf, and without delay he said thus to his spouse: "My wife," he said, "no creature can deny it; experience always proves the treason that women do to men. I can tell ten hundred thousand notable stories about your infidelity and frailty. O wise Solomon,[40] richest in wealth, filled with wisdom and earthly glory, your words are worthy to he remembered by every creature that knows wit and reason. Thus he praises the goodness of man: 'Among a thou-

---

[38] Wench. Woman of lower degree.

[39] Claudian. Fourth-century author of *De Raptu Proserpinae.*

[40] Solomon. Old Testament figure, king of the Israelites, who had 1000 wives.

sand men still I found one good, but of all women I found none.' These are the words of the king who knows your wickedness. And Jesus, the son of Sirach,[41] I believe he only seldom speaks respectfully of you. May a wild-fire and corrupt pestilence fall upon your bodies tonight!

"Do you see this honorable lord? Alas, because he is old and blind, his own man shall make him a cuckold. Lo, here in the tree he sits, the lecher! Now of my royal power I will grant to this old, blind, worthy knight that he shall recover his vision, when his wife will do him wrong. Then he shall know what a harlot she is, both to her dishonor and to others as well."

Proserpina said, "You shall, if you so wish; but by the soul of my mother's sire[42] I swear that I shall grant to her to return a sufficient answer, and for her sake to all women after; that, even if they are caught in a certain act, they shall excuse themselves with bold face, and bear down those who would call them to account. None of them shall die for lack of an answer.

"Even if a man may see something with both of his eyes, nevertheless, we women shall face it boldly, and weep, and swear, and craftily chide, so that you men shall be as ignorant as geese. What do I care for your authorities? I know well this Jew, this Solomon, found many fools among us women. But though he found no good woman, yet many other men have found women faithful, good, and virtuous. Witness those that dwell in Christ's house; they proved their steadfastness by their martyrdom. Also the Roman histories make mention of many a true faithful wife. But, sir (and be not angry), albeit he said he found no good woman, I ask you to grasp the man's real meaning. He meant this: that in perfect goodness there is none but God, and no man or woman.

"Ah, for the love of the one true God! Why do you make

---

[41] Jesus, the son of Sirach. Author of the Old Testament book *Ecclesiasticus*.
[42] My mother's sire. I.e., Saturn.

so much of Solomon? What does it matter that he built a temple, God's house? That he was glorious and rich? So likewise he made a temple to false gods; how could he do a thing more forbidden? By God! However beautifully you may whitewash his name, he was a lecher and an idolater, and in his old age he forsook the true God. As the Bible says, if God had not spared him for his father's sake, He would have rent the kingdom away earlier than He did. I care not a butterfly for all the dishonor that you men write of women. I am a woman; I must speak or else swell until my heart should burst.

"For since he said we are chatterboxes, even though I would not like to put my tresses in disarray, I will spare nothing out of any courtesy to speak harm of him who would do villainy to us."

"Lady," said this Pluto, "be angry no longer: I give it up. But since I swore my oath that I would grant him his sight again, I warn you that truly my word shall stand. I am a king; it is not fitting that I should be false."

"And I," she said, "am a queen of Fairyland. She shall have her answer, I maintain. Let us have no more words bout this. In truth I will oppose you no longer."

Now we return to January, who was in the garden with his fair wife, and sang more merrily than a popinjay, "I love you best, and ever shall, and no other." So long he wandered among the alleys until he had come near the pear-tree where this Damian sat on high, very merry among the fresh green leaves.

This fresh May, so bright and fair, began to sigh, and said, "Alas my side! Now sir, for anything that may happen, I must have some of the pears that I see, or I must die, so sorely I long to eat of the small green pears. Help, for the love of our Lady in heaven! I tell you truly, a woman in my situation may have so great an appetite for a fruit that she may die unless she could have it.'

"Alas" he said, "that I have not here a boy that could

climb! Alas, alas, that I am blind!"

"Yes, sir," she said, "no matter; but if you would agree, for love of heaven, to clasp that pear-tree within your arms (for I well know you distrust me); then, so I might set my foot on your back, I could climb up well enough."

"Surely," he said, "there should be nothing lacking here, if I could help you even with my heart's blood."

He stooped down, and she stood on his back and caught hold by a branch and went up. Ladies, I pray you, be not angered; I cannot avoid the truth; I am a rough man. And at once this Damian pulled up her smock, and in he thrust.

And when Pluto saw this great wrong, he restored his sight to January and made him see as well as he ever could. And when he had his sight again, never was there a man so glad of anything.

But his thought was evermore on his wife, and he cast his two eyes up into the tree, and saw Damian with his wife. And he set up such a roar and a cry as a mother does when the child is dying: "Out! Help! Alas!" he began to cry. "O rude, bold lady, what are you doing?"

And she answered, "Sir, what ails you? Have patience and reason in your mind. I have helped you in both your eyes. On peril of my soul, I lie not; it was taught me that to heal your eyes there was nothing better than to struggle with a man up in a tree. God knows, I did it with good intent."

"With a man up in a tree!" he said. "May God grant that you both die a shameful death! It was worse than that; he fornicated with you, I saw it with my eyes; if not let me be hanged by the neck!"

"Then," she said, "my medicine is all false; for certainly, if you were able to see well, you would not say these words to me; you have some glimmerings, but you do not have perfect sight."

He said, "I see with both of my eyes as well as I ever could, God be thanked! And by my word, I believe it was as I said."

"You are bewildered, good sir, bewildered," she said. "This thanks I have because I have given you your sight. Alas, that ever I was so kind!"

"Now, Lady," he said, "let us forget all of it. Come down, my love, and if I have spoken wrongly, God so help me as I am sorry for it."

"Yes, sir," she said, "you may think as you will; but, sir, a man that wakes out of his sleep cannot speedily comprehend a thing or see it perfectly, until he is thoroughly used to the daylight. Even so, a man who has been blind a long time cannot immediately see so well, when his sight is newly restored, as he who has seen for a day or two. Until your vision is settled for a time, many sights may beguile you. Be careful, I pray you; for by the Queen of heaven many men think they see a thing, and it is entirely otherwise than it seems. One who misapprehends, misjudges."

And with that she leaped down from the tree. Who was glad but this January? He kissed her and embraced her often and gently stroked her, and led her home to his palace. Now, good men, I pray you, be ever of good cheer. Thus ends my tale of January, and God bless us, and his mother, Blessed Mary.

Here is ended the Merchant's Tale of January.

Epilogue to the Merchant's Tale

"Eh! God's mercy!" said our Host. "Now I pray God keep me from such a wife! Lo what tricks and wiles are in women! They are ever as busy as bees to deceive us simple men, and they will ever swerve from the truth, it is well proved by this Merchant's tale.

"I have a wife as true as steel, without doubt, though she may be otherwise a poor one; but she is a blabbing shrew with her tongue and has a heap of other faults.

"No matter about that, let such things pass. But, do you know what? May it be said secretly, I sorely regret that I am tied to her. But if I were to count up every fault of hers, certainly I would be too foolish; and I say this with good reason, for it would be reported to her by some one of this company. For this reason there is no need to say, since it is women who know how to peddle such merchandise. And my wit suffices not to tell all. Therefore my tale is ended.

THE FRANKLIN'S TALE

Here follow the Words of the Franklin to the Squire, and the Words of the Host to the Franklin.

In faith, Squire,[1] you have conducted yourself well and nobly. I praise your wit highly," said the Franklin, with such delicate understanding. In my judgment there is nobody in this company who shall be your peer in eloquence as long as you live. May God give you good fortune, and send you perseverance in virtue, for I have great delight in your speaking. I have a son, and by the Trinity[2] I had rather he would be a man of such discretion as you, than have twenty pounds worth of land,[3] even if it were put in my hand right now.

"Fie on possessions, unless a man is virtuous as well! I have scolded my son, and shall still scold him, because he will not wish to pursue virtue; but his habit is to play at dice and to spend and to lose all that he has. And he had rather talk with a page than converse with any noble person from whom he might properly learn nobility.

"A straw for your gentle manners!" said our Host. "What, Franklin, well you know, by God, that each of you must tell at least a tale or two, or break your word."

"That I well know, sir," said the Franklin. "I pray you not to hold me in scorn if I speak a word or two to this man.

"Tell your tale now, without more words.[4]

---

[1] Squire. The Squire's Tale, which Chaucer seems to have left incomplete, precedes this one.

[2] Trinity. The divine trinity: the Father, Son (Jesus), and Holy Spirit.

[3] Twenty pounds worth of land. Land that would earn him twenty pounds in rent per year.

[4] Without more words. I.e., words before the tale begins.

"Gladly, sir Host," he said, "I will obey your will; now listen to what I say. I will not contradict you in any way to the extent that my wits will suffice. I pray to God that it may please you; then I will know well that it is good enough."

The Prologue of the Franklin's Tale

"These old gentle Bretons[5] in their time made lays[6] about various adventures, rhymed in their early British tongue; which lays they sang to their instruments of music, or else read them, for their pleasure. And one of them I have in mind, which I will relate with good will as best I can. But, sirs, because I am an unlearned man, at my beginning I pray you to excuse me for my homely speech. In truth, I never learned rhetoric; anything I speak must be bare and plain. I never slept on the Mount of Parnassus,[7] nor learned Marcus Tullius Cicero.[8] I know no colors of speech,[9] surely; only such colors as grow in the meadow, or else such as people dye or paint. Colors of rhetoric are too strange for me; my spirit has no feeling in such matters. But if you wish, you shall hear my tale."

Here begins the Franklin's Tale.

In Armorica, which is called Brittany, there was a knight who loved and served a lady in the best manner he could. And he underwent many labors and many great enterprises, before he won her. For she was one of the fairest women under the sun, and had come from such a noble family that

---

[5] Bretons. Celtic peoples of Brittany, a region is northwest France, well-known for its transmission of Arthuruan legends.

[6] Lays. Short narrative poems.

[7] Mount of Parnassus. Home of the Muses, from whom poets gain the skill to carry out their poems.

[8] Marcus Tullius Cicero. Most famous Roman orator (106-43 BC) whose *Rhetoric* is one of the central documents for the art of persuasion in the western world.

[9] Colors of speech. Figurative language, such as simile, metaphor, and hyperbole.

this knight scarcely dared for fear to tell her his woe and his pain and distress. But at last she took such pity upon his pains, because of his worthiness and primarily for his humble attentiveness, so that secretly she agreed to take him as husband and lord, in such lordship as men may have over their wives. And in order that they might live more in bliss, he swore to her as a knight, by his own free will, that never at any time in all his life would he take any authority upon himself against her will, nor show jealousy toward her, but obey her and follow her will in all things, as any lover shall do toward his lady; except that he wanted only the sovereignty in name, lest he should shame his rank as husband.

She thanked him, and said with great humility, "Sir, since through your noble mind you offer me so free a rein, God forbid that through my guilt there would always be war or contention between us two. Sir, I will be your true humble wife until my heart break; take here my pledge." Thus they were both in quiet and peace.

For one thing, sirs, I dare safely say, friends must comply with one another, if they wish to keep company long. Love will not be constrained by mastery; when mastery comes, the god of love soon beats his wings, and, farewell, he is gone! Love is as free as any spirit. Women by their nature desire liberty and not to be under constraint like a servant; and so do men, if I shall tell the truth. Note that the one who is the most patient in love has the advantage over all. Patience is a high virtue, certainly; for, as these scholars say, it conquers things that force could never reach.

Men should not scold or complain at every word. Learn to endure, or else, on my life, you shall learn this, whether you wish to or not. For certainly there is nobody in this world who sometimes does not act or speak amiss. Wrath, sickness, the constellation, wine, woe, and changing humors very often cause a man to act or speak amiss.

A man may not be avenged for every wrong; in every creature who knows how to rule his life, there must be moderation, according to the occasion. And therefore, so that he might live at ease, this wise worthy knight promised patience toward her, and she seriously swore to him that there never should be a fault in her. Here one may see a humble and wise agreement; thus she took her servant and her lord: servant in love, and lord in marriage. Then he was in both lordship and servitude. Servitude? No, but superior in lordship, since he has both his lady and love; surely, his lady, and his wife as well, who accepted that law of love.[10] And in this happy state he went home with his wife to his country, not far from Penmark, where his dwelling was, and where he lived in happiness and comfort. Who, unless he had been wedded, could tell the joy, the comfort, and well-being between husband and wife?

This blessed condition lasted a year and more, until the knight of whom I speak, who was called Arveragus of Kayrrud, laid his plans to go and dwell a year or two in England, which also was called Britain, to seek worship and honor in arms, for he set all his pleasure on such toils. And he dwelt there two years, as the book says.[11]

Now I will leave Arveragus, and will speak of Dorigen his wife, who loved her husband as her heart's blood. For in his absence she wept and sighed, as these noble wives do (when they will). She mourned, watched, wailed, fasted, lamented; desire for his presence so distracted her that she cared nothing for the whole wide world. Her friends, who knew her heavy thoughts, comforted her in all the ways they could. They preached to her; day and night they told her that she was slaying herself for no good reason, alas! And they comforted her all they could, to make her leave her heaviness.

Through the process of time, as you all know, one may

---

[10] Servitude…law of love. The Franklin is tinkering with different models of the ideas of serving and ruling.

[11] As the book says. The alleged but unnamed source of the Franklin's story.

engrave in a stone so long that some figure will be imprinted on it. They comforted her so long that, with the aid of hope and reason, she received the imprint of their consolation. Through this her great sorrow began to assuage; she could not continue forever in such frenzy.

And while she was in all this sorrow, Arveragus had sent home to her letters telling of his welfare, and that he would soon return; otherwise, this sorrow would have slain her heart. Her friends saw her sorrow began to slacken, and on their knees begged her for God's love to come and roam about with them, to drive away her dark imaginings. And finally she agreed, for well she saw that it was best.

Now her castle stood near the sea, and for a diversion she often walked with her friends high upon the bank, from which she saw many ships and barges sailing on their course, wherever they would go. But then that became a part of her grief. For often she said to herself, "Alas! Is there no ship of so many that I see that will bring home my lord? Then my heart would be fully cured of its bitter, bitter pains."

Another time she would sit there and ponder, and from the shore cast her eyes down. But when she saw the grisly black rocks, her heart would so quake for true fear that she could not hold herself on her feet. Then she would sit down on the grass and piteously look into the sea, and with sorrowful, cold sighs say just so: "Eternal God, who through Your providence guides the world by sure government, You make nothing in vain, as they say. But, Lord, these grisly, fiendish, black rocks, which seem more like a foul chaos of work than any fair creation by such a perfect, wise, and unchanging God: why have You created this irrational work? For by this work neither man nor bird nor brute is benefited, south or north, east or west.

"It does no good, in my mind, but harm. Do You not see, Lord, how it destroys mankind? Rocks have slain a hundred thousand bodies of mankind (although they may not be remembered), which is such a fine part of Your work that You made in Your own image.[12] It should seem that You had a great fondness toward humans; but how then may it be that You created these rocks to destroy them in such a way that do no good, but always harm? I know well that scholars will say as they please by arguments that all is for the best, though I cannot understand their reasons. But may the same God that made the wind blow protect my lord! This is my conclusion. I leave all disputation to scholars, but I wish to God that all these black rocks were sunk into hell, for his sake! These rocks slay my heart for fear." Thus she would speak to herself, with many piteous tears.

Her friends saw that it was no diversion for her, but only a discomfort, to walk by the sea, and devised for her amusements in other places. They led her by rivers and springs and in other delightful places; they danced and they played at chess and backgammon.

So one day in the morning, they went to amuse themselves for the entire day in a nearby garden, in which they had made their provision of food and other things. This was on the sixth morning of May, and May with his soft rains had painted this garden full of leaves and flowers. And truly the craft of man's hand had so curiously arrayed this garden that never was a garden of such beauty, unless it would be paradise itself.

The scent and the fresh sight of flowers would have gladdened any heart that was ever born, unless too great a sickness or too great a sorrow distressed it; so full was it of delight and beauty.

After dinner they began to dance and sing, except Dorigen, who always made complaint or moan, because she saw not her husband and her love enter into the dance. But nevertheless she must wait for a time and with good hope let her sorrow pass.

---

[12] In Your own image. An echo of Genesis 1:27: God created man in his image; in the divine image he created him; male and female he created them.

Upon this dance, among other men, there danced before Dorigen a squire who was fresher and more joyful in apparel than is the month of May, I believe. He sang and danced to surpass any man who is or was since the world was made. He was, if one would describe him, one of the most handsome men alive: young, strong, virtuous, rich, and wise; and well beloved and held in great honor. And in short, if I am to tell the truth, this servant to Venus,[13] this lively squire, who was called Aurelius, had loved Dorigen, entirely without her knowledge, more than any creature for two years and more, as it happened, but never did he dare to he tell her his woe. He drank all his penance without a cup.[14]

He was in despair, he dared say nothing except that in his songs he would reveal his woe to some degree, as in a general complaining; he said he loved, and was in no way beloved. Of such matter he made many lays, songs, complaints, roundels, and virelays,[15] about how he would dare not utter his sorrow, but would languish like a fury in hell; and he would die, he said, as did Echo for Narcissus,[16] who dared not tell her woe. In other manners than this that I speak of he dared not reveal his passion to her; except that, by chance, sometimes at dances, where young people perform their customs of courtship, it may well be that he looked upon her face in such a way as a man who asks for grace; but she knew nothing of his intent.

Nevertheless it happened, before they went from that garden, that because he was her neighbor and a man of good

---

[13] Venus. Goddess of love.

[14] Drank his penance without a cup. Had his share of sorrow.

[15] Lays . . . complaints, roundels, and virelays. Lays: short narrative poems. Complaints: poems that lament the troubles of love. Roundels: short poems, usually on light subjects and containing a refrain. Virelay: a variant on the roundel. Roundels and virelays were likely composed for dance as well.

[16] Echo for Narcissus. Narcissus, the beautiful youth, who pined away for love of his own reflection in a pool, was loved by Echo, who, because her love was unrequited, died of grief.

reputation, and she had known him for a long time, they began to speak. And Aurelius drew more and more toward his matter and when he saw his time, he said thus: "Madame, by God That made this world, If I had known it would gladden your heart, I wish that on the day when your Arveragus went over the sea, I, Aurelius, had gone to a place from which I never should have returned.[17] For I well know that my service is in vain; my reward is but the breaking of my heart. Have pity upon my bitter pains, Madame, for with a word you may slay me or save me. I wish to God that I were buried here at your feet! I have now no time to say more; have mercy, sweet, or you will cause me to die!"

She looked at Aurelius: "Is this your desire?" she said. "Is this what you wish to say? Never before did I know what was in your mind. But now, Aurelius, I know it. By that God that gave me breath and soul, never in word or deed shall I be an untrue wife. As long as I have any senses, I will be his to whom I am bound. Take this for my final answer."

But in sport after that she said, "Aurelius, by the high God in heaven, yet would I consent to be your love, since I see you so piteously lamenting. Whenever that day comes that all along the coast of Brittany you remove all the rocks, stone by stone, so that they no longer obstruct the passage of ship or boat – I say, when you have made the coast so clear of rocks that there is no stone to be seen, then I will love you best of all men. Take here my pledge, in all that I can ever do."

"Is there no other mercy in you?" he said.

"No," she said, "by that Lord that made me! For I well know that shall never happen. Let such follies pass out of your heart. What delight should a man ever have to go about loving the wife of another man, who has her body whenever he wishes?"

Aurelius gave many sore sighs. He was woeful when he heard this; and with a sorrowful heart he answered, "Ma-

[17] Never should have returned. I.e., that he would have died.

dame, this would be impossible! Then I must die of a sudden and horrible death." And with that word he turned back.

Then many of her other friends came roaming up and down in the paths, and knew nothing of this affair, but speedily began new revel; until the bright sun lost his hue, and the horizon had taken away from him his light (this is as much as to say, it was evening). And they went home in joy and contentment, except, alas, wretched Aurelius alone! He went to his house with sorrowful heart; he saw that he could never escape death, and felt his heart grow cold. Up to the heaven he held his hands and set himself down on his bare knees, and raving said his prayer; for true woe he was out of his wits and knew not what he spoke.

With piteous heart he began his complaint to the gods, and first to the sun: "Apollo,"[18] he said, "lord and ruler of every plant, herb, tree, and flower, who gives to each of them his times and seasons, according to your height in the sky, as your lodging changes toward north or south; lord Phoebus, cast your merciful eye upon wretched Aurelius, who is so lost. Behold, lord, my lady has decreed my guiltless death, unless your kindness should have some pity upon my dying heart. For well I know, lord Phoebus, that you may help me best of all except my lady, if you wish. Now promise to hear me tell you in what way I may be helped.

"Your blessed sister, Lucina[19] the bright, chief goddess and queen of the sea (though Neptune has his godhead in the sea, yet is she empress over him), you well know, lord, that just as it is her desire to be kindled and lightened by your orb, for which reason she follows you eagerly, so too the sea desires by its nature to follow her, being goddess both in the sea and in rivers great and small.

"Therefore, Lord Phoebus,[20] this is my prayer: perform this miracle or break my heart; that now at this next opposi-

---

[18] Apollo. God of the sun.

[19] Lucina. Goddess of the moon.

[20] Phoebus. I.e., Phoebus Apollo.

tion, which shall be in the sign of the Lion,[21] pray Lucina to bring a flood so great that it shall rise above the highest rock in Armorican Britanny by at least five fathoms, and let this flood last two years.

"Then, certainly, I may say to my lady, 'Keep your promise, the rocks are gone.' Lord Phoebus, do this miracle; ask her to go the same speed as you; I say, ask your sister that these two years she will go no faster in her course than you. Then shall she always be exactly at full, and the spring flood-tide will last day and night. And if she will not promise to grant me my dear sovereign lady in such a manner, pray her to sink every rock into her own dark region under the ground where Pluto[22] dwells, or nevermore shall I gain my lady. Barefoot I will go a pilgrimage to your temple at Delphi.[23] Lord Phoebus, see the tears on my cheeks, and have some pity on my pains."

And with that he fell down in a swoon and for a long time lay in a trance. His brother, who knew his trouble, caught him up and brought him to his bed. In this woe and torment I let this woeful creature lie in despair. He may choose, as far as I am concerned, whether he will live or die.

Arveragus had come home, with other valiant knights, in health and great honor as the flower of chivalry. Oh, now you are happy, Dorigen, who have in your arms your lively husband, the vigorous knight, the valiant warrior, who loves you as his own heart's life. He never thought to be suspicious whether any creature had spoken to her of love while he was gone; he had no fear of that. He gave no heed to any such matter, but danced, jousted, and showed her great enjoyment. Thus I leave them in happiness and bliss, and will tell of the sick Aurelius.

Two years and more the wretched Aurelius lay in languor and mad torment, before he could walk a step on earth;

---

[21] Sign of the Lion. The zodiacal sign of Leo.

[22] Pluto. God of the Underworld.

[23] Delphi. In Greece, near the foot of Mount Parnassus.

and he had no comfort in this time, except from his brother, a scholar, who knew of all this woeful matter. For in truth he dared say no word about it to any other creature. He carried it under his breast more secretly than Pamphilus carried his love for Galatea.[24] His breast was whole, to outward view, but ever in his heart was the keen arrow.[25] And you well know that in surgery the cure of a wound healed only on the surface is perilous, unless men could touch the arrow or get at it.

His brother wept and wailed privately, until at last it came to his mind that while he was at Orleans, in France, as young scholars who are desirous of studying curious arts seek in every nook and corner to learn this special knowledge, it came to his mind that, one day while he studied at Orleans,[26] he saw a book of natural magic, which his friend, who was then a bachelor of law, had secretly left upon his desk, though he was there for a different field of study. This book spoke much of the celestial influences concerning the twenty-eight mansions[27] which belong to the moon, and such folly as is not worth a fly in our day. For the faith of the Holy Church that is in our doctrine will not allow any illusion to harm us.

And as soon as he remembered this book his heart began to dance for joy, and he said quietly to himself, "My brother shall be cured speedily; for I am sure there are arts by which men create various apparitions, such as these deceiving magicians conjure up. For often at feasts, I have heard tell, within a large hall these magicians have made water and a barge come in and row up and down in the hall. Sometimes a grim lion has seemed to come, and sometimes flowers spring

---

[24] Pamphilus . . . Galatea. Lovers from the thirteenth-century Latin poem, *Pamphilus de Amore*, perhaps by Pamphilus Mauritianus.

[25] Arrow. I.e., Cupid's arrow.

[26] Orleans. I.e., the University of Orleans.

[27] Twenty-eight mansions. The daily positions in the twenty-eight day lunar cycle.

as in a meadow, sometimes a vine, with grapes white and red, sometimes a castle of mortar and stone. And when they wished, they caused it all to disappear immediately; so it seemed to every man's sight.

"Now then, I conclude thus, that if I could find some old comrade at Orleans who is acquainted with these mansions of the moon, or other natural magic besides, he should well cause my brother to possess his love. For by means of an illusion a clerk may make it appear to a man's sight that every one of the black rocks of Brittany be removed, and that ships come and go along the shore, and that this continue a day or two in such form. Then my brother would be entirely cured. Then she must keep her promise, or else at least he shall shame her."

Why should I make this a longer story? He came to his brother's bed and gave him such encouragement to go to Orleans that he started up at once and went ahead on his way in hopes to be relieved of his care. When they had almost arrived at that city, about two or three furlongs away, they met a young clerk roaming by himself who greeted them politely in Latin, and then said a marvelous thing. "I know the cause of your coming," he said. And before they went a foot further, he told them all that was in their minds. This scholar of Brittany asked him about the companions whom he had known in old days, and he answered him that they were dead; for which he wept many tears.

Aurelius alighted quickly from his horse and went forth home to the home of this magician, who made them well at ease; no provision that might give pleasure. Aurelius had never seen in his life a house so well appointed.

Before he went to supper, the magician showed him forests and parks full of wild beasts; there he saw harts with their lofty horns, the largest that eye ever saw. He beheld a hundred of them slain by dogs, and some bleeding from bitter arrow-wounds. When these wild deer vanished, he saw falconers upon a fair river, slaying the heron with their hawks. Then he saw knights jousting on a plain. And after this, the magician did him the pleasure to show him his lady in a dance, in which he himself was dancing, as it seemed to him. And when this master who created the magic saw that it was time, he clapped his hands, and, farewell, all our revel was gone.

And yet while they saw all this marvelous sight, they never stirred out of the house, but sat still in his study, where his books were, and no other creature but the three of them.

This master called his squire to him, and said thus: "Is our supper ready? It is almost an hour, I will swear, since I told you make our supper, when these honorable men went with me into my study, where my books are."

"Sir," said this squire, "when it pleases you it will be entirely ready, even if you wish to have it right now."

"Let us go to supper, then," he said, "that is best. These people in love must take repose sometime."

After supper they fell into talk over the sum which should be this master's reward for removing all the rocks of Brittany, from the Gironde to the mouth of Seine. He raised difficulties and swore that he would not have less than a thousand pounds, and he would be glad to do it for that sum, may God save him!

Aurelius answered directly, with a joyous heart, "Fie on a thousand pounds! I would give this wide world, which men say is round, if I were lord of it. This bargain is done, for we are agreed. You shall be paid faithfully, by my word. But take care now that you delay us here no longer than tomorrow, for any negligence or sloth."

"No," this clerk said, "take here my faith in pledge to you."

Aurelius went to bed when he wished, and rested nearly all that night. Despite all his labor and his hope of bliss, his woeful heart had relief from suffering. In the morning, when it was day, Aurelius and this magician took the shortest road to Brittany and dismounted at the place where they wished to be. And, as books remind me, this was the cold, frosty season of December. Phoebus grew old[28] and of hue like latten,[29] who in his hot declination shone with his bright beams like burnished gold; but now he had descended into Capricorn, where he shone fully pale, I dare well say. The bitter frosts, with sleet and rain, have destroyed the green in every garden. Janus[30] with his double beard sits by the fire and drinks the wine out of his ox-horn; before him stands brawn of the tusked boar, and every lusty man cries, "Noel!"

Aurelius offered his master all the hospitality and reverence he could, and asked him to do his duty to bring him out of his bitter pains, or with a sword he would slit his own heart. This cunning scholar so pitied this man that he made as much haste as he could, day and night, to look for the most beneficial time for his experiment; that is to say, to create an appearance, by such an illusion or crafty trick – I do not have vocabulary of astrology – that she and every person should think and say that the rocks of Brittany were gone, or else sunk under the earth.

So at last he found his time to work his tricks and stage his miserable performance of wicked superstition. He brought forth his Toledo tables,[31] well corrected; there was nothing missing, neither his tables of collected or expanded years, nor his roots, nor his other gear, such as his centers and his arguments, and his tables of proportional parts for his equations. And for his calculations he knew full well how far Alnath in the eighth sphere was pushed from the head of that fixed Aries above, which is calculated to be in the ninth sphere; cunningly he calculated by means of all this. When he had found his first mansion, by proportion he knew the

---

28 Old. The sun is at the end of the year.

29 Latten. A kind of brass or brasslike alloy, grey in color.

30 Janus. God of entrances and exits, for whom January is named. He is depicted as a bearded figure, facing forward and backward.

31 Toledo tables. Astronomical tables showing the progressive positions of the planets. The terms in the following sentences are rather specialized. See *The Riverside Chaucer* for further details.

rest, and he well knew the rising of his moon, in which was the planet's face and term, and all the rest. And he knew well the moon to be in a mansion favorable to his enterprise, and knew also the other matters to be observed for working such illusions and such misdoings as heathen people used in those days.

For this reason he no longer delayed, but through his magic it seemed for a week or two that all the rocks were gone. Aurelius, who was still despairing whether he should have his love or fare badly, waited night and day for this miracle. And when he knew that there was no hindrance, but that every rock was gone, he fell down at his master's feet immediately and said, "I, Aurelius, woeful wretch, thank you, lord, and Venus my lady, who have helped me from my cold misery." And he made his way forth to the temple where he knew he should see his lady. And when he saw his time, he then saluted his dear sovereign lady with a timid heart and humble face.

This woeful man said, "My own lady, whom I most fear and love as best I know how, and whom of all this world I would be most loathe to displease, if I did not suffer so much distress for the love of you that soon I must die here at your feet, I should never tell you how woebegone I am. But surely I must either die or make my complaint, as you slay me, an innocent man, with true pain. But though you have no pity for my death, consider this carefully before you break your pledge.

"For the sake of God in heaven, please repent before you murder me because I love you. For well you know what you promised, Madame; not that I claim anything of you as a right, my sovereign lady, but only ask it as a favor. Nevertheless, in a garden yonder, at such a spot, you know very well what you promised me, and you pledged your word in my hand, to love me best; God knows, you said so, though I may be unworthy of it. Madame, I say it for your honor, more than to save my heart's life; I have done as you said, and if you wish, you may go and see. Do as you wish; remember your promise, for, alive or dead, you shall find me right in that garden. It all depends on you, to make me live or die. But well I know the rocks are gone."

He takes his leave, and she stood astonished; not a drop of blood was in all her face. She thought never to have come into such a trap. She said, "Alas that ever this should happen! For I never deemed that such a monstrosity or marvel could happen, by any possibility. It is against the course of nature. And home she went, a sorrowful creature; scarcely could she walk for utter fear, and for a whole day or two she wept and wailed and swooned, so that it was pitiful to behold. But why she was so she told no creature, for Arveragus was gone out of town.

But with a pale face and sorrowful expression she spoke to herself, and said thus in her complaint as I shall tell you. She said, "Alas! I complain about you, Fortune, who has bound me unawares in your chain, from which to escape I know no help, except only death or dishonor; one of these two it is necessary for me to choose. But nevertheless I had rather forfeit my life than have shame on my body, or lose my fair reputation, or know myself false. And by my death, surely, I may escape.

"Alas, have not many noble wives and many maidens slain themselves before this, rather than do wrong with her body? Yes, surely; lo! These histories testify it. When the thirty tyrants,[32] full of cursedness, had slain Phidon at a feast in Athens, by their malice they commanded men to arrest his daughters and bring them before them entirely naked, to fulfill their foul pleasure, and they made them dance in their father's blood upon the pavement. May God give them damnation! For this reason these woeful maidens, in fear of this, secretly leaped into a well and drowned themselves, rather

[32] Tyrants. This and the following tales are drawn from the examples offered in Saint Jerome's *Adversus Jovinianum*, a treatise on the virtues of virginity.

than lose their maidenhood; so the books relate.

"The people of Messene[33] had fifty Lacedaemon[34] maidens sought out, with whom they wished to satisfy their lust; but of that entire band there was none who was not slain, and with good will chose to die rather than consent to be robbed of her maidenhood. Why should I, then, fear to die?

"Lo also, the tyrant Aristoclides. He loved a maiden named Stymphalides, who, when her father was slain one night, went directly to Diana's temple,[35] and laid hold of the image of Diana with her two hands, and would never let go. No creature could tear her hands from it, until she was slain in that very place. Now since maidens have had such scorn to be defiled with man's base pleasure, it seems to me that a wife ought indeed rather to slay herself than be defiled.

"What shall I say of Hasdrubal's wife, who slew herself at Carthage? For when she saw that the Romans had won the city, she took all her children and dropped down into the fire, and chose rather to die than that any Roman dishonored her.

"Did not Lucrece slay herself at Rome, alas, when she was violated by Tarquin, because she deemed it a shame to live when she had lost her honor?

"The seven maidens of Miletus also for true fear and woe slew themselves rather than the people of Gaul should violate them.

"I could tell now more than a thousand stories, I believe, concerning this matter. When Abradates was slain, his dear wife slew herself and let her blood flow into Abradates' deep, wide wounds, saying, "My body, at least, no creature shall defile, if I can hinder it."

"Why should I cite more examples of this, since so many have slain themselves rather than be defiled? I will end thus, for it is better for me to slay myself than so to be defiled. I

---

[33] Messene. Town in southern Greece.

[34] Lacedaemon. From Sparta, in southern Greece.

[35] Diana's temple. Diana, goddess of the moon, was the patron of women who wished to remain virgins.

will be true to Arveragus, or slay myself in some way, as did the dear daughter of Democion, because she would not be defiled. O Scedasus, it is a great pity to read how your daughters died, who slew themselves for the same cause, alas! It was as great pity, or indeed greater, for the Theban maiden that slew herself even for the same grief, to escape Nicanor. Another Theban maiden did likewise; because one of Macedonia had violated her, she redressed her maidenhood by her death. What shall I say of the wife of Niceratus, who for a like cause took her life? How true also was his love to Alcibiades, and chose rather to die than to suffer his body to be unburied! Lo, what a wife was Alcestis![36] What says Homer[37] of Penelope the good? All Greece knows of her chastity. It is written thus of Laodamia, in truth, that when Protesilaus was slain at Troy, she would live no longer after his days. I may tell the same of noble Portia;[38] she could not live without Brutus, to whom she had fully given her whole heart. The perfect wifehood of Artemisia is honored through all barbarian lands. O queen Teuta,[39] your wifely chastity may be a mirror to all wives. The same thing I say of Bilia, of Rhodogune and of Valeria."[40]

Thus Dorigen made her complaint a day or two, at all times intending to die. But nevertheless Arveragus, this worthy knight, came home the third evening, and asked her why she wept so sorely. And she began to weep ever more bitterly.

"Alas that ever I was born! Thus I said, and this was my oath," and she told him what you have already heard; there is no need to tell more.

---

[36] Alcestis. Exemplary wife featured in the Prologue to Cahucers' *Legend of Good Women.* She accepted death in place of her husband.
[37] Homer. Author of *The Odyssey*, which recounts the patience and chastity of Penelope as she awaits the return of Odysseus.
[38] Portia. Committed suicide, preferring not to live without her husband.
[39] Teuta. Queen of Ilyrica, famed for her chastity, as was Bilia,
[40] Rhodogune and of Valeria. Both refused to remarry after the deaths of their husbands.

This husband, with cheerful countenance and in friendly fashion, answered and said as I shall tell you; "Is there anything else but this, Dorigen?"

"Nay, nay," she said, "so may God help me; God forbid there would be more; this is too much."

"Yes, wife," he replied; "leave sleeping that which is quiet. It may yet be well today, by chance. You shall keep your pledge, by my faith! For may God so surely have mercy on me, for the true love I have for you I had far rather be stabbed to the heart, than you should not hold your pledge. A promise is the highest thing that a man may keep." But with that word he burst out weeping immediately, and said, "I forbid you, on pain of death, as long as your life lasts, to tell this matter to any creature. I will endure all my woe as best I can, and make no such sign of grief that people might judge or guess harm of you."

And he called forth a squire and maid, and said, "Go forth directly with Dorigen and bring her to such a place." They took their leave and went their way, but they knew not why she went there. He would tell his intention to no creature.

Perhaps in truth many of you will think him a foolish man in this, that he would put his wife in jeopardy; listen to the tale, before you exclaim against her. She may have better fortune than you might suppose; and when you have heard the tale, you may judge.

This squire Aurelius, who was so amorous of Dorigen, happened by chance to meet her amidst the town, right in the busiest street, as she was bound straight for the garden where she had promised to go. And he also was bound for the garden; for he always noted well when she would go out of her house to any place. But thus they met, by chance or good fortune; and he saluted her with joyous mood, and asked where she was going.

And she answered, as if she were mad, "To the garden, as my husband ordered, to keep my promise, Alas! Alas!"

Aurelius wondered about what had happened, and in his heart he had great compassion about her and her lament, and about Arveragus, the worthy knight who had told her to maintain everything she had promised, so loath was he that his wife should break her pledge. And Aurelius' heart was moved to great pity, and this made him consider carefully what would be best, so that he felt he would rather refrain from his desire rather than to be guilty of such a wretched and dishonorable act against nobility and all gentility.

For this reason he said thus in few words: "Madame, say to Arveragus, your lord, that since I see his great nobility to you (and I well see your distress), that it seemed better to him to suffer shame (and that would be a pity) than you should break your pledge to me, I would rather suffer perpetual woe than part the love between you. Into your hand, Madame, I release, cancelled, every assurance and every bond that you have made to me to this day from the time when you were born. I pledge my word that I shall never reproach you on the score of any promise. And here I take my leave of the best and truest wife that in all my days I have ever known. But let every woman beware what she promises; let her at least think of Dorigen." Thus surely a squire can do a gentle deed, as well as can a knight.

She thanked him upon her bare knees, and went home to her husband and told him everything, just as you have heard me tell it. And be assured, he was so well pleased that I could not tell how much; why should I explain this matter any further? Arveragus and his wife Dorigen led forth their days in sovereign bliss.

Never again was there trouble between them. Evermore he cherished her as though she were a queen, and she was true to him. Concerning these two people you will get no more from me.

Aurelius, who had forfeited all the expense, cursed the time when he was born. "Alas! alas!" he said, "that I promised a thousand pounds' weight of refined gold to this philosopher! What shall I do? I see nothing more but that I am undone. I must sell my heritage and be a beggar. I cannot remain here and shame all my family here, unless I can gain his mercy. But nevertheless I will seek of him to let me pay on certain days each year, and will thank him for his great courtesy. I will keep my word, I will not be false."

With sore heart he went to his coffer and brought to this clerk gold of the value of five hundred pounds, I believe, and asked him through his noble courtesy to grant him certain days to pay the remnant, and said, "Master, I dare well boast that I never failed of my word as yet. For truly my debt shall be paid to you, whatever may happen to me, even if I must go begging in my undergarments alone. But would you promise, upon security, to give me a respite for two or three years; then it will be well with me. For otherwise I must sell my heritage. There is no more to say."

This philosopher answered gravely and said thus, when he heard these words, "Have I not kept my covenant with you?"

"Yes, surely, well and truly," he said. "Have you not had your lady just as you desired?"

"No, no," he said and sighed sorrowfully.

"What was the cause? Tell me, if you can."

Aurelius began his tale immediately, and told him everything, as you have heard. There is no need to rehearse it again. He said, "Arveragus on account of his nobility would rather have died in sorrow and woe than that his wife would be false to her pledge." He told him also the sorrow of Dorigen, how loath she was to be a wicked wife, and that she had rather have died that day, and that it was through innocence she had sworn her oath. "She never heard tell before of magic illusion; that made me have pity upon her. And just as he sent her freely to me, so freely I sent her back to him. This is everything; there is no more to say."

This philosopher answered: "Dear friend, each of you did a gentle deed toward the other. You are a squire, he is a knight. But may God in his blessed power forbid, but a clerk may truly do a gentle deed as well as any of you.

"Sir, I release you from your debt of a thousand pounds, as freely as if you had only now crept out of the earth and had never known me before now. For, sir, I will not take a penny from you for all my skill and all my labor. You have paid well for my subsistence. It is enough. And farewell, and have a good day." And he took his horse and went forth on his journey.

Gentle people, I would ask you this question now: Which do you think was the most noble?[41] Now tell me, before you go farther. I know no more; my tale is finished.

Here is ended the Franklin's Tale.

[41] Noble. The term Chaucer uses here is "fre," which can mean noble, free, or generous. Likewise, the word "gentle," which is used in the preceding lines, implies nobility.

THE PARDONER'S TALE

❦

The Words of the Host to the Physician and the Pardoner.

Our Host began to swear[1] as if he were mad; "Help! Alas! By the nails and cross of Christ, this was a false churl and a false justice! May as shameful a death as a heart can devise come to these judges and their lawyers! But all the same, this poor maiden is slain, alas! She bought her beauty at too high a price; therefore I say, as we may see, the gifts of Fortune or Nature are the cause of death to many creatures.

Her beauty was her death, I dare well say. Alas, how pitifully she was slain! From both these gifts I spoke of now, people often have more harm than profit. But truly, my own dear master, this is a piteous tale to hear. But nonetheless pass it over; it does not matter. I pray God to save your gentle body, and your urinals[2] and chamber pots, as well as your Hippocrateses and your Galens,[3] and every container full of your syrup-medicine. God bless them and our Lady, Blessed Mary! As I live and prosper, you are a proper fellow and like a prelate,[4] by Saint Ronan.[5]

---

[1] Swear. The host is responding to the Physician's Tale, which recounts the slaying of the Christian maiden Virginia by her own father Virginius, who, with his daughter's consent, beheads her rather than allowing her to be possessed by a pagan Roman officer.

[2] Urinals. Clear flasks used to observe urine, by which the physician could analyze the patient's illness. Chamber pots were, of course, used for the collection of bodily fluids.

[3] Hippocrateses and your Galens. The two physicians of greatest authority in the Middle Ages. Hippocrates, ca. 460-370 BC, "the father of medicine," radically changed medicine in ancient Greece. Galen, 129-216 AD, Greek Physician whose works were the most widely followed throughout the Middle Ages.

Did I not say it well? I cannot speak like a scholar, but I know well that you so made my heart ache, so that I have nearly had a heart attack. By Christ's bones! Unless I take medicine, or else a draught of fresh malt ale, or hear a merry tale right away, my heart is done for, in pity for this maid.

"You there, you Pardoner," he said, "tell us at once some mirth or sport."

"By Saint Ronan, it shall be done," he said, "but first I will drink and eat a bit of bread here at this ale-house." But immediately the gentle people began to call out, "No, do not let him tell some ribald or coarse joke; tell us some moral thing that we may learn some wisdom, and then will we gladly listen."

"I agree, certainly," he said, "but I must have time to think up some virtuous thing while I drink."

Here follows the Prologue of the Pardoner's Tale.

Radix malorum est cupiditas; Ad Thimotheum, sexto.[6]

"Gentle people," he said, "when I preach in churches, I strive for a resounding voice, and I ring it out as round as a bell, for I know by heart all that I say. My theme is and always was one and the same: *Radix malorum est cupiditas*.

"First I pronounce where I come from, and then I show my bulls,[7] one and all, but first the seal of our liege lord the king on my patent.[8] I show that first to secure my body, lest any man, priest, or clerk would be so bold as to disturb me in Christ's holy labors. After that I then proceed with my tales, and show bulls of popes and cardinals and patriarchs and bishops, and I speak a few words in Latin to give a flavor to my preaching and to stir men to devotion. Then I show forth

---

[4] Prelate. A dignitary or officer of the Church.

[5] Saint Ronan. A Scottish saint.

[6] *Radix malorum est cupiditas.* Desire for earthly things is the root of evil. 1 Timothy 6.10.

[7] Bulls. Letters of authorization from the pope and other high-ranking officials.

[8] Patent. Leather patent, indicating his authority to sell pardons.

my long glass cases, crammed full of cloths and bones: all the people believe that they are holy relics.[9] I have a shoulder-bone set in brass which came from a holy Jew's sheep.[10]

"'Good men,' I say, 'mark my words; wash this bone in any spring, and if a cow or calf or sheep or ox swell up that has been stung or bitten by any serpent, take water from this spring and wash its tongue and it will be healthy then. And moreover, every sheep that drinks a draught from this spring shall be cured of pox or scabs or sores. And mark what I say.

"'If the man of the house who owns the beasts will, while fasting, drink a draught from this spring every week before cock-crow (as this holy Jew[11] taught our forefathers), his beasts and his stock shall multiply. And sirs, it will cure jealousy also; though a man be fallen into a jealous fury, mix his broth with this water and he will never mistrust his wife again, even if he knows the very truth of her fault – although she has taken two or three priests.

"'Here is a glove also. He who will put his hand in this glove shall see his grain multiply, whether it is wheat or barley; so he will offer pence, or else groats.[12]

"'But, good men and women, I warn you of one thing; if any person is now in this church who has committed a horrible sin and dares not to be confessed of it because of shame, or if any woman, old or young, has made her husband a cuckold, such people shall have no power or grace to make offerings here to my relics. But whoever knows himself to be free from such fault, let him come up and make an offering in the name of God, and I will absolve him by the authority granted me by bull.'

---

[9] Relics. Relics, any materials directly related to the physical presence of a holy person, were believed to have special powers of healing and were therefore valuable. The Pardoner's relics, of course, are not.

[10] Holy Jew's sheep. He may have Jacob in mind, but the reference may be more general, based on the belief that Jews often worked magic.

[11] Holy Jew. Again, the reference may be to Jacob, but without substantiation.

[12] Pence . . . groats. I.e., one small coin or another.

"With this trickery I have won a hundred marks, year by year, since I have been a pardoner. I stand like a cleric in my pulpit, and when the lay people are seated I preach as you have heard and tell a hundred more false stories. Then I take pains to stretch out my neck and bob my head east and west over the people, like a dove perched upon a barn. My hands and tongue move so briskly that it is a joy to see my movement.

"All my preaching is about avarice and such cursed things, to make them generous in giving their pence and especially to me. My aim is all for gain and not at all for the correction of sin. I do not care, when they are buried, even if their souls have gone blackberried![13]

"Surely, many sermons arise from an evil intention, how to please and flatter people, to aim for promotion through hypocrisy, from vain glory and some from hate. For when I dare not otherwise dispute with someone, then I sting him with my bitter tongue as I preach, so that he cannot escape being falsely defamed, if he has trespassed against me or my brethren. For though I do not mention his name, people shall know whom I mean by hints and other circumstances. Thus I pay back people who do unpleasant things to us, and thus I spit out my venom under the guise of holiness, seeming holy and faithful. I say again, in a few words, I preach for no motive but avarice from which my theme is and always was, *Radix malorum est cupiditas*. Thus can I preach against that same vice which I practice, avarice. But though I may be guilty of it, I can make other people depart from avarice and repent sorely. But that is not my primary purpose; I preach for nothing but greed; and this should suffice for this matter.

"Then I tell them many examples from old stories of long ago. For simple people love old tales; such things they

---

[13] Blackberried. Though this phrase is usually glossed as "going blackberry picking," the phrase clearly means more. The Pardoner does not care about the condition of their souls after death, whether they are pure white or black as a blackberry.

can well remember and repeat.

"What! Do you think that so long as I can preach and gain gold and silver through my teaching that I shall live in poverty willingly?

"Nay, nay, truly I never thought of it! I will preach and beg everywhere I go; I will not labor with my hands nor make baskets to live by, only because I will not be an idle beggar. I will imitate none of the apostles. I will have wool, wheat, cheese, and money, even if it is given by the poorest page or the poorest widow in a village, and even if her children are dying of starvation! I will drink liquor from the vine and have a merry wench in every town.

"But listen, gentle people, in conclusion. Your will is that I tell a tale. Now that I have drunk a good draught of malty beer, by the Lord I hope I shall tell you a thing that ought by reason to be to your liking. For though myself be a vicious man, yet I know how to tell you a moral tale which I am accustomed to tell in my money-getting homilies. Now hold your peace, and I will begin."

Here begins the Pardoner's Tale.

Once there dwelt in Flanders a company of young people who made a habit of folly, such as debauchery, gambling,[14] brothels, and taverns, where with harps, lutes and citterns[15] they danced and played at dice day and night, and ate and drank more than they could, through which they did the Devil's sacrifice in wicked fashion by unnatural excess within the Devil's temple.

Their oaths were so great and so damnable that it was grisly to hear them swear; they tore our blessed Lord's body into pieces anew (as if the Jews had not torn him enough), and each laughed at the others' sins. And then came graceful

[14] Gambling. Throughout the tale, the term "gambling" is used for Chaucer's "hasardrye," which refers to gambling in general, but may at times refer to the specific game of dice known as Hazard.

[15] Citterns. Guitar-like instruments.

and slim dancing girls, young girls selling fruit,[16] singers with harps, pimps and confectioners, who are all true officers of the Devil to kindle and blow that fire of lust, which is allied to gluttony. I take Holy Scripture as my witness that lechery is in wine and drunkenness.

Lo, how drunken Lot,[17] against nature, lay with his daughters, unwittingly; he was so drunk he knew not what he did.

Herod[18] (let any one look up the history), when he was full of wine at his feast, gave the command at his own table to slay the guiltless John the Baptist.

Seneca,[19] doubtless, also says a good word; he says he can find no difference between a man that is out of his mind and a man who is addicted to drink, except that madness, when it attacks a wretched creature, endures longer than drunkenness. O gluttony, full of cursedness! O first cause of our ruin! O origin of our damnation, until Christ redeemed us with His blood!

Lo, how dearly was this cursed sin paid for! This whole world was ruined by gluttony! Our father Adam and his wife in truth were driven from Paradise to labor and woe for that vice. For while Adam fasted, I say, he lived in Paradise, and when he ate of the forbidden fruit of the tree, he was cast out to woe and pain. O gluttony, well may we accuse you! If a man only knew how many maladies follow from gluttony and excess, he would be more moderate in his diet as he sits at table.

Alas! The short-lived pleasure of swallowing, the delicate mouth, causes men everywhere, east, west, north, and south, labor in every way, with earth, air, and water, to get fine meat and drink for a glutton. On this, O Paul, well can

---

16 Girls selling fruit. This is sometimes a metaphor for prostitutes, or at least the occupations have at times coincided.

17 Lot. See Genesis 19. 30-38.

18 Herod. See Matthew 14.1-12.

19 Seneca.

you explain: 'Meat into the stomach and stomach also to the meat, God shall destroy both,"[20] as Paul says. Alas! It is foul to say, by my faith, but fouler is the act, when a man drinks so of the white and red that he makes a toilet of his throat through this accursed excess.

The apostle, weeping, says piteously, "There walk many of whom I have told you, and I say it now weeping and with a piteous voice, they are enemies of the cross of Christ, their end is death; their god is their belly."[21] O belly! O stinking bag! Full of corruption! What a labor and cost it is to provide for you! How these cooks pound and strain and grind, and turn substance into accident,[22] to satisfy all your greedy taste! Out of the hard bone they knock the marrow, and cast away nothing that may go through the gullet soft and sweet. The glutton's delicious sauce is made of spices from the leaf, bark, and root and leaf, to get him ever a new appetite. But he that follows after such delights, surely, is dead while he lives in those vices.

Wine is a lecherous thing, and drunkenness is full of wretchedness and of contention. O drunken man, your face is disfigured: your breath is sour, you are foul to clasp in arms, and the sound through your drunken nose seems as if you always said, "Sam-son, Sam-son!" And yet Samson[23] never drank wine, God knows.

---

[20] God shall destroy both. See 1 Corinthians 6.13.

[21] Their god is their belly. See Philippians 3.18-19.

[22] Turn substance into accident. Turn that which is meant to sustain the body into something that is meant to be a delicacy. The Pardoner uses the philosophical terms "substance" (the essence or true purpose of the thing) and "accident" (the external form of the thing) to further his argument that eating fine gourmet food is a form of gluttony, while eating simple food is acceptable behavior.

[23] Samson. Old Testament Israelite strongman whose strength was in his hair (or his promise to God that he would not cut his hair). When his hair had grown again, after Delilah betrayed him and cut it off, he knocked down the temple pillars, killing his enemies (the Philistines) and himself. The story of his troubles with Delilah is told in Judges 16. 15 and retold in the Monk's Tale 2015-94.

You fall like a stuck pig, your tongue is lost, and so too is your sense of decency, for drunkenness is the very tomb of man's wit and discretion. He over whom drink has power can keep no secret, surely. Now keep yourself away from the wine white and red, and chiefly from the white wine of Lepe[24] for sale in Fish Street, or Cheapside.[25] This Spanish wine insidiously creeps through other wines growing nearby, and such fumes arise from it that after two or three sips, though a man may think himself to be at home in Cheapside, he is at the town of Lepe in Spain, not at Rochelle nor at Bordeaux;[26] and then he will say, "Sam-son, Sam-son!"

But listen to one word, I ask you, gentle people; the supreme acts of victory in the Old Testament, I dare say, were done through the help of the true omnipotent God in abstinence and prayer. Look into the Bible and there you may see it. Look too at Attila, the great conqueror, who died in shame and disgrace, bleeding at his nose in a drunken sleep. A great captain should live soberly. And furthermore, consider very carefully what was commanded to Lemuel – not Samuel,[27] I say, but Lemuel. Read the Bible and find it expressly set down with respect to giving wine to them that have oversight of justice. But no more now, for this may suffice.

Now that I have spoken of gluttony, I will forbid gambling to you, which is the very mother of lies, deceit, and cursed perjuries, of blasphemy of Christ, manslaughter, and waste of money and of time; and furthermore, it is a disgrace and against all honor to be known as a common gambler. And the higher a man's estate, the more abandoned he is considered to be. If a prince practices gambling, he will be held lower in reputation in all government and political af-

---

24 Lepe. Town in Spain, or the vineyard district surrounding it, near Cadiz.

25 In Fish Street, or Cheapside. In London.

26 Rochelle nor at Bordeaux. Regions in France producing fine wine.

27 Lemuel...Samuel. Lemuel, biblical king of Massa. Samuel: last of the judges of Israel, who anointed the Saul as the first king of Israel and later David as his successor. See Proverbs 31.4-5.

fairs, by common opinion.

Stilbon,[28] the wise ambassador, was sent to Corinth in great pomp from Lacedaemon to make an alliance; and when he came he happened to find all the greatest men of that land gambling. For this reason, as soon as he could, he went home again to his country and said, "I will not lose my good name there, nor will I take on me such a shame as to ally you to gamblers. Send other wise ambassadors; for by my word I would rather die than ally you with gamblers. For you who are so glorious in honors shall not be allied with gamblers by my will, or treaty of my making." Thus spoke this wise philosopher.

Note also how the king of the Parthians,[29] as the book tells us, sent in scorn a set of golden dice to King Demetrius because he had practiced gambling. For this reason the king of the Parthians held King Demetrius' glory and renown to be of no value. Lords may find other kinds of virtuous diversions to pass the day with.

Now I will speak a word or two about false and frequent oaths, which old books discuss. Violent swearing is an abominable thing, and frequent swearing is still more reprehensible. The almighty God, as Matthew witnesses, forbade swearing entirely;[30] but especially the holy Jeremiah says of swearing, "You shall say your oaths in truth, and not lie, and swear in judgment and righteousness."[31]

And idle swearing is a wicked thing. Behold how on the first table of the almighty God's glorious commandments[32]

---

[28] Stilbon. Perhaps a Greek philosopher.

[29] Parthians. Parthia is northern Persia, modern Iran. The king mentioned here may be Mithridates I, but it is yet uncertain. Demetrius I was the ruler of Sparta (139-127 BC).

[30] As Matthew witnesses. See Matthew 5.36.

[31] Righteousness. See Jeremiah 4.2.

[32] Commandments. I.e., the ten commandments. The first table, or tablet, would have presumably contained the first five commandments. Taking the name of the Lord in vain is sometimes named as the third commandment.

the second commandment is, "Take not my name in vain or amiss." Lo, He forbids such swearing before He forbids homicide or many other cursed things. I say that this is the order in which the commandments stand; anyone who understands His commandments, knows why it is the second commandment.

And furthermore, I tell you flatly that vengeance will not depart from the house of one who is too outrageous in his oaths. "By God's precious heart," and "By His nails" and "By the blood of Christ in the abbey of Hales,[33] my chance is seven; yours is five and three!" "By God's arms, if you play falsely, this dagger shall go through your heart!" This is the fruit that comes of the two cursed dice: perjury, anger, dishonesty, murder.

Now for the love of Christ Who died for us, forsake your oaths, great and small. But, sirs, I will now tell my tale. These three rioters of whom I speak, long before any bell had rung for prime,[34] were sitting in a tavern to drink. And as they sat, they heard a bell tinkle that was carried before a corpse to his grave. One of them called to his servant, "Go quickly," he said, "and ask without delay what corpse passed by here, and see that you report his name correctly."

"Sir," said the boy, "there is no need. It was told to me two hours before you came here; he was an old friend of yours, by God, and he was slain suddenly in the night, as he sat very drunk on his bench. A stealthy thief that men call Death, who slays all the people in this country-side, came with his spear and struck his heart in two, and went his way without a word. He has slain a thousand in this pestilence; and master, before you come before him, it seems to me that you would be best if you were wary of such an adversary. Be ready to meet him at all times; my mother taught me this. I

[33] Abbey of Hales. In Gloucestershire, which claimed to have a vial of Christ's blood, which was said to be visible only to those who were pure in heart.

[34] Prime. 9 am.

can say no more.

"The child speaks the truth, by Blessed Mary," said the tavern-keeper, "for over a mile from here, in a large village, he has slain both man and woman, child, servant, and page. I believe his habitation to be there. It would be a bit of great wisdom to be forewarned before he does him great dishonor."

"Yes, by God's arms!" said this reveler, "Is it really such peril to meet with him? I vow to God's bones I will seek to meet him in the highways and the byways. Listen, friends, we three are all one in this; let each of us hold up his hand and become the others' brother, and slay this false traitor Death. He shall be slain before night that slays so many, by God's dignity!"

These three pledged their word together, each to live and die for the rest as if he were their sworn brother, and up they all started in this drunken fury, and forth they went toward that village of which the tavern-keeper had spoken; and they swore many grisly oaths, and Christ's blessed body they rent to pieces – Death shall be dead if they can catch him!

When they had gone only a little way, just as they were climbing over a fence, an old and poor man met them, and greeted them meekly, and said, "Now, gentle people, God be with you!"

The proudest of these three revelers answered, "What, churl, bad luck to you! Why are you completely wrapped up except your face? Why live you so long to such a great age?"

This old man began to peer into his face, and said, "Because I cannot find a man, even if I should walk from here to India, in city or in village, who will exchange his youth for my age. And therefore I must keep my old age as long as it is God's will. Alas, death will not take me! Thus I walk, a restless wretch, and thus day and night I knock with my staff upon the ground, which is my mother's gate, and say, "Dear mother, let me in. Lo, how I vanish away, flesh and skin and blood! Alas, when shall my bones be at peace? Mother, I would exchange my treasure chest with you, which has been long time in my chamber, yes, for a hair-cloth shroud to wrap myself in!" But still she will not do me that favor; wherefore my face is pale and withered.

But sirs, it is not a courteous thing to speak rudely to an old man, unless he should trespass in act or word. You may read yourselves in Holy Scripture, "Before an old hoary head man you shall arise."[35] For this reason I counsel you, do no harm now to an old man, no more than you would like it to be done to you in your old age, if you remain so long. And now God be with you, wherever you may walk or ride; I must go where I have to go.

"Nay, old churl, not so fast, by God," said this second gambler without delay. "By St. John, you shall not depart so easily! You spoke just now of that traitor Death who slays all our friends in this country-side. By my word, you are his spy! Tell where he is, or, by God and the Holy Sacrament, you shall pay for it. Truly you are in conspiracy with him to slay us young people, false thief."

"Now sirs," he said, "if you are so glad to find Death, turn up this crooked path; for by my faith I left him in that grove under a tree, and there he will wait, and for all your boasting will he hide. Do you see that oak? There you shall find him. May God, Who redeemed mankind, save you and amend you!" Thus spoke this old creature.

And each of these revelers ran until he came to that tree, and there they found nearly eight bushels, as it seemed to them, of florins coined of fine round gold. They no longer sought then after Death, but each was so glad at the sight, for the florins were so beautiful and bright, that they sat themselves down by this precious hoard.

The worst of them spoke the first word. "Brethren," he said, "heed what I say; though I jest often and make sport, I have a good mind. Now Fortune has given us this treasure so that we may live the rest of our lives in mirth and jollity, and

---

[35] You shall arise. See Leviticus. 19.32.

as easily as it comes, so too we will spend it. Ah! God's precious dignity! Who would have thought today that we should have so wonderful a grace! Could this gold be but carried from here to my house or else to yours – for you know well all this gold is ours – then would we be in great joy. But truly it may not be done during the day. People would call us harsh thieves and hang us for our own treasure. It must be carried by night, as wisely and slyly as can be. Therefore I advise that we draw straws among us all, and he that draws the shortest shall run with a happy heart to the town and do so quickly, and secretly bring us wine and bread. And two of us shall secretly guard this treasure, and at night, if he does not delay, we will carry it where we all agree is safest."

One of them brought the straws in his fist and told them to draw, and see where the lot would fall. It fell to the youngest of them and he went forth without delay toward the town. As soon as he was gone, the second said to the third, "You well know you are my sworn brother, and now I will tell you something to your advantage. Here is a great abundance of gold to divide among the three of us; and you know well our friend is gone. Now if I can plan it so that it will be divided among the two of us, will I not have done you a friendly turn?"

"I do not know how that can be," the other answered. "He knows the gold is left with us two. What shall we do? What shall we say to him?"

"Shall it be a secret?" said the first villain. "I shall tell you in few words what we shall do to carry it out successfully."

"I agree," said the other, "not to betray you, by my word."

"Now," said the first, "you know well we are two and that two shall be stronger than one. See to it that when he is set down; you will arise and scuffle with him as in sport, and I will pierce him through the two sides, and you will see to it that you do the same with your dagger. And then shall all this gold be shared between you and me, dear friend. Then may we both fulfill all our desires, and play at dice at our own pleasure." And thus were these two villains agreed to slay the third, as you have heard me say.

The youngest, going to the town, turns over and over in his heart the beauty of those bright new florins. "O Lord," he said, "if only I could have all this treasure to myself, no man living under God's throne should live as merry as I!" And at last the fiend, our enemy, put it into his mind to buy poison with which to slay his two friends; for the fiend found him in such a way of life that he had permission to bring him to ruin, for utterly his full purpose was to slay them both and never to repent. And he went forth without delay into the town to an apothecary, and asked him to sell him some poison so that he might kill his rats; and there was a pole-cat in his yard, he said, which had killed his capons, and he would gladly avenge him upon the pests that ruined him by night.

"And you shall have such a thing," answered the apothecary, "that, so may God save my soul, no creature in all this world who can eat or drink the amount of a grain of wheat of this compound without dying immediately. Yes, he shall die, and will do so in less time than you can walk a mile, this poison is so violent."

This cursed man gripped the box of poison in his hand, and then ran into the next street to a shop and borrowed three large bottles. Into two of them he poured his poison, but the third he kept clean for his own drink, for he planned to labor all night long carrying away the gold. And when this reveler (may the Devil take him!) had filled his three great bottles with wine, he returned again to his friends.

What need to describe it more? For just as they had planned his death, even so they slew him, and did so quickly. When this was done, one of the two said, "Now let us sit and drink and make merry, and then we will bury his body."

And with that word he happened to take one of the bottles where the poison was, and he drank and gave his friend a drink also. Therefore, they both died soon. And surely Avicenna[36] never wrote in any canon or any chapter more wondrous signs of poisoning than these two wretches showed before they died. Thus these two murderers met their end, and the false poisoner also.

"O cursed sin,[37] full of cursedness! O treacherous homicide! O wickedness!

"O gluttony, lust and gambling! You blasphemer of Christ with insult and great oaths, habitual and proud! Alas mankind, how may it be that you art so false and unkind to your Creator, Who made you and redeemed you with His precious heart's blood, alas!

"Now, good men, God forgive you your trespasses and guard you from the sin of avarice. My holy pardon will cure you all, provided that you offer nobles and other sterling coin, or else silver rings, brooches, spoons. Bow your heads, bow them under this holy bull![38] Come up, wives, make an offer of your wool! See, I enter your name here in my roll; you shall enter into heaven's bliss; I absolve you by my high power, you that will make offerings, as clear and clean as when you were born. Lo, sirs, thus I preach). And may Jesus Christ, our soul's physician, grant that you may receive His pardon; for that is better than mine, I will not deceive you.

"But sirs, one word I have forgotten to say. Here in my bag I have relics and indulgences, as fair as any man's in Britain, which were given to me by the pope's own hand. If any of you in your devotion wish to make an offering and have my absolution, come forth now and kneel down here and meekly receive my pardon; or else take pardons all new

---

[36] Avicenna. Eleventh-century Arab (Persian) physician, who compiled the important treatise on medicine, "The Book of the Canon of Medicine."

[37] O cursed sin. Though there is no formal break in the manuscripts, the tale is clearly finished and the Pardoner's address to the other pilgrims begins. Thus the convention of adding quotation marks for the speech of the characters resumes here.

[38] Bull. A letter of authorization from the pope or another high-ranking official.

and fresh as you go along, at every town's end, so that you offer again and again nobles and pence which are good and sound. It is an honor to every creature here to have a competent pardoner to absolve you as you ride through the lonely country, in case of a misadventure which might happen.

"By chance one or two may fall down from their horses and break their necks in two. Look what a security it is to you all that I, who can absolve you all, high and low, when the soul shall pass from the body, fell into your company! I advise that our Host here be the first, for he is most enveloped in sin.

"Come forth, Sir Host, and offer first, and you shall kiss all the relics, yes, for a groat;[39] without delay unbuckle your purse."

"No, no!" he said, "may I have the curse of Christ if I do so!" he said. "Leave me alone; it shall not be, I swear. You would make me kiss your old breech and swear it is a saint's relic, no matter how foul it may be! But by the Holy Cross that St. Helen[40] found, I wish I had your testicles in my hand instead of relics or a sanctuary.[41] Let them be cut off, and I will help you carry them. They shall be enshrined in a hog's turd!"

This Pardoner answered not a word; he was so angry, he would not speak.

"Now," said our Host, "I will not talk with you longer, nor with any other angry man."

But when the worthy Knight saw all the people laughing, he said, "Enough, no more of this. Sir Pardoner, be cheerful, and I pray you, Sir Host, who is so dear to me, kiss the Pardoner. And Pardoner, I pray you draw near again, and let us laugh and make sport as we did before."

---

[39] Groat. Small coin.
[40] St. Helen. Mother of the Emperor Constantine, who was believed to have miraculously found the Holy Cross on which Christ was crucified.
[41] Sanctuary. Box for holding relics.

And without delay they kissed and rode forth on their way.

Here is ended the Pardoner's Tale.

THE PRIORESS'S TALE

The Prologue of the Prioress's Tale

Domine, dominus noster.[1]

O Lord, our Lord, how marvelously is Your name spread through this great world! For not only is Your worthy praise performed by worthy adults, but by the mouth of children Your goodness is celebrated, for sometimes when sucking at the breast they show Your praise. For this reason, as best I can, I will do my duty to tell a story in praise of You and of the white lily-flower[2] who bore You, who is a maiden[3] forever. Not that I can increase her honor, for she herself is honor and, next to her Son, the root of bounty and the remedy of souls.

O mother-maiden! O noble maid-mother! O bush unburned,[4] though burning in the sight of Moses, that through your humility did draw down from the Deity the Spirit that alighted in you; of whose virtue, when He had illumined your heart, was conceived the Father's Wisdom! Help me to tell my tale in your honor. Lady, no wit and no tongue can express your kindness, your nobility, your might, and your great humility. For sometimes, lady, through your benignity, you even go before men's prayers, and procure for us, through your intercession, the light to guide us to your dear Son.

My skill is so weak, O blessed queen, to declare your

---

[1] Domine, dominus noster. Lord, our Lord.
[2] Lily-flower. A symbol of the Immaculate conception of Christ, i.e., that Mary conceived and bore Jesus though still a virgin.
[3] Maiden. I.e., the Virgin Mary.
[4] Unburned bush. Another symbol of Mary's virginity.

great worthiness that I cannot sustain the burden; but I proceed like a twelve-month-old child that can scarce utter any word. Therefore I pray, guide my song which I shall say of you.

Here begins the Prioress's Tale.

In a great city in Asia among the Christian people was a Jewish quarter, maintained by a lord of that country for foul usury[5] and shameful profit, hateful to Christ and His followers. And people could ride or walk all through the streets of it, for it was open at either end. Down beyond the farther part stood a little school of Christian people, in which were many children of Christian blood. Year by year they studied such things as were in use in that country, that is to say, singing and reading, as small children do. Among these little school-boys was a widow's son, seven years old. On his way to school, day by day, wherever he saw the image of Christ's mother he would kneel down and say his *Ave Maria.*[6] Thus had the widow taught her little son to honor our Lady, Christ's dear mother, and he did not forget it, for a good child will learn quickly. But always, when I think of this thing, St. Nicholas[7] stands in my memory, because he did reverence to Christ so young.

As this little child sat in school, studying his little book of prayers, he heard the *Alma redemptoris*[8] sung, as the chil-

---

[5] Usury. The practice of charging interest on loans was largely unheard of at this time, and therefore it was termed usury.

[6] Ave Maria. Hail Mary, the name of one of the most popular prayers, the first sentence being derived from the words of the angel Gabriel at the moment of the annunciation, the second sentence being the words of Elizabeth (the mother of John the Baptist) when she hears the news that Mary is with child. (Hail Mary, full of grace, may the lord be with you. Blessed are you among women, and blessed is the fruit of your womb, Jesus.)

[7] St. Nicholas. Fourth-century bishop of Myra, who was a precocious child and, as an infant, would only nurse at his mother's breast on Wednesdays and Fridays, apparently in honor of God. Later he becomes a benefactor to poor children and, of course, is known as Santa Claus.

dren learned their book of antiphons, and he drew nearer and nearer as he dared, ever listening to the words and the melody until he knew the first verse entirely by heart. He knew nothing of what the Latin meant, he was too young and tender of age, but one day he begged his friend to explain this song to him in his own speech or tell him why it was in use. Many times on his bare knees he begged him to translate and explain it to him.

His friend, who was older than he, answered, "I have heard tell that this song was made to honor our blessed Lady and ask her to be our help and aid when we die. I cannot explain more of it. I study singing, but I know only a little grammar."

"And is this song made in honor of Christ's mother?" said this innocent one. "Now I will do my duty, surely, to learn it all before Christmas is past. Even if I will be scolded for not learning my own lessons, and beaten thrice in an hour, I will learn it in honor of our Lady."

On the way home from day to day his friend taught him secretly until he knew it all by heart, and then he sang it boldly and well word for word following the melody. Twice a day it passed through his throat, as he went to school and home again through the Jewish section, always singing and crying so merrily *O alma redemptoris*. His mind was set ever upon our Lady; the sweetness of Christ's mother had so pierced his heart that to pray to her he could not cease his singing on the way.

Our first foe, the serpent Satan, who has his wasp's nest in the Jewish heart, swelled up and said, "O Hebrew people, alas, is this honorable to you that such a boy shall walk at will in spite of you and sing of such matter as is against the reverence due your faith?"

From this point on the Jews conspired to drive this inno-

---

8 *Alma redemptoris*. "Glorious [mother] of the Redeemer," an antiphon sung in praise of Mary throughout Advent and until Candlemas (February 2).

cent one out of the world. To this purpose they hired a murderer who took up a secret place in an alley, and as the child went by, this cursed Jew seized and held him tight, and then cut his throat and cast him into a pit. I must say that they threw him into an outhouse, where these Jews purged their bowels.

O cursed race of modern Herods,[9] what good is your evil intent? Murder will be revealed, truly it will not fail, and chiefly where it touches the honor of God. Blood cries out on your cursed deed. O martyr made strong in virginity (the Prioress cried), now may you sing, following always the white celestial Lamb.[10] St. John, the great evangelist, wrote of you in Patmos,[11] and said that they, those who never knew women in the flesh, go before the Lamb and sing an ever-new song.

This widow waited all that night for her little child, but he did not come. Therefore, as soon as it was day, with her face pale from fear and anxiety she sought him at school and elsewhere, until finally she learned that he was last seen in the Jewish section. With mother's pity in her breast, as if half out of her mind she went to every place where she supposed it likely to find her little child, and ever she called on Christ's mother, the meek and tender; and at length she sought him among the cursed Jews.

She questioned every Jew that dwelt there and prayed them piteously to tell her if her child had passed by. They said "No." But Jesus through His grace presently put it into her mind that she cried out to her son, where he was cast in the pit beside the road.

---

[9] Herods. A line of Herods served as King of Judea, most notably Herod the Great who reigned at the time of the birth of Christ and ordered the execution of all the new-born Jewish males. His part on the medieval stage was a remarkable one, as, following the historical records, he was portrayed as a madman. See Chaucer's *Miller's Tale,* line 3384.

[10] Lamb. I.e., Christ, the Lamb of God.

[11] St. John . . . Patmos. The reference is to John's vision in the Book of Revelation, or Apocalypse.

O great God Whose praise is performed by the mouth of innocents, behold here your power! This gem of chastity, this emerald, and this bright ruby of martyrdom, where he lay with his throat cut, he began to sing *Alma redemptoris* so loudly that the entire place rang. The Christian people passing through the street came to marvel upon the deed and in haste sent after the magistrate. He came there and did not delay, and praised Christ, the King of heaven, and His mother as well, the glory of mankind. And then the magistrate ordered that the Jews should be bound. With piteous lamentations the child was taken up, ever singing his song, and carried to the nearest abbey with a great and noble procession.

His mother lay by the bier swooning; scarcely could the people draw this second Rachel[12] away from the bier. The magistrate ordered each one of the Jews who knew of this murder to be murdered in torment and by a shameful death, and immediately. No such cursedness would he tolerate. He who deserves evil shall have evil. Therefore he had them drawn with wild horses and after that hung them, according to the law.

Upon his bier before the chief altar this innocent one lay all the while the mass went on, and then the abbot and his convent hastened to bury him. But when they sprinkled holy water on him, the child spoke again, and sang, O *Alma redemptoris mater*! This abbot, a holy man, as monks are (or else ought to be), began to entreat this young child. "O dear child, I beseech you, in the name of the holy Trinity, tell me why you sing, since to my eyes your throat is cut."

"My throat is cut to my neck-bone," said this child, "and in the course of nature I should have died, yes, long ago. But Jesus Christ, as you will find in books, desires that His glory remain and be remembered. And for the honor of His dear

[12] Rachel. Biblical mother who was likewise inconsolable at the death of her children. Matthew 2:18 names her as one of the mothers of the innocents slaughtered at the command of Herod.

mother, I still may sing loud and clear O *alma.* I always loved Christ's sweet mother, this well of mercy, as best as I knew how; and when I was about to lose my life, she came to me and told me to sing this anthem in my death, as you have heard, and as I sang it seems to me she laid a grain on my tongue. For this reason I sing and sing I must in honor of that blessed noble maiden until the grain is taken from my tongue. And afterward she said to me, 'My little child, now will I come for you when the grain is taken from your tongue. Be not afraid; I will not forsake you.'"

This holy monk, the abbot I mean, drew out the child's tongue and took off the grain, and the child softly yielded up the spirit. When the abbot saw this marvel, his salt tears trickled down like a shower, and he fell flat upon the ground and lay still as if he had been bound. The convent as well lay weeping upon the pavement, blessing Christ's dear mother. At length they rose and went forth and took this martyr from his bier, and enclosed his little sweet body in a tomb of pure marble-stones. He is there now, God grant that we may all see him

O young Hugh of Lincoln,[13] slain also by cursed Jews, as all men know (for it is only a little while ago), pray also for us, sinful unstable people, that God in His mercy may multiply His grace upon us in reverence of His Mother Mary. Amen.

Here is ended the Prioress's Tale.

---

[13] Hugh of Lincoln. A child who was reportedly murdered during the reign of Henry III, who executed nineteen Jews for the murder in 1255. A contemporary ballad, "Sir Hugh or the Jew's Daughter," retells the story.

THE TALE OF SIR THOPAS

Prologue to Chaucer's Tale of Sir Thopas

Behold the merry words of the Host to Chaucer.

When this miracle[1] had been entirely told, everyone was rather sober, until our Host began to jest, and then for the first time he looked on me and said, "What sort of man are you? You look as if you are hoping to find a hare? I always see you staring at the ground. Come nearer and look up merrily. Now make way, sirs, and give this man room! His waist is shaped as well as mine, small and fair of visage; he would be a little doll for any woman to embrace in her arms, small and fine in face. He seems elf-like in his countenance, for he is sociable with no creature. Now tell us something, as other people have done. Tell us now a tale of mirth."

"Host," I said, "do not be displeased, for certainly I know no other tale but a rhyme that I learned long ago."

"Yes, that is good," he said. "Now it seems to me by his face we shall hear some excellent thing."

Here begins Chaucer's Tale of Thopas.

The First Fit[2]

"Listen, lords, with good will, and truly I will tell you of mirth and joy, all of a knight, fair and noble in battle and tournament, Sir Thopas was his name.[3]

---

[1] Miracle. I.e., of the Christian boy who was murdered in the Jewish ghetto, as told by the Prioress.

[2] Fit. Section, part.

[3] The short paragraphs throughout Chaucer's Tale of Sir Thopas are meant

Born he was in a far country, beyond the sea, in Flanders, at Poppering in the manor-house. His father stood in high degree, by God's grace lord of that country.

Sir Thopas grew into a spirited swain, with a face as white as wheaten bread and lips as red as a rosebud. His hue was like deeply-dyed scarlet cloth, and I tell you of a truth he had a seemly nose.

Like saffron were his hair and his beard, which reached to his girdle. His shoes were of Cordovan leather and his brown hose from Bruges. His robe was a rich silken material which cost many half-pennies.

He could hunt wild deer and ride along the river hawking, with a gray goshawk on his hand. He was a good archer as well and he had no peer at wrestling, wherever a ram was staked as the prize.

Many a maiden, bright in her bower, mourned for love of him when she had better have slept; but he was chaste, and not a lecher, and sweet as a flower of the thorn that bears the red hip.

One morning it so happened that Sir Thopas would ride forth, and he got upon his gray steed, in his hand a lance, and a long sword by his side.

Through a fair forest he spurred, where many wild beasts were, yes, both bucks and hares; but as he rode south and rode north, I tell you a sad misfortune had nearly happened to him.

There sprang herbs great and small, the licorice and ginger and many a clove and nutmeg to put in ale, whether fresh or old, or to put away in a box.

The birds, the sparrow-hawk and the popinjay, sang, and without a doubt that was a joy to hear; the male thrush as well made his ditty, and the wood-dove on the branch sang loud and clear.

Sir Thopas fell into love-longing when he heard the singing of the thrush, and spurred on like a madman; his fair

---

to imitate, however weakly, the clumsy meter of the original.

steed sweated so with the spurring that one might have wrung out water, and his sides were all bloody.

Sir Thopas too was so weary from riding over the soft grass, so fiery was his spirit, that he laid him down in that place and rested his charger and let him feed.

"Oh St. Mary, God bless you! What ails this love to bind me so sorely? By God, I dreamed all the night long that an elf-queen shall be my love and sleep under my cloak.

"I will truly love an elf-queen, for in this world is no woman worthy to be my mate; I renounce all other women, and I will take myself over dale and hill to an elf-queen."

He climbed straight into his saddle and spurred over stile and stone to find his elf-queen; until he found in a secret retreat the Fairy Land so wild; for there was no other who dared to ride into that country.

At length came a great giant, Sir Elephant by name, a perilous man in his deeds, and said, "Young knight, by Termagent,[4] unless you spur out of my haunt, I will slay your charger with my mace. Here dwells the queen of Fairy Land with harp, and pipe and tabor."[5]

The knight replied, "As I hope for bliss, tomorrow I will meet you when I am in armor. And I hope, by my faith, you shall yet very bitterly pay for it by this lance's point. I will thrust through your maw, I trust, before prime of day; and here shall you be slain."

Sir Thopas drew back quickly. The giant cast stones at him from a fierce staff-sling;[6] but Sir Thopas escaped, entirely through God's grace and his own noble bearing.

---

4 Termagent. Imaginary god believed by Christians to be the god of the Saracens (or Muslims).

5 Tabor. A small drum.

6 Staff-sling. Sling on the end of a stick.

The Second Fit

Yet listen to my tale, lords, that is merrier than the nightingale, for I will whisper to you how Sir Thopas, with his slender flanks, spurred over hill and dale and came to town again.

His merry men he told to make glee and jollity, for he must fight a giant with three heads; all for the love and joy of one who shines fair.

"Call here my minstrels, to recite tales while I arm myself; and royal romances, of popes and cardinals and of love-longing!"

First they fetched him sweet wine and mead in a wooden bowl; royal spicery, gingerbread and licorice and cumin with excellent sugar.

Next to his white flesh he donned breeches and a shirt of fine clear linen, and over his shirt a quilted tunic and over that a coat of mail to save his heart from piercing.

Over that he wore a hauberk of strong plate, all of Jews' work, and his coat of armor white as a lily.

His shield was all of red gold, and bore a red gemstone and a boar's head. There he swore by bread and ale how that the giant should die, come what may!

His leg armor was of hard leather, the sheath of his sword of ivory, and his helmet of bright brass, his saddle of whale-ivory, his bridle shone like the sun or as the moonshine.

His spear was of fine cypress and boded war, and no peace, with its head ground sharp. His steed was dapple-gray and went a soft and gentle amble all through the land.

Lo, my lords, here is the end of a fit! If you will have more, I will seek to tell it.

The Third Fit

For charity's sake, now hold your tongues, knight and gracious lady, and hearken to my story. I will tell you now of battle and knighthood and of ladies' love-longing.

Men speak of noble romances, of Horn Child[7] and of Ypotis, of Bevis and Sir Guy, of Sir Lybeaus. But Sir Thopas bears the flower[8] for royal knighthood.

He bestrode his good steed and glided forth upon his way like a spark out of the burning log. His crest was a tower with a lily within it. May God shield his body from harm!

And because he was an adventurous knight, he would not sleep in a house, but lay outside in his hood; his bright helmet was his pillow and his courser grazed beside him upon the herbage fine and fresh.

He drank of water from the spring, like Sir Percival[9] the knight, who was so worthy under his garments; until one day –

Here the Host stops Chaucer of his Tale of Thopas.

"No more of this, for God's dignity!" said our Host; "you so weary me by your very silliness that my ears ache with your rubbish-prattle, God so bless my soul! To the Devil with such a rhyme, well may men call it doggerel!"

"Why so?" I said. "Why will you stop me in my tale more than another, since it is the best rhyme I know?"

"By heaven," said, he, "because, to speak plainly, your stinking rhyme is not worth a turd; you do nothing but waste time. Sir, flatly, you shall rhyme no longer. Let us see whether you can tell us anything in worthy poetry, or at least something in prose, in which there may be some mirth or instruction."

"Gladly," I said, "in God's name! I will tell you a little thing in prose that ought to please you, I believe; or truly you are too hard to please. It is an edifying moral tale, though it

---

[7] Horn Child. King Horn, the hero of a fourteenth-century adventure Romance. (Child is an antique word for a knight.) Ypotis, Bevis of Hampton, Guy of Warwick, and Lybeaus Desconus ("The Fair Unknown"), all fit roughly the same description.

[8] Bears the Flower. Takes the prize.

[9] Sir Perceval. A knight of the Arthurian Round Table; one of the knights who quested for the Holy Grail.

may be told in various ways by various folk, as I shall show you.

In this way: you well know that each evangelist who tells of Jesus Christ's passion tells not everything as his fellows tell it; but nevertheless their substance is all true, and all agree in their substance, albeit their telling differs. For Mark and Matthew, John and Luke, some say more and some less when they tell of His piteous passion; but doubtless their meaning is all one.

Therefore, gentle people all, I pray, if you think I vary in my speech, as thus – though I tell somewhat more proverbs in this little treatise to enforce my matter with than you have heard other people tell, and though I do not say the same words that you have heard before, yet I pray you all do not blame me. For in my meaning you shall not find much variance from the meaning of that little treatise after which I write this pleasant tale. Therefore, I ask of you to listen to what I shall say, and let me tell my entire tale."[10]

Here ends the tale.

[10] Entire tale. Chaucer's Tale of Melibee follows, a story of the rape of Melibee's daughter, and mostly of his wife Prudence's deliberation on the sentencing of the rapists. Though the shallow plot is stretched over one of the longest of the collection, the other pilgrims allow it to be told in its entirety.

THE NUN'S PRIEST'S TALE

The Prologue of the Nun's Priest's Tale

"Ho, good sir,[1] no more of this," said the Knight. "What you have told is enough, in truth, and much more, for a little sorrow goes a long way with most people, I believe. As for me, it is a great distress to hear of the sudden fall of people who have been in great wealth and ease. Alas! And the contrary is joy and delight, as when a man who has been in a low station climbs up and becomes prosperous and remains there. Such a thing is joyful and pleasant to speak of."

"Yes, by St. Paul's bell," said our Host, "you tell the truth. This monk's mouth rings loudly; he told about how Fortune 'covered with a cloud' I don't know what. And you also heard right now of a 'tragedy,' and yet it does not help, by God, to bewail or complain of what is past. And also it is grievous, as you have said, to hear of such sorrow. Sir Monk, no more of this, for the love of heaven. Your tale distresses this whole party. Such talk is not worth a butterfly, for there is no joviality or sport in it.

Therefore, Sir Monk, or, by your name, Sir Peter, tell us something else, I pray you heartily; for in truth, were it not for the clinking of your bells, hanging over all your bridle, by heaven's king, I would have fallen from this horse into slumber by now, even if the mud is not very comfortable or deep. Then your tale would have been told in vain, for truly, as these scholars say, 'Whenever a man can find no audi-

[1] Sir. The knight is addressing the Monk, who has been telling short tales (fifteen at the point he is interrupted) of men who had good fortune but fell from it.

ence, it does no good to offer one's opinions.' I know how to understand a good tale well told, I believe. Sir, tell something about hunting, I ask you."

"No," said the Monk, "I do not wish to make sport. Let another tell, as I have told."

Then our Host, with rough and bold speech, said without delay to the Nun's Priest, "Come nearer, you priest, Sir John,[2] come here and tell of something to gladden our hearts. Be cheerful, even though you ride upon a nag. What does it matter that your horse is foul and lean! If he serves you, don't care a bean about it. See that your heart will always be merry.

"Yes, sir," he said, "yes, Host, in faith if I am not merry, you may rebuke me well." And without delay he began his tale and spoke thus to us all, this goodly man, this sweet priest, Sir John.

Here ends the prologue.

Here begins the Nun's Priest's Tale of the Cock and the Hen, Chanticleer and Pertelote.

A widow, poor and somewhat advanced in years, dwelt once in a little cottage that stood in a dale beside a grove. Since the day she was last a wife, this widow of whom I tell this tale had lived patiently and simply; for her goods and earnings were small. By managing carefully what God sent, she provided for herself and her two daughters; she had three large sows and no more, three cows and a sheep named Molly. Her bedroom and living area, where she ate many slender meals, were rather sooty; she never needed a bit of pungent sauce, nor did a dainty morsel ever pass her throat; her diet was in keeping with her livestock shed. She was never sick on account of overeating; her only treatment was a temperate diet, with exercise and heart's content. The gout never kept her from dancing, nor did the apoplexy bother her

[2] Sir John. Usually a name of contempt for a priest, but apparently his real name in this case.

head. She drank neither red wine nor white; her table was served for the most part with white and black – milk and brown bread, of which she found no lack, with broiled bacon and at times an egg or two, for she was a kind of dairy woman.

She had a yard enclosed all around with sticks and a dry ditch, and in it she had a cock, who was called Chanticleer. In all the land there was no match for his crowing; his voice was merrier than the merry organ that goes in church on mass-days. More trusty was his crowing in his yard than a clock or an abbey timepiece; he knew by nature each coming of the hour in that place for when each fifteen degrees were ascended,[3] then he crowed so well that it could not he bettered. His comb was redder than fine coral and crenellated like a castle-wall. His black bill shone like jet; his legs and toes were like azure; his nails, whiter than the lily flower; and his hue, like burnished gold. To do all his pleasure, this noble cock had in his governance seven hens, his sisters and paramours, and very much like him in their markings; of these the one with the fairest hue on her throat was named lovely Mademoiselle Pertelote.

She was courteous, discreet, generous and sociable, and bore herself so fairly since she was seven nights old that truly she held the heart of Chanticleer completely locked, and she bore the key. He loved her so that he was full of happiness. But such a joy as it was to hear them sing in sweet accord when the bright sun began to rise, "My love has gone to the country"[4] – for at that time, as I have learned,

---

[3] Fifteen degrees were ascended. The time was measured by the movement of the sun, each of the twenty four hours being fifteen degrees.

[4] My love has gone to the country. A popular song of Chaucer's time:

My love has gone to the country;
Alas! Why is she gone!
And I am so sorely bound,
I may not go to her.
She has my heart in her hold
Wherever she rides or walks,

beasts and birds could sing and speak.

Now it so came to pass, one day at dawn, as Chanticleer sat on his perch among his wives in the hall, and next to this fair Pertelote, that he began to groan in his throat as a man grievously troubled in his dream. When Pertelote heard him roar this way, she was aghast, and said: "Oh dear heart, what ails you to groan so? A fine sleeper you are; fie, for shame!"

And he answered, "Madame, don't take it the wrong way, I pray you. It is God's truth, I dreamed right now that I was in such trouble that my heart is still sorely frightened. Now may God" he said, "let my dream be interpreted favorably, and keep my body from foul prison! I dreamed how I roamed up and down within our yard, and saw there a beast like a hound, who wished to seize my body and kill me. He was between yellow and red in color, his tail and ears tipped with black, unlike the rest of his coat; his snout was slender and his two eyes glowing. For fear of his looks I almost die, even now. This caused my groaning, without a doubt."

"Shame!" she said. "Fie upon you, heartless coward! Alas! For by that God above you have now lost my heart and all my love. In faith, surely, I cannot love a coward. Regardless of what any woman will say, all of us desire to have husbands bold, wise, and noble, and trusty with secrets, not a miser nor a fool, nor afraid of every weapon, nor yet a boaster, by God above! How dare you, for shame, say to your love that anything could make you afraid? Have you not a man's heart, though you have a beard! Alas, can you be afraid of dreams?

"There is nothing in dreams but vanity, God knows. Dreams are engendered by excess and often by vapors[5] and by people's temperaments, when their humors are too abundant in a creature.[6] Truly this dream that you have dreamed

---

With true love a thousand-fold.

[5] Vapors. Vapors rising from the humors in the stomach to the head.

[6] In medieval medicine, one's health depended upon the balance of the four humors, or elements in the bloodstream. The correspondences be-

comes from a excess of your red choler. This causes people in their dreams to have fear of arrows and of fire with red blazes, of huge beasts (that they will bite them), of fighting, and great and small dogs; just as the melancholy humor causes many people to cry out in sleep for fear of black bears or black bull, or else that black devils will seize him as well. I could tell also of other humors that cause woe to many men in sleep, but I will pass on as lightly as I can. Lo, Cato,[7] who was so wise, did he not say this: 'Take no heed of dreams'?

"Now sir," she said, "for the love of heaven, when we fly down from these rafters, please take some laxative. On peril of my life and soul, I do not lie, and I counsel you for the best, that you should purge yourself both of choler and of melancholy, And since you should not delay, and because there is no apothecary in this town, I will myself direct you to herbs that shall be for your health and wellbeing; and I shall find the herbs in our yard that have the natural property to purge you both beneath and above. Do not forget this, for God's own love! You are completely choleric in your temperament. Beware, lest the sun as he climbs up should find you full of hot humors. And if he does, I dare lay a wager that you will have a tertian fever,[8] or an ague that may be the death of you. For a day or two you shall have a light diet of worms before you take your laxatives – your spurge, laurel, centaury, and fumitory, or hellebore, that grows there, your

---

tween the humors and the physical and psychological dispositions of humans are outlined as follows.

- Red Bile (Blood); Air; Hot & Moist; Sanguine; Amorous, Happy, & Generous.
- Yellow Bile; Fire; Hot & Dry; Choleric; Violent & Vengeful.
- White Bile (Phlegm); Phlegm; Water; Cold & Moist; Phlegmatic; Dull, Pale, & Cowardly.
- Black Bile; Earth; Cold & Dry; Melancholic; Gluttonous, Lazy, & Sentimental.

[7] Cato. Cato the Elder, Marcus Porcius Cato (234-149 BC). Roman statesman. The second half of the quote is, "for dreams deceive many).

[8] Tertian fever. A fever that recurs every third day or forty-eight hours.

caper-spurge or buck-thorn berries, or herb-ivy growing in our yard, and pleasant to take. Peck them right up as they grow and eat them up. By your father's soul, husband, be merry and fear no dreams. I can say nothing else."

"Madame," he said, "God have mercy, for your advice! But nevertheless, as to Sir Cato, who has such a name for wisdom, though he instructed to fear no dreams, by God, one may read in old books of many of more authority than ever Cato had, who say the complete reverse of Cato's opinion, and have well found by experience that dreams are significant both in the joys and the tribulations that people endure in this present life. There is no need for argument in this; experience itself shows it.

"It is told by one of the greatest authors[9] that one may read that once two companions went with very good intentions on a pilgrimage, and it so happened that they came into a town so full of people and so scant of lodgings that they found not so much as one cottage where they could both be lodged. Therefore they had to part company for that night, and each went to his quarters as it would happen. One was lodged in a stall far off in a yard, with plow-oxen; the other was well enough housed, as was his chance or his fortune, which governs all of us.

"It so happened that long before dawn this man dreamed, as he lay in his bed, that his friend began to call upon him, saying, 'Alas! For I shall be murdered in an ox's stall this night. Now help me, brother dear, before I die! Come to me in all haste!" This man started out of his sleep for fear, but when he had waked he turned over and took no heed of this, thinking his dream was only vanity. Thus he dreamed twice in his sleep. And at the third time his fellow seemed to come to him and say, 'I am now slain. Behold my wounds, deep, wide, and bloody. Arise early in the morning, and at the west

---

[9] One of the greatest authors. Either Cicero, who wrote *De divinatione*, or Valerius Maximus, who wrote *Facta et dicta memorabilia.* Both contain the following two stories.

gate of the town you shall see a dung-cart in which my body is secretly hidden; stop that cart boldly. In truth, my gold caused my murder.' And with a pale pitiful face he told him every point of how he was slain.

"And trust well, his friend found the dream entirely true, for in the morning, at earliest day, he took himself to his friend's lodging, and when he reached the ox-stall, he began to shout after him. The inn-keeper answered directly, 'Sir, your friend is gone. At daybreak he left the town.' This man began to become suspicious, remembering his dream, and he went forth without delay to the west gate of the town and found a dung-cart, ready to fertilize a field, and in such condition as you have heard the dead man say. And with a bold heart he began to call for vengeance and justice upon this felony. 'My friend is murdered this very night and lies face upward and mouth open in this cart on his back. I cry out upon the magistrates who should rule and watch over the city. Help! Alas! Here my friend lies slain!

"What more should I tell of this tale? The people rushed out, cast the dung-cart over, and in the middle of the dung they found the dead man, freshly murdered. O blessed God, faithful and just! Lo, how You always reveal murder! Murder will be found out – we see that daily. Murder is so horrible and abominable to the God of justice and reason that He will not permit it to be covered up. Though it may lie hidden for years, murder will be found out: this is my conclusion. And right away the magistrates seized the carter and tortured him so sorely, and the inn-keeper as well, on the rack, that they soon acknowledged their wickedness and were hanged by the neck.

"We may see by this that dreams are to be feared. And surely I read in the same book[10] in the very next chapter (I do not lie, as I hope to be saved) about two men that for a certain cause wished to pass over the sea into a distant land, if the wind had not been adverse and made them to wait in a

[10] In the same book. In either Cicero or Valerius, as noted previously.

city standing pleasantly on the shore of a haven. But shortly before dawn, in the evening, the wind changed and blew just as they wished. Merry and glad they went to rest, and planned to sail early.

"But a great marvel came to one man as he lay asleep, who dreamed toward day a wondrous dream. He thought a man stood beside his bed and ordered him to wait; 'if you go, tomorrow, you shall be drowned; my tale is done.' He woke and told his friend his dream, and prayed him to give up his journey. His friend, who lay on the other side of the bed, began to laugh and sorely mocked him. "No dream can so frighten my heart that I will stop my business; I would not give a straw for your dreams, for dreams are but vanity and tricks. People are always dreaming of owls or apes and of many other bewildering things; they dream of things that never were nor shall be. But since I see that you intend to stay here and thus by your free will lose your chance through sloth, God knows, it will grieve me. But may you have a good-day!"

"Thus he took his leave and departed. But before he had voyaged over half his journey, I do not know why or how that misfortune arose, but by some mishap the ship's bottom was torn open, and ship and man went down in sight of other ships that had sailed at the same time.

"Therefore, fair Pertelote so dear, you may learn by such old examples that no person should think too lightly of dreams, for I tell you that without doubt many dreams are to be sorely feared.

"Lo, I read in the life of St. Kenelm[11] the son of Kenulph, the noble king of Mercia, how he dreamed a dream; one day a little before he was murdered, he saw his

[11] St. Kenelm. According to the legend, in 821, Kenulph, only seven years of age, succeeded his father to the throne of the Mercians. In a dream he foresaw his own death, which was instigated by his own aunt; his body was afterward revealed by a heavenly light. A verse narrative of his life is one of the standard works of Middle English.

murder in a vision. His nurse expounded his entire dream and warned him to beware of treason; but he was no more than seven years old and paid little heed to any dream, so holy he was in spirit. By God, I would give up my shirt to have you read his legend, as I have! I tell you truly, Madame Pertelote, that Macrobius,[12] who wrote the vision of the noble Scipio in Africa, affirms dreams to be forewarnings of things that men see afterward.

"Furthermore, I pray you look well in the Old Testament and see if Daniel[13] held dreams to be in vain. Read about Joseph[14] also, and there you will find whether dreams be sometimes (I say not always) warnings of future things. Look at the king of Egypt, Sir Pharaoh, and at his baker and his butler, and see if they felt no virtue in dreams! Whosoever wishes to turn to the chronicles of various realms may read many wondrous things about them.

"Lo, Croesus,[15] once king of Lydia! Did he not dream that he sat upon a tree, which signified that he would be hanged? Lo, Andromache, Hector's wife![16] She dreamed the very night before the life of Hector should be lost if he went that day into battle; she warned him, but it did not matter, for

---

[12] Macrobius. Late roman author (fl. c.400) who wrote a commentary on the *Dream of Scipio* (*Somnium Scipionis*) by Cicero, which is included in his *Republic*. The story is retold in Chaucer's *Parliament of Fowls* 29-84.

[13] Daniel. Biblical figure who interpreted the dreams of Nebuchadnezzar and his son Belshazzar. See the Book of Daniel; also Chaucer's *Monk's Tale* 2143-82 and 2183-2246, and *Man of Law's Tale* 471-78.

[14] Joseph. Biblical figure who interpreted the dream of the Egyptian Pharaoh and was subsequently given much favor. In Genesis 41:1-36, the Pharoah's dream of seven fatted cows followed by seven emaciated cows is interpreted by Joseph to be seven years of good harvest followed by seven years of famine.

[15] Croesus. King of Lydia who saw his own death in a dream but did not recognize it. His daughter interpreted it correctly, but this fact made no difference. See Chaucer's *Monk's Tale* 2727-66.

[16] Hector's wife. Andromachae's dream was included in Dares' account of the Trojan War (*De excidio Trojae Historia.*), but not in most other accounts.

he went nonetheless to fight, and soon after was slain by Achilles.

"But that tale would be entirely too long to tell, and I must not delay, for it is nearly day. In short, I conclude that I shall have adversity after this vision; and I say, moreover, I put no confidence in laxatives. I know well that they are poison; I defy them; I like them not a bit. Now let us speak of mirth, and stop all this. God has greatly blessed me in one thing, Madame Pertelote, and thus I have joy; for when I see how scarlet-red you are about your eyes, and the beauty of your face, all my fear dies away. For as true as the Gospel of John says, "*Mulier est hominis confusion*,"[17] Madame, the meaning of this Latin is that "Woman is all of man's bliss and joy!"[18]

"For when I feel your soft side at night – albeit I cannot ride on you, because our perch is so narrow, alas – I am so full of joy and comfort that I defy all dreams and visions."

And with that, down he flew from the rafter, and with him all his hens, for it was day. He began to call them all with a cluck, for he had found a grain of corn lying in the yard. He was royal, and he was afraid no longer; twenty times before prime[19] he clasped Pertelote in his wings, and he coupled with her just as often. He looked as if he were a grim lion, and roamed up and down on his toes, he chose not to set his foot to ground. He clucked when he came upon a grain of corn, and his wives ran to him. Thus royal, like a prince in his hall, I will leave this Chanticleer in his feeding-ground, and afterward I will say what happened to him.

When March, the month in which the world was made, and when God first created mankind, was complete, and there had passed thirty-two days since March began, it hap-

---

[17] *Mulier est hominis confusio.* Woman is the ruin of man.

[18] Man's bliss and joy. Of course, Chaunticleer's translation is incorrect. Why it is incorrect, from the perspectives of both Chaucer and Chaunticleer, is the subject of much speculation.

[19] Prime. 9 am.

pened that Chanticleer in all his glory, with his seven wives walking beside him, cast his eyes to the bright sun, which had sped through twenty-one degrees and somewhat more in the sign of Taurus. By nature and not education he knew that it was prime, and he crowed with joyous voice. "The sun," he said, "has climbed through the heavens forty-one degrees and more. Madame Pertelote, my world's bliss, listen to how the happy birds sing, and see the fresh flowers springing up; my heart is full of revelry and joy."

But suddenly a sorrowful event occurred. For the latter end of joy is always woe, God knows. The joy of this world is soon gone, and if an orator could compose beautifully, he could confidently write it in a chronicle as a notable fact. Now let every wise man listen; this story is every bit as true, I dare swear, as the book of Lancelot of the Lake,[20] whom women hold in great reverence. Now I will return to my text.

A coal-fox,[21] sly and unrighteous, who had dwelt three years in the grove, by decree of almighty Providence burst through the hedges that same night into the yard where stately Chanticleer was accustomed to stroll with his wives. And there the fox lay quietly in a bed of cabbage until it was past eleven o'clock, awaiting his time to fall upon Chanticleer, as do all these homicides that lie in wait to murder men are glad to do.

False murderer, lurking in your lair! You new Iscariot,[22] new Ganelon,[23] false deceiver, just like the Greek Sinon that brought Troy utterly to woe![24] May that morning be ac-

---

[20] Lancelot of the Lake, Famed Arthurian knight, lover of Queen Guinevere, both of whom fell from grace when their affair was made public.

[21] Coal-fox. A fox with black markings, as made with coal.

[22] Iscariot. Judas Iscariot, who betrayed Jesus Christ.

[23] Ganelon. Betrayed Roland in *Song of Roland*. See Chaucer's *Monk's Tale* 2389 and *Shipman's Tale* 194.

[24] Sinon . . . woe. Deceived the Troys into accepting the Trojan Horse, in which the Greeks were hidden. See Vergil's *Aeneid* 2.57-267, and Chaucer's *House of Fame* 152-56 and *Squire's Tale* 209-10.

cursed, O Chanticleer, on which you flew from your rafter into the yard! Well you were warned by your dreams that this day was perilous to you. But what God foresees must come to pass, according to certain scholars. You may witness it from any perfect scholar that there is great difference of opinion in the schools and great disputation about this matter, and there always has been among a hundred thousand people.

But I cannot sift the wheat from the chaff,[25] as can the holy doctor Augustine or Boethius or Bishop Bradwardine;[26] whether God's glorious foreknowledge compels me by necessity to do a thing (by necessity I mean absolute necessity), or if I am granted free choice to do or not that same thing, though God foreknew it long before; or whether His knowing does not constrains at all except by a conditional necessity. With such matters I will not concern myself.

My tale is all about a cock, as you may hear, who took his wife's counsel, to his sorrow, to walk in the yard that morning, after he had dreamed his dream of which I told you. Women's pieces of advice are often fatal. Woman's advice brought us first to woe and made Adam depart from Paradise where he was merry and at ease. But because I know not whom I might disturb if I should insult women's advice, let us pass it over, for I said it only in sport. Read what authors, who treat such matters, say of women. These are the cock's words and not mine; I cannot imagine harm by

---

[25] Chaff. The non-essential matter. Chaucer often distinguishes the kernel or fruit of the wheat (or corn), the essential matter, from the chaff, the full description (perhaps non-essential) of the matter.

[26] Augustine . . . Bradwardine. Controversy over the relations between the divine will and the human will, especially in relation to foreknowledge and free will. Originally a dispute between St. Augustine (man was born in original sin and could be saved only by divine grace) and Pelagius (man was born innocent and had the free will to do good or evil). In the fourteenth century, Thomas Bradwardine, Oxford professor, revived the controversy with *De causa Dei contra Pelagium et de virtute causarum* (The cause of God versus Pelagian and concerning the nature of causation).

any woman.

Pertelote lay elegantly in the sunshine with all her sisters nearby, bathing herself merrily in the sand, and the gallant Chanticleer sang more merrily than the mermaid in the sea; for Physiologus in truth says that they sing merrily and well.[27] And it so happened, as he cast his eye upon a butterfly among the cabbages, that he noticed this fox who lay hidden. He had no mind then to crow, but cried at once, "Cok! cok!" and started up like a man frightened in his heart. For by instinct a beast is glad to flee from his natural enemy if he should see it, even if he had never seen it with his eye before.

This Chanticleer, when he first detected him, would have fled, except that the fox immediately spoke, "Alas, gentle sir, where do you want to go? Are you afraid of me, your own friend? Now surely I would be worse than a fiend if I desired harm or indignity to you. I have not come to spy upon your privacy, but in truth only to listen how you sing. For truly you have as merry a voice as any angel in heaven, and more feeling in music than Boethius[28] had, or any singer. My lord your father (may God rest his soul), and your mother too, by her courtesy, have been in my house, to my great content; and you, sir, I would gladly please, surely. And speaking of singing, I must say, may I be struck blind if I ever heard anyone, except you, sing as did your father in the morning.

"Surely, all that he sung was from the heart. And to make his voice stronger he took such pains that he had to shut both his eyes, he cried so loud, standing on tip-toe as well and stretching forth his long, slender neck. And he was also of such discretion that there was no man in any land who could surpass him in song or wisdom.

---

[27] Physiologus. Author of the very popular *Bestiary*, which described real and imaginary animals and attributed to them moral qualities.

[28] Boethius. Late Roman philosopher (c.475-525), best-known for his *Consolation of Philosophy*, but also the author of the standard treatise on music in the Middle Ages, *De Musica*.

"I have indeed read in the life of Burnel the Ass,[29] among the verses, about a cock, who, because a certain priest's son, when he was young and foolish, gave the cock a rap on his leg, the cock in later years made him to lose his benefice. But certainly there is no comparison between his wisdom and subtlety and discretion and your father's. Now sing, sir, for sweet charity's sake. Let's see – can you imitate your father?"

Chanticleer began to flap his wings, like one who could not detect his treachery, so ravished he was by the flattery. Alas! You lords, in your courts are many false flatterers and parasites, who please you more, in faith, than he who tells you the truth. Read about flatterers in Ecclesiasticus,[30] and beware of their treachery.

Chanticleer stood high on his toes, stretching his neck and shutting his eyes, and began to crow loudly. Up started Sir Russel the fox at once, seized Chanticleer by the throat and bore him away on his back toward the wood, for as yet nobody gave chase.

O destiny that may not be eluded! Alas that Chanticleer flew down from the rafters! Alas, that his wife did not care about dreams! And all this bad fortune fell on a Friday! O Venus, goddess of pleasure, why would Chanticleer, who was your servant and did all within his might in your service (more for delight than to multiply the world), endure to die upon your day?

O Geoffrey de Vinsauf,[31] dear sovereign master, who

---

[29] Burnel the Ass. *Speculum Stultorum* (Mirror of Fools), a popular Latin satire of the donkey who hoped to increase the length of his tail. In the story told here, the young man, named Gundulfus, having overslept, missed his ordination and lost his benefice (Church career appointment).

[30] Ecclesiasticus. Biblical book that reflects this thought often.

[31] Geoffrey of Vinsauf . Author of the *Poetria Nova,* an early thirteenth-century treatise on the art of poetry, who had considerable influence on Chaucer's early poetry. Geoffrey of Vinsauf offered a model lament on the death of Richard I (1157-1199), the somberness of which Chaucer, in a sense, burlesques in the following passage.

when your noble king Richard was slain by shot did mourn his death so sorely, why do I not have your learning and your pen now to reproach Friday as you did! (For truly it was on a Friday he was slain.) Then I would show you how I could mourn Chanticleer's dread and torment. Not since Ilium[32] was won and Pyrrhus had seized King Priam by the beard and slain him with his drawn sword, as the *Aeneid*[33] says, was ever such cry and lamentation made by ladies as by the hens in the yard, when they saw this sight of Chanticleer.

Above all Madame Pertelote shrieked, louder than Hasdrubal's wife[34] when her husband perished and the Romans had burned Carthage; she was so full of torment and frenzy that she leapt into the fire and burned herself with a steadfast heart. O woeful hens, even so you cried as did the senators' wives when Nero[35] burned the city of Rome and their guiltless husbands all perished, slain by this Nero.

But now I return to my tale once more. This poor widow and her two daughters heard these hens cry and lament, and started out the door immediately and saw the fox make toward the wood, bearing the cock away on his back. "Out! Alas! Help!" they cried. "Ho! Ho! The fox!" and after him they ran, and many other people with cudgels. Colle, our dog, ran, and Garland and Talbot,[36] and Malkin with her distaff[37] in hand; the cow and calf ran and the hogs themselves, so afraid were they for the barking of the hounds and the shouting of the men and women; they ran till they thought their hearts would burst.

---

32 Ilium. The walled city of Troy.

33 *Aeneid.* Vergil's epic poem, which describes the end of the Trojan war (including the death of Priam, 2. 469ff.) and Aeneas' search and fight for the land that will eventually become Rome.

34 Hasdrubal's wife. Hasdrubal, King of Carthage, was defeated by the Roman Scipio (Africanus Minor) in 146 BC.

35 Nero. Decadent Roman emperor who did not care when Rome burned. See Chaucer's *Monk's Tale* 2463-2550.

36 Talbot and Gerland. Also dogs.

37 Distaff. The staff used to hold the wool in the process of spinning.

They yelled like fiends in hell. The ducks quacked as if they were being slaughtered, and the geese in fear flew over the tree-tops. A swarm of bees came out of the hive, so hideous was the noise. Ah, God bless! Surely Jack Straw[38] and his rabble never made shouts half so shrill when they were slaughtering a Fleming, as were made this day after the fox. They brought horns of brass, of wood, of horn and bone, and blew and bellowed in them, and so shrieked and whooped indeed until it seemed as if the heavens would drop.

Now, good men, I pray you all listen. Lo, how Fortune suddenly overturns the hope and arrogance of her foe! This cock, lying upon the fox's back, in all his fright spoke to the fox and said, "Sir, if I were you, so may God help me, I should say, 'Turn back, all you proud churls! May a true pestilence fall on you! Now that I have come to this wood's edge, the cock shall remain here, in spite of anything you can do. I will eat him, in faith, and do so at once.'"

"In faith, it shall be done," answered the fox. And as he spoke that word, at once the cock broke away nimbly from his mouth and flew immediately high upon a tree.

And when the fox saw the cock was gone, "Alas! Chanticleer!" he said; "alas! I have done you wrong to frighten you, when I seized and brought you out of the yard. But, sir, I had no ill intent; come down and I shall tell you what I meant. I shall tell the truth to you, so may God help me!"

"No then," said the cock, "I curse both of us, and first I curse myself, both blood and flesh, if you should trick me more than once. No more shall your flattery make me sing and shut my two eyes. For he who willfully shuts his eyes when be should see, may God let him never thrive!"

"No," said the fox, "but God give him bad fortune who is so indiscreet as to prattle when he should hold his peace!"

---

[38] Jack Straw. One of the reported leaders of the Peasants' Revolt in and around London in 1381, in which many of the Flemish (Belgian) merchants and manufacturers were killed because their great success was perceived as the result of unfair competition.

Lo, such a thing it is to be negligent and heedless and trust flattery! But you who maintain this tale to be foolishness, about nothing but a fox and a cock and a hen, take the moral, good sirs. For St. Paul says that all that is written is written for our learning, in truth. Take the fruit and leave the chaff.[39] And now may the good God, if His will be so, as says my lord,[40] make us all good Christians and bring us to His heavenly bliss. Amen.

Here is ended the Nun's Priest's Tale.

Epilogue

"Sir Nun's Priest," said our Host, "may your breeches be blessed for this merry tale of Chanticleer! By my word, if you were a secular man, a very hearty fellow you would be with women. See what brawn and what a neck this gentle priest has, and what a chest! He looks with his eyes like a sparrow-hawk. He does not need to dye his color with brasil or Portugal.[41] Now may goodness come to you for your tale, sir!

And after that, with a merry look, he spoke to another as you shall hear.

---

39 Fruit and Chaff. See note above.

40 My lord. The Ellesemere manuscript includes a note that this is a reference to the Archbishop of Canterbury, but the relevance of the reference is not clear.

41 Brasil or Portugal. Red dyes.

THE MANCIPLE'S TALE

Here follows the Prologue of the Manciple's Tale.

Do you know[1] where a little village called Bob-up-and-down stands, under Blean forest on the Canterbury road? Our host began to jest and to make mirth there, and said, "What! Sirs, Dun is in the mire! Is there no one who for prayer or pay will awaken our friend in the rear of the company? A thief might easily bind and rob him. See how he is napping! See, for Christ's bones, as if he would soon fall off his horse. Is that a London cook – bad luck to him! Make him come forth, he knows his penance, for he shall tell a tale, although it may not be worth a bottle of hay, by my faith! Awake, you Cook, God give you sorrow! What ails you to sleep in the morning? Have you had fleas all night, or been laboring with some trollop, or are you so drunk that you cannot hold up your head?"

This Cook, who looked very pale, said to our Host, "So God bless my soul, such heaviness has fallen on me, I don't know why, that I had rather sleep than have the best gallon of wine in Cheapside."

"Well," said the Manciple[2], "if it would help you, sir Cook, and annoy no person who rides here, and if our Host is willing, through his courtesy, I will excuse you of your story for now; for your face is pale, your eyes also look dazed, it seems to me, and I well know your sour breath stinks, which well shows you are indisposed; good faith, you

---

[1] Do you know. As this tale begins, it is unclear if it reflects anything that has come before it. *The Canterbury Tales* is a collection of various fragments, and this tale is usually taken to be the beginning of a fragment.

[2] Manciple. A purchaser of provisions, usually for a college, abbey, or monastery.

shall never be flattered by me!

"Lo, this drunken creature! See how he yawns as though he would swallow us right now. By your father's soul, man, keep your mouth shut; may the Devil of hell set his foot in it! Your cursed breath will infect us all. Fie, stinking swine! Fie, may bad luck come to you! Ah, take heed, sirs, of this lusty fellow. Now, will you joust at the vane of the quintam? It seems to me that you are in great shape for that! I believe you have drunk ape-wine, and that is when people will play with a straw."

At this speech the Cook grew upset and angry, and began to shake his head heatedly at the Manciple for lack of speech, and threw himself down from the horse, where he lay until men picked him up. This was quite a feat of horsemanship for a cook! Alas that he had not kept to his ladle! And before he was once more in the saddle there was a great deal of shoving to and fro to lift him up, and so much trouble and woe, so unwieldy was this sorry, pale ghost.

And our Host then said to the Manciple, "Because drink has dominion over this man, I believe by my salvation that he would tell his tale lewdly; for whether it was wine or old and musty ale that he has drunk, he speaks through his nose and puffs hard, and he has a head cold as well. He also has more than enough to do to keep himself and his horse out of the swamp.

"And if he should fall from his horse again, then we shall all have enough to do to lift up his heavy drunken carcass. Tell your tale; don't worry about him. But nevertheless, Manciple, you are too foolish, in faith, to reprove him so openly with his fault.

"Perhaps another day he will recall you and bring you down as a hawk to the lure. I mean he will speak of small matters, such as finding fault with your account books, which, if it came to the test, would not be honest."

"No," said the Manciple, "that would be a great misfortune; so he could lightly bring me into the trap. Yet I would rather pay for the mare that he rides on than have him quarrel with me; I will not anger him, as I hope to prosper! What I spoke, I said in jest. And what do you know? I have a draught of wine in a gourd here, yes, of a ripe grape, and soon you shall see a merry jest. This Cook shall drink from it, if I can make him, and he will not say no to me; I'll stake my life on it."

And truly, to tell it all, the Cook drank deep out of this vessel, alas! What need did he have? Already he had drunk enough. And when he had blown in this horn, he handed the gourd back to the Manciple. And he was extremely glad for this drink and thanked him in such a fashion as he was able.

Then our Host began to laugh marvelously loud and said, "I well see we will need to carry good drink with us wherever we go for that will turn rancor and discomfort into accord and love, and appease many wrongs. O Bacchus, blessed is your name, which so can turn earnest to sport. Worship and thanks to your godhead! But you will get no more of that from me! Tell your tale, Manciple, I pray you."

"Well, sir," the Manciple said, "now listen."

Thus ends the Prologue of the Manciple.

Here begins the Manciple's Tale of the Crow.

When Phoebus dwelt down here on this earth, as old books make mention, he was the hardiest young knight in this entire world, and the best archer as well. He slew Python, the serpent, one day as he lay sleeping in the sunshine; and he completed many other noble worthy achievements with his bow, as one may read.

He could play on every type of instrument, and sing in such a way that it was a heavenly melody to hear the sound of his clear voice. Surely Amphion, king of Thebes, who walled that city by his singing, could never sing half so well as he. And he was the handsomest man that is or was since the world was made. What need is there to describe his features? For no man so handsome lived in this world. Likewise, he was full of gentle manners, of honor and of perfect worthiness.

This Phoebus, flower of all young men in both chivalry and in generosity, for his sport and also in sign of his victory over Python, as the history tells us, was accustomed to bear a bow in his hand. Now this Phoebus had in his house a crow, which he fostered for a long time in a cage and taught to speak, as one may teach a jay. This crow was white as a snow-white swan, and when he was to tell a tale, could counterfeit the speech of every man. And no nightingale in this entire world could sing one hundred thousandth as merrily or well.

Now this Phoebus had in his house a wife whom he loved more than his soul, and was ever busy night and day to please her and treat her with respect, except only, if I am to tell the truth, that he was jealous and anxious to guard her well; for he was loath to be tricked. And so is every creature in this case, but all in vain; it does not help. A good wife, clean in deed and thought, should not be watched, in truth; and truly the labor is in vain to watch an evil one, for that can not be done. This I believe to be true folly, to waste labor in watching wives; thus write old scholars.

But now to my purpose, as I first began. This worthy Phoebus did all he could to please her, thinking that with such pleasure and with his manhood and handsome looks nobody should remove him from her grace. But this, God knows, there is no man who can constrain a thing that Nature has placed in a creature's very being.

Take any bird, put it in a cage, and set your mind and heart entirely on fostering it tenderly with food and drink, with all dainty things you can imagine, and keep it as cleanly as you can; even if its cage may be ever so delightful with gold, this bird would still twenty thousand times rather go eat worms and other such wretched things from the cold and crude forest. For he will do his best at all times to escape from his cage, if he can; this bird always desires his liberty.

Take a cat, and foster him well with cream and tender meat and make him a silken couch; and let a mouse run by the wall. At once he forgets cream and fine meat and every dainty thing in that place, as he has such an appetite to eat a mouse. Lo, here desire has its dominion, and appetite banishes discretion.

A she-wolf also has a villainous low nature; at the time when she wishes to have a mate, she will take the most scurvy wolf she can find, or the one of least honor.

I speak all these examples concerning these men who are untrue – and never a bit concerning women! For men always have a wanton appetite to take their pleasure with lower creatures than their wives, no matter how beautiful or true or meek they may be. Flesh is so eager for something new – unfortunately – that not for long can we find pleasure in anything that is in pursuit of virtue.

This Phoebus thought of no deceit, and was deceived for all his good-heartedness; for behind his back she had another, a man of small reputation, worth nothing in comparison to Phoebus, which made it more painful! Thus it often happens, and much harm and woe comes from it.

And so it happened when Phoebus was away that his wife sent then after her lover. Lover? This is a churlish word surely; forgive me for it, I pray you. The wise Plato says, as you may find in the books, that word and act must be in agreement; if one shall tell a thing as it is, the word must be cousin to the deed. I am a plain man, I speak just so: there is truly no other difference between a wife of high degree that is dishonest with her body, and a poor wench, other than this: if they both act wrongly, the gentlewoman, high in estate, shall be called his lady in love; and because the other is a poor woman, she shall be called his wench. And God knows, my own dear friend, men lay the one as low as the other.

Just as between a usurping tyrant and an outlaw or a roving thief, I say the same: there is no difference. This definition was told to Alexander, because the tyrant is of greater power by the force of his retainers to slay downright and to burn house and home and lay everything low, behold, he is therefore called a captain; and because the outlaw has only a small band and cannot do such great harm nor bring a country to such harm, men call him an outlaw or a bandit. But because I am not a bookish man, I will not retell any more sayings from books, but I will go to my tale, as I began.

When Phoebus' wife had sent for her lover, the white crow, which always hung in the cage, watched them, and never said a word. And when Phoebus the lord had come home, this crow sang "Cuckoo! cuckoo! cuckoo!"

"What, bird!" said Phoebus. "What song are you singing? Were you not accustomed to sing so merrily that it was a joy to my heart to hear your voice? Alas, what song is that?"

"By God," he said, "I am not singing the wrong thing.. Phoebus," he said, "despite all your worth, your beauty and your noble birth, despite all your sweet singing and all your melody, and despite all your vigilance, you have been hoodwinked by a man of small reputation, not worth a gnat alongside you, by my head!"

What more would you like to know? Soon the crow told him, by trusty tokens and bold words, how his wife had sinned, to his great shame and reproach; and he told him once and again that he had seen it with his eyes.

This Phoebus turned away; it seemed to him his sorrowful heart would burst in two. He bent his bow and set an arrow in it, and then in his rage he slew his wife. This is the conclusion; there is no more to say. And for sorrow of this he broke his instruments of music, his harp, lute, gittern, and psaltery; and he broke also his arrows and bow.

And after that he spoke thus to the bird: "Traitor," he said, "with a scorpion's tongue you have brought me to destruction. Alas that I was ever created! Why am I not dead? O dear wife, gem of delight, who was so constant to me and so faithful, now you lie dead with face pale of hue, so guiltless, that I dare truly swear! O rash hand, to do so foul a wrong! O troubled mind, O reckless anger, that heedlessly strikes the guiltless! O distrust, full of false suspicion, where was your wisdom and discernment? Let every man beware of rashness, and believe nothing without strong testimony; do not strike too soon, before you know why, and consider soberly and well before in wrath you execute anything upon suspicion. Alas! Rash anger has fully destroyed a thousand people, and brought them to the dust. Alas! I will slay myself for sorrow!"

And to the crow he said, "O false thief, from this point I will pay you back you for your false talk! You sang once like a nightingale; now, false thief, you shall forego your song and all your white feathers as well, and never in all your life shall you speak again. Thus shall men be avenged on a traitor; you and your offspring shall forever be black, and shall never make sweet sound but always cry before the tempest and rain, as a sign that through your fault my wife is dead."

And he rushed upon the crow, and swiftly plucked out every one of his white feathers and made him black, and bereft him of his song and of his speech as well, and slung him out the door to the Devil, to whom I commit him! And for this cause all crows are black.

Gentle people, by this example I pray you to take heed, and mark what I say: as long as you live never tell a man of his wife's frailty; in truth he will mortally hate you. Sir Solomon, as wise scholars say, teaches a man to guard his tongue well; but as I said, I am not a learned man.

Yet thus my mother taught me: "My son, in God's name, think carefully about the crow! "My son, hold your tongue and keep your friend. A bitter tongue is worse than a devil; [3]

[3] Against a devil. People may protect and bless themselves (with the sign of the cross) against the devil, but they have no such protection against their own words, which can thus harm them more than the devil.

my son, one may bless themselves against a devil. My son, God, through His endless goodness, formed a wall around the tongue with teeth and lips as well, because one should consider well what one speaks. My son, many have been undone on account of too much speech, as scholars teach; but nobody is ever harmed for little speech cautiously given.

"My son, you should restrain your tongue at all times, except when you take pains to speak of God in worship and prayer. The first virtue, son, if you will learn it, is to restrain and guard well your tongue; children learn this when they are young. My son, there comes great harm of much speech and ill-advised, where less speech would have been enough; so was I told and taught. In much speaking there is no lack of sin.

"Do you know what a rash tongue results in? Just as a sword cuts and carves an arm in two, so, my dear son, a tongue cuts friendship in two. A prattler is abominable to God: read Solomon so worthy and wise, read David in his psalms, read Seneca. My son, speak not, but nod with your head. Make as if you were deaf, if you hear any gossip speak of perilous matters. The Flemish say (and learn this, if you please), that 'little prattling causes much rest.'

"My son, if you have said no ill word, you need not fear to be betrayed; but one who has spoken ill, I affirm, can in no way recall those words.

"What is said, is said; it goes forth, whether or not one repents, or however unfavorable it may be. One is a slave to whom one has spoken a thing for which one is sorry now. My son, beware, and do not be the author of any new tidings, whether they are true or false. Wherever you go, among gentle or simple people, guard your tongue well, and think carefully about the crow."

Here is ended the Manciple's Tale of the Crow.

Chaucer's Retraction

❦

Here the maker of this book takes his leave.

Now I pray to all who read or listen to this little treatise, that if there may be anything in it that pleases them, that they may thank for it our Lord Jesus Christ, from whom all intelligence and all goodness proceeds. And if there be any thing that displeases them, I pray them also that they ascribe it to my lack of skill and not to my will, all of which I would have gladly said better if I had had the skill. For our book says, "All that is written is written for our instruction,"[1] and that is my intent.

Therefore, I beseech you meekly, for the mercy of God, that you pray for me that Christ may have mercy on me and forgive me my sins; and namely for my translations and compositions of worldly vanities, all of which I revoke in this retraction: namely the book of Troilus; the book also of Fame; the book of the twenty-five Ladies; the book of the Duchess; the book of Saint Valentine's day of the Parliament of Birds; the tales of Canterbury, those that pertain to sin; the book of the Lion; and many another books, if I could remember them, and many songs and many lecherous ditties, that Christ for his great mercy may forgive me the sin.

But of the translation of Boethius' Consolation, and other books of Legends of Saints, and of Homilies and moral and devotional works, for which I thank our Lord Jesus Christ and his blessed Mother, and all the saints of heaven, beseeching them that they from this point to the end of my life may send me the grace to lament my sins and to study for the salvation of my soul, and grant me the grace of true peni-

---

[1] For our instruction. See Romans 14.4; 2 Timothy 3:16.

tence, confession and satisfaction to carry out in this present life, through the gentle grace of he who is king of kings and priest over all priests, of he who ransomed us with the precious blood of his heart, so that I may be one of those who shall be saved at the Day of Judgment.

Qui cum Patre et Spiritu Sancto vivit et regnat
Deus per omnia secula.[2] *Amen.*

Here is ended the book of the tales of Canterbury, compiled by
Geoffrey Chaucer, on whose soul may
Jesus Christ have mercy.
Amen.

[2] He with the Father and Holy Spirit lives and reigns, God, through all ages.

MINOR POEMS

INTRODUCTORY NOTES

In addition to the more ambitious poems that fill the pages of this volume, Chaucer also composed dozens of shorter poems, some for specific purposes or occasions, mostly in the courtly style that was popular in France. In this type of poetry, we may find the gentle complaint of an unrequited lover, as in "To Rosamonde," or a complaint about the changeable ways of the world, as in "Lack of Steadfastness," which is, as many poems were in Chaucer's day, directed to the King.

Chaucer also created poems from different impulses as well. For example, his "A.B.C." is a poem in praise of Mary, the mother of Jesus. His "Complaint of Chaucer to His Purse" is a sort of begging poem, of which there are several other examples in England and the Continent. The last poem in this collection, "Chaucer's Words to Adam, His Scribe," can only have been written by Chaucer. Though the sentiment echoes what we might find in other texts, the poem is written from Chaucer's unique position to his actual scribe, Adam. Chaucer was unable to write with his right hand (since he was missing his thumb and forefinger: such was the punishment for archers who were prisoners of war) or his left (as he had developed a palsy).

Please note that two of the poems end with an "envoy." This is a common feature of occasional or lyric poetry of Chaucer's day. In a poetical context, an envoy is a postscript addressed either to a specific individual or to the poem itself (a bidding for the poem to go to a specific individual).

TO ROSAMONDE

Madame, you are the shrine of all beauty, as far as the map of the world extends, for you shine as glorious as crystal, and your round cheeks are like ruby. Furthermore, you are so carefree and joyful, that when I see you dance at a merry-making, it is an ointment to my wound, even if you do not dally with me.

For though I weep a tub full of tears, yet that woe cannot put a stop to my heart; your lovely voice, that flows out so softly, fills my thought with joy and bliss. So courteously I move, so bound by love, that I say to myself in my pains, it suffices me to love you, Rosamond, even if you do not dally with me.

Never was a pike so wallowed in spicy sauce as I am wallowed and immersed in love; and for this reason so often I see myself to be the true second Tristram.[1] My love can never cool or fail. I ever burn in amorous pleasure. Do as you wish, I will always be your lowly servant, even if you do not dally with me.

The Very Genteel Chaucer.

---

[1] Tristram. Famous lover of Isolt, in the Arthurian tradition. Isolt, though married to King Mark of Cornwall, loves Tristram, who is Mark's most able and dedicated knight.

LACK OF STEADFASTNESS

❦

A Ballad

At one time this world was so steadfast and stable that a man's word was a sufficient bond; now it is so false and deceitful that, in effect, word and deed are in no way alike, for the whole world is so turned upside-down by willfulness and corruption that all is lost for the lack of steadfastness.

Why is this world so variable, except that people rejoice in dissension? Among us now a man is believed to be impotent unless by some conspiracy he can wrong or oppress his neighbor. What except wretched willfulness causes all to be lost for the lack of steadfastness?

Truth is put down, reason is esteemed a fable; virtue has now no dominion, pity is exiled, no man is merciful, through covetousness discernment is blinded. The world has made a transmutation from right to wrong, from fidelity to instability, so that all is lost for the lack of steadfastness.

The Envoy to King Richard

O prince, desire to be honorable, cherish your people, hate extortion! Allow no thing to be done in your domains that may be a reproach to your office. Show forth your sword of chastisement, fear God, execute the law, love fidelity and worth, and wed your people again to steadfastness.

Here ends the Poem.

THE A.B.C.

Here begins the song according to the order of the letters of the alphabet.

Almighty, all-merciful Queen, to whom all this world flees for succor, to have release from sin, sorrow and trouble, glorious Virgin, flower of all flowers, to you I flee, confounded in error! You mighty, gracious lady, help and relieve me, pity my perilous malady! My cruel adversary has vanquished me.

Bounty has so fixed his tent in your heart that well I know you will be my succor; you can not reject him who with pious mind asks your aid. Your heart is ever so bounteous; you are the liberal giver of full felicity, haven of refuge, of quiet and rest. Lo, how the seven thieves pursue me! Help, bright lady, before my ship goes to pieces!

Comfort is there none, save in you, dear lady, for lo! my sin and confusion, which ought not to come into your presence, have brought against me a grievous suit, founded on strict justice and my despair. And in justice they might well maintain that I were worthy of condemnation, were it not for your mercy, blessed queen of heaven.

Doubt is there none that you, queen of mercy, are the source of grace and mercy on earth. Through you God vowed to be reconciled with us. For surely, dear, blessed mother of Christ, were the bow of justice and wrath bent now in such wise as it was at first, the righteous God would hear of no mercy; but through you we have favor, as we desire.

Ever has my hope of refuge been in you, for in divers manners you have received me into mercy heretofore full oft. But grant me favor, lady, at the Great Assize, when we shall come before the high Judge! So little fruit shall be found in me then that, unless you well chasten me before that day, by strict justice my work will destroy me.

Fleeting I come to your tent for succor, to hide me from the tempest full of terror, beseeching you, though I be wicked, that you withdraw you not. Ah, help me yet in this need! Though I have been a beast in will and in act, vet, lady, clothe me with your grace. Take heed, lady, your enemy and mine is in point to pursue me unto my death.

Glorious maid and mother, who never in earth or heaven was bitter, but ever full of sweetness and mercy, help, that my Father may be not angry with me. Please speak, for I dare not behold Him! Alack the while! I have done such things on earth that surely, unless you will be my succor, He will exile my spirit to eternal stench.

He vowed, tell Him, to become a man, to have kinship with us, as was His will; and with His precious blood He drew up the contract upon the cross as general release for every penitent that believes in Him. And therefore, bright lady, pray for us! Then you shall both but to rest all His displeasure, and snatch his prey from our foe.

I know it well, you will truly be our succor, you are so full of bounty. For when a soul falls into sin, your pity goes and hails him back again. Then you make his peace with his Lord and bring him out of the crooked path. Whosoever loves you shall find he loves not in vain, as he leaves this life.

Kalendars and illuminated texts are those in this world who are lighted with your name; and whosoever takes to you by the straight path need not fear to be maimed in soul. Now, queen of comfort, since you are she from whom I seek my medicine, let my foe no more re-open my wound; I commit my health all into your hand.

Lady, I cannot portray the sorrow you had beneath the cross, nor His grievous suffering. But by the pains of both I pray you, let not the foe of us all make his boast that he has vanquished in his fatal lists what You both have ransomed for such a great price. As I first said, you ground of our being, continue to keep your pitiful bright eyes upon us.

Moses, who saw the bush burning with red flames, of which was never a stick consumed, saw the sign of your unspotted maidenhood. You are the bush which Moses deemed had been afire, on which descended the Holy Ghost; and this was in symbol. Now, lady, defend you us from the fire which shall last eternally in hell.

Noble princess, who never had any peer, surely, if there may be any comfort for us, it comes from you, you beloved mother of Christ. No other melody or song do we have to make us rejoice in our adversity, no other advocate who will and dare so pray for us; and you do so for such small payment, and help us for an Ave-Maria[1] or two.

O true light for blind eyes, O true delight of them in labor and trouble, O treasurer of grace to mankind, you who for your humility God chose as mother! From His handmaiden He made you mistress of heaven and earth, to offer up our petition. This world ever waits upon your goodness, for you never fail any creature in need.

[1] Ave Maria. The Hail Mary prayer.

Purpose I have at times to seek out why the Holy Ghost sought you, when Gabriel's voice came to your ear. He worked not such a marvel to make war upon us, but to save us whom afterwards He redeemed. Then we need no weapon to save us; but only needful penance, when we have not done it, and to ask and receive mercy.

Queen of comfort, yet when I consider that I have sinned toward both Him and you, and that my soul is worthy to sink, alas, churl, where can I go? Who shall be my mediator to your Son? Who but yourself, who are the fount of pity? More pity do you have on our adversity than any tongue in this world can tell.

Reform me, mother, and chasten me, for truly my Father's chastening I dare in no way to endure, so hideous is His just reckoning. Mother, from whom all mercy to humankind has ever sprung, may you be you my judge and my soul's healer as well. For pity always abounds for all who will beg you for pity.

Sooth[2] is it that God grants no mercy without you; for God of His goodness forgives none unless it should please you. He has made you vicar and mistress of all the world and empress of heaven as well; and He restrains His justice according to your will, and in token of that He has crowned you in such a royal fashion.

Temple of devotion, where God has His abode from which infidels are forbidden, to you I bring my penitent soul. Receive me; I can flee no further! O queen of heaven, with those venomous thorns for which the earth was accursed so long ago I am so wounded, as you may well see, that I am almost lost; it pains me so grievously.

---

[2] Sooth. True.

Virgin so splendid in apparel, who leads us unto the high tower of Paradise, counsel and guide me, how I may obtain your grace and your succor, although I have been in filth and error. Lady, please summon me to that court that is called your bench, O fresh flower, where mercy shall ever remain!

Xristus[3] your Son descended into this world to suffer His passion upon the cross, and that Longinus[4] also should pierce His heart and let His heart's blood run down; and all this was to save me. I am false and unkind to Him, and yet He desires not my damnation. For this I thank you, succor of all men.

Young Isaac was truly the prefigurement of His death; he so obeyed his father that it troubled him not to be slain; even so your Son wished to die as a lamb. Now lady full of mercy, since He measured out His mercy so liberally, I entreat you, please do not be scant; for we all sing and say that you are ever our shield against vengeance.

Zachary calls you the open spring to wash the sinful soul from its guilt. Therefore I ought well to read this lesson, which teaches us that, were it not for your tender heart, we would be lost. Now, lady bright, since you can and will be merciful to the seed of Adam, bring us to that palace that is built for penitents who are deserving of mercy. Amen.

Here ends the song.

---

[3] Xristus. The name of Christ was often abbreviated with an X, which stood for the cross on which he died. The form Xristus is rare.

[4] Longinus. The Roman soldier who pierced the side of Jesus when he had died upon the cross. Many legends grew up around him, including the notion that he was blind and that the blood that poured out from Christ's side cured his blindness.

THE COMPLAINT OF CHAUCER TO HIS PURSE

To you, my purse, and to no other creature, I lament, for you are my lady dear. I am so sorry now that you are light! Surely, unless you make me heavier in spirit, I may as well be laid upon my bier. For this reason I cry for your mercy – be heavy again, or else surely I must die.

Promise this day, before it may ever become night, that from you I may hear the blessed clanking or may see your color like the bright sunshine, which never had a peer in terms of golden glow. You are my life, only you, queen of comfort and of good company. You are the compass of my heart. Be heavy again, or else surely I must die.

Now, purse, you who are to me my life's one light, my life's one savior, down in this world here, help me out of this town through your might, even if you will not be my treasurer. For my purse is as bare of money as a shaven friar's head. But yet I pray you by your courtesy, be heavy again, or else surely I must die.

The Envoy of Chaucer.

O conqueror of *Brute's Albion*,[1] who, through your lineage and free choice, are the true King of it, this song to thee I send. And you, who have the power to amend all our woes please be mindful of my supplication.

---

[1] Brute's Albion. Brute, a descendent of King Priam of Troy, was the legendary founder of Britain, also known as Albion.

CHAUCER'S WORDS TO ADAM, HIS SCRIBE

Adam my scribe, if it should ever happen that you write my *Boece* or *Troilus* in some new way, may you have scales and scabs under your long locks, unless you copy in true fashion in accord with my lines. So often I must revise your work and correct it and erase it and scrape it; and all is on account of your negligence and haste.

ABOUT THE TRANSLATOR AND EDITOR

Gerard NeCastro is Professor of English at The University of Maine at Machias and Visiting Professor of English at The University of Maine. He teaches courses in Humanities, Creative Writing, Theater History, World Literature, Art History, Latin, Shakespeare, and Chaucer. He is the founder of Medica, The Society for the Study of Healing in the Middle Ages, and he has published on a variety of medieval and other subjects. For fourteen years, he has been the editor of *The Binnacle: The Literary Journal of Coastal Maine*. After many years of academic writing, translations, web pages, short stories, and poems, he has completed his first novel, *Columbine AS3*.

The Primavera Press

The Primavera Press was established in 2011 to publish high-quality books and e-books. We are starting slowly, but are proud of our expanding catalogue. Here are some of our recent titles.

- A Rump-Sprung Chair and a One-Eyed Cat: Poems by Down East Maine's Salt Coast Sages – M. Kelly Lombardi, Sharon Bray, Donald Crane, Gerald George, Philip Rose, and Grace Sheridan
- Jack in the Cracks, A Memoir. Jack Dennis
- Double Double: Tales of the Double: Tales by Chaucer, Conrad, Dostoevsky, James, Melville, Poe, and Salvia
- Essential Readings in the Humanities
- King Arthur and the Knights of the Round Table
- Troilus and Criseyde – Geoffrey Chaucer

The Primavera Press invites proposals for publications by authors, especially of certain varieties: 1. poets who have published volumes of poetry and would like to publish e-book reprints; 2. writers of tales of or about ancient times, especially books for young readers; and 3. authors of memoirs.

All of our titles are now available through Amazon on Kindle. Several of them are now available in print, and all of them will be soon.

Please visit us at www.primaverapress.com.

www.ingramcontent.com/pod-product-compliance
Lightning Source LLC
Chambersburg PA
CBHW020257030726
47499CB00001B/229
* 9 7 8 0 9 8 9 4 2 6 3 1 2 *